The English Heritage

North Stands
Gate 9
Section S
Seat 13, 11, 9
row RR

The English Heritage

SECOND EDITION

Frederic A. Youngs, Jr.
Henry L. Snyder
E. A. Reitan

FORUM PRESS, INC.
ARLINGTON HEIGHTS, ILLINOIS 60004

This book, or parts thereof, must not be used or repro-
duced in any manner without written permission. For
information, address the publisher, Forum Press, Inc.,
3110 North Arlington Heights Road, Arlington
Heights, Illinois 60004–1592.

Library of Congress Cataloging-in-Publication Data

Youngs, Frederic A., 1936–
The English heritage.

Rev. ed. of: English heritage. c1978.
Bibliography: p.
Includes index.
Contents: v. 1. To 1714—v. 2. Since 1689.
1. Great Britain—History.   2. England—Civiliza-
tion.   I. Snyder, Henry Leonard, 1929–
II. Reitan, E. A. (Earl Aaron), 1925–
III. Title.
DA30.Y68   1988   942   87-30475
ISBN 0-88273-360-5 (v. 1)
ISBN 0-88273-361-3 (v. 2)
ISBN 0-88273-359-1 (set)

Designed by Roger Eggers
Maps designed by James Bier

Manufactured in the United States of America
97 96 95 94 93 92 EB 3 4 5 6 7 8

CONTENTS

Volume One, chapters 1–9
Volume Two, chapters 9–18

MAPS

PREFACE

The English Heritage, Second Edition introduces one of the most remarkable national heritages the world has known. We may share that heritage directly because some of our ancestors were English in origin; yet, even if our families have no English roots, the English heritage is ours because it exists in so many places and has influenced so many societies throughout the world. It belongs to whites in North America and Australia, to blacks in Nigeria and Jamaica, and to orientals in Hong Kong and India. The English heritage is itself a fusion of cultures—of Celts, Germans, Vikings, and French—and today is diffused to every continent.

The English Heritage, Second Edition reflects the authors' belief that a brief introductory text serves both the student and the professor. It sketches for the student the main aspects of England's heritage and introduces briefly the themes that will be developed more fully in class. It is a reference work to which the student can return for clarification and is a source of auxiliary aids, such as maps and illustrations, which stimulate and reinforce learning. This book establishes the chronological framework into which can be set the information in lectures, discussions, outside readings and resources—all of which together are the heart of the course. A brief text allows the professor great flexibility in combining a variety of resources that meet student needs and that reflect the professor's special interests, talents, and experience. *The English Heritage, Second Edition* is intended to be only part of the assignments that comprise the course.

The English Heritage, Second Edition is written as an integrated whole. Although of necessity politics and government form the chronological framework, considerable attention is also given to English society: to the conditions in which English men and women lived, worked, prayed, studied, and enjoyed life. This balance in treatment justifies the use of the inclusive concept of *heritage*. The book includes character sketches, not

ix

only of political leaders but also of people in many walks of life whose contributions shaped England's social and cultural heritage. Among the special features of *The English Heritage, Second Edition* are periodic overviews of London, including Chaucer's London, Shakespeare's London, the urbane eighteenth-century London of Samuel Johnson, Victorian London when English power was at its height, and modern, swinging London. Because the story of the English heritage spans over a thousand years, there are special pauses or "stocktakings" to evaluate where England stood at crucial points in its development—in 1485, near the close of the Middle Ages; in 1660, after the agony of the Civil Wars; in 1783, when the loss of the American colonies ended the "first Empire"; and at 1850, when industrialization had profoundly altered British society. An extended stocktaking in the last chapter analyzes the United Kingdom's present problems and promises.

In the second edition, *The English Heritage* has been substantially reworked to build on the success of the original book and to make it even more effective as a teaching tool. The chapters on the medieval, Tudor, and Stuart periods have been expanded and restructured. New sections on cultural developments have been added in many places, and the treatment of London—already a major feature of the first edition—has been enlarged in all parts. The text of the chapters and also the suggestions for further reading have been revised to take account of the most recent scholarship. A new chapter on Britain under Margaret Thatcher provides an opportunity for a thoughtful and provocative analysis of the role of the United Kingdom in today's world.

Because many students will want to find additional information on the personalities and themes developed in *The English Heritage, Second Edition,* there is a section at the end of most chapters (Suggestions for Further Reading) that lists helpful books and articles. There are a number of books that are basic to the fuller understanding of British history, and they are listed at the end of Chapter 18.

The authors owe a debt of appreciation to their students, whose realistic, often delightfully irreverent comments and suggestions represent the greatest test of any book. Special gratitude is due to David M. Fahey of Miami University of Ohio, whose part as an author in the first edition and as a helpmate in the second is particularly appreciated. Many of our colleagues have been most helpful in comments on both editions: Roy A. Austensen of Illinois State University, Richard Boyer of the University of Toledo, Robert C. Braddock of Saginaw Valley State College, Lawrence E. Breeze of Southeast Missouri State University, Suzann Buckley of the State University of New York at Plattsburgh, John Byrn of Milford, Connecticut, Charles Carlton of North Carolina State University, Valerie Cromwell of the University of Sussex, Ronald H. Fritze of Lamar University, John F. Glasper of Ripon College, James M. Haas of Southern Illinois University, W. Kent Hackmann of the University of Idaho at Moscow, Thomas F. Hale of Idaho State University, Paul H. Hardacre, formerly of Vanderbilt University, Dale Hoak of the College of William and Mary, Daniel W. Hollis, III, of Jacksonville State University, Henry G. Horwitz of the University of Iowa, Ray Kelch of San Francisco State University, Donald Lammers of Michigan State University, the late Arthur Marder of the University of California at Irvine, James I. Miklovich of the University of West Florida, Patrick V. O'Dea of St. Bonaventure University, Jerome V. Reel, Jr., of Clemson University, Charles Ritcheson of the University of Southern California, William B. Robison, III, of Southeastern Louisiana University, Timothy J. Runyan of Cleveland State University, James Schmierchen of Central Michigan University, Lois G. Schwoerer of George Washington University, Beverly A. Smith of Illinois State University, Harry Snapp of North Texas State University, Leo F. Solt of Indiana University, and R. Dean Ware of the University of Massachusetts—Amherst.

The authors also wish to express their appreciation to the staff of Forum Press for assistance in the publication of this second edition, particularly to Maureen Hewitt, vice president and editor-in-chief.

Frederic A. Youngs, Jr.
General Editor

The Earliest Britons

to 1066

*W*hen the glaciers of the ice ages receded, Britain was part of the European landmass, but about 8000 B.C. glacial melting raised the level of the sea to form the North Sea and the English Channel and to leave Britain as an island. The sea was no real protection—wave after wave of invaders came from continental Europe so that the story of the creation of the English state is at first an appreciation of what the different invading people—Celts, Romans, Anglo-Saxons, and Vikings—successively contributed to an emerging British culture.

Early Invaders and the Celts

The earliest large migration of Europeans across the Channel came around 2750 to 2500 B.C. These settlers are called Windmill Hill people after the name of the archaeological site where the remains of their camps were found. Because the weapons and utensils of their Stone Age culture were not very versatile, they settled on the open unforested plains of the south and east where hunting, the grazing of animals, and some light plowing were possible. For protection they dug circular ditches around the camps and used the dirt to form stockades.

The Celtic Tribes. From about 2000 B.C. onward, the invaders of Britain were the Celts, the people of an ancient civilization probably originating in the lower area of the Danube River in eastern Europe. Although they were not a distinct ethnic group, they were a linguistic group with a shared culture. Their military prowess was such that they spread across the European continent. Among the earliest documented Celts in Britain were the Beaker people, so called by archaeologists of modern time because of the characteristic shape of their drinking vessels. This wave of Celtic invaders became so economically successful from grazing and breeding animals that they were able to undertake trade with lands thousands of miles distant, selling not only agricultural products but also beautifully fashioned bronze ornaments and jewelry, which symbolized the transition from the Stone Age to a more sophisticated one.

Celtic tribal life was characterized by holding the area they occupied in common. Although some lands were set aside for the chieftain and his associates in rule and some for the poor and ill, most land was held without individual ownership. There were six classes in society, ranking upward from the unfree who had broken tribal law to the chieftain. Some were distinguished by the right freely to till the soil, others by profession, as for example the poets or bards, or the priestly druids. Women had equality of status with men. The idea of common ownership and the ease of moving from one class to another prompted a cooperative activity in which advanced techniques such as making better plows, manuring, and harvesting implements were developed.

Celtic Culture. The cultural activities of the Celts were many and varied. They fashioned ornamental jewelry of exquisite beauty and made musical instruments such as harps and trumpets on which accomplished artists developed a musical heritage that still lives today in Scottish and Irish tunes. The Celts believed in immortality. Death merely marked the passage of a soul from this world to the other world, a process which came full circle in due time when the soul migrated from there to another person in this world. The druids or priests were a caste of great prestige, an international order whose influence spread far beyond religious ritual to education and natural science. Among the four great religious festivals was one on the last day of October. Spiritual contacts with the other world, with all attendant fear and mystery, were celebrated by a feast transformed in a later Christian era into a feast of All Hallows (All Saints). The evening before the feast gained the name of Hallowe'en.

Some idea of the Celtic people's level of development can be gained from their impressive monuments. At Avebury the largest of the concentric circles of massive stones had a diameter of 1,400 feet and included nearly thirty acres. At Stonehenge the inner ring consisted of vertical stones thirty feet high, which weighed five tons apiece, joined by equally large stones laid horizontally across them. The whole site included outer concentric rings and was probably a temple for sun worship, but from recent computer-assisted calculations an astronomer has argued that Stonehenge was also an astronomical calendar and clock of great sophistication. The far-reaching implications of such a theory suggest that the monument's builders had the economic means and religious commitment

Stonehenge *(E. A. Reitan)*.

needed to dedicate labor and material to a construction project that took many years, the mathematical competence to make alignments and take measurements of celestial movements with amazing accuracy, the engineering skill to move huge stones hundreds of miles from the quarry, and perhaps the political unity that guaranteed the peaceful conditions needed to erect the monument.

From the eighth to the first centuries B.C. there were successive waves of Celtic invaders who used iron in their weapons, tools, and implements. Iron plows could turn the soil and make agriculture more productive, and the Celts worked skillfully with iron and other metals to fashion swords, daggers, shields, and luxury goods such as brooches. As regions began to specialize in different products, trade between them was facilitated by the use of minted coins. The new Britons exported to continental Celts many products such as grain, leather, animals, and highly prized tin, which was mined in the western regions.

The increase in populations from newer migrations caused a severe competition for land. The Celts grew more warlike and aggressive, erecting hillside forts and venerating the warriors as an aristocracy. As a result of continued fighting several more stable kingdoms were formed from the smaller tribal groups. About 75 B.C. a particularly fierce group of Celts called the Belgae occupied Britain, and they continued to assist their relations who had remained behind in northern Gaul. When nearly twenty years later the Roman general Julius Caesar conquered Gaul, he became convinced that Gaul could be held only if he also subdued Britain.

Roman Britain

The Military Conquest. The 47-year-old Julius Caesar was a man of boundless energy, ability, and ambition, a statesman who had earlier shared rule in Rome with two other outstanding politicians and who had then embarked on military campaigns as a way to gain the glory and prestige necessary to catapult him into single rule back in Rome. His conquest of Gaul, modern-day France, in the years just before 55 B.C. opened up the possibility of continuing conquest in the British Isles.

The attack that Caesar and his two Roman legions mounted in 55 B.C. nearly cost him his reputation: the Celts resisted fiercely, gaining a technological edge by using chariots against which the Romans had not previously fought and a psychological edge as many Celts, their naked bodies painted blue to instill terror, temporarily restrained the invading Romans to the beachhead. A few subsequent Roman victories not far from the point of invasion did demonstrate enough Roman might and discipline so that Caesar could salvage his reputation, then withdraw until a better-prepared force could make a better-prepared invasion the following year.

When the Romans brought five legions in 54 B.C., their disciplined troops carried the fight to the home area of the most powerful Celtic chief, and the decisive victories established the reality of Roman domination so well that when Caesar's forces left, the Celts acknowledged the Roman lordship and continued to pay tribute for 100 years in the absence of any sustained Roman presence in Britain. During those years the Celts took advantage of the great opportunities for trading within the Roman Empire and gained a breathing space for political consolidation, but chafed at their dependent status. In A.D. 43 the Romans decided to invade and to occupy Britain in order to end the military and political dangers which the Celts posed.

This time the Roman invaders skillfully separated the Celtic forces and won decisive victories at the onset. In the next thirty years the Romans moved their control westward and northward into the mountainous regions. They suffered occasional defeats as when Queen Boudicca led her people in rebellion in A.D. 60 and destroyed nearly an entire Roman legion in battle. When in A.D. 70 a previously friendly buffer state in the north turned hostile, the Romans mounted a massive military effort and

Hadrian's Wall *(E. A. Reitan)*.

then erected the town of Eboracum (later called York) to consolidate the hard-won successes.

The Roman Military Frontiers. The Romans succeeded because their army was such a formidable fighting force. Each legion was a self-sufficient and mobile town which carried the equipment needed to overcome man-made fortresses and to deal with natural barriers by erecting bridges and roads. The soldiers were extensively trained in marching and fighting, and the state offered them special privileges after twenty-one years of well-paid and respected service if they would settle in areas near the frontier to be available if their military talents were ever needed again.

Such a settlement of retired soldiers and their families was called a *colonia*. The *colonia* usually retained marked military characteristics: as at Roman York, for instance, where the headquarters of the legion defending the northeastern frontier occupied half the town's area, all the settlement on the north side of the river. Although there were probably three other *coloniae*—at Colchester guarding the eastern shore on the English Channel, at Gloucester guarding the western frontiers, and at Lincoln—the Romans built other fortified towns. These were called *castra*. The survival of names in variant English forms—as, for example, Chester, Chichester, and

Roman baths, Bath *(Bath City Council, Department of Leisure and Tourist Services)*.

Exeter—shows how extensively the Romans organized the conquered country. Three legions, about a tenth of the Roman Empire's entire fighting force, were normally stationed in Britain, but the Romans were still unable to conquer all the island. The northern frontier was set soon after the troops in the north suffered a severe defeat in A.D. 122; the Emperor Hadrian then had a wall built across an eighty-mile narrow stretch to keep out the Picts who occupied what later would become Scotland.

Life in Roman Britain. Secure behind the military shield, the civilian areas of Roman Britain enjoyed the most advanced civilization in the western world in common with the rest of the Empire. "Civilization" refers generally to the social heritage of ideas, attitudes, and style of living which one people passes on to its descendants. For the Romans civilization meant life in cities, and thus Roman Britain was a network of cities linked together by well-engineered, straight roads.

The cities had wide streets laid out at right angles and enclosed within protective walls. The center was the forum, an open square onto which faced the basilica, the hall for public meetings. There were temples, baths, shops for the highly developed economic life of the town, and homes whose exteriors were often shops but in which the domestic area centered interiorly on open courtyards. The floors of the richer homes were made of tiled mosaics, the walls were plastered and colorfully painted, the windows were made of glass, and the whole was heated by central heating which used a system of pipes and water. Underground sewers kept the cities clean, and outside the walls there was sometimes an arena for pageants and sports.

Life within the cities was varied and cultured. Young men and women were tutored in Greek and Roman literature and philosophy and practiced oratory. There were theaters for plays and baths for relaxation and gambling. The emperor was worshipped officially for the sake of political unity, but other gods were venerated as well. Christianity came to Britain at first as one of many religions, then in later years finally became the religion of the Empire.

Roman London. In his second campaign Julius Caesar had sought a place at which his armies could successfully ford the broad river Thames, a natural barrier along his invasion route from extreme southeastern England to the homelands of the major Celtic chiefs. Just to the east of the fordable site he located was a rudimentary settlement destined to be a major part of subsequent British history. The area came to be called London, a site geographically distinguished by the commanding presence of two major hills, by two rivers flowing from north and west through the site into the Thames, and by being the meeting point of several adjoining Celtic tribal lands.

Within five years after the successful invasion of A.D. 43, which established permanently a Roman presence, the conquerors turned London into the provincial capital. Within the first hundred years the Romans erected a fifteen-foot-high wall to encircle all but the river frontage of the nearly square mile area, heavily protected the five gates that opened through the massive walls onto the Roman roads which acted as spokes of communication into the hinterlands, and built a bridge across the river Thames. In addition to the full range of typical Roman buildings—a forum of unusually large size and the temples, basilicas, baths, and other monuments to the Roman presence—there was a palace for the governor of the province. At the height of the Roman period, the population of London perhaps reached 50,000.

The upper ranks of British society were greatly influenced by Roman culture, but the vast majority of Britons were completely unaffected. Their lives were focused in the rural settlements on farming and raising animals. The only important Roman presence in the countryside was on estates known as villas. They differed considerably in size but in general were large-scale farming operations with many workers under a well-to-do and highly romanized owner. Because the villas were self-sufficient they had little impact on the native Britons nearby.

The first decay in Roman life in Britain came when many city dwellers started to move to the countryside to escape the high taxes and public demands of city life. The decline in urban living sapped the cultural vitality of Roman Britain and contributed to a loss of political unity. In the third and fourth centuries many soldiers stationed in Britain were recalled to the continent because of political difficulties in the crumbling Roman Empire.

Faced with the prospect of being left defenseless, the British appealed to Rome for assistance—only to be told by the Emperor Honorius in 409 to look after their own safety. The Britons were ill-prepared for fighting because the Roman soldiers had guaranteed the peace for centuries. Thus the British sought the services of German mercenaries to protect their island. Ironically, in time the Germans would be responsible for totally eradicating Roman culture from Britain. Roman ways would indeed have a role in shaping later Britain, but that came only when in later centuries the Christian church reintroduced many Roman practices.

Anglo-Saxon Britain, 450 to 870

The Anglo-Saxons. The Angles and Saxons of northern Germany were closely related in language, customs, culture, and especially in their reputation as fierce fighters. Their territories had never been part of the Roman Empire so that they were untouched by Roman civilization and Christianity. Loyalty to the tribe was paramount and military skill was highly praised, but because they were illiterate the details of their gradual conquering of Britain from about 450 to 600 are sparse. Some evidence of their settlements can be gained from archaeological remains and from such place names as *ingas,* which survives in the names Reading and Hastings, and *tun,* as in Southampton.

Legend has it that when the Romans left and the Saxons were hired, the mercenaries liked what they saw and began to conquer Britain, coming up the rivers to penetrate deep into the interior. At first the British were able to resist the small bands of invaders, and under the leadership of Arthur they stopped the Germans temporarily at Mount Baldon. Although Arthur's existence and military skill cannot be doubted, the legends about him and his Round Table are many, and the site of the battle and of his kingdom of Camelot, if indeed he was a king, are actually unknown.

By about 600 when the conquest was complete there were nearly a

Anglo-Saxon Migrations

dozen independent Anglo-Saxon kingdoms. In time many of the names of the settlers had become the names of the kingdoms so that the lands of the East Saxons, West Saxons, and South Saxons had become, respectively, Essex, Wessex, and Sussex, and the East Angles had given their name to East Anglia. A slower advance northward produced several kingdoms, notably Bernicia and Deira, which were later unified as Northumbria ("north of the river Humber") and Mercia ("the borderers' area") in the midlands. The old cities were naturally inhabited, but the urban Roman style of life was totally foreign to the invaders. Many of the Romano-Britons had fled northward and westward into the mountainous areas to avoid the waves of pagan invaders. By the end of the seventh century the native British people had been forced into three geographically separate kingdoms. In the far southwest was Cornwall, which would later be conquered by the Anglo-Saxons. The kingdom of Wales in the west would flourish until well into the Middle Ages. The Scots, who were originally from Ireland, and the Picts created the northern Celtic kingdom known from about 850 as Scotland.

The Conversion of the Anglo-Saxons. There were two distinct missionary efforts to bring Christianity back to Britain, one from the Celts in the north and west and the other sent from Rome. About the year 575 a monk in Rome had seen several youths from Anglo-Saxon Britain and had been deeply moved by their ignorance of Christ. When he became pope soon after, the monk (known to history as Pope Gregory the Great) commissioned another monk named Augustine to lead a band of missionaries to

Britain, and in 597 they arrived in the extreme southeast corner of the island. Augustine and his companions preached to various kings in the hope that a converted king would allow the evangelization of his kingdom. The first to be won was Ethelbert of Kent, a well-disposed ruler whose wife had been raised a Christian in her native Frankland. As the faith was spread the gains were consolidated by the erection of dioceses, geographic areas under the supervision of a bishop, such as Canterbury where Augustine himself settled.

The Celtic missionaries, the second missionary group, had a distinctly different character. The Roman traditions had been learned by the Celts during Roman rule, and St. Patrick (ca. 389–461) had established the church in Ireland by erecting dioceses which were coterminous with the tribes. But soon after his death the diocesan organization was abandoned, and the tribal chiefs established monasteries whose influence was unlimited by geographic borders. When Oswald became king of Northumbria in 633 he opened his realm to the Celtic monks who had been responsible for his earlier conversion.

The Roman and Celtic missionaries also differed in religious customs. A particular problem arose over the different ways of calculating the date of Easter, the central feast of the Christian year. The clergy in Rome had accepted newer and improved mathematical techniques for measuring cycles upon which the church's liturgical calendar was based, but the Celts who had been isolated from Rome when the Anglo-Saxons invaded had retained the older ways of calculation.

The issue over the date of Easter was merely one of many which arose from the fundamental question of whether British Christianity would develop in union with the universal church based on Rome or would maintain its by now unique features. At a Council in Whitby in Northumbria in 664, which both groups attended, they agreed to follow the Roman ways and to develop monasticism in the diocesan framework. The ecclesiastical unity that resulted made the missionaries' work easier and provided an example for and a stimulus to political leaders to bring about themselves the ideal of political unity instead of the multiplicity of the Anglo-Saxon kingdoms.

The Legacy of the Law. One of the most precious gifts of the invading Germanic tribes was their tradition of an unwritten but binding customary law. As they settled in different parts of Britain their tribal law became the law of the territory they occupied. The laws of the kingdoms were generally similar but there were differences, just as there were differences between the East Saxons and the West Saxons. All the laws sought to provide protection and to ensure a fair way to handle disputes.

The Germanic law had been intended as an alternative to the endless feuds and bloodshed between families seeking revenge for what outsiders had done to their kin. Each person had his own "peace," and it was far more serious to attack someone and break his peace within the privacy of his home than elsewhere. If a crime was committed the law sought to prevent revenge by ordering the guilty to pay money as damages. If the accused had not been caught in the act or if there was no other presumption of guilt, he was allowed to swear an oath asserting his innocence. The value of his oath was based on his rank so that a nobleman's was many times more valuable than any other person's. If his oath was not deemed sufficient to free him from the accusation, he could bring in oath-helpers who swore to his trustworthiness, and the latter were unlikely to support a guilty person because of the penalties for perjury. When guilt had been determined then damages were assessed depending on the extent of the injury and the victim's rank. Thus the damage for the loss of a nose was twice that for a thumb or ear and nearly seven times as much as for a finger. The damage for causing a death, called the wergeld, was of course the highest amount that could be assessed.

If the procedures of oath-taking had not determined guilt or innocence, and after elaborate safeguards for the rights of all parties, the decision was left to God through one of several types of ordeal. In the ordeal by water, for example, the defendant first prepared himself by prayer, fasting, and the sacraments. Then a priest blessed a body of water such as a small pond. The defendant was thrown into the water and a struggle on his part was taken as a sign of guilt because the purified water would not receive a defiled criminal. If the water received him unstruggling, he was in time brought up and declared innocent.

Toward Political Unity: The Bretwaldas. Not until the tenth century was there political unity in Britain. From about 600 the different Anglo-Saxon kingdoms struggled for political dominance, with warfare the tactic and overlordship the result. The victorious kings who dominated others were called Bretwaldas. The crucial question was the quality of that overlordship: was it to be a recognition as the first among many essentially independent kings, or was it to be so effective politically that the lesser kingdoms under a Bretwalda's control would lose their independence and become absorbed within his own kingdom? To a striking extent the answer depended on the leader's strength of character. A series of able rulers could consolidate their predecessors' gains, but a weak successor could lose in a single battle the advances made over many years.

Kent was the first of the dominant kingdoms, but when Ethelbert died in 616 Kent's overlordship ended. Northumbria dominated during the remainder of the seventh century. Of necessity it was militarily oriented because as the northernmost Anglo-Saxon kingdom it was exposed on its frontiers to the hostile Celts, Welsh, Picts, and Scots. King Edwin (616–632)* won Northumbria's independence from the Celts, and his successor Oswald reunified the kingdom; a third Bretwalda maintained Northumbria's dominance until late in the century when weak kings gained the throne.

Mercia dominated during the eighth century, principally because of the ability of two kings who ruled for a total of eighty years. Ethelbald (716–757) combined military power with a ruthless personality, if a letter by the saintly missionary Boniface, which condemned the king's morality, accurately reflects the situation. Offa (757–796) enjoyed the greatest esteem of any Anglo-Saxon king up to that time. His wisdom in government was profound, his reputation on the continent so renowned that the great king of the Franks, Charlemagne, considered marrying one of his sons to Offa's daughter, and his importance to the church sufficient to move the pope to send a legate to him and even found (temporarily, as it turned out) a third archbishopric at Lichfield in Mercia. Under Mercia's control there was a striking acceleration of the movement toward political unity. The kingdoms of East Anglia, Essex, and neighboring areas were wholly incorporated in Mercia and lost their independence so that the number of competitors for power was significantly reduced. Thus London became a Mercian city and lent its prestige to the kingdom.

The dominant power in the ninth century and later was Wessex. Mercia had attempted to divert the crown in Wessex from Egbert, the proper successor, and placed one of its own claimants on the throne. Egbert fled to Charlemagne's court where in time he absorbed a thorough schooling in statecraft at that most important of European kingdoms while awaiting a promising time to return from exile. In 825 he came back to win a crushing victory over Mercia and in the next several years he became overlord of all southern Britain as well. But the logical advance toward political unity which he represented was interrupted by an external force of great power, the Vikings.

The Vikings. Out of the north swept the fierce Vikings, attacking not only Britain but most of Europe as well. These Scandinavians were well schooled on the seas: the mountain ridges that dominated their homelands had rendered internal travel difficult and forced them to rely on the sea, and the extreme climate turned them away from the land to seek a living by trade or by fishing, or by the much more lucrative profession of piracy. The long, sleek Viking boats, propelled either by sails or by oars, had such an extended range that they even reached North America.

The Viking raids on Europe began in the eighth century. Their vessels

---

*Dates given are the dates of the reign.

were so swift that they could strike quickly and surprise victims both along the seacoast and even many miles inland along rivers which emptied into the sea. They terrorized the inhabitants of towns, looted extensively in nearby areas, and then withdrew before any help for the hapless victims could arrive. The undefended wealthy monasteries of Britain's eastern seacoast were particularly ripe targets.

Although the name Viking is used generically of all Scandinavians, the Danes concentrated their attacks against Britain and the Norse struck at Ireland. The Danish efforts against Britain continued intermittently for many years, but from 865 onward they abandoned the tactic of strike and withdrawal and began to make permanent settlements in Britain. As the Norse had begun their settlements on Ireland's eastern coast at Dublin, so the Danes settled Britain's eastern shore first. Their roving army quickly reduced the east and then subdued major parts of Mercia. Within a few years the only English kingdom totally free of Danish occupation was Wessex.

Alfred the Great and the Creation of England

Alfred the Great. The only English king ever to be called "Great" succeeded to Wessex's throne, determined to overcome the Vikings. Alfred (871–899) began to build his military strength, rallying the men of Wessex and forming an alliance with the unoccupied part of Mercia. The combined forces stopped the Danes' second campaign in 875, and in 878 Alfred led his forces to defeat them decisively when they mounted a third attempt. An agreement left eastern Britain to be governed by Danish custom (the area came to be known as the Danelaw) and the west to the Saxons. Alfred then used the twenty remaining years of his life to lead and inspire the kingdom, developing its military and naval strength. He organized the navy to protect the coastline and cut off the Viking lines of communications, and on land he consolidated his victories by erecting fortified strongholds to protect the countryside and people. Although the time to begin a sustained campaign to recapture the Danelaw was not yet ripe, he had prepared the military base which his descendants would need.

Alfred was an inspiration to his people culturally as well. If it had not been for his zeal, few writings in English (as the Anglo-Saxon language came to be called) would have survived. In addition to the *Anglo-Saxon Chronicle,* in which Alfred had a role, and legal documents from his government, Alfred translated Pope Gregory's *Pastoral Care* from Latin so that his bishops might be guided in properly shepherding their flocks. To give his people a sense of their heritage he translated the *Ecclesiastical History of the English People,* written by the Northumbrian monk Bede. To encourage learning he rendered Boethius' *Consolation of Philosophy* into English, and to stimulate his subjects' piety he had lives of the saints translated. There can be few more appealing pictures than that of this king who lamented his own lack of an early education, but who painstakingly worked to learn to read and write, first English and then Latin, and who later gathered around him educated men to instruct others. His encouragement of learning led other Englishmen to study Latin, the international language of scholarship and of the church. Thus horizons to European culture were expanded.

The Creation of England. At Alfred's death there were five major and a number of smaller kingdoms in Britain. The two Saxon kingdoms of Wessex and Mercia controlled the southwest and had been united politically by marriages between their royal families. The east was controlled by the Danes, primarily in the Danelaw but also in a few lesser kingdoms in the northeast. There were two Celtic kingdoms, Wales in the far west and Scotland in the north, the latter dating from a union of the Scots and Picts about 850. The most important steps toward political unification were the successive military victories of Alfred's son Edward (899–924) and grandson Athelstan (924–939) which resulted in the conquest of the Danelaw and the minor Danish kingdoms in the north and in the stopping of any Celtic movements southward. By the middle of the tenth century an agreement had been made with Scotland as to territories, the entire area south of the river Tweed to be the one unified kingdom of England.

Thenceforth England was a political unit never to be subdivided. When outside kingdoms threatened to invade, the whole of England was to be the prize. The kings were now the kings of England, solemnly bound to the realm as was demonstrated by the coronation oath of Edgar in 973. The ceremonies of coronation were traditional and included crowning, anointing, and investing with the royal insignia; the oath was new—the king's sworn promise to govern England well and lawfully, to give justice to his people and protection to the church.

The Powers of Kingship. An Anglo-Saxon king's immediate claim to power had rested on his military ability; thus he was the greater as he conquered or subdued more territory. But once England had been unified, kingship had to be expanded to include nonmilitary tasks as well, and the king's prestige grew accordingly. Because the Germanic kingdoms had been communities which stressed the law, the preeminence of the king developed first in that area.

The king grew to paramount importance in the law in three ways. First, the wergeld on his life was set so high that no one could pay it, and thus an offender would be executed. The king, therefore, had a unique form of

Alfred the Great *(The Bettmann Archive)*.

protection. The crime of taking his life came to be considered a separate legal offense, treason. Second, the king became the normal person to make the decisions about the unclear or undeveloped areas in the customary law. His decisions, called "dooms," were in fact accepted as declarations of law—indeed, the first written law while remaining, however, of much less importance than the main body of unwritten law. Third, the kings began to develop a system of separate royal law administered exclusively by royal agents. The kings took the notion of "peace" which was so important in Germanic law and expanded the "king's peace" greatly. It was made to apply to persons other than the king (such as his family and royal officers), to places other than his royal court (churches, fairs, highways), and to times other than the king's ceremonial wearing of his crown (Sundays, feast days of the church). A small number of offenses were defined as breaking the peace on those occasions, and the case was to be heard before a royal officer. The guilty party upon conviction had to pay a fine to the king as well as damages to the injured.

The king was advised by a council, a group of his closest advisors called the witan. He was not bound to take their advice, but it was to his advantage to consult them since he thereby associated the leading men of the realm with royal policies. The witan had the right to designate the successor to the throne; usually it chose the king's son although this was not always done since a hereditary right to the crown was not yet an unquestioned legal right. In practice the witan chose the obvious candidate, often passing over a very young son of a deceased king to choose an older relative or someone else who could actively exercise the office.

As nonmilitary administration became more important with an expanded kingdom, two offices within the royal court grew to greater importance. The chamberlain, who was at first the keeper of the king's bedding and personal effects, began to keep the king's treasure as well and thus received and disbursed royal funds on command. The clergy, who cared for the king's spiritual needs, were often the only literate men in the court and also served by writing the king's orders (the writs) and his grants of privileges and rights (the charters). These documents were cut so that a tongue of parchment hung down from the main writing, to which wax shaped with a mold (the royal seal) was affixed as an authentication.

Local Administration. As Wessex led the unification of the realm the kings needed to assert and assure their control over an increasing number of localities. A system of shires was developed, shire meaning "a share" or part of the whole. When former kingdoms such as Essex or Sussex were deemed small enough for administrative efficiency they became shires in themselves, but larger kingdoms such as Wessex were subdivided into several artificial shires as was done also for the land won back from the Vikings. Eventually over thirty shires were formed.

The king's representative in the shire was at first an ealdorman, but so many new shires were eventually created that it became unwieldy for the king to have to deal with so many of them. Alfred's successors began to group three or four shires under one ealdorman, but this increased responsibility made the ealdorman so important that he could even pose a threat to the king's exclusive power, and thus in time the ealdormen were relieved of any administrative responsibility. From the tenth century onward the principal royal officer in the shire was the sheriff (*shire reeve*). He collected the revenues of the king (rentals of land and profits of justice primarily), transmitted royal writs, oversaw the militia of the shire, and assisted in keeping the peace, especially by presiding over the shire court. The shire in turn was subdivided into hundreds or wapentakes, the latter a name which prevailed where the Vikings had had influence. It is not clear whether "hundred" referred to men, to units of land, or to units capable of producing a certain revenue. The constable was in charge of the hundred, below which were tithings ("tenths") which were charged with keeping the peace.

Standing outside this system were the boroughs. The word *burh*, which was the root of "borough," implied a fortified place, often strategically located at the junction of rivers or on hilltops which commanded an area. It was natural that these centers would come to have economic and governmental importance as well and so the boroughs acquired grants of privileges through royal charters, one of the most important of which was exemption from supervision by the sheriffs and constables. The population of boroughs remained generally small, a reflection of the new emphasis on rural life which differed so markedly from when the Romans had dominated Britain.

Early English Society

The People of Saxon England. To understand the people who made up early English society first requires putting aside more modern terms such as upper, middle, or lower class because those terms are based primarily on differences in wealth and occupation. Anglo-Saxon society was almost totally agricultural, and distinctions were based on degrees of legal and economic freedom. There were three basic grades: slaves who had no freedom at all, ceorls who enjoyed legal but not economic freedom, and a nobility who enjoyed both legal and economic freedom. Persons became slaves when they were captured in battle by men of another kingdom, when they were punished for very serious crimes, or when they voluntarily exchanged their freedom for protection or for food during times of acute strife or famine.

The ceorls were husbandmen, tillers of the soil who headed agricultural households and worked in part on their own behalf and in part for their lord. The lowest ranking ceorls spent most of their time in unpaid labor for the lord—in sowing, tending, and harvesting his crops, in minding his animals, and in performing many other menial tasks. They were able to work on their own lands only after completing their legal obligations. The ceorls with the greatest freedom were those who merely paid the lord some rent and did not have to perform personal services. Because their energies could be spent on developing their own lands they could prosper and settle their obligations that much easier. Many ceorls owed a combination of personal and money services. The state of legal freedom but economic unfreedom which English ceorls and men of similar standing on continental Europe had is generally called serfdom.

The nobility of early English society gained their special privileges in the period of the Saxon conquests by their military services to the king. In later centuries they were rewarded also with land and were called thegns. Many thegns served the kings as administrators, most notably the ealdormen. As the latter were relieved of administrative duties and replaced by sheriffs in the shires, the Danish title of *eorl* (later earl) was adopted, and to its holders it became a more important rank of nobility with preeminence over the others.

Mobility between grades of society was possible. It was to the lord's advantage to make enterprising slaves ceorls, not only because the church encouraged this Christian act but also because the ceorl then became responsible for maintaining himself and yet still owed the lord service. A ceorl might accumulate enough wealth to buy exemptions from the economic services he owed and thus become economically and legally free even though not of noble status. It was also possible to move downward—many were unable to protect themselves from the constant dangers of the Viking invasions or were wiped out by a series of bad harvests and so voluntarily gave up some freedom to a lord in return for protection and the necessities of life. This practice was called commendation and became common in later years so that many people were less free than in the early part of the Middle Ages.

The Countryside. Early English settlements consisted not of single dwellings scattered around the countryside but of villages which were surrounded by the fields that people worked. Some villages were clusters of houses around an open space and others had a single road lined with dwellings through the village. Rarely would there have been any buildings of stone, although some more important churches and the homes of some nobles used stone in construction. The rest of the buildings varied as much as the social standing of the village's families. Prosperous ceorls might live in timbered structures with walls made of mud and wattle, but the poorer ones often lived in hovels, sunken huts covered with straw. The villages usually had a common pasture on which all could graze their animals.

The fields which surrounded the villages were divided, half to be sown while the other half lay fallow to regain its fertility. By the tenth century a system of strip farming had become quite common, perhaps introduced by the Danes. A ceorl would have several strips of land just over twenty yards wide in various parts of the fields, none adjacent but rather separated by the strips of other ceorls. Because oxen were used to pull the plow the strips would be as long as possible so that the team did not have to turn often. When the harvesting was completed in one field the other was immediately sown with wheat and rye, to lie dormant over the winter until germination in the spring, at which time barley and oats were also sown.

Barley was the most important crop and was ground in mills for making bread and also made into malt for brewing beer, the staple drink. Pigs and sheep were raised, but because it was so hard to keep animals alive in the winter due to the lack of fodder, most animals were slaughtered in the autumn; the rest often occupied the houses along with the people. Many areas of Britain were simply not suited for farming, and thus animals were grazed in the steep pastures.

Christian Life. The pattern for early Christianity had been set by its rapid spread in earlier periods, and by 700 it had been accepted in all of Britain. Dioceses were created, sometimes coinciding with smaller kingdoms as London did for Essex, sometimes consisting only of part so that Canterbury and Rochester served eastern and western Kent, respectively. The archbishop of Canterbury supervised the southern dioceses and the archbishop of York the northern. The real importance of Christianity lay in the impact it made on the lives of each person, substituting Christian ideals of love, respect, and unselfishness for pagan values. These new virtues were exemplified in the person of Theodore of Tarsus, a Greek who in his service of the universal church came to be archbishop of Canterbury from 669 to 690. He actively formed new dioceses and set a personal example of tireless devotion to his flock through teaching, preaching, confirming, and ordaining. He convened the clergy to draft codes for morals and penance in order to insure the sound formation of the people in Christian life, and his personal supervision of the higher clergy kept them zealous and dedicated.

The life in monasteries was a jewel of Christian living. Men and women who wished to dedicate themselves to God in lives of worship and contemplation came to monasteries to withdraw from the world's distractions, binding themselves by vows of poverty to be rid of concern for worldly goods, chastity so that family responsibilities did not occupy their time, and obedience so that by losing their own will they might better do God's. In time the monasteries became centers of learning, especially when founders and benefactors presented them with handwritten manuscripts which were so rare in England. Some of the most beautiful examples of copied Bibles were made in northern monasteries such as Jarrow, and a particularly beautiful one of the early eighth century from Lindisfarne is an outstanding work of early English art. It was at Jarrow that the monk Bede prepared his *Ecclesiastical History of the English People,* an invaluable source for the history of Anglo-Saxon society which Alfred had translated. The manuscript has a rich and vivid style with unusually advanced descriptions of complex historical events.

The conversion of Britain did not exhaust the missionary vigor of the church. Northumbrians such as Wilfrid and Willibrord brought Christianity to Saxony and neighboring areas which were the original home of the Germanic invaders of Britain. The West Saxon Boniface evangelized down the Rhine in Germany to found Christianity there and to assist in reforming it in nearby Frankland. So famous was the monastery school at York under Alcuin that in 782 he was called by Charlemagne to head the school at his own court at Aachen.

The first Vikings had been pagans whose attacks on monasteries and churches dealt a crippling blow to Christianity. Gradually their conversion, both in England and in Scandinavia, led to a good deal of restoration, but the state of religion in the early eleventh century had not yet recovered to its earlier situation.

England in the Early Eleventh Century

For several generations the brilliance and wisdom of Alfred had continued in his descendants, but in the late tenth century there had been a considerable decline in the standards of English society which was personified in great part in King Ethelred the Unready (978–1016). He seemed to reflect the weakness, treachery, and selfishness of the time and his character was blemished by his contemporaries' suspicion that his mother had been implicated in the murder of Ethelred's older brother. When the second wave of Viking invasions began in the early years of his reign he sought to stop the invaders by paying them huge sums of money. England was greatly burdened in raising the thousands and thousands of pounds of precious metals which came to be known as the danegeld. The new invaders were a professional fighting force whose training and discipline made them a more effective army than western Europe had ever known before.

Although this explains in part why Ethelred gave in, his flight in 1013 before another band of raiders, led this time by the Danish king, made many of his subjects esteem him as a coward.

Canute's Viking Empire. The successful invading Danish king died soon afterward and power passed to his son Canute. Most of the English recognized Canute as their king and when he defeated Ethelred's son Edmund Ironside in battle, and at Edmund's death soon afterward, Canute's acceptance was complete. Ethelred the Unready had been married to a Norman woman, Emma, whom Canute now married to further solidify his status in England. He thus became stepfather to the children of Ethelred and Emma.

Canute actively ruled a Scandinavian empire made up of the English, Danes, Norwegians, and Swedes. He was a remarkable man who combined the severity and cruelty of the military conqueror with the wisdom which realized that England's government was far superior to the Scandinavian institutions. Unlike earlier invaders he adopted England's government and law and by his military strength he guaranteed the opportunity for its economic growth. He safeguarded the church and appreciated English culture.

After Canute's death in 1035 his two sons who had little ability squandered his legacy. The last of them invited back from Normandy his half brother Edward, the son of Emma and her first husband, Ethelred the Unready, and thus made the transition of the crown easier. When Edward began to reign (1042–1066) he theoretically blended the three traditions which at Edward's death in 1066 would compete for the throne of England—the Saxons, the Vikings, and the Normans.

Edward the Confessor. Edward's religious devotion was inspiring to his contemporaries, and as "Edward the Confessor" he was recognized as a saint by the church soon after his death. Scholars today debate whether his saintly reputation was exaggerated, but they agree that the realm was certainly not peaceful. He had spent the first twenty-five years of his life in Normandy and had little appreciation of Englishmen or their values, so that when vacancies arose in the English government or church he filled them with trusted Normans. A resentful native opposition arose which was led by Godwin, Earl of Wessex, by his sons whose earldoms included most of southern England, and by his daughter Edith who was Edward's wife. The quarrels between these mighty English subjects and the king were complicated because Edward had no children, probably as a result of a vow of celibacy which he took just before his marriage.

It seems certain that in either 1051 or 1052 Edward had promised England's crown to his second cousin, William, Duke of Normandy. In later years when Edward withdrew from public life to devote more time to religion and to the building of his beloved Westminster Abbey, he allowed his cousin and brother-in-law Harold (a son of Godwin, who had died in 1053) to assume the practical direction of English affairs. Harold was a good fighter whose victories over the Welsh won much admiration. It seemed natural that when Edward died early in 1066 this capable English noble would be chosen king by the witan. His title was compromised, however, by Edward's promise to William and by an oath which Harold himself made to William, although the terms of the latter are still uncertainly known.

Harold's reign as king lasted but nine months. In September 1066 Harold Hardrada, the king of Norway, assisted by the English king's brother, landed on the northeastern coast of England to reassert the Scandinavian claim to the crown. King Harold of England marched his forces northward, and on September 25 at Stamford Bridge repelled the invasion, killing his brother and the Norwegian king in battle. But on September 27, William of Normandy set sail to demand the fulfillment of the promise of Edward the Confessor, so that King Harold of England had to turn his troops and march 250 miles southward to face yet another contender.

Suggestions for Further Reading

The earliest times are treated in Jacquetta and Christopher Hawkes, *Prehistoric Britain* (1965). Two useful studies of the Celts are Nora K. Chadwick's *Celtic Britain* (1963) and T. G. E. Powell, *The Celts* (1958). The theory that Stonehenge was a sophisticated astronomical observatory is argued in Gerald S. Hawkins with John S. White, *Stonehenge Decoded* (1965). Geoffrey Ashe and others introduce the vexed question of King Arthur in *The Quest for Arthur's Britain* (1968).

Among excellent surveys of Roman Britain are I. A. Richmond, *Roman Britain* (1955), Peter Hunter Blair, *Roman Britain and Early England, 55 B.C.–A.D. 871* (1963), and Peter Salway, *Roman Britain* (1984). A specialized, fascinating study is Peter Beresford Ellis' *Caesar's Invasion of Britain* (1980). The urban style of life is reflected in John Wacher's *The Towns of Roman Britain* (1974).

An excellent survey of the Anglo-Saxon period is Peter Hunter Blair's *An Introduction to Anglo-Saxon England* (1956), while Sir Frank Stenton's *Anglo-Saxon England* (2nd edition, 1947) is a longer classic. The two major contemporary sources have been often edited, such as G. N. Garmonoway, *Anglo-Saxon Chronicle* (1953) and *Bede* by T. Sherley-Price (revised by R. E. Latham), *A History of the English Church and People* (1955). The best guide to governmental developments is Bryce Lyon, *A Constitutional and Legal History of Medieval England* (2nd edition, 1980), and a penetrating discussion of Germanic contributions appears in the early chapters of J. E. A. Jolliffe's *The Constitutional History of Medieval England* (1961).

There are studies of important Anglo-Saxon figures in Eleanor S. Duckett's

Alfred the Great: The King and His England (1956) and the same author's *Anglo-Saxon Saints and Scholars* (1947), and in L. M. Duckett's *Alfred the Great* (1912). A good study of the childless king who precipitated the crisis over the succession is Frank Barlow's *Edward the Confessor* (1970). Early agriculture is well treated in H. P. R. Finberg's *The Formation of England, 550–1042* (1974). A great emphasis on social and economic matters is in Dorothy Whitelock's *The Beginnings of English Society* (1952), while an illustrated brief guide to early culture is in *Art Treasures in the British Isles* (1969).

2

Anglo-Norman England

1066–1189

*W*hen Edward died early in 1066 Harold was the logical successor to the crown, and in fact the witan proclaimed him king. Harold's title was at least in part compromised, however, by the promise Edward had made to William and by an oath which Harold himself made to William, although the terms of the latter are still uncertain. As has been discussed, Harold's reign as king lasted but nine months: after defeating his brother and the king of Norway in the northeast of England in September, King Harold of England had to march southward to meet a new threat. On September 27, William of Normandy set sail to demand the fulfillment of the promise of Edward the Confessor.

The achievements of William the Conqueror and his successors—the Anglo-Norman kings—shaped England into a much more powerful realm than it had been. The Anglo-Norman kings and the first of the Plantagenets, Henry II, fused Norman ideas and experiences with the best of the earlier Anglo-Saxon and Viking elements. By 1189 England had the most sophisticated governmental institutions in western Europe.

The Norman Conquest

The Vikings had attacked and permanently conquered Normandy in the ninth and tenth centuries and had gradually fused their culture with the French, but early in the eleventh century Normandy was still a weak and divided duchy where great nobles were often competitors with the duke for power. William's resolute leadership dramatically changed that. He was a unique blend of statesman and soldier—a determined, courageous, and often brutal fighter who won control within the duchy and secured its

24

borders against neighboring powers. He elaborated on feudal principles to subordinate and to harness the abilities of the Norman nobles. So that the Norman church served both God and the duke faithfully, William reformed the church vigorously according to the principles of the religious revival of the eleventh century. The promise of Edward the Confessor to Duke William gave him the opportunity to expand greatly his area of control.

England Conquered. The battle that Duke William fought against King Harold nine miles inland from Hastings on October 14, 1066, was a dramatic clash between two men who each claimed to be England's rightful ruler. Harold's army was drawn up in close order on a hilltop which could only be approached from the south. William sent charge after charge against the English, but neither the Norman soldiers nor their rain of arrows could break the English lines. The attackers soon discovered that a feigned retreat could cause some of the impulsive English soldiers to break ranks in pursuit, and then the Normans could ambush them piecemeal. This tactic was used repeatedly, and then a stray arrow struck and killed King Harold. Leaderless and with dwindling forces, the English retreated, and the first stage of the Conquest was complete.

William's political success depended on capturing London, but he advanced on it slowly to let the tales of his brutality toward townspeople who resisted him reach the Londoners. When his initial demands were rejected, he marched his army in a large arc through the areas neighboring London, burning as he went, until the Londoners capitulated to avoid the same fate. On Christmas Day, 1066, William was crowned king of England in Westminster Abbey.

In the next four years he gained effective control over northern England, at first confirming the titles and privileges of many English nobles in power if they would support him. William appreciated the more sophisticated practices of English government and wished to emphasize his claim to be heir to the crown by preserving the English nobility. In 1075 a rebellion of most English nobles brought this to an end, and, after William rewarded the Norman lords who helped him repress the rebellion with the rebels' lands, only a few English nobles remained.

The Feudal System. Although William retained English governmental institutions he did begin gradually to feudalize England. He acted as a lord in granting land called fiefs (from the Latin *foedum*, the root of the word feudalism) to vassals for which they did homage by kneeling before him to swear their fealty, an oath of honor, loyalty, and service. The exact details of the manner and the pace with which William imposed feudalism are not known. It seems that as more and more lands were forfeited to him as the native English lords rebelled, the lands were regranted according to the new system. He also imposed the Norman custom of primogeniture, according to which the eldest son alone inherited his father's lands. William avoided the common continental European practice of granting all land within large areas or provinces to a single nobleman; by granting nobles many scattered fiefs he avoided making them all-powerful in their locality and denied them the means of mounting a concentrated opposition to royal policies.

Under the feudal system a lord kept part of his lands for his own use (as his demesne) and granted the remainder to a vassal in return for certain specified services. The obligations that the vassal owed to the lord were called the *servita debita* and varied considerably. The most common was knight service, in which a vassal had to furnish a certain number of men armed and ready for military duty at a set time. Churchmen usually owed prayer and religious services, officers in the king's administration owed their time and talents under the tenure of serjeanty, and occasionally a vassal merely paid a money rent.

Among the vassal's other responsibilities were attending the lord's court, offering him counsel, and paying "aids" and "incidents." Aids were paid when a lord's eldest son was knighted, when his eldest daughter was married, and as a ransom if the lord was captured in battle. The most important incident was the "relief," a money payment from a vassal's heir so that the lord would regrant the fief to him. Since a vassal often left minor heirs who were incapable of military or any other service, the lord managed the fief until the heirs came of age under a system known as wardship, and he could arrange the marriages of minor heiresses in order to protect his interests. If a vassal broke the feudal agreement he forfeited the fief to the lord, but if the lord was unfaithful then the vassal was entitled to rise in rebellion.

These elements were common to any lord-vassal relationship, but as the system was implemented the layers of subordination multiplied. A man who was a king's vassal could retain part of his grant as his own demesne and regrant the remainder to other men who became his own vassals. This regranting was called subinfeudation and was quite common in England, doubtless because the possessions of individual lords had been purposely scattered by William. The result was a hierarchical structure of landholding, often schematically described as a pyramid, with the king at the apex and a number of tenants-in-chief holding land directly from him. There were many layers below as further subinfeudation took place. Because it was possible for one vassal to hold fiefs from different lords, the figure of a web can also be used for illustration to stress the tangle of interrelated loyalties implicit in feudalism. Because a vassal's loyalties were most immediately dedicated to his own lord, feudalism tended to make minor

Knight and his Lady, monumental brass rubbing.

vassals less concerned with tenants-in-chief or even the king who was far removed above in the pyramid. This diffusion of power and loyalties away from the king who stood at the center of the feudal kingdom can be likened to the centrifugal motion of ripples away from the center of a pond where a stone has been cast. William I attempted to mitigate this diffusion of loyalties by requiring all important men of the kingdom to take an oath of loyalty to him directly.

By means of the feudal system the Norman kings of England were able to weave the aristocracy into the fabric of the English state and to bind them to loyal service; approximately 200 tenants-in-chief were direct vassals of the king. The common people of England were little touched by the new developments. The fief was the smallest legal unit of feudalism but, since it often coincided with the village which was the social and economic unit, the rights and duties which had long characterized the obligations of agricultural society were merely restated in newer legal terms.

Normans and the Church. The monasteries had a well-established and traditional place in English life before the conquest, and at first only the leadership changed as Norman abbots were appointed. The Normans gradually began to appreciate the fervor of the English monks. As the new abbots introduced the continental reforms which had brought a revitalized spirit to monastic life, the abbeys fused the best of the old and the new. New orders of monks came to England, among them the Cistercians (often popularly called Trappists) who were a particularly austere and fervent order with a preference for settling in remote parts of the country.

The greatest ecclesiastical effect of the conquest was the Norman elaboration of the territorial structure of the church. England had long been divided into geographic dioceses under the direction of bishops, but the Normans rearranged the dioceses for greater efficiency. Later, smaller churches were built throughout the dioceses to serve people in geographic areas known as parishes. This expansion made it imperative to develop further the administrative machinery of the dioceses. Archdeacons were appointed in every diocese to handle administration and legal matters such as cases on marriages and morals; where a diocese included several shires, an archdeacon was usually appointed for each.

There was a special organization for the cathedral church of the diocese, a corporate body called the chapter which was made up of important churchmen called canons. The canons elected one of their number to head the chapter as its dean. In addition to their responsibilities for maintaining the cathedral, the dean and chapter elected a new bishop when one died or was moved to a new diocese. This was only a theoretical right because the Norman kings told the deans and chapters whom to elect. The bishops were skilled administrators who had often begun their careers as chaplains in the royal court. Piety and spiritual dedication were important but, in many cases, were neglected in favor of managerial skills so that the zeal encouraged by the reforms and the effectiveness of this well-organized system was at times compromised by the character of some of its leaders. The archdeacons developed a reputation for pressing legal claims down to the last penny. In later centuries waggish university students were known to debate, half-seriously and half-mockingly, whether it was possible for an archdeacon to save his soul.

The Conqueror's Sons

William the Conqueror and his nobles were forced to divide their time between England and Normandy, at times crushing rebellions of resentful English lords and at other times fighting less successfully to defend the Norman possessions from hostile neighboring French rulers. As William I neared death he adhered to tradition by willing Normandy to his eldest son, Robert, and England to his second son, William. The hard-won unity between the two possessions would be destroyed. The nobility who held lands in Normandy and England feared that if conflicts arose between the brothers they might be forced to choose one and thereby face the loss of possessions in the other's domains.

William Rufus. William II (1087–1100, called "Rufus" by his contemporaries because of his ruddy coloring) was an unappealing ruler who combined all the vices of a soldier with a blasphemy and immorality that scandalized a believing age. Only the code of the camp captured his respect; thus, he valued England merely as a source of revenue for battle. When some of his nobles supported rebellions to supplant him with Robert and to reunite England and Normandy under one ruler, he responded with a military skill as effective as his father's and with a personal brutality which led him to blind, castrate, and hang the rebels. The governmental officials whom he left in charge in England were ruthlessly efficient and therefore very unpopular. William also took advantage of his brother Robert, an affable and courageous man who was irresolute in governing Normandy. When Robert wished to go on a crusade in 1095 he pawned part of his duchy to William to gain the funds. William in turn used Robert's absence to gain control of Normandy and to advance its frontiers militarily.

William often refused to fill vacant bishoprics so that he could appropriate their revenue, but, in 1093 when he believed that he was dying, he decided to make his peace. He accepted his councillors' advice to name Anselm archbishop of Canterbury—a man renowned for his holiness and

England and Wales

as the most outstanding philosopher of the time. When William unexpectedly recovered his health he began to regret the choice. Anselm's behavior was a reproach to the king, and the archbishop combined a lack of administrative experience with a stubborn streak that further strained his relations with the king. These differences were worsened by the investiture controversy. English feudal custom required a bishop to swear an oath of fealty to the king, as did other feudal lords, after which he was invested with his fiefs and the symbols of ecclesiastical office. The pope objected to the king as a layman presuming to confer a spiritual office. Anselm insisted on the papal position, and William resisted lest his control over a feudal lord be reduced. At William's death matters were strained, and Anselm was in exile; only in the following reign was a compromise reached which was acceptable to all parties.

Henry I. William's successor was the Conqueror's third son who had been left a large treasure and no kingdom. Henry had played both sides in the struggle between his older brothers and had earned the distrust of both so that Robert and William each made the other his heir to exclude Henry. When Rufus was on a hunting trip in 1100 he was "accidentally" struck in the neck with an arrow and killed. Henry just happened to be nearby and rode at once to Winchester to seize the English treasury and to proclaim himself king of England. William's body lay unclaimed for hours. Several years after he had been buried at Winchester Cathedral the roof fell in over his tomb, and it was taken as a certain sign of divine disfavor. Henry (1100–1135) was a capable statesman who immediately bid for the support of important leaders in order to gain their acquiescence in his usurpation. He issued a Charter of Liberties which promised to repudiate William II's abuses in the church and government, and he kept most of the promises by ruling fairly. He was called the "lion of justice." His governmental skill consolidated the achievements of his father, and he began new procedures which further enhanced the power and authority of kingship. In 1105 to 1106 he turned on his brother Robert and mounted an English conquest of Normandy, thereby reuniting Normandy and England.

Anglo-Norman Government

Most English administrative agencies were more developed than those were in Normandy, and the Anglo-Norman kings retained them and expanded them greatly. The Anglo-Saxon writing office that prepared writs and charters acquired the new name of the Chancery and grew in importance as writs became important in law as well as in administration. A council of advisors was retained but was now called by the Latin name *curia regis* rather than the witan. The greatest Norman contribution to government was feudalism, with its contractual ties that bound the aristocracy to serve the monarchy. Now the *curia regis* was to consist exclusively of the king's feudal tenants-in-chief, but because there were nearly 200 of them most of the day-to-day advice to the king came from the council's members who held the major administrative posts.

Because the kings were often away on the continent to attend to Norman business, William II and subsequent monarchs established the office of justiciar to direct English affairs during their absence. Later the office was expanded to direct the administration even when the king was in England. William Rufus chose Rannulf Flambard as his justiciar, a man who worked with such a ruthless efficiency and an ability to make royal rights lucrative that the king had to remove him in order to placate a growing opposition. Under Henry I, Roger, bishop of Salisbury, held the office and expanded the judicial and administrative powers of government.

It was under Roger's direction also that the first administrative office went "out of court," ceasing to travel with the king and his royal court as they moved throughout England but instead settling down in one central location with a degree of independence. The Anglo-Saxon kings had entrusted the collection and dispersal of funds to the chamberlain in the royal household, and before Roger's time the members of the *curia regis* had superintended the sheriffs' accounting for the king's revenue. Roger developed a new office called the exchequer, which took its name from the checkered cloth upon which the sheriffs accounted after the fashion of an abacus. The cloth was marked in vertical columns to represent units of currency such as pounds and hundreds of pounds, and upon it were placed counters to represent the total revenue which the sheriff was expected to produce.

Because the sheriffs had been ordered many times during the previous year to make disbursements on the king's behalf, counters were removed from the cloth to symbolize these proper deductions, leaving a total to be paid into the exchequer as a result of a process which even the illiterate could follow easily. Pegs of wood shaped like modern tent pegs were notched to indicate the sums paid by the sheriff, wider notches for larger sums down to bare nicks for fractions of pounds, and then the wood (called a tally) was split lengthwise. If disputes arose, the sheriff was able to produce his half to match that kept in the exchequer.

Thus there was a growing number of administrative agencies—the *curia regis*, the justiciar, the chancery, the exchequer, and the royal court in which much was still done. The legal system grew more complex as well. The Anglo-Norman kings retained two existing systems of law, the Anglo-Saxon local courts with their Germanic principles and the system of royal pleas, and added a third with the introduction of feudalism. The feudal system of justice created many courts because each lord was obliged to hold a court for his vassals. A village might spread over several manors, and thus the duty of keeping order and other public duties were often assigned to the village—adding another layer of public justice which grew up alongside the private feudal jurisdiction. William I also separated the church's courts from those of his government. Although this merely followed the Norman practice, in time numerous conflicts would arise over the proper jurisdiction that each type might claim.

Anglo-Norman Society

Feudalism and the Upper Ranks of Society. When William I replaced rebellious English nobles with loyal Norman and French lords he affected nothing less than an aristocratic revolution. The new nobility differed considerably in their outlooks, attitudes, and values. These changes were evident above all else in their use of the French language which had supplanted English in high society, in their military attitudes which led them to mock the "softer" English with their long hair and finer clothes, and in their lack of interest in the arts and literature which many English nobles prized.

Because a much smaller number of new nobles replaced the substantially larger group of English aristocrats, the former tended to be richer and of more individual importance. In time they came to appreciate the more cultured English ways, as had William I. Growth in wealth had an important part in mellowing the Norman attitudes. As men of property, the new nobles began to devote more time to the management of their estates and less to military skills which had first brought them to prominence. At a later time the Norman kings capitalized on this attitude by allowing the nobility to commute the personal knight service that they owed into money payments, which sufficed to hire a smaller number of mercenary fighters.

The character of the knights who stood immediately below the nobility changed as well. At first a knight had been little more than a hired soldier, but once he received property through the process of subinfeudation he too wished to spend more time in managing his estates. As the gradual consolidation of the Norman Empire reduced the frequency of combat there were fewer opportunities for military service. Even the nature of warfare tended to change: the beginning of the Crusades to recover the Holy Land from non-Christians provided an idealistic motive for fighting, and the church promoted elaborate rules of chivalry in the twelfth century to mitigate the worst features of battle. Soon it became more profitable to

Bodiam Castle, Sussex *(Aerofilms, Ltd.)*.

capture a knight, seize his expensive armor and horses, and then hold him for ransom rather than to kill him.

Because military preparedness was a necessity, a new style of architecture came to England. There were few castles from pre-Conquest days, but between 1066 and 1100 over eighty were built as strongholds to dominate and control the areas that the Normans conquered. Most of the early castles were of the motte and bailey type where a protective ditch was dug around the limits of some prominence, such as a hill, and then a timber fortification was built on top of the dirt heaped from the ditch within the enclosure. As the haste of the period of Conquest gave way to more settled times, these early castles were rebuilt in stone. When the style of building was fully developed in later centuries, there were a number of characteristics: castles' exterior walls were smooth with few openings through which an arrow could penetrate, there was but one entrance so that defenses could be concentrated, and the interior was of sufficient size to house a noble family in proper style, although such a damp, cold building with little light penetrating from outside was not comfortable. These castles were designed to enable a loyal force to hold out against an enemy for a considerable time until the royal forces could raise a siege.

Domesday Book and the Peasantry. In 1086, probably fearing a Scandinavian invasion and wishing to understand his realm's resources, William I sent commissioners throughout England to survey landholding and wealth. County by county, hundred by hundred, manor by manor, the commissioners recorded who had held the land before the Conquest, who held it in 1086, what obligations were owed, and what other resources there were such as plows and cattle. Men marveled that one could sooner escape the day of doom and judgment than the questions of the king's men, and so the name stuck to the results of the inquiry. Domesday Book helped the king be better informed, provided a record of landholding which was invaluable for settling later disputes at law, and showed clearly the extent of the aristocratic revolution. It also showed that the primary implications of the Conquest were restricted to the upper ranks of society and to a very small number of people.

Domesday Book was not a survey of population but rather of adult landholders; modern demographers who are interested in population studies have used the scientific aspects of their discipline, nevertheless, to attempt to estimate England's population from that unique survey. Granting that any estimate must be tentative, and that its accuracy depends on the proper selection of a multiplier by which one extends the known number of landowners to take account of the landless and of family size, it has been estimated that England's population in 1086 was about 1,600,000.

Most agricultural workers—the landless for the most part—saw little more than the substitution of a new lord for the old and the requirement to attend the new manorial courts. Otherwise the rhythm of the seasons with the traditional sowing and reaping continued. English was used as a language on the nonaristocratic level, and at first the resentment at the conquerors spawned periodic violence which meant hardship for the common people.

The number of offenses that were considered to be a breach of the king's peace was expanded and reached thirty-seven under Henry I. The Normans had to introduce a murder fine to protect themselves. In English law the victim's family prosecuted someone who had murdered one of their kin, but the Normans usually had no family to avenge them and so there was a great temptation for the English to attack the invaders with little fear of retribution. The murder fine set by the Norman leaders was very high, and all the inhabitants of a hundred in which a Norman was slain had to contribute if the murderer went undetected.

Religion and Society. The creation of new parishes made the church better able to serve people's spiritual needs but also created a number of problems. Parishes were often created when a wealthy patron donated land and other endowments sufficient to erect a church and support a parish priest. Because the patron reserved the right to nominate the next priest every time the office became vacant, the priest's primary loyalty was often to the patron. The training before a priest's ordination was usually inadequate so

Domesday Book (page of entries for Somerset) *(The Bettmann Archive/BBC Hulton)*.

that many lacked the spiritual leadership demanded by the office. Since the priest farmed the land that was the parish's endowment he was subject to the same attitudes, trials, and temptations that beset the flock which he was to guide.

In spite of the problems, the reforms of the period kindled a great deal of religious zeal, and the stone churches which the Normans erected were the centers of both village and town life. These churches were erected in a style called Romanesque or Norman and are a testimony to the preeminence of spiritual aspirations. This was a massive style of construction limited only by the requirement that the walls and columns be strong enough to support the entire weight of the roof, so that the girth of the columns was usually the same as their height. The floor plan was usually of cruciform shape with the altar and choir on the eastern end to catch the rays of the morning sun, the nave to the west forming the remainder of the long part of the cross, and the north and south transepts making the shorter crossbar. The walls were usually constructed in three tiers with windows only at the highest level lest the wall be weakened, and the circular arch was characteristic of the style. The Norman cathedral thus mirrored the strength and even militant attitude that was characteristic of the feudal period. The cathedral at Durham is one of the finest examples in England of the Romanesque style.

Monasticism and the Spiritual Life. The clearest enunciation of the spiritual ideal of the time was to be found in the monastic life where men and women withdrew to live according to a rule of prayer and worship. A good example of early monastic fervor which came close to the ideal was the community at Fountains Abbey. A small number of Benedictine monks at St. Mary's Abbey in York had begun to yearn for a more ascetic and less comfortable life than was normal in their wealthy monastery, and so in the winter of 1132 to 1133 they left York to choose a remote site twenty-five miles away where abundant springs suggested the name Fountains. The following year the monks petitioned for adoption into the Cistercian Order, and under the direction of Abbot Richard endured winters of near starvation until at last their reputation for saintly lives brought both recruits and endowments. Within a decade there were probably 500–600 monks so that three times in ten years offspring monasteries were founded from Fountains Abbey.

Assuming that the daily routine at Fountains was similar to that at other Cistercian abbeys, the gray-clad monks would rise in the dormitories about 2 AM to go to the massive church built in the Norman style, where they would begin the first of an eight-part combination of prayers called the divine office—a blend of psalms, scripture readings, prayers, and hymns which complemented the two daily masses. About two-thirds of the day would have been spent in the church or in reading and prayer in the cloister, to which the monks added periods of manual labor in the fields. The business of the monastery was conducted in the chapter house and the one or occasionally two meatless meals of the day were taken in the refectory. Silence was maintained except for necessary business, and the rhythms of the seasons were seconded by the regular cycle of the liturgical year which represented Christ's life and held it up for the monks' imitation.

It was difficult to maintain such an austere life in full rigor, and many monasteries fell short of the ideal. The wealth that abbeys received from admiring benefactors often caused the monks to spend so much time in worldly management that it intruded on their otherworldly ideals, and ambitious building programs plunged some monasteries into debts and eroded the spirit of prayer. Nevertheless, the impact and attractiveness of the ideal were great, and the zeal of the reformed houses was an inspiration.

Religion and Education. There was a mutual dependence between the church and education: the church needed educated clergy, and the clergy were the only educated people who could staff schools. At the lowest levels were the "reading" or "song" schools, the closest equivalent to what today would be called elementary education, in which reading and singing were taught to boys primarily to meet the church's liturgical needs. In the twelfth century, as an intellectual renaissance swept across Europe, "grammar" schools grew up for students about 11 or 12 years old or older, usually as cathedral schools in major centers. The grammar that was taught was Latin grammar, the prerequisite not only for liturgical service but also for participation in the European intellectual world—one language common to all well-educated Europeans. Two Englishmen illustrate the mutual dependence of church and education—Anselm from the earlier part of the period and John of Salisbury from the later.

Before Anselm became archbishop of Canterbury under William II, he had been a monk at the great Norman abbey of Bec and had there established a scholarly reputation in philosophy and theology. He was well-known across Europe for his erudition. He set forth an argument to prove the existence of God with such intellectual force that his work still commands interest and debate among philosophers today. Anselm thus not only represents profound thought but exemplifies the central role of monastic schools in early education, especially in the eleventh century.

John of Salisbury was a contemporary of his friend and patron, Thomas à Becket, archbishop of Canterbury under Henry II, to whom he dedicated his two greatest books. In his early twenties he left England to go to the famous University of Paris, one of the earliest universities in north-

The nave of Durham Cathedral *(BBC Hulton Picture Library)*.

ern Europe and by far the most renowned in the entire Middle Ages. There he studied under its most famous early teacher, Abelard, and then John went to Chartres in France to complete his studies. He spent several years in the service of the pope and the papal curia, writing a history of the papacy. Because he served also in English government he had an idea of the state and of service to it, which animated his writings on that topic. He compared the political state to a human body: the priesthood corresponded to the soul, the king to the head, the judges to the eyes, the soldiers to the hands, and the tillers of the fields to the feet. John thus represents two important late twelfth century educational advances: the study at universities started to supplant monasteries as centers of learning and the employment of education in the service of both church and government.

England and Anjou

The greatest threats to the English king's Norman possessions came from France which bordered Normandy on the southeast and from Anjou directly southward. William I and II had resisted their incursions, and Henry I by reuniting England and Normandy had increased his ability to resist. In Henry's reign the French King Louis VI began attempts to expand his territories beyond the areas immediately surrounding Paris and thus saw Anglo-Normandy as the principal obstacle to his plans. Although France was occasionally at war with the Anglo-Normans, Louis VI assisted Anjou and other more immediate foes in attacking Normandy. Henry I remained there over half the years of his reign after 1106 to meet the increased threats.

Matilda and Stephen. Henry feared that his realm's capacity to resist would be seriously crippled by the succession to England's crown. Of his numerous children, one boy and one girl only were legitimate and, thus, heirs to the throne. In 1120 his son drowned when a ship in which he and a number of equally drunk companions had embarked sank in the English Channel. Henry had no choice but to order his barons to swear to allow his daughter Matilda to become queen and reign after his death. A woman ruler was a novelty that few lords could anticipate without dread: Matilda was mismatched by a political marriage to Geoffrey, count of Anjou, a youth fourteen years old and eleven years her junior when Henry I died in 1135, yet the marriage offered Anjou the potential for dominating England. Furthermore, Matilda was extremely arrogant, fond of recalling that by her former marriage with the late German emperor she had been an empress.

Matilda never realized her claim because Henry's nephew Stephen seized the throne when the old king died. Stephen (1135–1154) was a popular man whose accession was greeted with relief by most of the nobility. As the grandson of William I through the Conqueror's daughter he was Matilda's cousin. Most nobles acquiesced in the extraordinarily hasty events of the first three weeks during which time he seized the treasury and had himself elected king, as had Henry before him. But this initial decisiveness and foresight were deceptive because for the remainder of the reign he was usually incapable of concentrated and sustained effort. Above all else he showed himself "soft" (as a chronicler put it), ever able to be prevailed upon and to make concessions to powerful forces in the vain effort to sustain an effective control over affairs.

Matilda's arrogance and Stephen's inability were a perfect match—Stephen lost effective control of Normandy to Matilda and neither could decisively win in England during the civil wars which lasted from Geoffrey and Matilda's invasions in 1139 until 1148 when they left England. Five years later an agreement was made between them which allowed Stephen to remain king as long as he lived and to be succeeded by the son of Matilda and Geoffrey, Henry.

Henry II and the Angevin Empire. Few kings have been as personally compelling as the twenty-one-year-old man who began to rule as Henry II (1154–1189). He was a bundle of energy, always on the move, able to spend the day in strenuous hunting and other sports and then the evening in conducting the business of his realms. He was up earlier than his ministers and retired later than they did—and he was so taken with nervous energy that his stocky body, which was topped with red hair, often trembled with uncontrollable rage and fury. Few could love a man of such intensity, but all respected him.

His inheritance was breathtaking: Anjou and other areas in what is now central France from his father, England as a result of the agreement with Stephen, and Normandy from his mother. When he married Eleanor of Aquitaine he assumed effective control over her territories which included most of the southwest of modern France. The total domain, often called the Angevin Empire (Angevin is the adjective derived from Anjou, his patrimony; the name Plantagenet is also often used for this dynastic line, from the devices on the family coat of arms), stretched 900 miles from England's border with Scotland to the Pyrenees which are the modern French border with Spain. Only the strongest of rulers could hope to hold together so many diverse territories, and then only if there was a strong government by which to rule. England alone offered the potential but first Henry II had to restore the powers of the monarchy that Stephen had frittered away. Within the first year of his reign Henry had regained the

Medieval England and France

crown lands which had been alienated, had ridded the country of the hated mercenaries who had fought much of the civil wars, and had taken back the royal castles which the barons had occupied or erected without authorization as havens for resisting the royal power.

The barons' loyalties were won back by Henry's vigorous reassertion of his and their feudal rights. Officials wrote down in the *Cartae Baronum* (Charters of the Barons) the exact terms of feudal obligations. Henry re-established the effectiveness of the royal administration, choosing the exceptionally able Ranulf de Glanville to direct the government and to fashion a staff of loyal administrators who oversaw the enforcement of royal policy. The greatest area of his achievements was in the development of royal law, and the greatest difficulty was in his dealings with the church.

Henry II and the Law. William I had retained English law and fused with it important Norman elements such as feudalism. Henry I, the "lion of justice," introduced a number of innovations which gave royal justices great flexibility. It was Henry II's regularization, systemization, and expansion of justice which made all that had gone before into a coherent and efficient hole. The *curia regis* heard important feudal cases and other important matters for the king, and the exchequer which by now had gone "out of court" heard cases over disputes on royal revenue. The great elaboration was the provision for hearing cases at royal law throughout England's many localities by the itinerant justices.

The name itinerant (from the Latin *iter,* meaning journey) was appropriate because the royal justices divided England into circuits composed of several counties in which they travelled several times a year. Their judicial sittings on disputes over property were called assizes (from the French *assis,* meaning seated or a sitting); on criminal matters, the trials over which they presided were called gaol delivery because they cleared the gaol (as the English spell jail) of all suspects whom the sheriff had detained to await trial. Property matters were heard before a jury (from the Latin word *jurati,* meaning "men sworn on oath"). Not until the thirteenth century were juries used in criminal matters. Men were not ready earlier to decide a neighbor's guilt when that might result in the death penalty and when God's judgment was able to be ascertained through the ordeal. The origin of the jury was the Norman inquest, the seeking of information from men under oath. William I used it to compile Domesday Book, and from 1176 onward it was used for informational surveys of local conditions which were called general eyres. The latter were very unpopular because men resented having to respond under oath to questions that were felt to be mere fishing for information to which the king had no right. In time the informational eyres were dropped, but the jury remained as a regular part of the judicial process.

A plaintiff began a case at royal law by purchasing royal writs. Some writs were jurisdictional, transferring cases from the feudal courts into the royal courts, while others provided means for determining the right to property or the lawful possession of it. The question of the right to property was the most important, and so the writ for this was called the Grand Assize (from the French *grand*, meaning large and implying importance). All parties to the suit had to present full documentation and proof about the ownership of the land, and the defendant was allowed many delays before the case was heard. Therefore, many plaintiffs decided to purchase writs that, without any delay, settled the more restricted question of rightful possession. These writs were called Petty Assizes (from the French *petit*, meaning small or of lesser importance). If through their processes a plaintiff was presumed to be entitled to possess the property he was restored to it until the lengthy and final processes of the Grand Assize were completed. For example, he was restored to the property if the jury found him to be the heir apparent at the time of the "death of his ancestor" (hence the writ *mort d'ancestor*) or if he had been "recently dispossessed" by the defendant (writ of *novel disseisin*).

In time the system of writs was expanded to over 500 types. The king gained financially from the sale of the writs and from the fees for his justices who heard the cases, but more important he gained prestige as the protector of his subjects' rights. By the end of the Middle Ages the local courts in the shires and the feudal courts of the lords heard only the most minor matters, and royal justice had become the dominant system. The kings' subjects used the system because it guaranteed them the right to a speedy and relatively inexpensive trial by a jury of their peers, which was felt to be a far-superior process than in the feudal courts where the landlords were the judges.

Henry II and the Church. One area of conflict between the kings and the church was the proper relationship between the Papacy and England, but the settlement of the investiture controversy in Henry I's reign had cleared up most of these problems. The second difference was the degree of control that the kings could exert over the church in England, a problem which often concerned the proper spheres of jurisdiction between the separated ecclesiastical and secular courts for an offense such as murder. The church claimed that a spiritual person should be tried in a spiritual court; the monarchs argued that, because the church's courts did not inflict the death penalty but only penance and other spiritual punishments, the culprits escaped serious retribution. Many clerics were only in minor orders, the initial stages in the process toward ordination as priests and thus enjoyed full protection yet were not fully members of the clergy. Henry II hoped to solve this problem and all difficulties with the church by appointing as archbishop of Canterbury his loyal friend and Lord Chancellor Thomas à Becket. Surely together they could compromise the matter.

Becket surprised Henry and everyone else—from a cleric hardly renowned for piety, a carefree, pliant royal servant, Becket became the dedicated ascetic changed by a religious conversion and became devoted to defending every privilege of the church no matter how unimportant. When Henry II drew up in 1164 a codification of royal rights in the church called the Constitutions of Clarendon, matters came to a head. Becket refused to accept the Constitutions and in particular objected to the claim that clerics convicted before spiritual courts of a serious secular crime should be degraded by the church and handed over to the secular arm for execution. The conflict that ranged over the next years combined the personal bitterness of a former friendship gone sour with exaggerated claims of principles on both sides. Late in 1170 matters had gotten so bad that Becket excommunicated several bishops who had cooperated in a plan of Henry's, and in exasperation the king uttered the words "Will no one rid me of this troublesome priest?"

Taking him literally, four of Henry's knights went to Canterbury and murdered Becket in his cathedral. The effects of this act were profound. Although Henry disavowed the literal intention of his words he was made to do public penance for his carelessness. Becket was canonized in 1173, and the shrine at Canterbury of St. Thomas à Becket became a center of pilgrimage for Europeans. More important, the event forced Henry II and the Papacy to come to an agreement: Henry conceded that felonies of clergymen should be tried in spiritual courts while secular courts should retain jurisdiction over the lesser misdemeanors of clerics, and that appeals in some cases would be allowed from church courts in England to Rome. But in other matters that related directly to Henry's control over the church, such as nominating bishops and allowing papal orders to come into England only with his permission, Henry retained the ancient rights of English kings. Because both sides had been forced to come to an explicit agreement, England was not to be subject to the same running disputes with the Papacy during the rest of the Middle Ages as were many other European kingdoms.

As marked as Henry's achievements were in so many areas, the seeds for undoing much of his work lay in his own family. Rule as he would throughout his lands, he could not rule Queen Eleanor, who was as formidable and cunning as he was, nor his sons, who spent much of their later years plotting against their father to increase their own inheritances. These family struggles were the more serious because they coincided with the accession to France's throne of Philip Augustus (1180–1223) who dreamed of driving the English out of France and who knew how to exploit the greed and rapacity of Henry's children. Henry II's Angevin Empire stood challenged.

Suggestions for Further Reading

David C. Douglas' *William the Conquerer: The Norman Impact upon England* (1964) is an excellent study of how William first developed effective control over Normandy and then used that experience in England. A special treatment of the fateful year is Alan Lloyd's *The Making of the King, 1066* (1966). A fierce debate on whether Saxon England or Normandy contributed more to the Anglo-Norman experience has long raged, and the varying interpretations are ably presented in C. Warren Hollister's *The Impact of the Norman Conquest* (1969).

Bryce Lyon explains feudalism and Anglo-Norman government well in *A Constitutional and Legal History of Medieval England* (2nd edition, 1980); of special interest for its lucid explanations are S. B. Chrimes, *An Introduction to the Administrative History of Medieval England* (1966). The anarchy of the civil wars between Stephen and Matilda is described in R. H. C. Davis, *King Stephen* (1967). A newer study by W. L. Warren, *Henry II* (1973) replaces several older studies of that important monarch.

There are studies of important churchmen in R. W. Southern's *St Anselm and his Biographer. A Study of Monastic Life and Thought* (1963) and in David Knowles' *Thomas Becket* (1971). The intricacies of the church's organization are explained in Felix Makower's *Constitutional History and Constitution of the Church of England* (1895). The best study of early monasticism is David Knowles' *The Monastic Orders in England, 943–1216* (1940).

Social and economic topics are admirably treated in Doris Mary Stenton, *English Society in the Early Middle Ages, 1066–1307* (1959, first published 1951), and much on the clothing of the era can be gained from the plates of *The Bayeux Tapestry* (edited by F. M. Stenton and others, 1957). Other topics are covered in A. L. Poole, ed., *Medieval England* (2 vols., 1958) and in Sidney Painter, *Medieval Society* (1951).

3

High Medieval England

1189–1327

*T*he thirteenth century was the high point of medieval culture in Europe, and England participated fully in its achievements. It was a century of aspirations, characterized by a religious revival led by the friars who called men to a life of simplicity and an imitation of the Lord's poverty; by the building of cathedrals in the new Gothic style which used height, light, and color to lift man's spirit heavenward; and by the flourishing of medieval philosophy which sparked such an interest in scholarship that universities were developed as centers of learning.

It was a century of change in many of the workaday aspects of life as well. Although rural life continued its traditional practices and rhythms, and agriculture was the way of life for most Englishmen, the countryside came to be dotted with flourishing walled towns whose newly won charters of privileges and new trade organization of the guilds made them ever more important centers for economic growth. As feudal society was broadened by these new styles of life, the century witnessed also a fuller development of England's own unique system of common law, a supplement to and at times a competitor with feudal justice.

It was in the years 1189 to 1327 that England became the first European power to work out a concept of government, the "community of the realm," which significantly broadened participation in government and altered relationships between king and subject. The king was both sovereign and servant of the kingdom, one with many privileges and also many responsibilities, the ruler *for* as well as *of* England. Should a king not satisfy the norms of good government, he could be restrained by the community—as Edward II learned in 1327.

The leaders in the struggle to realize this notion of community were the great feudal barons of England. They did not have a fixed theoretical goal toward which to work, nor did they attempt to wrest from the king his right to make policy and serve as England's leader. But through conflict and chance, through efforts at times inspired by great idealism and at other times merely by personal selfishness, they sought to define the king's and their own place in English life. In the process were forged many precedents and institutions that were unique in the European experience and which are at the heart of British government, most notably the Magna Carta and the beginnings of Parliament.

Richard, John, and Magna Carta

Richard the Lion-Hearted. Henry II, great king and master of many lands, spent his last years in anguish, his sons fighting among themselves and even rising in rebellion against their father, each asserting his right to be the heir to England's crown. Richard, the eldest surviving son and the best fighter, sought the assistance of the king of France, the young Philip Augustus. Wily Philip knew that the expansion of France required winning back French provinces like Normandy, now under English control, and so he played many roles to Richard—confidant, supporter, perhaps even lover—and was rewarded when, in a particularly vengeful act of defiance to old Henry, Richard did homage to Philip for all England's French possessions. Should ever a pretext be found to allege that Richard or his successor was an unfaithful vassal, Philip now had the legal authority under the feudal system to declare those fiefs forfeit.

As King Richard I (1189–1199), Henry's eldest son became Europe's most formidable fighter; his chivalry and shining sword won him the title "Lion-Hearted" and the fear and respect of many. So consumed was he with fighting that he spent nearly all of his time in battle on the continent and only six months of his ten-year reign in England. England became merely his war treasury, with its offices, titles, and lands for sale to finance the costly wars. Because Richard was strong enough to prevent English discontent from erupting into a serious domestic rebellion, Philip Augustus had no opportunity to turn Richard's act of homage into any gain of territory for France. The machinery of government that Richard's father had developed was capable of promoting justice and good government, but it was also possible to use its capabilities for sinister purposes. Richard demanded more feudal service from his tenants-in-chief than could be justified by custom, exercised undue influence in the royal courts, and sought to wring every penny out of the system of royal administration. A less firm ruler would reap bitter fruit from his legacy.

King John. When Richard died from an infection of a minor wound, his brother John came to the throne (1199–1216). John was a talented man

Knight and King, west facade, Exeter Cathedral *(E. A. Reitan)*.

capable of brilliance, the favorite son of his father and as such pampered and indolent, a man who hardly ever achieved anything because he could not sustain a course of action. His secretiveness, moodiness, and intransigence provoked distrust, and he had the uncanny ability to alienate almost everyone. John played right into Philip Augustus' hands. While travelling through France, he fell in love with a young woman, Isabelle, who was legally betrothed to Hugh the Brown, one of John's vassals. When John married her, Hugh sought justice from Philip Augustus, John's lord. When John refused to answer Philip's summons to appear at the French court to answer for his actions, the French king declared all of England's French possessions, for which Richard and then John had done homage, to be forfeited.

John's efforts to win back the French territories by the sword failed. At the same time, he had run afoul of the most powerful pope of the era, Innocent III, over the choice of a cleric to be archbishop of Canterbury. As was traditional, John nominated a candidate, but another candidate was elected by the dean and chapter of Canterbury Cathedral. When the case was appealed to Rome, Innocent disallowed both procedures and installed his own choice. A series of retaliations on both sides followed, escalating finally to the point at which Innocent excommunicated John, a spiritual censure that denied the king any ministration of the church and forbade all from having any contact with him. John could neither withstand such a public reprimand, nor allow his barons the pretext for their continued opposition to him because of grievances, so he submitted to the pope and had the excommunication lifted.

The barons had come to feel more keenly a sense of outrage at the way in which John continued Richard's abuses and added his own. Not only did he pervert good government, but he was a failure. They agreed that the king should be forced to accept, in writing, a statement of the proper norms for government, articles that would spell out the proper relationship between the king and his feudal nobility. On June 15, 1215, John met a delegation of barons on the meadow at Runnymede near Windsor and put his seal to the document known as Magna Carta.

Magna Carta. Over a third of the sixty-three clauses of the "Great Charter" set out the exact feudal obligations of the king's vassals—these included the terms of wardship, the amount of reliefs, and the occasions when feudal aids were to be paid. Another third was directed against abuses in the royal courts, particularly at John's practice of seizing a defendant's property before judgment was made against him, and the remainder of the clauses dealt with a number of other problem areas, including a promise from the king to respect the church's independence. Magna Carta asserted that the king could receive more financial assistance than

Benedictine monk (*Dugdale*, Monasticon Anglicanum).

was already due him only if granted by the assent of the "community of the realm," that is, by the approval of his feudal tenants-in-chief. Although this document dealt primarily with the relationships between the king and his feudal barons, and only incidentally with other Englishmen, it was of fundamental importance to everyone. It stated a crucial principle—the king was not above the law but rather was subject to it. John's assent to this document was an acceptance of the principle that he and all Englishmen belonged to a community of law and that the law governed the ruler as well as the ruled.

Within a year John had repudiated Magna Carta, claiming that his assent was coerced and thus that his oath was not binding, and when he died in 1216 England was in the midst of a civil war as a result of his action. But every succeeding monarch reissued Magna Carta, and its role as a precedent was assured. Because tradition and custom were so highly esteemed in England, nothing made an argument more effective than to cite historical precedents to support a claim, but a precedent could be made enforceable only if the aggrieved party had the military or political power to insist upon it. Succeeding kings attempted to evade the law and repeat abuses that John or his predecessors had promised to reform; but in time the rule of law would prevail, and Magna Carta would be vindicated as the fundamental precedent.

Henry III and Parliament

Henry III, only nine years old when his father died, became England's first minor ruler (1216–1272). The regent appointed to look after Henry reissued Magna Carta in the young king's name. With the civil wars caused by John's repudiation of Magna Carta at an end, peace returned. The barons banded together to preserve the crown and kingdom for Henry, but, when he began to rule on his own, they increasingly felt that their trust had been betrayed. Although the king was cultivated, gracious, and generous in endowing fine new buildings, he was generally contentious in matters of state.

Household Government. The barons particularly resented Henry's reliance on foreign favorites, kinsmen of his French mother and his queen. He refashioned his council, ignoring the barons who had a feudal right to give him counsel, and appointed instead the non-noble favorites who were bound to him by a special oath of loyalty. The king found it hard to control the day-to-day operation of the government because important administrative bodies had "gone out of court" (page 32), so he shifted many important financial and administrative tasks away from the exchequer and the chancery and into household departments of his royal court, such as the wardrobe and the chamber, which attended him daily. The growing resentments of the barons over the new council and the household government of Henry reached the breaking point in 1258. Henry sought to provide for his second son by accepting an offer of the pope to make him king of Sicily. But the pope did not control Sicily—to win the crown for his son, Henry would have to conquer it himself and pay all the debts the pope had incurred in his own unsuccessful wars of conquest. The barons, who would have to go to war in order to make these ludicrous terms work, had had enough.

Remembering how John had been forced to accept Magna Carta in 1215 when the barons acted together, and realizing that they would have to go further now to regain their rightful share in the government of England, the barons framed a series of articles, the Provisions of Oxford, and forced Henry to agree to them in 1258. The provisions bound Henry to embark on a plan of reform, and gave supervisory control of the royal government to a council of barons. Henry soon rallied enough support to repudiate his acceptance of the baronial council, and, because the barons did not have a single leader capable of stiffening their resolve, the king's promise to reform bought him time. When it became clear that he was insincere, and when the brilliant Simon de Montfort stepped into the leadership of the baronial party, the barons began a civil war that ended in 1265 with Henry's capture. De Montfort had been born in France, had come to England to claim an inheritance, and then had married Henry III's sister. He served the king until they had a falling out. Although the motives of this mercurial man are as unclear today as they were to his contemporaries, he was shrewd enough to see that opposition by a small group would not suffice to counter the king.

The Beginning of Parliament. De Montfort realized that success in achieving governmental reform was possible only if the demand for it was broad based and not limited to a handful of baronial tenants-in-chief. In 1265 he called together a Parliament. This was to be composed not merely of the feudal nobility but also of representatives of England's shires and principal towns. The name "parliament" (from the French *parler*) was not new, because it had been used when the king met with his feudal advisors to discuss matters of state. The notion of representation was not new: the system of juries was based on the selection of men to act for their neighbors, and kings early in the thirteenth century had convened representatives of the localities—some who were even elected—to perform certain specific duties. The importance of the Parliament of 1265 was that it fused into one truly national body concerned with broad affairs of the kingdom the heretofore separate elements of feudal advisors and elected representatives. The two representatives from each county were called knights of the shire, and the two from each of the major boroughs were called burgesses. Although these representatives and the feudal barons might divide into smaller groups to discuss certain matters, they met as a unicameral (one house) assembly.

Later in 1265, Henry III's talented son Edward led the royalists against the barons at Evesham where he smashed their armies and killed de Montfort. But the notion of a truly national Parliament that had arisen out of the conflict was much too valuable to be lost, and Parliaments were frequently convened in the remainder of Henry's reign. At this early stage Parliaments were not legislative in character; after consultation the king could pronounce a law or statute in Parliament on his own initiative, as was done in 1267 when many of the reforms sought in the Provisions of Oxford were granted by the king in the Statute of Marlborough. The real development of Parliament as an institution lay in the future, and we shall see later in this chapter how important Edward was in the process.

The Common Law and Juries. The legal system fashioned by Henry I and Henry II came to maturity in the thirteenth century, primarily because it attracted a greater part of the litigation as a quicker and more impartial alternative to feudal justice. The procedures of the system of writs were uniform, the personnel were homogeneous because the same judges who sat in the royal courts at Westminster went throughout England twice a year on circuits to hear cases locally, and the principles that they followed were the same. This caused the system to be called the common law, based on the principles of *stare decisis,* to "stand in decisions" in earlier cases which were to be the precedents in similar matters later. This "judge-made law" based on the outcome of court cases naturally called forth a large body of legal literature to quote and comment on the precedents and required a learned profession of attorneys to plead in the courts.

In the thirteenth century the jury system was also applied to criminal cases. Previously it had been used only in disputes over property, according to the terms of the writs, and people were reluctant to judge a neighbor's actions in criminal matters where a conviction brought the death penalty. The notion of leaving the determination of guilt to God through the process of the ordeal had been severely compromised by the Norman practice of allowing a defendant to hire a champion to represent him in the ordeal of battle. The church recognized this and in 1215 ordered priests not to sanction ordeals any longer, significantly hastening the acceptance of juries.

There were two criminal juries, one for each stage of the process. A large representation was desired when accusations of criminal misdoings were sought, and so the name grand jury was adapted from the French

August corn harvest *(BBC Hulton Picture Library)*.

grand, meaning large. The grand jury indicted offenders (from the Latin *in,* meaning against, and *dictum,* meaning speaking) or "spoke against" an individual. A smaller jury, called a petty jury after the French *petit,* meaning small, heard the evidence and determined whether the defendant was guilty or innocent. It was asked to "truly speak" about guilt or innocence, that is to render a verdict (from the Latin *vere* for truly and *dictum*). At this early stage the size of the petty jury varied greatly, but in time twelve became the accepted number.

New Economic Growth

Perhaps 90 percent of England's population worked in agriculture with its traditional attitudes and techniques. But there were new economic developments that formed the prerequisites for a substantial and relatively sophisticated economic growth in the centuries to follow.

The Towns and Trade. The importance of towns was out of proportion to their size. Only a few towns such as London, Bristol, and York had as many as 10,000 persons, and the average size of the slightly over 100 boroughs at the beginning of the fourteenth century was about 2,000. The towns became important for a variety of reasons. Some were important because they commanded a harbor or the confluence of two rivers or some other prominent geographical feature, and some were important because they were centers of administration, such as a shire, or were the seat of a diocese with its cathedral. In the latter case they were properly called "cities," regardless of size. Townspeople often helped with the harvest or farmed land within or near the town. The heart of a town's prosperity, however, was trade, and, when town became borough, the seeds of its trading growth were sown.

The transformation was made when a borough was chartered. A charter normally gave a town a degree of political independence from the shire's officers, conferred economic privileges such as markets and fairs, and enabled the burgesses to have legal rights that reflected their different style of life. Some towns were boroughs before 1066 and had traditional privileges, but the practice of granting written charters coincided with the great financial needs of Richard I. Officials often hoped to improve the terms in new grants that would let the town have prized privileges such as those enjoyed by London and Bristol. Important lords and bishops also granted charters for boroughs. If a borough prospered, it became a potential source of greater royal income, and kings developed new types of taxation. But a charter was no guarantee of success, and many boroughs languished or even disappeared.

The political structure of the boroughs was rather uniform. If a borough was large enough, it was divided into wards, each of which elected an alderman. The alderman formed the upper and most important of two councils, electing one of their members to serve as mayor for a year's term. The other council was larger, consisting of a number of representatives from each ward. The borough's officers enforced the laws, punished criminals, collected taxes, and kept "foreigners," as nonresidents were called, from usurping the privileges of the burgesses.

The economic control of the borough rested with the guilds. In smaller boroughs and in the early years of the larger ones, there was only one guild to control all economic activities—the guild merchant. It enforced the rules of the markets, supervised the quality of the products that were traded, and generally directed the town's economic life. If a town flourished, an economic specialization nearly always followed, and in time guilds for each of the crafts were organized, such as weavers, tailors, butchers, brewers, and goldsmiths. These guilds established regulations that governed the reception of apprentices and certified them afterward as journeymen (day workers) entitled to exercise the trade and, in due time, as masters. The transition from a single guild merchant to many craft guilds often involved acrimonious disputes as men fought for control of the economic life of the borough, but in time the craft guilds supplanted the guild merchant.

Although in theory the political and economic control of the borough were vested in different bodies, in practice the same men ran both; to this day, the buildings that house the governmental offices of English towns are called guildhalls. The town's lifeblood was the weekly or twice-weekly market; foreigners were welcome to buy or to sell at wholesale those specialized products not made in the town, but the borough's success depended in large part on restricting sale at retail to its own burgesses. A fair might be held once or twice a year, specializing in products peculiar to the area. There was entertainment and fun, but its success depended on drawing merchants from throughout England and the continent.

The Wool and Cloth Trade. England was the greatest wool-producing kingdom in Europe. From the vast numbers of sheep that dotted the hills of northern England came the fleece to make the wool cloth which most northern Europeans wore. Although it was possible merely to ship raw wool abroad, its value was considerably enhanced if it was made into finished cloth. So many stages were involved in the process that large numbers of persons were employed full-time on estates which specialized in making woolen cloth. Farmers everywhere worked at it part-time to supplement their income. In order to make cloth, shearers removed the fleece from the animals and sent it to carders who combed it so that the wool fibers lay parallel. Spinners fashioned this into thread, and weavers wove this into cloth. Fullers bleached the cloth, dyers added the desired coloring, and then it was stretched back into shape and trimmed to size. The cloth was sold either at fairs, or special marketing halls in England, or abroad.

In the early years the English were distinctly inferior to continental Europeans in making finished cloth, and the conduct of the market for the sale of the cloths was dominated by aliens as well. To learn to make cloth better, the English allowed aliens to enter and to teach the trade. By the beginning of the fourteenth century the English had begun to use the capitalistic method of controlling the manufacture of cloth. An entrepreneur gathered materials prepared at one stage of the process and delivered them to the next, and so assumed the responsibility of seeing the product through all its complicated preparation. In 1326 the English moved to gain control of the marketing stages as well. They forbade, as before, purchasers from abroad to travel throughout England to the various fairs to buy cloths and instead allowed them to buy only in a few regulated halls stocked with cloth gathered by English middlemen. With such a small number of set places for purchase, called "staple towns," the government was better able to supervise the trade, to collect a new type of tax in the form of customs duties, and to enforce the laws which controlled the quality of the products. Customs duties were also collected on the commodities that the English imported: wine from France, spices from Venice and other areas which traded with the Far East, and naval stores such as timber and pitch for building ships from Scandinavia. From these modest beginnings would develop an ever-increasing volume of trade, until in the eighteenth and nineteenth centuries England would be the greatest trading nation in the world.

Medieval York. Few towns better illustrate the importance of the new municipal government and the wool trade than York in northern England. On the moors and other hilly terrain to the north and west of this city grazed countless sheep, many on the estates of the Cistercian monks who had introduced the raising of sheep into England. York's location on the River Ouse gave it direct access to the North Sea and thus to continental markets. It was important militarily because it lay astride the only lowland route from England to Scotland and administratively as the center of Yorkshire and as the cathedral city of the diocese of York.

As the headquarters of the Roman garrison whose legions protected the northern frontier of Roman Britain (page 5), York had been laid out on neat military lines. The seventy acres within the walls housed barracks and other military buildings which had been built in rectangular fashion at right angles to the river. Medieval York was different in a number of ways. The neat pattern of streets was gone and was replaced by wandering lanes at helter-skelter angles, spilling out beyond the old walls to cover an area three times as great, even though the walls were kept as a fortification. The costly buildings were no longer military but ecclesiastical—forty-seven parish churches, several abbeys, and the jewel of the city, York Minster, the archbishop's cathedral with its captivatingly lovely gothic arches and windows. These churches were aligned not with the river, but with the morning sun in the east so that it spilled through the windows to illumine the divine services. There was a guildhall for the borough's officers and separate buildings to house the guilds of the various trades.

York was alive with activity. Food and drink were sold from dawn to dusk in the open market on the broad expanse of the center of town, called the Pavement, on Tuesdays, Thursdays, and Saturdays, while cloth and household needs were sold in another market on Thursdays and Saturdays. The areas in which the approximately sixty craft guilds were concentrated were revealed in the street names such as Tanner Lane and the Shambles, the latter where the butchers slaughtered animals in the street, letting the blood and offal ooze toward the Ouse. The narrow, paved streets allowed little sunlight or breeze to disperse the smells and sounds of trade, and, because the upper stories of the houses extended further into the street than those on the ground level, the streets felt even more constricted.

York's burgesses were prospering. Aside from the laborers, the largest guilds were those of the weavers and tailors. The guilds and the religious confraternities of the city sponsored the mystery plays and pageants that provided much color and entertainment. The city's officers policed the markets to supervise quality and proper measures. The deceitful merchant suffered the ignominy and the appropriate punishment of having to drink his putrid beer in public or to eat the spoiled food he had attempted to sell. Urban problems and pollution know no bounds of time or place, but they arose in York to greater degrees because the fleece of the sheep and the success of trade brought increased population, prosperity, and plenty.

High Medieval Culture

The late eleventh and the twelfth centuries were times of an intellectual revival in Europe. Some call it a "renaissance," a "rebirth," because the rediscovery of classical Roman and Greek writings had a major part. By the late twelfth and thirteenth centuries, the attitudes and institutions of this revival had become a mature part of English life.

The Intellectual Revival. The great rediscoveries that sparked the renaissance were in the fields of literature, law, and philosophy. Medieval scholars studied Roman literature to learn how to improve their own writing style and to discover the virtues and ideals which had let Rome dominate the ancient world. Medieval persons were especially intrigued by the study of law and philosophy because they found them highly amenable to synthesis, the drawing together into one coherent and organized system of a tremendous breadth of knowledge. The rediscovery in the eleventh century of the magnificent codification of Roman law made centuries earlier by the Emperor Justinian spurred medieval scholars to adapt this to the church's needs. The study of canon law flourished in England and helped provide the theoretical underpinnings for Henry II's legal innovations and for Becket's insistence on the church's privileges in his quarrels with Henry.

Theology was the most important medieval study: it placed God at the center of things and began with His revealed truths, which were the surest knowledge. The contribution of the intellectual revival was to make philosophy the handmaid of theology—to provide the tools of logic which would allow scholars to deduce useful knowledge from revelation. The Greeks had been the great philosophers of antiquity, but many of their ideas were unknown in the West. The conquest of the East by the Moslems put them into direct contact with Greek thought.

Eager Moslem intellectuals translated the works of Plato, Aristotle, and other philosophers into Arabic and incorporated them into Moslem thought. In the twelfth century translations from Arabic into Latin were the key to reopen a study of classical philosophy in western Europe. A Dominican friar at the University of Paris, St. Thomas Aquinas, "baptized" Aristotle, combining pagan philosophy and Christian dogma to produce a stunningly magnificent synthesis of theology. Before long the contents and techniques of this new learning had captured most European schools.

Universities. The broadened content of medieval knowledge demanded better facilities for study. Good teachers drew good students. However, it was easy for landlords and civic officials to victimize teenage students, and a teacher might collect fees and then not teach. The first reaction was for students to form a guild to protect themselves, and professors formed their own guild to ensure proper qualifications for instruction and to protect their interests. In time a single corporate body called a university developed, with specific privileges and responsibilities set out in a charter. The first English university was at Oxford, to which many of the English students came when called home from the University of Paris by Henry II in 1167 during his quarrels with Becket. Gradually a center of learning developed, interrupted by quarrels between the townspeople and the often rowdy students, called "town and gown" riots (the students' academic dress was a gown). These difficulties were overcome at the beginning of the thirteenth century by the bishop's supervision and control. A second university grew at Cambridge but was a good deal smaller than Oxford in its early years.

Oxford and Cambridge were in reality loose confederations of colleges, as the residential centers of instruction were called. A college was a corporation whose members, later called "fellows," were nearly always priests. Many of the students went on to become priests, and the students' day was much like that in a monastery. They arose before dawn for prayer and mass and returned for prayer at stated intervals during the day. In the usual three years it required to earn a B.A. degree, they studied the seven liberal arts of grammar, rhetoric, logic, arithmetic, geometry, astronomy, and music. Books were rare, so the students took notes during lectures, memorized them, and then formally disputed selected topics—all in Latin, of course.

Although most European universities were similar, Oxford did have some distinguishing features. Bishop Robert Grosseteste, who once headed the university, was interested in science and urged that the normal deductive process of learning be supplemented by observation, the forming of hypotheses, and experimentation. This uncharacteristic process was also advocated by a Franciscan friar interested in science, Roger Bacon. Another Franciscan, John Duns Scotus, was an influential philosophical thinker who was a critic of the accepted system of Thomas Aquinas.

The Friars and the Religious Revival. A spiritual revival was sparked by the creation on the continent of new religious communities, the friars. St. Dominic formed an order of preaching friars in Spain to teach true doctrine and to combat heresies, and on the Italian peninsula St. Francis of Assisi renounced his well-to-do heritage to embrace "the lady poverty" and teach his followers to imitate the humility and simplicity of the Lord.

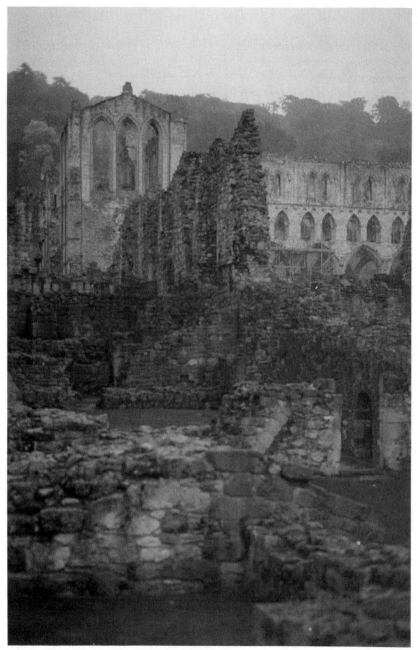

Ruins of Rievaulx Abbey, Yorkshire *(E. A. Reitan)*.

Fan vaulting, Gloucester Cathedral *(Dugdale,* Monasticon Anglicanum*)*.

The Dominican and Franciscan friars did not live in monasteries but went among the people, especially in towns, to preach and teach by pious example.

Both communities of friars came to England in the 1220s. Because they believed in the importance of education and sound religious instruction they were well-prepared, especially when compared with the often inadequate training of the normal parish priest. Their emphasis on education led many to the universities; we have seen how important the Dominicans were at Paris, and the Franciscans at Oxford. The friars often aroused the jealousy of the parish priests, but their emphasis on preaching to the poor and unlettered made a significant impact on English spiritual life.

Gothic Architecture. The piety of the age was also expressed in stone and mortar, in new churches and in extensions built on the older ones. The Romanesque style of the tenth and eleventh centuries tended to be squat and massive because the walls had to support the entire weight of the roof. The emphasis was on the horizontal. The Gothic style which developed in the twelfth and later centuries utilized the discovery that the weight of a roof, if concentrated over a center of gravity atop a pointed arch, could be supported by slender columns in the walls. Since the walls proper were no longer supporting the roof, they could be considerably lighter and include large windows that were usually decorated with stained glass. Above all, the walls and the interiors were higher, the emphasis on the vertical.

The change was immediately apparent when one entered a gothic cathedral: with an interior height reaching and even exceeding 100 feet, the effect was to sweep the eye and, perhaps, the spirit heavenward. The ceilings were beautifully decorated in fan vaulting. The columns of the walls branched out in fingers along the roof to reach the center of gravity and to carry the weight downward. The stained glass windows became textbooks of Bible stories and pious legends to instruct the unlettered faithful. The airy and light effect of Gothic architecture was as refined and reflective of the intellectual outreach of the twelfth century renaissance as the massive Romanesque or Norman style was of the more military emphasis of the eleventh century.

Edward I and Edward II

Edward I (1272–1307) was one of the strongest medieval kings, well-schooled by the difficulties of the reign of his father, Henry III. He was a tall, imposing man who commanded great respect, a talented administrator whose effective use of household government and of Parliament produced monuments to his energy and control. Domestic affairs flourished under his leadership, but wars in France, Scotland, and Wales caused no end of difficulty.

Edward I and Parliament. Edward had seen how useful a national Parliament could be; he called as many as two Parliaments a year. Although at first the representatives of the shires and boroughs were called infrequently, his growing need for revenue to finance his wars suggested that the representatives of his subjects who would pay the parliamentary taxes should be present regularly. In 1295 a Parliament met, which much later was to be called the "Model Parliament." It was not called this because its organization became a precedent to be followed invariably thereafter but because all the categories of membership were present. These would be included when the exact composition of Parliament would be fixed in the following century. It must have been a magnificent sight—twenty bishops and seventy abbots in their ecclesiastical robes, fifty earls and barons, representatives of the lower clergy from each diocese, and representatives of the shires and 110 towns, more soberly clad as befitted their common rank.

After the opening prayers and sermon, the king addressed the community of the realm and presented his needs. The burgesses withdrew across the way to Westminster Abbey to deliberate, the king and his inner council moved to a nearby chapel, and the others remained in the Great Hall of Westminster Palace. Over a period of about ten days, these various groups received petitions which protested grievances, considered the grant of taxes, heard cases of great importance, and counseled the king on important matters. This completed, all met together again in the Great Hall to hear the king promulgate as statutes the new laws he granted, which were based on some of the petitions, and thank the assembly for the grant of taxes.

Edward used Parliament very effectively to codify much of the law. "Judge-made law," with its reliance on precedents hammered out in numerous trials, had been the basis of the common law, but now Edward restated the laws on property, criminal offenses, and other matters succinctly in statutory form. Common law did not disappear—an offense could be punished at common law even if it had not been defined in a statute—but the principle gradually developed that the law could be changed only with Parliament's consent.

A crucial precedent for Parliament's future importance was won in 1297 when Edward was fighting to maintain control of Gascony, the area of southwestern France that was not included in Richard I's homage to the French king and was still one of England's possessions. So great was Edward's need for funds that Parliament resisted, asking that as a sign of good faith the king reissue many charters of privileges. Included in this Confirmation of Charters of 1297 was Edward's promise not to seek extraordinary funds without the consent of the "community of the realm." Magna Carta in 1215 stated that extraordinary feudal income could be granted only with the community's consent, but at the time the "community" meant the feudal barons; the Confirmation of Charters set conditions for grants of nonfeudal revenues, but now "community" meant Parliament—quite a broadening of the political nation in 82 years. Over future centuries, with much travail and long periods of reversal, these two precedents would give Parliament the control of finances, and eventually of the monarch.

Edward I and Scotland. Scotland had kept its independence by withstanding invasions attempted by the Romans, Anglo-Saxons, and Normans, but its separateness from England was gradually weakened as the Scottish royalty married into the English royal family. In 1173 Henry II had used a minor border clash as the first step in a full-scale battle with the Scots, and the defeated Scots king did homage to Henry for Scotland. Later, Henry III had improved relations by marrying his daughter to the king of Scotland, a minor. By 1290 the young Scottish king and all his direct descendants were dead, and the Scots saw no other way out of a complicated disputed succession than to leave the decision to Edward I as overlord. Edward insisted before hearing the case that the claimants and Scotland's leaders take oaths which explicitly reasserted his superior position. Even after choosing a new king of Scotland, Edward kept intervening in their affairs and Scottish patriotism was awakened.

The Scots began to ignore Edward I, and they sought an independent alliance with France. In 1296 Edward I deposed the king whom he had chosen and sent him into exile. Robert Bruce, the descendant of the unsuccessful claimant of the same name in the disputed succession case, then had himself crowned king of Scotland and began to rebel against Edward. Edward's military victories won him the title "Hammer of the Scots," but his opponents would not give up. Edward died in 1307 during a battle in the tenth year of the struggles.

Wales and Ireland. The Welsh had retained their independence from England longer than the other Celtic kingdoms on the British Isles. The mountains had been an effective barrier against invaders, but, because the Welsh leaders were continually bickering among themselves, they were really no threat to England. Llewelyn the Great (died 1240) was the first Welsh leader to succeed in uniting the Welsh against England, but Henry III had defeated him and conferred on his son Edward many Welsh lands to make an English presence felt there. Opposition to England began again in the 1260s, this time led by Llywelyn ap Gruffudd who took the title "Prince of Wales." His early victories especially humiliated Edward, whose estates were overrun. On his father's behalf (and then on his own when he became king), Edward completely defeated the Welsh. The statutes for Wales in 1284 symbolized the English domination, as did Edward I's gift of the title of Prince of Wales to his son, a title to this day born by the heir apparent to the English crown.

England had had far more success at an earlier date in Ireland, which Henry II had conquered with papal approval because of the sad state into which the church had fallen. Two-thirds of the island was under English control, and the remainder was the battleground of clan leaders who continually fought among themselves. Under later kings the English system of government and common law was introduced, but the fights of the Scots and Welsh against English control awakened Irish patriotism which in future centuries caused trouble for England.

Edward II. Edward I's son was unworthy of his father's legacy. Indolent and willing to seek any amusement rather than work at government, Edward II brought ruin upon England's military ventures and then upon himself. He scandalized his subjects because his foreign favorite, Piers Gaveston, was his lover and monopolized his attention. The Scottish situation was not attended properly, in part because of Edward's vacillation and weakness of character but more important because he was protecting Gaveston whom the English barons particularly wanted to remove. English forces in the north lost the military advantage, and Scottish victories such as at Bannockburn in 1314—which guaranteed the Scots a respite from English attacks—added to the king's ignominy. He refused to recognize Bruce as king, and only a series of truces kept the Scots from occupying even more of northern England.

The barons reacted to Edward by forcing upon him in 1311 a set of Ordinances that committed the king to reform and imposed a baronial council to control government. Edward was able to rally support and repudiate the Ordinances, as John had done with Magna Carta and Henry III had done with the Provisions of Oxford, but the defeat at Bannockburn led the barons to impose the plan of reform once again. Another precedent was invoked: just as Magna Carta had been reissued later, and the Statute of Marlborough granted much the Provisions had sought, so Edward II had to yield in a Statute of York in 1322 to many of the reforms sought in the ordinances. The barons did not stop there but captured Gaveston and had him executed, sparking the king to further vengeance and obstinacy. Later, Edward's wife took a lover, Roger Mortimer, and together they and others of the baronial party who were sick of misgovernment persuaded Parliament to debate how Edward had ignored his promises to govern justly and wisely. Edward was forced to abdicate and allow his minor son to rule as Edward III; within a year Edward II was murdered in prison.

Suggestions for Further Reading

Henry II's troublesome family is described in Amy Kelly, *Eleanor of Aquitaine and the Four Kings* (1950), and separate studies of her royal sons are James A. Brundage, *Richard Lion Heart* (1974) and Sidney Painter, *The Reign of King John* (1949). A lengthy treatment of John's son is F. M. Powicke's *King Henry III and the Lord Edward* (2 vols., 1947). L. F. Salzman's *Edward I* (1968) is very brief, and Caroline Bingham's *The Life and Times of Edward II* (1973) is profusely illustrated.

The best study of the Magna Carta is J. C. Holt, *Magna Carta* (1965). Useful for the background to the Parliament of 1265 is Margaret Wade Labarge's *Simon de Montfort* (1962). The organization and powers of the early parliaments have attracted a raft of extremely capable scholars, and so voluminous are the writings that a guide is needed, such as Gerald Bodet's *Early English Parliaments. High Courts, Royal Councils, or Representative Assemblies?* (1968). W. S. Holdsworth, *History of English Law* (7th edition, 16 vols., 1956) treats medieval law, including the development of common law and the origin of juries, in the first three volumes of his work.

H. S. Bennet's *Life on the English Manor* (1937) is a classic; different strata on the social scale are studied in Labarge's *A Baronial Household of the Thirteenth Century* (1965) and R. H. Hilton, *The English Peasantry in the Later Middle Ages* (1975). Aspects of medieval life and customs are presented in the many separate essays edited by Austin Lane Poole as *Medieval England* (new edition, 2 vols., 1958). Eileen Power's *The Wool Trade in English Medieval History* (1941) is a short introduction. A great amount of historical reconstruction, rarely possible for long lost days, is a result of post–World War II aerial photography and is reflected in M. W. Beresford and J. K. S. St. Joseph, *Medieval England. An Aerial Survey* (1958).

David Knowles treats the friars in Vol. I of *The Religious Orders in England* (3 vols., 1950) and puts intellectual advances, including the medieval renaissance and the origin of universities, in a European context in *The Evolution of Medieval Thought* (1962). Doreen Yarwood's *The Architecture of England from Prehistoric Times to the Present Day* (1963) is an excellent brief presentation, and more detail can be found in Hugh Braun, *An Introduction to English Mediaeval Architecture* (1951).

4

Late Medieval England

1327–1485

*I*n these nearly 160 years, 1327 to 1485, if England is considered from the aspect of strong political power, or of peace and tranquility, or of military success in the wars against the French, then certainly England was in decline. The feudal bonds that had knit society together were unravelling, the Hundred Years' War gained neither territory nor the French crown, and the civil wars of the fifteenth century severely dislocated the political state.

Yet if the intangibles that give a country its unique character are considered, it was a period of transition and not of decline. In the early fourteenth century, the leaders of England spoke French and followed French ways. In the late fifteenth century, Englishmen spoke English and attended to domestic business, and distinctly English institutions such as Parliament became increasingly important. Even the political decline was arrested in 1485 when the Tudors captured the crown and revived royal power and ended the drift of the civil wars. The peace and prosperity that they brought were the preconditions of England's reassumption of an important place in European affairs.

The Fourteenth Century: Growth and Disruption, 1327–1399

Edward III and the Hundred Years' War. Edward III (1327–1377) was a warm, cheerful, and inspiring leader, at once a practical man of affairs and an idealist. He had learned from his father's reign how deeply the barons resented their exclusion from the inner circles of power. As a valiant and generous warrior he led his realm to war and gave his nobility the sweet taste of victory and the comradeship of a shared mission—no aristocratic rebellion ever scarred his reign. In all of this he set a high moral tone: he made chivalry and pageantry points of policy and, by founding the Order of the Garter as an honorific society, he had the means for rewarding men of similar ideals.

The Hundred Years' War which Edward began lasted from 1338 to 1453, but in reality the war was a series of intermittent campaigns of limited fighting often interrupted by long years of truces. The war was distinctly new in several important aspects. When England fought in the thirteenth century it was to regain territories such as Normandy that John had forfeited to Philip Augustus, but in the fourteenth and fifteenth centuries the English king fought as a claimant for the crown of France. Edward's mother Isabelle was the sister of the childless French king (the last of the house of Capet) who died in 1328. The French had no intention of letting the end of the Capetian line result in their crown descending to an English king. By "inventing" the Salic law, which excluded descent through a female, the French denied Edward the crown; instead it passed to a French cousin, Philip VI, the first of the house of Valois.

The tactics of warfare changed also when the English began to use the longbow as a weapon. Before the Norman Conquest the English had relied on the militia of the shires and, after 1066, on the feudal host in which heavily armored knights acted as a cavalry. Edward III's bowmen were capable of shooting arrows with a force sufficient to pierce chain mail, so that when the French knights charged the English at Crecy in 1346 the English bowmen slaughtered the flower of the French nobility. This success was repeated in 1356 at Poitiers, when the French king was captured and held for ransom. It was impossible to convert these individual triumphs into total victory. The cost of sustained warfare was staggering, England lacked the financial resources, and France had a substantially greater area and population. Belatedly the French adopted new military tactics and erased the English advantage, and the capable French leader Bertrand du Guesclin began to wage a war of guerilla tactics that relentlessly destroyed the English forces. By 1377 England's military gains had evaporated and its original holdings in southwestern France had been severely curtailed.

The Growth of Parliamentary Powers. When Edward I promulgated the Confirmation of Charters in 1297 he established the principle that Parliament alone could grant the king extraordinary revenues; Edward's financial needs thus gave Parliament a tremendously increased importance. It was quickly agreed that the consent of the elected representatives of the counties (two knights of each shire) and of the boroughs (two burgesses apiece) was needed to grant taxes. These representatives were present at every one of Edward's nearly annual Parliaments, and in 1339 these two classes of elected members met together to act jointly for the first time;

Battle of Crécy, Hundred Years' War *(The Bettmann Archive)*.

these "men of the commons" were eventually to be the House of Commons. The secular and ecclesiastical lords formed the House of Lords. The representatives of the lower clergy ceased to attend Parliament but instead met with the bishops in a separate ecclesiastical parliament called convocation, which granted the king taxes on the church's wealth.

As Edward grew older his control of affairs lessened, tempting nobles and parliamentary leaders to wrest power. Edward's third son, John of Gaunt, duke of Lancaster, felt that he could grasp power by replacing the king's councillors with men loyal to himself, but by 1376 the king's eldest son, Edward the Black Prince, led a reaction. In the "Good Parliament" of that year the process of impeachment was used for the first time to remove John of Gaunt's "evil councillors," a process thus initially and henceforth directed at a king's advisors and never at the king. Even though John of Gaunt's faction was able to reassert itself a year later, the precedent had been set of Parliament's control of a royal minister.

Richard II and Absolutism. At Edward III's death in 1377 his grandson Richard II (1377–1399) was only ten (Richard's father, Edward the Black

Edward the Black Prince *(The Bettmann Archive)*.

Prince, had died in 1376). This thoughtful boy had a goal, the restoration of the monarch's powers to the strength of Edward I's reign. He wished to reverse the loss of power wrung from Edward II and the voluntary losses Edward III endured to win taxes to pay for his wars. As a youth, Richard gathered about him a "court party" that shared his absolutist goals, but, as soon as his domineering uncle, John of Gaunt, went abroad in 1386, Richard was left unprotected and exposed to the barons who abhorred his absolutist views.

In 1386 Parliament impeached Richard's most able minister and imposed a baronial council to reform his government. Richard obtained judicial opinions that supported his views and that denied the propriety of Parliament's actions, but the latter had the power. In 1388 five leading lords, the Lords Appellant (they "appealed" against Richard's supporters and thus earned their name) removed Richard's supporters so thoroughly that it became known as the "Merciless Parliament." His powers temporarily eclipsed, Richard quietly bided his time to rebuild his court party.

By 1397 the king was strong enough to pack Parliament with his supporters, and this compliant assembly "appealed" against three of the five Lords Appellant and sent the other two into exile, including John of Gaunt's son Henry Bolingbroke. When John died in 1399, Richard refused to allow the normal succession of the Lancastrian lands and titles to Henry, so he returned to England with an army and rallied the lords to his cause. Parliament debated and then received Richard's abdication when he returned from a campaign in Ireland. Within a year Richard was dead, probably murdered. Although Parliament played a role in the abdications in 1327 and 1399, the precipitating cause in both cases was nonparliamentary military might. But in 1327 the normal heir apparent became king, whereas in 1399 there were cousins with better claims to succeed the childless Richard than Henry IV (as Bolingbroke styled himself). Royal absolutism had been stopped, but tampering with the legal descent of the crown would dictate much of the strife of the fifteenth century.

Economic and Social Strain and Change

The early part of the fourteenth century was struck by economic crises. Most notable of these was the famine of 1315 to 1316, caused primarily by changes in the weather. The immediate problem was excessive rain which ruined the harvests; equally as important were long range weather changes, especially the lower than average temperatures (the period from 1309, when the Thames froze at London, to about 1700 is known by the exaggerated name "Little Ice Age"). Although the usual cycle of good and bad agricultural years continued, the overall trend was disruptive. England was relatively overpopulated in these years, perhaps with 5 to 6 million persons, and the suffering contributed to a general malaise.

The Black Death and the Peasants Revolt. No generalized or particular crisis could ever approach the horror and magnitude of the "Black Death," which struck all of Europe at midcentury. The bubonic plague that destroyed so much of England's population in the first attack in 1348 to 1351 had begun fifteen years earlier in China and had travelled across Europe along the trade routes. Rats on the ships carried fleas that bore the bubonic plague. Infected persons suffered a grotesque swelling of the glands before death, and the asphyxiation and discoloration that often resulted from a buildup of fluid in the lungs contributed to the name Black Death. The number of lives lost, if not accurately measurable, was appalling.

Perhaps close to 40 percent of the entire English population died, reducing the population perhaps to around 3.5 million. Particular segments of the population suffered differently: nearly half of the clergy died, scores of densely populated settlements such as towns, villages, and monasteries were decimated, while those in the countryside who lived somewhat apart—notably the aristocracy and gentry—suffered much less. Even after the first attack had subsided, the plague recurred often in England for 300 years. The sense of personal tragedy at the horrible toll was profound and the fear evoked by such a visitation was gripping.

The immediate reaction of the propertied class was repression—a Statute of Labourers (1351) that attempted to hold wages to pre-plague levels. The agricultural workers felt deeply grieved by the Statute and by novel taxes. Previously, the wealthy alone had paid the taxes, but in 1377 a poll tax was levied, a flat tax on each person 14 years or older. The combination of unrealistic wage regulation and taxes levied on the lower classes produced the first broad uprising in England, the Peasants' Revolt of 1381.

The Peasants' Revolt initially took place only in two English counties, Essex and Kent, but it was a major threat to the realm. From those localities the rebels marched on nearby London, which was the key to the kingdom's security. The initial strengths and actions of the rebels—the dynamism of Wat Tyler who led the forces, the freeing of men held in a royal prison, the burning of the palace of King Richard II's uncle, and then Richard's conciliatory meeting with the rebels—were lost when the rebels overstepped by pressing for wider and more revolutionary demands such as the abolition of lordships and a dispersal of church wealth. The mayor of London got into a scuffle with Tyler in which he stabbed the rebel leader to death. Quickly the king's forces took the initiative in dispersing and killing the rebels, not only in the London area but in other parts of England where news of the initial rebellion had spread.

Although the government relented in its taxing policies and the Statute of Labourers became a dead letter, the long-term consequences for society were far-reaching and revolutionary. Before 1348 England had been relatively overpopulated, and many peasants were in effect tied to the soil to render servile labor to their feudal lords on their vast demesnes. This system, known as "high farming," was characterized by vast labor forces working under the immediate supervision of the landowning class. Because the plague caused a severe labor scarcity, workers heretofore bound to the soil (the name "serf" had been used for those legally free but economically unfree workers) now had a valuable and avidly sought commodity. They could easily run away from a lord who did not end their servile status, and another lord who was desperate for help to harvest his crops would hire them, no questions asked. The king and aristocratic landowners were now unable to maintain the vast labor force that had made high farming possible. Lords instead began to lease out parts of their lands to independent laborers, and the nobility became collectors of rents rather than superintending estate managers. Serfdom became a thing of the past.

Changing Notions of Aristocracy and Gentry. There were other factors at work to change the notion of rank and class in the fourteenth century. Up to this time there were only two traditional ranks of the nobility, the barons and the earls. By the fourteenth century there was no clear definition of what set those in the lower rank of baron apart from many others in the class of those who bore arms. Earlier a particular type of land tenure had distinguished them, but because of changing times and divisions of estates there was no certainty by the fourteenth century.

When Parliament started to sit, however, kings summoned certain barons to Parliament by individual summonses. Thus some who did not hold land by the traditional tenure were called and some who did were not called—the list that was developed throughout Edward I's reign became by Edward II's a definite list not only of who were summoned to Parliament but also of the extent of the peerage. In 1387 a man was made a noble by a specific grant in writing. Henceforth either individual summons or a particular grant in writing were the distinguishing characteristic of a noble.

In 1337 Henry III created a new rank of nobility when he made his first son a duke. This title, like that of earl, carried no office or special rights but did bestow prestige and precedence. A duke ranked right below the monarch and above earls; the first duke not of royal blood was created in 1351. In the fifteenth century two new ranks were created, marquess and viscount, so that then the order of precedence from highest to lowest

Cottages, Longstocks, Hampshire *(BBC Hulton Picture Library)*.

in the peerage was duke, marquess, earl, viscount, and baron. All of these distinctions were social, not economic.

The rank of knight was the highest in that group called the gentry—a group as ill-defined in the early fourteenth century as the peerage had been. Knighthood was granted through a special ceremony so that it was relatively easy to distinguish them, but as with other titles it could receive a related but nonspecific use, as for country representatives to Parliament who were "knights of the shire" but who did not have to hold the rank of knight. The Hundred Years' War and other military employments kept the rank high, perhaps regularly in the range of 1,000 to 1,200 persons, but there was a serious decline in the number of knights in the fifteenth century.

As the ranks of knights contracted, there was a growth in the two other ranks, which with the knights constituted the gentry, the esquires and the gentlemen. A tax return of 1436 indicated there were about 1,200 esquires; it is more difficult to ascertain from that return exactly how broad the class of gentlemen was, but it was in the range of 1,000 to 2,000. There was such a fluidity about what constituted any group that exactness is not possible and was no clearer to persons of that time than to us today. When involved in public service, most of the gentry did so on the local

Geoffrey Chaucer, Ellesmere MSS *(Henry E. Huntington Library and Art Gallery)*.

level. Of all such employments, the most prestigious was to be a justice of the peace, an office arising in the fourteenth century originally as "keepers of the peace."

Chaucer's England

Chaucer and the Revival of English Letters. English had remained the language of the lower classes after the Norman Conquest, the language of the towns and byways of rural England where wandering minstrels sang English ballads, versified narratives of heroic deeds such as wars against the French and Scots, and recounted episodes of chivalrous romance. Because French had been the language of the upper classes since the Conquest, there was no literature composed thereafter in English until the fourteenth century. The exact reasons for a revival of English in literature and in the common speech of the upper classes remain mysterious, but certainly the Hundred Years' War in which the French were the enemy provided a powerful psychological impetus.

Geoffrey Chaucer (ca. 1343–1400) led the revival of English letters. He combined an extraordinarily wide range of personal experiences with a keen eye for detecting the strengths and weaknesses of men and women and with a flair for setting down his characterizations in striking poetry. He was well acquainted with the world of business because his father and grandfather had been wine merchants in London, and he served later as comptroller of customs there. He had served with Edward III's army in France, had been captured and ransomed, and in later years went abroad on the king's behalf on diplomatic missions. He knew the nobility well and was befriended by the Lancastrians. He was a justice of the peace and sat in Parliament.

As one of the first major writers to use and prefer English instead of French, Chaucer allowed his countrymen to experience the richness and suppleness of their native language. One of his greatest gifts was the ability to portray vividly the ideals and prejudices of many different classes and walks of life. In *Troilus and Criseyde* he described the world of the king and court, and in *The Canterbury Tales* he immortalized a monk, a friar, a worldly prioress, and other pilgrims who amused themselves by telling stories as they walked to the shrine of St. Thomas à Becket in Canterbury. Chaucer, the master storyteller, was strikingly secular in his approach to his characters.

Chaucer was the greatest of many writers who wrote in English, but other authors as well increasingly chose to use English rather than Latin, although there does not seem to have been a correspondence or exchange of ideas between any of them and thus no "school" of English letters. The legends of King Arthur were very popular, and the greatest medieval work in English in this vein was *Sir Gawayne and the Grene Knight*, written anonymously about 1370.

In addition to the more courtly works of Chaucer and those of the author of *Sir Gawayne*, there were writings in English on the life of ordinary people as well. The greatest medieval English work concerned with everyday people was William Langland's *Piers Plowman*. This work satirized all social strata but did nevertheless provide accounts of life on a level far removed from knights and the court. The lives of ordinary people also were reflected in the ballads, which sometimes reflected social discontent. The Robin Hood legends were in circulation by the time Langland wrote because he referred to them in *Piers Plowman*. In these legends a man of common stock and uncommon abilities harassed immoral sheriffs and kings. There is speculation today that the protests in the Robin Hood legends were in origin protests of the gentry who suffered from the legal system, but the stories gained a much wider audience because they touched on an exposed nerve of nearly universal discontent.

There were other means of popular instruction in English as well. The stained glass windows in churches, with their vivid colors, had long taught

Bible stories to the illiterate flocks; now the church's drama spilled out into churchyards and towns in plays called mystery stories. These recreated Bible episodes and pious legends always taught a moral, but sometimes they upset stern officials because the moral lesson was often interspersed with stretches of broad humor which all too accurately portrayed the foibles of sinful man.

The Church and Wycliffe. There were problems within the church from many sources, some of which were satirized in literature, as noted, but others of far greater importance. The plague had a profound impact on religious life. Men analyzed it in terms of the divine wrath and began to conceptualize God as the God of judgment and retribution rather than of love and popular devotion. The death of so many clergymen curtailed proper religious instruction so that superstition increased. The prestige of the institutional church was hurt when from 1309 to 1377 the popes were French and resided in Avignon in southern France rather than in Rome. Their stay in France coincided with the Hundred Years' War and strained relations between England and the Papacy. For a short time in 1378 there were two popes, one at Avignon and one at Rome, each fulminating against the other and thus lowering the church's prestige.

There was no fourteenth century religious revival as there had been in many earlier centuries, and the uncorrected abuses called forth criticism and satire. The Oxford scholar John Wycliffe at first merely criticized these faults but then moved on to doctrinal heresy. He denied the efficacy of the sacraments as channels of divine grace and rejected Jesus' real presence in the consecrated Eucharist. In turn this led him to denigrate many of the church's roles and to insist that the Scriptures be translated into English to allow personal religious instruction. Wycliffe's followers came to be called Lollards. Although he died in 1384 of natural causes, the seeds of doubt that he had sown and that the Lollards nurtured in an underground movement had challenged the church's authority.

Chaucer's London. The 40,000 Londoners lived in the area of less than a square mile within the city's ancient walls, yet the city was alive with the sights and smells of the nearby countryside. There were signs of the ancient past now abutted by the commercial present, as in the wharves which lined the riverside. Although London was distinctly English, it did house many aliens who were part of the international trading community.

The ecclesiastical buildings were the most striking and most numerous—over a third of the city's area was occupied by church buildings. The cathedral of St. Paul was the largest. That massive building was 560 feet long and nearly 300 feet wide, with an interior height of nearly 200 feet and a spire reaching nearly 500 feet. (The medieval cathedral was much

Medieval town, Lavenham *(E. A. Reitan)*.

larger than the present cathedral built after the great fire of 1666). It was also the largest employer in London. The number of priests who staffed the cathedral chapter was about sixty. The size of the staff needed for the church's liturgy was very large. There were those to take care of the vestments, chalices, and other items needed for mass, seamstresses to make the vestments, men to light and replace the candles which were the only illumination, and a very large choir that included boys who sang the higher parts. The choir meant a school for the boys, not only to learn the music but also for their general education, and librarians to copy and prepare the music. Grave diggers were needed for funerals, archivists for the church's records, and estate managers for the vast lands held by the cathedral as its endowment, not only near London but throughout the realm. The size of the staff needed for expansion and repair was vast, including stonemasons, painters and gilders, carpenters, and a host of others in the construction trades.

The most numerous ecclesiastical buildings were the 100 or so parish churches within the walls, with another 20 in nearby areas—it has been estimated that there was a parish church for every 3.5 acres. London's parishes were not only centers of worship but also served particular craft guilds, whose members often worshipped as a group, and housed parish guilds that looked after the poor and cared for widows and orphans. There were also numerous abbeys and friaries that housed men and women of

Chaucer's London

almost every religious order in England. Some abbeys served the city in ways other than prayer. The priory of St. Bartholomew was a hospital for the poor, and the Hospital of St. Mary of Bethlehem cared for lunatics— the name "Bethlehem" was pronounced "Bedlam," a name now popularly associated with irrational sounds and disorder. Because friars located in towns by preference, major houses existed for each in London, Blackfriars for the Dominicans and Greyfriars for the Franciscans, the names taken from the color of the capes worn by the former and the religious habit of the latter.

The many buildings dedicated to trade reflected London's position as the commercial hub of England. There were numerous markets to feed London's masses, and names such as Poultry, Ironmonger Lane, Fish Street Hill, and Honey Lane testify to concentrations of tradesmen. Small industry dotted the city, so that workshops and forges were a common sight. Over half of the wool exported from England passed through London, and Londoners also dominated cloth export. Foreign merchants such as the German Hanseatic League maintained massive trading complexes in London.

The craft guilds were so important that they dominated the city's government. A man was a citizen of London only if he belonged to a guild, and so less than a fourth of the city's residents were eligible to participate in government. Thus a trading oligarchy ruled the city, and the greatest guild had a privileged position—the Mercers and Drapers who dealt in clothing, the Fishmongers and Grocers who provided food, the Vintners who controlled wine, and a handful of other major companies. Power was further concentrated when major guilds absorbed smaller but related trades, as the Haberdashers did with the Capmakers. London had become so wealthy and important that after 1392 no monarch attempted to tamper with the city's government, but rather he courted it for the support and financial assistance his royal government needed.

The city's population also included a number of specialized and important occupations. The king's ministers lived in the western suburbs near Westminster and in eastern London near the military complex in the Tower of London and near the royal mint. Many lawyers lived in and near London because they pleaded cases in the royal courts, and students wishing to enter the profession prepared at the numerous Inns of Court and Inns of Chancery which were centers for legal education. These were concentrated just west of the city's gates. Chaucer's London was glittering—sumptuous pageantry and elaborate processions were frequent; there were many luxury shops that supplied jewels and the newly fashionable embroidered, colored clothing. The homes of the wealthy, larger than ever before, featured handsome furniture and tapestries. But London had the appalling problems common to all English and European cities—poor sanitation, overcrowding, and the threat of the plague and other diseases.

The Fifteenth Century: Dislocation and Strain, 1399–1485

The Lancastrians and the War with France. Richard II had tried to deny Henry Bolingbroke his Lancastrian dukedom and lands when John of Gaunt died in 1399, and so Bolingbroke's forces had won for him not only the dukedom but the crown of England as well. Henry IV had the strength to face many difficulties. Richard II had been childless so that there was no line of descent through the first of Edward III's sons; Henry was the third son, and his seizure of the crown excluded the second son, Lionel, duke of Clarence. Not until 1410 did Henry IV put behind him the last of many rebellions raised by Clarence's descendants and their Welsh allies.

Meanwhile the French had seized the initiative in the wars and had landed raiding parties on the south coast of England. Henry IV's finances were so precarious that resuming a full-scale war was not possible. Luckily two factions of the French royal house, the Burgundians and the Orleanists, began in 1407 to feud among themselves. This gave Henry breathing space which stilled the mounting criticism in Parliament but increased the scheming of his son Henry. He was so anxious to press the seeming military advantage that he was willing to plot with his father's enemies.

Upon his accession Henry V (1413–1422) renewed the war immediately. He was an effective and self-confident fighter who insensitively dominated his friends and foes alike. The barons rallied to his side, and the English victory over the French at Agincourt in 1415 was so overwhelming that it evoked memories of Crecy and Poitiers nearly a century earlier. In 1420 Henry sided with the Burgundian faction, and together they controlled northern France. Henry and the duke of Burgundy made an agreement by which Henry would become king of France as soon as the present but insane French king died. It was while Henry was moving southward against the Orleanists that he died of dysentery a few months before the French king died.

It seemed that England was on the verge of its greatest achievements, but the reality was just the opposite: under Henry VI (1422–1461) the English monarchy reached its lowest point in foreign and domestic affairs. Henry VI became king of France according to the terms of the agreement between his father and the duke of Burgundy, but the Orleanists under the inspiration of Joan of Arc began a military effort that led to ultimate victory and the expulsion of the English from France. So convinced was the young peasant maiden Joan of the message which she heard from heavenly voices that she conveyed her sense of mission to the head of the Orleanists who was consecrated as Charles VII. As Joan rode in armor with his revitalized forces they swept to victory after victory. Even though the Burgundians captured and delivered her to the English who burned her as a witch, the duke of Burgundy recognized that English forces had lost the momentum to the French and allied himself with the Orleanists. By 1453 when the Hundred Years' War ended France was a unified country, and England had been left with only one town on the French mainland, Calais.

The domestic legacy of the Lancastrians was nearly as ruinous. Parliament gained many important powers because of the instability and military failures of Henry IV and because of the concessions Henry V made to secure funds for his wars. The House of Commons gained power in particular when it began to dictate to the king how taxes were to be spent and to examine his accounts to insure that he had complied. Parliament began to frame its own bills rather than to allow the king to dictate the provisions of remedies for grievances.

Henry VI was merely the puppet of his uncles during his long minority and was so inept as an adult that the government nearly collapsed. He had some personally attractive characteristics, such as a love for the arts and a generosity in founding schools, but his nearly total withdrawal from public affairs led to a breakdown in law and order and internal feuding between the different Lancastrian factions. This vacuum in political leadership coincided with severe economic depressions to make England's prospects grim.

The Yorkists and the Wars of the Roses. Since Henry IV had earlier repressed uprisings by the duke of Clarence's descendants there had been little further agitation over the Lancastrian usurpation of the crown. Meanwhile a female descendant of the Clarence line had married the duke of York (a descendant of Edward III's fourth son), and although their offspring bore their father's title they retained the superior theoretical claim of the Clarence line over the Lancastrians.

During the wars with France a Yorkist official had been removed from command, and gradually the relations between the two families worsened. In 1455 they fought the first of a series of battles in a civil war for the throne which centuries later was dubbed the "Wars of the Roses" because the Yorkists' coat of arms included a white rose and the Lancastrians' (a mistaken assumption) a red rose. The battles were intermittent and restricted for the most part to small armies, but many nobles were killed. This, and the collapse of government under the inept Henry VI, and the bickering of the different Lancastrian factions contributed to a Yorkist victory. In 1461 the mad Henry VI was replaced by the duke of York who became Edward IV.

Edward IV (1461–1483) was a strong, forceful man whose vision of kingship went beyond mere Yorkist dynastic ambitions. He realized that his subjects wanted an end to the civil wars and that England's renewal of the wars with France would squander the fragile kingdom's resources. He restored law and order and won confidence; by reviving household government, which placed important financial and administrative powers under his direct supervision in the royal court, he restored the prestige and effectiveness of the monarchy.

Parliament's exclusive right to grant extraordinary revenue had made it nearly indispensable in the Hundred Years' War and gained it many constitutional powers. Edward's refusal to revive the war obviated the need for frequent parliamentary taxes and allowed him to call Parliament less frequently. The king's greatest potential wealth was his vast holdings of land which now included not only the Plantagenet domains but also the Lancastrian lands added at Henry IV's accession in 1399 and the Yorkist estates added by Edward himself in 1461. By insisting on new techniques of land management he greatly increased the yield from the crown lands and thus reduced further his reliance on parliamentary grants.

Edward IV relied heavily on the abilities and strength of his brother

Richard, duke of Gloucester; realizing that when he died his son would be a minor, Edward stipulated that Richard be regent for the young king. At the death of Edward IV in 1483 the family of Woodville, to which Edward IV's wife belonged, seized the regency and excluded Richard. Richard in turn argued that the marriage of Edward IV and Elizabeth Woodville had been illegal, and thus Edward V (1483) was illegitimate. Richard had himself crowned king, and no one had the strength to resist him.

Richard III (1483–1485) placed Edward V and his brother in the Tower of London. Nothing was ever heard of them again. There is no proof that Richard had any complicity in their disappearance, but contemporaries believed that he did, and that was part of his undoing. He attempted to purge the commissions of the peace in many counties of England, replacing justices of the peace who had long held that office with men more pliant to his ways, in an attempt to solidify his control over local as well as central government. These actions prompted a number of local rebellions—so that Richard had trouble in the localities as well as in his own administration. The time was ripe for revolt—and Henry Tudor, earl of Richmond, was waiting to step forward on behalf of the Lancastrians to do battle with Richard III and the Yorkists. In 1485, at the Battle of Bosworth Field, Henry defeated and killed Richard in battle. Few could have guessed what a turning point in British history that battle was to be.

A Stocktaking: England in 1485

Politics and Government. In the later Middle Ages a number of limitations on royal power had been imposed. It was clear that the law limited the king, a principle enunciated explicitly in the established convention that law could be changed only by the king acting in Parliament. It was also clear that the king's power tended to diminish in direct correlation to increased expenses in foreign wars, and so wise kings such as Edward IV freed themselves from parliamentary surveillance merely by declining to fight. The forum for holding a king and his ministers accountable was now Parliament, but in the depositions of 1327, 1399, 1461, and 1485 it was military power which made Parliament's role possible.

Yet any monarch who was willing to rule by law, to cooperate with Parliament and include the great feudal lords in the realm's policy and planning, and to avoid costly wars, possessed extraordinarily great powers of government. He controlled policy-making; directed an effectively organized and sophisticated royal administration; provided a system of royal justice which with its writs and jury system protected Englishmen's rights better than did any other European monarch; enjoyed feudal rights; and in general presided over a kingdom protected from continental involvements by the sea. This potential royal power could reach even greater heights when combined with that all-important intangible, success.

Even in local affairs the king's power was great. Borough charters rested on the royal favor, the king's management of trade brought prosperity to merchants and port towns, and the office of justice of the peace which had been developed from the fourteenth century enabled the king to have royal officers close to local happenings. Local communities had been delegated important powers of self-government, not only in the institutional sense but in other responsible activities such as juries.

Society and the Economy. The aristocratic upper class had been the dominant group in society throughout the entire Middle Ages. In the early years of feudal England they were the indispensable military arm and the exclusive advisors of the monarchy, men who employed vast numbers of villeins in high farming. The Black Death had made these nobles landlords living from rents; the use of the longbow and the decline of the knights had made the nobles' military service less important, although their military leadership was still recognized; and the rise of the House of Commons lessened their political status but did not take away their predominant place in government. The greatest change was the bloodletting of the Wars of the Roses which left only twenty-nine surviving secular nobles.

In early feudal England the knights were immediately below the lords, but their military role had declined and they had become socially allied with the aristocracy but politically allied with the burgesses in the House of Commons. The expansion of professions such as law and the royal administration had begun to create a nonagricultural middle class that was swelled by the merchants who managed England's expanded trade. Life in the cities was structured and sophisticated, temporarily diminished by depressions in the fifteenth century but soon revived in the sixteenth. London had become more than a trading center—like an octopus, its tentacles reached out to take away the economic importance of lesser port towns and to monopolize trade.

Many of the agricultural workers in the lower strata of society had been economically unfree in the early Middle Ages, but nearly all had been freed by the cataclysmic changes from the Black Death. This economic freedom did not, however, guarantee economic success. Most of the peasantry continued to live by subsistence farming, at the mercy of the weather which governed the crops and could in bad times send famine to decimate the countryside.

Religion and Culture. Although religion was certainly one of the unchallenged values in English life, the institutional church had suffered greatly and became a less effective force in England. The Black Death had swept away half the clergy and wreaked havoc on the monasteries and friaries that, in earlier centuries, had been the principal repositories of reformed religious ideals and centers of inspiration. The Papacy's prestige had been lowered by the Avignon "captivity," and Lollardy had first rent the doctrinal unity of English Christianity. From the time of the Conquest, French cultural values had supplanted the English in the upper echelons of society, so that in the cosmopolitan literate society and the intellectual community with its Latin learning England had been part of a truly pan-European world.

The flowering of the English language at the upper as well as the lower levels of society from the fourteenth century had reawakened an ancient heritage, and even in areas such as architecture the later Middle Ages had witnessed a separate, more austere native development. When considered together with the distinct political and governmental institutions, England was well on the way toward an appreciation of uniqueness that was soon to be assiduously cultivated.

Suggestions for Further Reading

The politics of the later Middle Ages and the Hundred Years' War can be followed in May McKisak, *The Fourteenth Century, 1307–1399* (1959) and in E. F. Jacob, *The Fifteenth Century, 1399–1485* (1961). Other useful overviews are Michael Prestwich, *The Three Edwards: War and State in England, 1272–1377* (1980) and John A. F. Thompson, *The Transformation of Medieval England, 1370–1529* (1983). The constitutional implications are treated in S. B. Chrimes, *English Constitutional Ideas in the Fifteenth Century* (1936) and in B. Wilkinson, *Constitutional History of England in the Fifteenth Century, 1399–1485* (1964), the latter with selected documents and a good bibliography. K. B. McFarlane's *The War of the Roses* (1965) and *The Nobility of Later Medieval England* (1973) show changes in upper society. The Yorkist revival is shown in Charles Ross, *Edward IV* (1974), and P. M. Kendall's *Richard III* (1956) is also very good.

G. C. Coulton, *Chaucer and His England* (1957) places that versatile man in context, and Basil Cottle's *The Triumph of English, 1300–1500* (1969) traces the rise of the vernacular. A good short treatment of London is A. R. Myers, *London in the Age of Chaucer* (1972), and a fuller study is Gwyn A. Williams, *Medieval London. From Commune to Capital* (1963). The commercial importance of that city is shown in Sylvia L. Thrupp, *The Merchant Class of Medieval London (1300–1500)* (1948). An excellent study of another medieval town is Sir Francis Hill's *Medieval Lincoln* (1965).

The depopulating effects of the Black Death on so much of England is evident in Maurice Beresford's *The Lost Villages of England* (1954). P. M. Kendall, *The Yorkist Age: Daily Life During the Wars of the Roses* (1962) is a good study of mid-fifteenth century family life. The upheaval in religion is well outlined in K. B.

McFarlane's brief *John Wycliffe and the Beginnings of English Nonconformity* (1952), and a good survey of the state of the church's clergy at the end of the medieval period is Peter Heath's *The English Parish Clergy on the Eve of the Reformation* (1969).

5

The Early Tudors

1485–1558

Richard III's reign was brief: his governmental actions had led to swift and violent reactions. More important, the action of which he was suspected—killing his nephews imprisoned in the Tower of London—caused the scandal that stirred others to rebel. Whether or not Richard ordered the killing of twelve-year-old Edward V and his nine-year-old brother Richard, duke of York, is still a lively matter of debate. Because Richard was widely suspected of the crime, it was the ideal moment for the Lancastrians to strike. When the nearest Lancastrian claimant defeated Richard III in battle in 1485, he set on the throne the Tudor dynasty (1485–1603) whose reign would be one of the most monumental England had ever witnessed.

Henry VII: Consolidation and Transition, 1485–1509

The Emergence and Triumph of the Tudors. Henry Tudor was the best Lancastrian claimant in 1485 as a result of a number of unusual links. Owen Tudor, a younger son of a Welsh gentry family, had married Catherine, the widow of Henry V, and thus became stepfather to Henry VI. Two children of Owen and Catherine's were ennobled, including Edmund, earl of Richmond. Edmund married Margaret Beaufort, a descendant of the line which traced itself back to a liaison between Edward III and his mistress, Katherine Swinford, and thus the Tudors assumed a tenuous potential link to royal succession. In 1471 when the Yorkists defeated a Lancastrian uprising, they executed Henry VI and his son, leaving as the nearest surviving Lancastrian claimant Henry Tudor, earl of Richmond, who had inherited the title from his father Edmund. Henry Tudor met Richard III at the

Battle of Bosworth Field in 1485, and the victorious Henry placed on his head the crown of the slain Richard III and began to rule as Henry VII.

The Battle of Bosworth Field was the end rather than merely the continuation of the Wars of the Roses due to the ability of Henry VII (1485–1509). This tall, reserved, shrewd, calculating, aloof monarch was willing to spend long hours supervising every detail of government—consolidating, reviving, strengthening, expanding, searching for means to secure and develop English kingship and his own Tudor line.

Establishing the Tudor Dynasty. Henry's claim was tarnished. The children of Edward III by Katherine Swinford were illegitimate, and, although Henry IV had legitimized his cousins, he had forbidden any of that line ever to inherit the crown. Furthermore the claim of the Tudors to royal descent was not direct but was only as a result of Edmund's marriage to a female descendant of that line. In reality Henry had won by military might and thus was in a position to "convince" others of the truth of his theoretical claims. By sagacity and skill at government, he assured the maintenance of his line on the throne and also made royal power a present reality.

It took Henry ten years to secure the Tudor reign. He sought to merge the Lancastrian and Yorkist claims by marrying Elizabeth, the best female Yorkist claimant. He removed the males either by imprisoning them, forcing them into exile, or defeating them in real or imagined plots against himself. Several boys claimed to be the brother of Edward V, and Henry had to restrain these imposters and the men who attempted to manipulate them.

In order to ensure the end of the civil wars, he dealt effectively with the "over mighty subjects" who had led the fighting in the aristocratic Wars of the Roses. He first took away from them the potential of gathering a rebellious army. Many lords had kept private armies of retainers, giving their supporters special clothing and badges known as livery. Henry had laws passed that severely reduced the number of persons a lord could retain, reducing a lord's entourage to a few honorific liveried servants much too small to be the nucleus of a private army. Henry then prohibited maintenance, a practice whereby lords often intimidated juries and local officers by appearing in armor when the lords's retainers were accused of lawbreaking.

As a place to discipline "over mighty subjects" and others who might threaten the new Tudor regime, Henry VII revived the medieval Court of Star Chamber, a judicial arm of the council which gained its name from the painted roof in its chamber. Because this court was so closely linked with the king—its judges were the members of his council—the noblemen did not dare challenge its authority, and the "over mighty subject" could be held to account in it.

The Revival of Effective Government. Henry VII was one of England's most effective monarchs not because of innovation but because he revived those institutions and practices of strong government that kings before him had developed. In domestic affairs Henry continued to use household government, as Edward IV had done so effectively. Henry greatly increased royal revenues by insisting on the payment of all feudal obligations, including some that had long gone uncollected. He vigorously supported foreign trade and took steps, with varying degrees of success, to increase the competitive power of English merchants against foreign traders, increasing customs revenues in the process. He became the patron of the Genoan sailor, John Cabot; when that enterprising sailor led ships under the English flag across the Atlantic, Cabot discovered and claimed for England the eastern seaboard of America, even though his untimely death meant that the claim would go untended for many years. By the end of the reign Henry had nearly trebled the ordinary revenue of the crown. He left his son Henry a secure and wealthy kingdom, one which had risen from the internal divisions of civil war to a place of importance and respect in Europe. Henry VII had revived the medieval rights of kingship and made them effective once again.

Henry VII used traditional means, especially marriage, in his foreign policy as well. He named his eldest son Arthur to evoke memories of that legendary British king, and then married him to Catherine of Aragon, a princess of the Spanish house that was one of Europe's first powers. He married his eldest daughter, Margaret, to the king of Scotland to cement friendly relations with the other independent kingdom on the British Isles. Even after Arthur died, Henry attempted to continue the Spanish alliance by urging his second son, the future Henry VIII, to marry her. Although Henry VII seemed at times ready to forward his foreign policy by war as well as marriage, and even though he sometimes won parliamentary taxes to support the anticipated hostilities, he never really fought and thus conserved and augmented his own revenues.

Henry VIII: The Early Years, 1509–1527

The young Henry VIII (1509–1547), who succeeded his respected but unloved father in 1509, was a magnificent specimen—an athlete who excelled in hunting, riding, and tennis and an educated prince with broad intellectual interests and the ability to speak Latin, French, and Spanish as well as English. He was a cultured Renaissance man who played instruments and composed music (he is thought to have written Greensleeves). He was also extraordinarily indulgent and vain, a boisterous lover of good times and carousing, a man who had been flattered all his life and had

Henry VIII *(National Portrait Gallery)*.

never had to work to achieve fame. He had a flaming and mercurial temper that quickly turned from pettiness into rage and vindictive cruelty.

Catherine of Aragon and the Imperial Alliance. Soon after his accession Henry VIII married his brother's widow, Catherine of Aragon. Lest there be any future question that the children of their union would be legitimate, Henry requested and received a dispensation from the pope specifically allowing the marriage to take place. Catherine, a well-educated Renaissance princess, was the daughter of Ferdinand of Aragon and Isabella of Castille, whose marriage in 1469 had been instrumental in the creation of Spain. In their early years a genuine love and trust grew between Henry and Catherine.

In 1516, Catherine's nephew Charles became king of Spain; in 1519 as Charles V he was elected emperor of the Holy Roman Empire. This monarch's domains were unprecedented: he ruled Spain, the Spanish Netherlands (modern-day Belgium and Holland), the Habsburg dominions (modern-day Austria, Hungary, and adjacent territories), and the new American territories opened by another Genoan sailor, Christopher Columbus. As emperor he exercised a nominal leadership over all of central Europe, particularly modern-day Germany. Because Henry VIII conceived of monarchy in the traditional manner and thus was eager to win glory in the customary way, through war, Henry became the willing partner of his wife's nephew in the latter's expansionary activities on the European continent.

Henry's early years were dominated by planning for English participation in warfare on continental Europe in support of Charles' actions. Henry was distinctly the junior partner in the enterprises, a king who had little part in the grand imperial strategy, whose battles were minor sideshows, and who had no part in the spoils of victory. Henry won occasional military glory, but his treasury was continually depleted.

Cardinal Wolsey. Henry VIII was unwilling to attend to the details of everyday administration as his father had, and so the burden fell on the willing shoulders of the king's chief minister, Thomas Wolsey. Because Wolsey was not of aristocratic birth, he entered the church where it was possible for a talented and bright young man to rise merely on ability, and after a budding career at Oxford he entered the royal service. Under Henry VIII he became lord chancellor, taking precedence over other ministers to head the legal system. In the church he was first a bishop, then archbishop of York, later a cardinal, and finally, at Henry VIII's request of the pope, a papal legate. In this last capacity Wolsey had the theoretical right to exercise in England the pope's own powers, a grant made to allow him to reform the church.

Wolsey was generally unsuccessful as the king's minister. The aristocratic power elite were offended at his humble origins and resented his ostentatious display of the trappings of power. His arrogance ill-equipped him for the delicate tasks of managing Parliament and for the delegation of responsibilities which was the key to effective administration. In foreign affairs Wolsey substituted a pro-French alliance for friendship with Spain, risking England's wool and cloth exports that flowed through the Spanish Netherlands. He did serve well in the law, especially in the Courts of Star Chamber and Chancery where he presided and increased the jurisdiction.

His greatest failings were ecclesiastical. Although made a papal legate to reform its abuses, he was seen by his contemporaries to personify the very abuses in the Church that needed reformation. Priests were called to be chaste and celibate, but he had an illegitimate son. Priests were called to serve their offices faithfully, but he was a pluralist who multiplied office holding and was therefore nonresident in most posts. Priests were called to administer their posts faithfully and without gain, but instead he accepted bribes for favors.

Wolsey did leave his mark on Britain. He suppressed several religious houses and used the revenues to endow a new college at Oxford for the training of secular priests; after the Reformation its chapel was to become a cathedral for the new diocese of Oxford. He purchased a manor at Hampton and began a lavish building program that made it a showplace known as Hampton Court that evoked the envy of Henry VIII himself. He took the palace of the archbishops of York that lay just between the western edge of London and Westminster and began a massive rebuilding plan. In addition, he had two other magnificent country houses. Worse yet he never visited York where he was the archbishop.

Early Renaissance and Reformation Ideas in England

The Beginning of the English Renaissance. Early sixteenth-century England was starting to share in the flood of ideas and attitudes from continental Europe. The Renaissance that began in fourteenth-century Italy had been primarily cultural, philosophical, and artistic: writers such as Dante created early literary masterpieces in vernacular Italian, the thought of the Greek philosopher Plato was restudied, and artists such as Michelangelo and Leonardo da Vinci painted, sculpted, and designed magnificent palaces and churches in Florence, Rome, and elsewhere on the Italian peninsula.

The Renaissance in northern Europe beginning in the fifteenth century had a different character. It was more concerned with Christian than pagan scholarship, particularly in the study of the ancient biblical texts and the writings of the fathers of the Christian church in the second through fifth centuries. The most famous light of the Northern Renaissance was Erasmus of Rotterdam who researched and produced as scholarly correct a revised text of the Greek New Testament as was possible. Erasmus and others also very interested in church reform wrote tirelessly (and bitingly) about its unreformed state. In both the Italian and the Northern Renaissances, the attention paid to the human condition produced the name by which Renaissance thinkers were known, "humanists." The development of printing in the mid-fifteenth century in Germany meant that the ideas of the humanists in the sixteenth century could be spread quickly and widely in a manner unparalleled in the western world.

Henry VII had invited Italian humanists to England, and during his son's lifetime Erasmus lived and worked in England, particularly at the University of Cambridge. William Caxton set up the first printing press in England, and from 1476 the English press played an important part in the Renaissance. John Colet, an Oxford-educated priest who had travelled three years in France and Italy, returned and became dean of the chapter of St. Paul's Cathedral. The statutes he wrote for the cathedral school about 1509 became one of the earliest documents of educational reform in the humanistic mold. Thomas Linacre, the physician to the royal court, illustrated that well-rounded goal of learning which humanists so prized: in addition to his own medical studies and founding the Royal College of Physicians in 1518, he translated medical works from Greek and Latin into English and wrote on Latin grammar and composition.

The most renowned of the Tudor humanists was Sir Thomas More. The son of a London lawyer, the young More studied first in the household of the archbishop of Canterbury and then at Oxford. He thought first of becoming a priest but instead chose to devote himself to a legal career, to humanistic writing, to married life, and to public service. In time he rose to be speaker of the House of Commons and eventually lord chancellor, the highest legal office in the land and the titular head of the royal administration. Indeed, More was the first layman to hold that office which theretofore had been reserved for a bishop.

More was a close friend of Erasmus, and both wrote to forward humanistic ideas and the reform of the church. More's concern for his children was exemplary; in particular he wished his daughter to be as well educated in the classics and letters as any young man. His book, *Utopia*, describes an ideal city in profound contrast with the realities of the time; some have seen it as a frustrated admission that an ideal human state was an impossibility in his own time.

Early Reformation Ideas in England. Although the ideas of the Christian humanists were well received, the teachings of the continental Protestant

Utopia illustration *(The Bettmann Archive)*.

reforms were officially suppressed. Martin Luther began his public confrontation with the Catholic church in Germany in 1517 and unleashed a flood of religious controversy and interpretation. Henry VIII showed his opposition to these ideas when he wrote an answer to Luther, a book entitled *Assertion of the Seven Sacraments*. For this display of orthodoxy he was rewarded by Pope Leo X with the title "Defender of the Faith." Wolsey, More, and other leaders in the royal government and the church worked to suppress Lutheran books, including William Tyndale's English translation of the Bible (1525) which had numerous Lutheran explanatory notes.

Henry VIII and the English Reformation

Henry VIII's early loving relationship with Queen Catherine had cooled. She had six children, of whom only Princess Mary survived; of the two boys, one had lived fifty-two days and the other was stillborn. Henry had a bastard son by a mistress, but, with no legitimate male to succeed him, he feared his dynasty would be short-lived. He had lately become infatuated with a witty young woman at court, Anne Boleyn, which doubtless intensified his dissatisfaction with the aging queen.

In 1527 Henry VIII made public his belief that his marriage to Catherine of Aragon was invalid. He sought an annulment of his marriage, a declaration by the church that he was never really married because religious impediments barred a valid marriage. Such a declaration would leave him free to marry, whereas a divorce (a statement that a valid marriage was now terminated) would not allow remarriage. The chain of events that followed his announcement constituted the English Reformation.

The English Reformation differed markedly from that on the continent and was accomplished in two stages. It is useful to consider the differences before considering the details. The first stage, from 1527 until Henry's death twenty years later, was made not by religious leaders but instead by the English government, by king and Parliament; it broke the jurisdictional ties between the universal Catholic church and England but did not sweep away all of the old. In particular, it did not make doctrinal changes. The second stage occurred in the reign of the son eventually to be born to Henry, the future Edward VI (1547–1553), and was distinctly religious in character. In the first stage, Henry's jurisdictional break was epitomized in the Act of Supremacy that declared him supreme head of the Church of England; in the second stage, a way had to be found to make England legally Protestant. The means then found was to command, through the Act of Uniformity, the exclusive use of the *Book of Common Prayer* in which the services of worship were distinctly Protestant. The theology of the new church would be learned from its liturgies. While continental reformers led the break from the Catholic church over religious convictions and took the initiative in the changes, the English Reformation was led not by religious reformers but by king and Parliament, and was effected by changes in English law.

The "King's Great Matter." Henry's argument for the annulment was based on his reading of a scriptural text which stated that God would punish anyone who had relations with a brother's wife (Leviticus 18:16). Henry and his advisors argued that the prohibition of such a union, stated in scripture, was part of the divine law and was beyond the powers of papal dispensation, so that the union of 1509 was invalid. The motives prompting him to such an argument are unknown and therefore highly debated: did he have a genuine religious scruple? was he motivated by reasons of statecraft, eager for another marriage that might produce a son so there would be no repetition of the civil war which happened in the twelfth century when Matilda attempted to succeed Henry I? was he uncontrollably swayed by lust, his passion for Anne Boleyn kindled to flame by her refusal to be his mistress? Regardless, a speedy resolution of the matter seemed likely, because as a papal legate Cardinal Wolsey could exercise many of the pope's judicial powers.

Henry and Wolsey had not reckoned on the proud and stubborn resolve of the devout Catherine of Aragon who refused to allow so many years of her life to be cast aside as sinful and her daughter Mary to be declared a bastard or on the pope's refusal to allow Wolsey to handle the matter completely. Spanish soldiers had captured a great deal of the Italian peninsula, and the pope could not afford to antagonize the Spanish king by allowing his aunt to be judged a paramour. Wolsey was only allowed to hear the evidence, and the pope's intention to stall indefinitely became clear when many obstacles were raised even in that preliminary stage.

Wolsey's usefulness was clearly at an end. In vain he tried to recapture Henry's favor; he gave Henry his rebuilt estates at Hampton Court and at York Place in the hopes that Henry would be content with the magnificent buildings that he coveted. Henry accepted the gifts but still sought a way to be rid of Wolsey. Henry found an unusual weapon to remove him. The fourteenth-century statute of Praemunire had forbidden appealing from English church courts to the papal court at Rome any suits about the legal right a patron of a church had to nominate men to serve as parish priests (a right called an advowson). That law had been passed when the popes were living at Avignon and were all French, at a time when anti-French feeling had been fanned by the Hundred Years' War between England and France. The law had long since become ignored, a dead letter extremely limited in its scope. Henry twisted, enlarged, and distorted the original meaning of the statute to argue that it was in force and that it forbade *any* appeals to the Papacy. The king therefore conclude that Wolsey's papal legateship made him the worst offender of the law. Wolsey realized that the king's intention to be rid of him was as firm as the law's intention was dubious. He had enough common sense not to fight the trumped-up charges but instead sought a pardon without a trial, retired from his governmental posts, and died a year later of natural causes.

The Break with Rome. The Parliament which first sat in 1529 was so cooperative that Henry kept it in existence for seven years. The legislation which Henry proposed and Parliament passed earned it the title "Reformation Parliament." But from 1529 to 1531, the years immediately following Wolsey's fall, there was no positive plan of action. Although Parliament, with Henry's blessing, passed acts to reform minor clerical abuses, the impasse over Henry's marriage remained. From 1532, however, there was a definite plan, and because Thomas Cromwell rose to the position of Henry's chief minister at that time it has been argued that Cromwell was the architect of the political Reformation.

Efficient, calculating, expert in administration, the superb parliamentary manager, the stable counterpart and often bullied foil to the exuberant, emotional, and sometimes vindictive king, Cromwell brought purpose and organization to Henry's government. His plan was breathtakingly simple: separate the church from Rome and make it a department of the English state with the king as its head. The groundwork was laid in 1532 when king and Parliament acted to end the church's legislative independence and stop the flow of funds to the Papacy from England. The church had always made its own rules (called "canons"), and now the king gained control over all of the canons then in force through a commission he appointed. They were to determine which canons should continue. Henry gained the right to license all future canons. This was only a potential power, as was the authority to stop funds flowing from the realm. The purpose was still to pressure the pope. Threatening to break the financial powers tying England to Rome and to revoke the legislative independence of the church were powerful threats, but as yet there was no final break.

The need for actions and not threats became obvious in January 1533 when Anne Boleyn was found to be pregnant. Henry secretly married her, but it would not do to have the future heir tainted with illegitimacy. In March Parliament passed a law forbidding appeals out of England in matrimonial cases; the judicial action was added to the financial and legislative actions. In May an English court granted the annulment, and Henry's marriage to Anne was revealed. The pope excommunicated Henry who had violated an earlier papal ban against his remarriage while the case was in litigation. In turn Henry implemented the legislation of 1532. To Hen-

Catherine of Aragon *(The Bettmann Archive)*.

ry's dismay all of the promise of 1533 was not realized—Anne did not bear Henry a son but rather a daughter, Elizabeth. The new queen's days were numbered, and in May 1536 she was executed on apparently trumped-up charges of adultery.

The separation of the church from Rome was only a prelude to its total subordination to the English state, a process completed in 1534 to 1535 in a series of statutes. The king gained not only the revenues generated by two taxes and heretofore paid to the papacy but also a fee paid by parish priests to their bishops at the time the latter installed the former into their offices. The archbishop of Canterbury gained the powers of dispensation needed for effective administration, powers previously held by the popes, and the king gained the power to visit religious institutions to inquire into the state of religious life and to correct any abuses. Cases that had earlier been appealed from English church courts to the papal courts were now to be appealed to the English Court of Chancery, so that the state became the ultimate court of appeal for religious matters. An oath was devised so that men could be tested for their agreement with the new arrangements. Finally a law was passed which epitomized the break from the Catholic church: in the Act of Supremacy of 1534 Parliament recognized Henry's claim as supreme head of the Church on earth, under God's direction. It is to be noted that the act *recognized* Henry's headship of the church; merely to *grant* him that title would be to make the granting power, Parliament, superior to the king in religious matters, something Henry would find abhorrent. The law provided penalties of treason for those who would not conform. Now Henry was the head of a sovereign national state, which owed no allegiance to any foreign power, and of all the subjects of the realm, whether laymen or clergymen.

The Dissolution of the Monasteries and the Aftermath. Parliament had cooperated in the changes in part because of Cromwell's skill as a parliamentary manager, but more important because Henry seldom asked for new grants of revenue—a loss he more than made up from the proceeds of the dissolution of the monasteries between 1536 and 1540. Henry appointed the new vice-regent for spirituals to use the powers granted the king to investigate and reform religious abuses. Cromwell made as the subject of his inquiry the spiritual life of the monasteries. There were abuses, but probably nowhere near the degree pictured in Cromwell's lurid reports, which served as the basis for the legislation to abolish the monasteries and friaries. Since they controlled between a quarter and a third of the land of England, the king was greatly enriched. The monks and nuns were dispensed from their religious vows, a welcome relief for those who had no religious vocation but a tragedy for the majority. In time Henry and his successors gave or sold at reduced rates most of the newly acquired lands.

The purchasers received the land and the priceless social standing which it conferred, and in turn the king gained their loyalty in the implementation of the Reformation—were the nation to return to the Catholic church, the lands would have to be returned from lay persons to the church.

For most, the severe penalties of the new legislation were an effective deterrent against protest. There were a few outstanding resisters, notably the saintly Bishop John Fisher and Henry's own chancellor, Sir Thomas More, renowned throughout Europe for his humanism and integrity. He resigned his office rather than give an opinion on the changes of which he certainly disapproved and was convicted by perjured testimony. More and Fisher were both beheaded. The single popular uprising was the Pilgrimage of Grace in 1536, a futile rebellion in two northern counties. Although the rebels demanded a return to Catholicism, they were also inspired by a number of socioeconomic grievances which arose from the decay of traditional feudal values. Henry was quickly able to defeat them and hang the leaders.

A more serious problem was the division in the king's own council. Cromwell and Archbishop Thomas Cranmer had been strongly influenced by continental Protestantism and wanted religious reform, while the faction led by Thomas Howard, duke of Norfolk, resented Cromwell's humble social origins and Cranmer's great influence on the king and wished to maintain traditional Catholic beliefs in the new English church. Henry had married a third time, gaining at last a son and heir but losing Edward's mother Jane Seymour soon after she gave birth. The Cromwell-Cranmer faction urged a fourth marriage to Anne of Cleves, a German whose Protestantism was known. Henry's dislike of her plain appearance helped provide the lever for Norfolk's triumph over Cromwell who was executed in 1540. Henry's fifth wife was Catherine Howard, Norfolk's niece, but her adulteries cost her her head and cost Norfolk his seeming ascendancy in Henry's favor. The sixth wife, Catherine Parr, agreed with the more Protestant party. Although Henry was able to master and control both factions, the unity of purpose that marked the earlier years was lost.

Early Modern Government. Cromwell had spent much of the 1530s in reorganizing the royal administration so that it would function for the king without his detailed supervision. In part this recognized that Henry VIII did not care to invest as much time in day-to-day affairs as his father had; in part it reflected Cromwell's vision of the state which looked beyond medieval traditional practices to newer roles of governmental service. In the place of the traditionally large advisory medieval council, Cromwell substituted a Privy Council of fewer than twenty. The council's function was not only to advise but also to act as an executive agency to supervise the royal administration. He then developed and held the office of principal secretary—receiving reports from royal officers and agents, preparing the Privy Council's agenda, and then drafting and issuing the letters and commissions needed to implement conciliar decisions.

The king's decision prevailed on important matters, but the Privy Council made lower-level decisions. Financial offices were created to handle the new revenues produced by the Reformation, but these were absorbed into the exchequer in Mary's reign and did not survive as permanent governmental institutions. Cromwell's dedication to the management of parliamentary affairs reflected the growing importance of Parliament in English government.

As the Tudor prosperity increased the wealth of the gentry and they came to see the House of Commons as a focus for their political energy, and especially as Henry VIII increasingly made the Commons partners in the Reformation, the lower house became more important. Thomas Cromwell, the commoner, sat there, bringing in government bills, attempting to keep the proposals intact as independent-minded members of Parliament considered them in the three readings and committee investigations, and keeping relations between the king and the House of Commons harmonious. The king and Parliament were both beneficiaries of this cooperation, a far cry from the acrimony not uncommon in the Middle Ages.

Years of Tension and Uncertainty: Edward VI and Mary I

With Parliament's approval, Henry VIII had stipulated in his will that his son Edward accede to the throne and, were that young prince to die childless, then his daughters in the order of their birth, Mary first and finally Elizabeth. Henry had no illusions about the problems in store for the Tudor dynasty: Edward would be a minor at his accession, and, should a daughter reign later, there would be unprecedented difficulties. To forestall these problems, Henry ordered that a council and not an individual should serve as the regent for his son. But this precaution turned out to be in vain, and the next decade proved how prophetic his fears were.

Government on Behalf of Edward VI (1547–1553). The provision for a council was quickly set aside by the nine-year-old king's uncle, Edward Seymour, who as duke of Somerset directed the government as his nephew's protector. Somerset was necessarily concerned with sustaining his irregular position, which meant he made concessions of power to court the House of Commons and tolerated dissent in the hope of winning men's minds and assent.

Even the most resolute leader would have had difficulty in coping with

England's problems, and the protector was not successful. In 1549 Somerset was swept from his position by a fellow council member, John Dudley, who as duke of Northumberland assumed control of the young Edward and a few years later had Somerset executed on trumped-up charges of treason. Northumberland was self-centered and grasping, an impetuous leader whose own faults were magnified by the corruption of those around him.

England Becomes Protestant. The death of Henry VIII had removed the principal obstacle to the development of Protestantism in England, and Archbishop Cranmer with Somerset's encouragement had begun gradual reforms. Early in 1549 Parliament enacted the first Act of Uniformity and its *Book of Common Prayer*, which was worded with some ambiguity in order not to alienate the Catholics. But there were unmistakable signs of new changes, particularly when the chantries were suppressed just as the monasteries had been in the previous reign. Reformed Protestantism did not believe in a purgation after death from the effects of sin, and thus on theological grounds argued that the chantries in which masses were sung for the dead should be suppressed. The monasteries closed by Henry were usually rural, but the chantries were often in larger centers and their priests often served as schoolmasters, so that the impact of the suppression caused significantly more discontent. Under Northumberland a second Act of Uniformity and a revised *Book of Common Prayer* were adopted in 1552 which made a definite break with Catholic teachings on the mass, the real presence of Christ's body in the Eucharist, and many other beliefs repugnant to Protestantism. Priests were allowed to marry and other changes were made, but Edward's early death ended further reform.

These monumental religious changes provoked reaction and rebellion, not only because of religious disaffection from Catholics and Protestants but also because of keenly felt economic and social grievances aggravated by economic distress (see pages 105–106). The insecurity of Northumberland's position as he faced a growing conservative opposition led him to side with radical Protestantism, which in turn became a test of political loyalty. But because young Edward who had approved of this protestant emphasis lay dying in 1553 of lung disease, all that had been begun was in jeopardy because the Catholic Mary Tudor was next in the succession. Northumberland's desperate plan was to avert this by proclaiming as queen a great-niece of Henry VIII, the appealing Protestant Lady Jane Grey, to whom he married his own son. Such blatant self-interest awakened a nearly universal opposition, and within two weeks Mary and the forces of legitimacy had overthrown the plot, so that Lady Jane is not recognized as having ruled.

Mary I (1553–1558) and the Return to Catholicism. Mary Tudor—the fiercely proud thirty-seven-year-old daughter of Catherine of Aragon, the woman whose childhood was scarred by the dishonor of her mother, the disinterest of her father, and the legal stigma of judicial bastardy, the ruler who was the focus of all the fears of the Protestant party—had little ability or inclination to face or to deal with England's mounting problems. She desired only to restore Catholicism, a policy that would be resisted by the governing elite. The accession for the first time in history of a reigning female monarch posed a dangerous issue: marriage. If she married an Englishman, she would marry beneath her rank. If she married a reigning monarch of another realm, the result would probably be to make England's policy subordinate to that of her husband's nation.

Mary decided to marry Philip of Spain, heir to his country's throne and an ardent Catholic. Although he was a willing participant, Philip did not care for his wife and her hopeless wish to bear a child, but rather he sought Parliament's recognition of the title "King of England" for himself and England's participation in Spain's wars against France. Mary's proposed marriage to Philip produced a multicounty plot, dangerously near London, led by Sir Thomas Wyatt. The rebellion was crushed, the marriage was made, but Philip won the title of king that lasted only as long as his wife was alive. England did go to war as an ally of Spain, but the war was so unsuccessful that England lost its last possession in France, the town of Calais, which it had retained after the Hundred Years' War. Philip gained the hatred and distrust of his wife's subjects.

Mary's desire to return England to her Catholic religion involved two elements: the repeal in Parliament of the Edwardian Protestant statutes and the reconciliation of England with the Papacy. The first was made palatable to Parliament because Mary wanted a modified Act of Supremacy which would keep state control over the church, but especially because it was made clear that reconciliation would not require returning the lands seized at the dissolution of the monasteries. It is interesting that so doctrinally Catholic a queen was not willing to sacrifice the power over the Church which had been won by her father and half brother.

With the legal preliminaries finished, the Papal absolution for England was pronounced late in 1554. Mary next tried to uproot Protestantism in England. With the queen's tacit approval, most of its leaders left England voluntarily to go to European Protestant centers such as Geneva and Frankfurt; but, while they drank at the pure springs of reformed Protestantism abroad, their fellow religionists suffered mightily in England. The government had reenacted the harsh medieval laws against heresy which Edward's government had repealed, and nearly 300 were martyred for their heresy by burning at the stake, many for radical Protestant views which were equally intolerable to Edwardian Protestants. Most were of

Death of Thomas Cranmer *(Foxe,* Acts and Monuments).

lower social ranks, but a few had been notable leaders of the earlier movement, including Thomas Cranmer. It is still not clear if the burnings were
at the insistence of the coldly unbending queen, of her Spanish advisors
whose own country had a reputation for ferocity in dealing with heretics,
or of the queen's English councillors, but such severity was unprecedented
in England although very common in Europe. When Catholic Mary was
succeeded by the Protestant Elizabeth, the reputation of "Bloody Mary"
as a great religious persecutor was assured.

Economic Crisis During the Reigns of Edward and Mary. Edward and Mary
had no monopoly on economic problems, but two crises which affected
the whole century became particularly acute in their reigns. The inflation
that was felt throughout all Europe intensified, and in 1552 the wool
market, which served England's principal export, collapsed.

Prices had been relatively stable in the fifteenth century, but in the sixteenth century before Edward's accession, prices had risen nearly 50 percent. In the troubled decade thereafter prices nearly doubled again. There
were many causes: the wars against France and Scotland led to huge governmental deficits, and there was a bloated money supply. The latter was a
result of the practice of Henry, Edward, and Mary of stretching the value
of English coins by mixing base alloys into the pure metal to increase their
number (called "debasement") and in part a result of participation in the
European inflation from the flood of precious metals from America via

Spain. In an agricultural society where land was the main source of wealth, landlords were faced with the problem of increasing the yield from the land, whether in produce or rents, to keep pace with rising prices. Before 1552 one of the most appealing alternatives was to switch from farming to raising sheep because the wool produced a higher return than did the sale of crops. Some landlords sought to increase their efficiency by forcing small farmers off the strips of land they held and then consolidating all the holdings into a more efficient, larger farm, while others began to enclose the commons and wastes which had been such a valuable source of supplemental income for the villagers. This process of enclosing was bitterly resented.

The social effects of enclosure wrought a major though gradual change in English life. The aristocrat who traditionally lived lavishly found it increasingly hard to maintain his economic standing when compared with the more industrious smaller landowner whose thrift and efficiency allowed him to buy land (much of it formerly monastic property) on the market. The monarch, as the largest and often the most inefficient holder of lands, was particularly vulnerable to this relative decline. Many small landowners were forced off their holdings through unscrupulous lawsuits and became leaseholders in a subordinate position to a landlord or perhaps became merely wage earners. The gap between rich and poor widened. To the extent that men forced off the land could not find another job, the number of unemployed and vagabonds rose, intensifying the already serious job of maintaining law and order. The extraordinary rise in English prices meant that the cost of English wool abroad continually rose and in 1552 reached such a height that it was priced out of competition, and the market collapsed. It was nearly thirty years before the exports rose to the pre-1552 level, and the unemployment that resulted in England was particularly severe. Governments of the sixteenth century, English and European, had no tools of economic analysis to discover the roots of the problem or to suggest remedies. In vain they attempted to treat the symptoms and to return to the days of stability by ordering that as many men be employed or that as much land be tilled as before.

A Legacy of Unrest. The short reigns of Edward and Mary left a legacy of unresolved problems. In addition to the major rebellions already noted, there were other spasmodic eruptions of violence so that governmental fears of insurrection at times bordered on paranoia. In Parliament the lack of leadership occasionally meant that private members dared to introduce bills on religion, heretofore the exclusive concern of the government. This precedent when repeated in Elizabeth's reign provoked a constitutional issue. Both the Edwardian and Marian religious settlements were imposed upon the ordinary subject. The rapid changes and reversals bred confusion and suspicion, and the intolerance of the times which was an English and a European characteristic meant a legacy of enduring bitterness.

Mary died alone in 1558, leaving a country repulsed by her religious policies, humiliated by unsuccessful war, and bereft of leadership. Her death probably resulted from a uterine cancer, the first manifestations of which suggested pregnancy and eventually led to ridicule of the pitiful queen when her term was up and she was still childless. England's first female monarch had been a failure as a ruler; the next, Mary's half sister Elizabeth, would completely reverse that experience.

Suggestions for Further Reading

The best introduction to political events in England in the sixteenth century is G. R. Elton, *England Under the Tudors* (2nd edition, 1974). Elton's thesis that Thomas Cromwell inspired the plan for the Reformation, and that his administrative changes mark the watershed between medieval and early modern government, was argued in *The Tudor Revolution in Government* (1953), with elaboration in other works such as *Policy and Police: The Enforcement of the Reformation in the Age of Thomas Cromwell* (1972) and *Reform and Renewal, Thomas Cromwell and the Common Weal* (1973). A differing view is found in W. C. Richardson, *Tudor Chamber Administration, 1485–1547* (1952). The whole issue was debated by Elton and some of his opponents in the journal *Past & Present*, 1963–1965. The role of Parliament in the crucial years of the English Reformation is masterfully surveyed by Stanford E. Lehmberg in *The Reformation Parliament, 1529–1536* (1970) and in *The Later Parliaments of Henry VIII, 1536–1547* (1977).

The troubled years of midcentury are argued from one point of interpretation by Whitney R. D. Jones, *The Mid-Tudor Crisis, 1539–1563* (1973) and from another point by Jennifer Loach and Robert Tittler (eds.), *The Mid-Tudor Polity c. 1540–1560* (1980). Useful corrections to established views about Edward VI's reign are in Dale Hoak, *The King's Council in the Reign of Edward VI* (1976) and in M. L. Bush, *The Government Policy of Protector Somerset* (1975). The best account of Mary is in D. M. Loades, *The Reign of Mary Tudor: Politics, Government, and Religion in England, 1553–1558* (1979); a more sympathetic treatment of Mary is in H. F. M. Prescott, *Mary Tudor* (2nd edition, 1972). The best survey of foreign affairs is in R. B. Wernham, *Before the Armada, The Emergence of the English Nation, 1485–1588* (1966).

Religious change in the first half of the sixteenth century is surveyed in A. G. Dickens, *The English Reformation* (1964). Foxe's account of the Marian martyrs has often been edited, as in Marie Gentert King, *Foxe's Book of Martyrs* (1968). Recent work in the Reformation is well represented by essays edited by Felicity Heal and Rosemary O'Day, *Church and Society in England: Henry VIII to James I* (1977) and *Continuity and Change: Personnel and Administration in the Church of England, 1500–1642* (1976).

A most useful restatement of the scope and results of current studies in Tudor social and economic issues is in Joyce Youings, *Sixteenth-Century England* (in the series The Pelican Social History of Britain, 1984). The workaday world of rural England is reflected in the essays in John Thirsk, ed., *The Agrarian History of England and Wales,* Vol. IV, *1500–1640* (1967). The Renaissance in England is shown in Arthur B. Ferguson's *The Articulate Citizen and the English Renaissance* (1965); intellectual history is well surveyed in Christopher Morris' *Political Thought in England from Tyndale to Hooker* (1954).

6

The Elizabethan Era

1558–1603

*T*he heir to the promise and problems of England's crown was its second reigning queen, Elizabeth Tudor, the twenty-five-year-old "Reformation child," the daughter of Henry and Anne Boleyn. Elizabeth's lengthy reign (1558–1603) was to be so successful and distinctive in so many areas that the "Elizabethan Age" is seen as the springtime of early modern England. The often overromanticized adulation of the period need not blind anyone to its serious problems, but the stability and progress that characterized the era arose in great part from the remarkable acumen of Elizabeth Tudor.

Elizabeth was popular, an indispensable element for success. She had impressive personal qualities that helped her fulfill the duties of the office. The policies of her government were successful, in part from her and her minister's sagacity and in part from the luck that all political leaders need. She often delayed making decisions, and her procrastination often worked to advantage when she was confronted with insurmountable problems. Also, she knew how to cultivate affection but could have retained it only because her subjects believed she cared for England above all.

Her subjects loved her, because they could see themselves in her. She mirrored their zest for the bawdy and bloody amusements of the day, attending with relish the cock fights, bear baitings, and plays. She reflected their extravagance, wearing ornately jeweled, outrageously ruffed and decorated clothing. Even in personal items—the reddish wig, the heavy white makeup, the blackened teeth—she was characteristic of the premedical age, hiding, as did many subjects, the ravages of smallpox, which left people hairless and pockmarked, and the indulgence of an excessive consumption of sweets.

In later years, when it became clear that she would not marry, the "Virgin Queen" claimed with sound reason and not a little hyperbole that she was married to the realm. Elizabeth was remarkably secular-minded in a

109

century of religious passion. France was torn by religious civil wars, and the advancement of Catholicism was a principal motive of Spain's foreign policy; in contrast, Elizabeth made her church serve England first, then Protestantism.

The Elizabethan Settlement and the Early Years, 1558–1570

The Young Queen. The first arena in which Elizabeth would demonstrate her considerable talents was in the formation of an administration that could command respect, restore confidence, and govern effectively. Because she was an astute judge of character, Elizabeth was able to surround herself with advisors whose fierce dedication to England's welfare matched hers. Yet with those ministers, and with complex matters of state that had to be faced, the queen was iron-willed, cold, and calculating. At first the ministers feared that her sex would be a liability, as potentially harmful as it had been for the indecisive Mary, but Elizabeth made her femininity a powerful asset—and when she wished, a weapon she could use to paralyze into submission those male advisors who were defenseless against her emotional fury, her resolve, and her unwillingness to yield to their "reason."

Among the queen's strongest assets was her ability to choose capable, loyal, and dispassionate ministers of government. Her earliest and best choice was that of Sir William Cecil (1520–1598) for the post of principal secretary. That shrewd, calculating, ambitious yet levelheaded thirty-eight-year-old man was already well seasoned, not only in government service (he had been a principal secretary under Edward) but especially in the necessary Tudor exercise of survival in factional intrigue and infighting. His role as virtual head of the English administration went well beyond his title of principal secretary; Elizabeth trusted him implicitly with all matters.

The Elizabethan Settlement. The earliest problem was religion. Elizabeth's intentions were moderate, a return to Henry's national church, and so she sought only political control through a new Act of Supremacy. But the Protestant exiles who returned from the continent were successful in getting passed in Parliament renewed religious changes through a Protestant Act of Uniformity that revived the *Book of Common Prayer* of 1552. Elizabeth wisely yielded to these pressures but eased tensions by refusing to insist on a zealous enforcement of the new religious settlement.

Another problem related to religion was the question of marriage. Should Elizabeth remain unmarried and childless, the crown would most likely go to Mary Queen of Scots, Elizabeth's Catholic cousin and closest

Queen Elizabeth I *(National Portrait Gallery)*.

relative. The Englishman most attractive to Elizabeth was her childhood playmate, Robert Dudley, a son of the duke of Northumberland who had been the second lord protector in Edward's reign. Elizabeth's infatuation with Dudley was matched by the consternation felt by Cecil and the other ministers at their relationship. Dudley had married in 1550; unwilling to have any other, Elizabeth was not eager to marry and so kept alive the possibility of a Catholic succession through Mary Queen of Scots. When Elizabeth nearly died of smallpox in the early years of her reign, the marriage issue became acute. It led to strains in Parliament, where she was urged to marry for the realm and for the Protestant succession.

Foreign and Domestic Affairs. Religion was an important factor in Elizabeth's first foray into foreign affairs, intervening in Scotland which was religiously and politically torn between two powerful forces. There was on one hand the hegemony France exercised in Scottish affairs, and on the other Scotland's growing commitment to the Protestant Reformation. England sent troops into Scotland successfully to help the Scots oust the French; the Treaty of Edinburgh of 1560 cemented the Anglo-Scottish accord.

The intervention of the Protestant English had been welcomed in much of Scotland, especially by John Knox, Scotland's great religious leader. Knox had lived in Geneva under the direction of John Calvin; upon his return to Scotland from Geneva in 1558, Knox directed the establishment in Scotland of Presbyterianism, as Scottish Calvinism was called, in the absence of Scotland's queen. Mary Queen of Scots (1542–1587) had become queen when only six days old when her father died in 1542, but had married into the French royal family. When her husband died in 1562, she returned from France to Scotland, determined to reverse Scotland's new Protestant settlement. Her return threatened the new Anglo-Scottish accord.

Mary's reign was increasingly weakened by scandal in her choices of husbands and lovers, intrigue and plots, and was weakened by her inability to rule effectively. Faced with an impossible situation, she abdicated in 1568 in favor of her nine-month-old son, James VI, and then she went to England where her self-exile became a virtual house arrest.

Elizabeth and her ministers also took actions aimed at restoring confidence in the economy. By calling in the debased coins of earlier reigns and issuing in their place coins of pure metal, the queen helped slow inflation and rebuild the prestige of the English government. The successes of the first decade were particularly apparent in the ease with which two crises were handled. In 1569 two earls from families that had enormous feudal importance in earlier centuries led a rebellion which sought a restoration of Catholicism and which reflected the frustration over the severe socioeconomic dislocations felt acutely in northern England. Elizabeth's officials repressed the uprising easily, executing one earl while the other fled the country. In 1570 the pope excommunicated Elizabeth, an action involving a theoretical deposition of the queen and an invitation to other monarchs to invade England to bring it about. Nearly twelve years had convinced the pope there was no hope of Elizabeth's conversion. Governmental officials were able to prevent copies of the bull from distribution in England by vigilance at seaports. That the queen suffered no immediate difficulties at home as a result of these two crises showed how firmly and successfully she had ruled in her first eleven years. Elizabeth was secure in the affections of her subjects, and neither threat could topple her.

Growing Religious Discord, 1570–1585

After the settlement of religion made in the Parliament of 1558 to 1559, there was relatively little conflict over religion until about 1570. The Anglican church, established by law, was in fact a new recreation, and neither its leaders nor its members had yet time to reflect on its character. Religious dissent from the other religious groups was surprisingly muted in this period. Beginning about the year 1570, however, conflict over religion increased markedly and became a major determinant in English policy and life.

Anglican, Papist, and Puritan. Because only the Church of England was legally established, everyone was theoretically an Anglican, the name derived from the Latin word "Anglicana," meaning "English." The organization of the church was the same as existed when Henry VIII separated the English church from the papacy: bishops headed geographic dioceses, parishes constituted the dioceses, and all of the church officials and institutions were part of the medieval Catholic church except, of course, the monarch who was now the head of the state church. Elizabeth took the name "supreme governor" in deference to those who objected to a woman being "supreme head" of the church as Henry VIII had been styled, and she did not exercise direct leadership as he had done, working instead through her bishops and especially through the archbishop of Canterbury, the normal titular head of the church hierarchy.

In doctrine, however, the Elizabethan Anglican church was far removed from that of Henry: the settlement of 1559 had reimposed the *Book of Common Prayer* that had been drafted in 1552, and thus Protestant liturgy imparted Protestant ideas. Financially the church continued to suffer at the hands of the Tudors. As Henry VIII had had the monasteries and friaries suppressed and their revenues transferred to the crown, as Edward

VI had done the same with the chantries, so Elizabeth continued to profit at the expense of the church, sometimes keeping dioceses whose bishop had just died without a new bishop for an inordinately long time so that she could enjoy the profits of the diocese herself in the interim, sometimes forcing church leaders to "exchange" church lands for royal lands, but always so that the rather uneven exchanges meant greater revenues for the crown.

The settlement of 1559 was of course most disastrous for the Catholics who had enjoyed a brief respite when Queen Mary had reversed the Reformation in England. Most high-ranking leaders—the bishops, many of the upper clergy, university theological professors—chose to leave England at Elizabeth's succession, not unlike the exodus of Protestant leaders at the beginning of Mary's reign. A number of these self-exiles settled in the Spanish Netherlands, particularly at the University of Louvain. Because Catholicism requires priests for its most sacred functions—to offer mass and consecrate bread and wine into the Body and Blood of Christ, to hear confessions and grant absolution, and so on—the absence of the priests meant a steady decline in the adherence of ordinary men and women to the Catholic faith. They were sheep left without shepherds.

The uprising in the north in 1569 had left the impression that Catholics were disloyal subjects, and the papal excommunication in 1570 added to that impression. Because in the public mind Catholics seemed more loyal to the pope than to their nation, the derisive name "Papists" was often accorded them. Nevertheless, Elizabeth had left Catholics relatively undisturbed in their faith in the period 1558 to 1570, provided they conformed outwardly by attending the Anglican religious services weekly.

A more serious problem of dissent existed within Protestantism itself. A substantial number within the established national Anglican church felt that the English Reformation had not gone far enough, that some things still needed to be "purified," hence the derisive name "Puritan" given by others who resented their "holier-than-thou" self-righteousness. Because the Bible was to them the sole source of religious instruction and the test of all practices, they found many things in Anglicanism without Biblical warrant. However, these Puritans were not of one mind over what needed to be removed as part of reform: some wished to remove the hierarchal structure from bishops downward, others only to be rid of vestments and other symbols kept from Catholicism; some wanted to revise the church's liturgical year to remove times and practices not mentioned in the Bible, as for example the keeping of Lent before Easter.

While all Puritans were "against" something—opposed to some "unreformed" abuse—a smaller group within Puritanism known as Presbyterians was "for" a positive alternative—the form of worship developed in John Calvin's Geneva, where many Englishmen had lived in Mary's reign.

To Presbyterians the key to a proper Reformation was the removal of the Anglican episcopal structure and the *Book of Common Prayer*. These were to be replaced with the translation of the Bible into English with their own interpretative notes—the "Genevan" Bible in England—and the strict organizational and disciplinary tenants of Calvinistic practice. Because positive programs of reform such as these are a more dangerous form of opposition, the Presbyterians would become the greatest threat within Puritanism; all Presbyterians were Puritans, but of course not all Puritans were Presbyterians.

Still other Protestants were so impatient at the unreformed elements that they wished to dissociate entirely from the Church of England, and they were called "Separatists." These were often very small groups, perhaps only a single congregation, as were the Brownists in eastern England, or a dispersed group of like-minded persons motivated by a charismatic leader, such as the Family of Love which looked to a Dutch Anabaptist as their spiritual father. In sixteenth-century England, Separatism never grew to a large number; however, in the seventeenth century, it would become more important—from the Pilgrims who left for America to the Baptists and others who flourished.

The Threat from Catholics in the 1570s and 1580s. The vigor of Catholic practice had been sapped by a slow process of attrition during which priestless Catholics conformed by attending Anglican services. In 1574, however, the first of what was to be a steady stream of "missionaries" began to arrive secretly in England. The Catholic self-exiles had established seminaries abroad to train young Englishmen as priests who would, after ordination, return secretly to England to reconvert their countrymen. These "seminary priests" were joined in 1580 by English members of the Jesuits, a community that was the most important element in the Catholic Counter-Reformation in Europe. The Jesuits were more of a threat because they were unabashedly confrontational: as learned men they directly challenged the leaders of Anglicanism to debate which was the "true Church" founded by Christ, and as pastors concerned for their flocks' souls, they instructed the faithful not to attend Anglican services.

The government of Elizabeth was driven to respond to the renewed challenge from Catholicism, and anti-Catholic legislation was produced in many Parliaments in the 1570s and 1580s. The slowly elaborated legislation was twofold, aimed primarily at forbidding the ministries of the priests and then secondarily at those Catholic laypeople who sheltered the priests in their secret ministry.

The culmination of a number of laws against the priests was one passed in 1585 that defined a priest's mere presence in England, with no overt act whatsoever, to be treason. Under this law and several less inclusive laws passed earlier, over 100 priests were martyred. They usually suffered the agonizing and barbaric practice of hanging, drawing, and quartering by which they were hanged until nearly dead and, while still alive, castrated, arms and legs amputated, entrails cut out and burned, and finally the heart cut out and the body decapitated.

The legislation against laymen was aimed at their financial ruin rather than physical punishment; by striking at a Catholic's patrimony and thus threatening the end of a family's social status, the government sought to draw the gentry and nobility away from Catholicism and to set examples that the lesser orders would certainly imitate. The penalty for nonattendance at Anglican services was raised to £10 per month (the average agricultural worker earned just over £5 per year).

Persecution, propaganda, and financial pressure spelled the beginning of the end to an effective domestic Catholicism. An unrelenting propaganda campaign branded the Catholics as traitors, citing not only the pope's excommunication of Elizabeth but the more recent fact that certain English leaders abroad who felt that only force could prevail, particularly those influenced by the Jesuits, urged King Philip of Spain to invade England. When Philip did indeed mount the Spanish Armada against England in 1588 for that purpose, English Catholics remained loyal to queen and country.

The Threat from Puritanism in the 1570s and 1580s. Puritanism involved less of a confrontation but more of a sustained threat. Because the Marian Catholic bishops had fled on Elizabeth's accession in 1558, the new queen had had to rely greatly on those returning self-exiles who had spent Mary's reign abroad, the greater part in Geneva where they had become strongly Calvinistic. Equally as great a reason for Puritanism's success was that laymen as well as churchmen shared its leadership, so that its pressures for reform were made not only in the church but also in Parliament, where a disproportionate number of reformers were elected, and even in the royal court, where sympathizers such as Sir William Cecil and Robert Dudley were very influential.

The early efforts at reform in the 1560s had been piecemeal, seeking the removal of pre-Reformation religious practices. The reformers believed that the queen favored further reform, and they sought to hasten matters by making proposals in the church's convocation and in Parliament. They were surprised when she refused to let the proposals be discussed in the House of Commons, arguing that, as head of the church, its reform was her exclusive right. Some in the Commons recalled contrary precedents for parliamentary initiatives in the two earlier reigns, but Elizabeth refused to let a religious matter became a constitutional issue and promised to make reforms herself.

In the early 1570s Thomas Cartwright, a professor of divinity at Cambridge who came to Presbyterianism by an academic route, and other Presbyterian leaders who had learned at the feet of Calvin himself at Geneva, began to write and surreptitiously print books urging change. Not only Cartwright but even an archbishop lectured the queen on her religious duty to delay a "complete" and thoroughgoing reformation no longer. Elizabeth struck back by ordering the enforcement of religious uniformity against Puritanism.

Not unnaturally the movement went underground but resurfaced in the 1580s in more threatening guises. A clandestine Presbyterian organization was established in some parts of England, particularly in eastern England where Puritanism was strongest, alongside of and completely ignoring the Anglican church. The pressure within Parliament to replace Anglicanism with Presbyterianism or at least a milder form of Puritanism was as unrelenting as it was unsuccessful. Elizabeth's counterattack triumphed when her anti-Puritan new archbishop of Canterbury, John Whitgift, made his own diocesan tribunal into a nationwide Court of High Commission in which Puritan churchmen were charged, tried, and removed from office and influence. Laymen who wrote books urging reform were branded "seditious," and thus, for example, John Stubbs, a Puritan author who wrote against the queen's consideration of marriage to a French Catholic prince, had his right hand cut off. More important, government agents sought out and suppressed the growing Presbyterian underground counter-church, so that by the late 1580s Puritanism was nearly as ineffective as Catholicism.

Meanwhile, three decades of internal growth had enabled Anglicanism to develop and enunciate its principles. The most mature expression was in Richard Hooker's *The Laws of Ecclesiastical Polity*, an argument that Anglicanism was a *via media*, a "middle way" between unreformed Catholicism and radical Protestantism. Anglicanism accepted as a valid norm for the church not only the Bible but also the tradition of the first five centuries of the church before the great growth of papal influence—thus it accepted the episcopal form of government, creeds, and practices, which had flourished in the early Christian church during and after the Biblical first century, and rejected the belief of Puritans and others that man's will was not free.

Elizabethan Society

In many respects Elizabethan society was shaped and changed by the continued importance of movements and trends previously considered. Inflation continued especially because of the rise of population; to counter inflation more and more persons converted leases to shorter terms to enable more frequent raises to keep pace, while inefficient landowners—the crown foremost among them—continued a relative economic decline. The flood onto the land market of former monastic and other church lands provided the opportunity for enterprising and well-connected Elizabethans to acquire the social as well as economic prestige of landowning. The movement toward enclosure continued unabated, although for a different reason: earlier there had been enclosure for pasture since owning sheep and selling wool provided a higher rate of return than growing crops; the advantage now slowly tilted back toward tillage of crops after the collapse of the cloth market in 1552.

But in the Elizabethan era there were newer sources of prosperity as well, such as overseas trading companies and new industries based on improved technology, whether in mining where coal was produced more efficiently from deeper mines or in marshy areas such as the fens in the east, which were drained for land reclamation. There were important social consequences of all these economic trends.

The Aristocracy and Gentry. Throughout the Middle Ages the small number of nobility had had a stunningly disproportionate share of power and responsibility: their military role had made them indispensable, their castles and vast estates dwarfed the landowning status of all except the king and the church, and they held the major positions in royal administration. The decline in the importance of the aristocracy was a constant in Tudor England, however. Henry VII and Henry VIII had not only been sparing in the creation of new nobles to replace those killed in the Wars of the Roses but had used many "new men" in administrative positions—had not Henry VII rewarded so many of his many wives' relatives with peerages, the number would have been even less. Elizabeth made only seventeen peers during her entire reign, and only two of these were from families that had not had a peerage earlier (Sir William Cecil was made Lord Burghley in 1571).

Meanwhile the size of the gentry grew strikingly. At Elizabeth's death there were perhaps 16,000 to 18,000 persons with a coat of arms, the greater number by far in the two lowest ranks of gentlemen and esquires. The entree into the ranks of the gentry was the possession of a coat of arms from the College of Heralds. Because land was now available—the market in lands arising from the dissolution of the monasteries assured that—the indispensable prerequisite of landowning which "qualified" one for a coat of arms was at hand. It was not surprising that an official from the College of Heralds could be induced for a price to search energetically and successfully for the gentle origins of a wealthy landowner's ancestors, provided of course that no official did violence to gentility by promoting manifestly unworthy persons.

The employment of the gentry showed their rising importance. There could be no question of menial work: the higher the rank, the greater the expected adherence to the principle that work was beneath their dignity. The gentry, like the aristocracy to whom they were often related, instead served in the public arena. The stepping stone to public trust was service as an unpaid local official—perhaps as a commissioner to collect the taxes voted by Parliament, or as a commissioner with special legal responsibilities for an important local case, or as a vice admiral who supervised the harbors for commercial reasons and also to keep out unwanted persons, especially the seminary priests.

The epitome of local service was being selected as one of thirty to fifty men on the local county's Commission of the Peace. These justices of the peace regulated wages according to the Statute of Artificers, licensed alehouses and other places of amusement, committed those who broke the peace to prison until trial, enforced the laws passed by Parliament, served as the trial judges for important matters of royal justice, and otherwise controlled all aspects of local life. To be selected as a justice of the peace, a member of the ruling county elite, was a stunning show of prestige, and faithful service (aided by proper connections) marked a justice of the peace for preferment on the national level.

The most successful became courtiers, serving in the royal household or court or on the monarch's Privy Council. Many sat as members of the House of Commons; indeed, by the end of the century members of the gentry had come to fill the seats in Parliament theoretically allotted to town burgesses because the latter were honored to have such influential yet nonresidential representatives in Parliament.

Elizabethan Country Homes. Another sign of prestige was to engage in the Elizabethan building mania. The huge stately mansions of the nobility and upper gentry were monuments to the peace and prosperity of the era and symbols of the owner's importance. The new buildings ignored the irregular floor plans, ornate decoration, and gothic features which had prevailed early in the century, adopting instead cleaner classical lines, with symmetrical floor plans in the E- or H-shape and an extravagant use of glass. Lord Burghley had three mansions, the second largest of which (like many other new homes) was built out from a former monastic building at the east end. The interiors of these homes featured elaborate wood panelling, sculptured plasterwork ceilings, and tapestries hung on the walls to provide color and keep out the cold. The homes of the middle gentry had a distinctive new style called half-timbering, in which the darkened wood

Longleat, an Elizabethan stately home *(E. A. Reitan).*

of the beams used in construction was contrasted with white exterior plasterwork.

The leisure activities of the aristocracy and gentry were prodigal. The brilliant possessions and pastimes of the Elizabethan era were thoroughly and gustily enjoyed although not widely shared, and the degree to which one participated in them depended on rank. A multitude of outward signs bore witness to gentle birth and its privileges: gentlemen could bear arms and amuse themselves at gambling while ordinary men could not; gentlemen wore hats and workers caps, and even within the upper ranks the gradations were apparent from whether one wore cloth-of-gold, silk, velvet, or more ordinary cloth in his apparel. Amusement in the country homes was extravagant: Elizabeth and her court of nearly 500 visited Burghley a dozen times, each time costing him huge sums (perhaps £5,000) in hospitality. Even the primary amusements of the country life, hawking and hunting, were restricted to the upper classes.

The Lower Classes. The enlargement of the ranks of the gentry and their increasing economic importance often cost lesser men dearly. The unemployed victims of enclosure tended to drift into cities, especially London, only to find endemic outbreaks of the plague, squalor, overcrowding, and a distinct loss of amenities. Crime was one possible solution, begging another. Even criminals and vagabonds lived according to rank, from the confidence man at the top down through levels of thievery such as "priggers of prancers" (horse thieves) to beggars—some of whom elicited sympathy with feigned wounds or intentionally maimed children. Living in close quarters in manifestly unsanitary conditions made the city poor particularly susceptible to the plague, which occasionally took its grim toll. The pockets of human misery, the stench of sewerless streets, and the many other hardships of city life were all-too-constant remainders that the poor had often left one type of misery for another.

In rural settings the lot of the poor was difficult as well. Most lived in hand-to-mouth subsistence dependent on the vagaries of weather and good crops. There were periods in the middle 1580s and especially in the late 1590s when steady rains for several years in a row left crops stunted and rotting in the fields. Prices for the inadequate supply of grain soared, and even those lucky enough to escape starvation suffered from severe malnutrition. In an act of 1597 and in its fuller elaboration in 1601, the Elizabethan government enacted a poor law which remained in its essence until the nineteenth century. It commanded that mandatory taxes be collected by local officials for the relief of the poor of the parish. Any poor person found away from his or her native parish was to be sent back there—a provision obviously aimed (and as obviously unsuccessful) at reducing the number of the poor who flocked to London and other larger towns. All of these conditions and the halting initial steps to remedy them are a pointed reminder that, although the Elizabethan age was glittering for the elite, the participation in the good things of life was yet very shallow.

The Attractions of the Sea. A major new outlet at this time was the rediscovery of the sea. Elizabethans came to realize that what the Mediterranean had been to the ancient world, the Atlantic would be to the modern, and that their location on it offered exceptional advantages. Henry VII had authorized the Genoan John Cabot to sail on voyages of discovery on behalf of England; that intrepid explorer had sailed across the Atlantic and down the American eastern seaboard, thus staking England's claim in the New World. No one followed up on his pioneering; all had been forgotten by midcentury, but now interest was reawakened, often through the writings of Richard Hakluyt who recounted *The principall Navigations, Voiages, and Discoveries of the English nation*, or urged colonization in his *The Discourse on the Western Planting*. In 1585 Sir Walter Raleigh began a colony at Roanoke Island on what is now the shore of North Carolina. When the first attempt failed a second was made, but locked among history's secrets is the fate of the first colonists who could not be found three years later when a relief ship arrived.

If the time was not yet ripe for sustained colonization, it was for other sea-related efforts. The navy was completely reorganized, and fighting ships were redesigned and armed with heavy guns capable of inflicting damage from a distance. The successes on the sea helped make naval heroes as important as soldiers in the national imagination. The most promising venture, however, was the development of the joint-stock company, a means for pooling the funds of many investors to finance sustained shipping trade with distant areas of the world. By 1588 companies existed to conduct trade with such far-flung places as Russia, the Barbary Coast of North Africa, and the west coast of Africa. A significant signpost to a later empire was the chartering in 1600 of the East India Company, and thus England's claim was made in that remote part of the world, the beginnings of a presence that would later blossom in India and the Orient.

The Elizabethan Renaissance

Elizabethans knew their time was exciting, adventuresome, alive to new opportunities—a quickening time. But doubtless they would have been as hard-pressed to analyze its spirit as we are to describe our own. It was marked in part by a discovery of their own realm and of new horizons, and as always the printed word was often the key to discovering new experiences.

Caxton's world of printing a century before emphasized the theological, legal, and philosophical; Elizabethan booksellers also offered practical how-to books on better farming, navigation, correct manners for polite society, planning a garden, interpreting dreams, or being an effective justice of the peace. England itself was open to discovery in the pages of William Camden's *Magna Britannia,* written in Latin for the educated elite both in England and abroad. John Stow described the hub of Renaissance England in his *A Survay of London.* Freshly printed maps could be bought, often brightly colored by hand, awakening the imagination with sketches of sea monsters, the Indians of the New World, and strange animals in faraway lands. Elizabeth's tutor, Roger Ascham, argued for new teaching techniques in *The Scholemaster,* and Sir Thomas Gresham founded a college in London where merchants were taught mathematics, business, and science in English.

Elizabethan Literature. One of the proudest proofs of the Elizabethan love of language and letters was the splendid outpouring of poetry and prose, mirroring the themes that fascinated the Elizabethan imagination: courtly

Anatomy lecture, 1581 *(The Wellcome Trustees, Wellcome Institute of the History of Medicine)*.

and human love, violence and savagery, human emotions in turmoil, a search for national identity through the pageantry of past kings, and the confident realization of uniquely English values. The exclusive use of English and the predominance of secular themes distinguish this literary outpouring from the medieval.

The most polished literary expression was poetry in its myriad forms. Although the themes might reflect past times, the manner of composition pointed to the new. Edmund Spenser's epic poem, *The Faerie Queene*, was set in the medieval world of virtue personified, but the imagery was intended for Elizabethan ears hungry for sumptuous description. The original plan was for twelve books, each to set forth the adventure of a different knight of Gloriana, the queen herself. Another outstanding poet was Sir Philip Sidney. He had first served his queen as a soldier but added to that calling a literary career, using his artistry to express the soldier's ideal of chivalry. He wrote often in the new sonnet form that Elizabethans gave to the world: his *Arcadia* was a heroic prose romance, and in *Astrophel and Stella* he expressed his own unrequited love.

Elizabethan Drama. The crowning glory of the Elizabethan Renaissance was drama. In medieval times drama had been religious and staged in the church or just outside it. Sixteenth-century drama was greatly different: the themes were rarely religious, and the use of language as the vehicle for vivid description was its greatest characteristic. Classical drama was emphasized in the universities: it demanded the keeping of the "unities," so that all the action occurred on the same day, in the same place, and in the same literary genre. It was unacceptable to mix tragedy with comedy. Drama written for the new playhouses around London often violated the rules, to the delight of the penny-paying audiences drawn from all ranks of society. James Burbage built the first playhouse in 1576, and before Elizabeth died a number flourished in the area of London—not in London itself because the Puritan officials of that great city thought the drama and the theater were immoral.

The second-most renowned Elizabethan dramatist was Ben Jonson (1572–1637). This erudite man could write in majestic prose or in lyric poetry. He could describe the most amusing and slapstick of situations to delight the most unlearned theater goer, or could bring into his works plots borrowed from Greek and Latin literature, or comments upon the state of scientific learning in his time. His career flourished to a greater extent in the reign of James I, Elizabeth's successor in 1603: in that time he produced the best known of his major plays, such as *Volpone* and *The Alchemist*, and entered into a partnership with the talented Inigo Jones to stage the masques which were the most prominent form of entertainment at the royal court.

William Shakespeare. The greatest literary figure of the Elizabethan Renaissance was William Shakespeare. He was an accomplished actor and wrote beautiful sonnets, but of course he was best known for the works he produced for the stage. The tragedies, histories, and comedies that he wrote rank among the greatest masterpieces of English literature. He had the uncanny knack of describing the complexities of human character: he brought alive ambition in *Macbeth,* the tragedy of young love in *Romeo and Juliet*, the panoply and triumph of English history from monarchs of the Middle Ages such as *King Henry IV* to his own century, frolicking comedic froth in *A Midsummer Night's Dream*, and the drama of the classical world in *Julius Caesar.* As a member of the Lord Chamberlain's Company (after the accession of James I, The King's Company or the King's Men) he and his troupe enjoyed aristocratic protection. Shakespeare's plays were as much to be heard as to be seen: the English language con-

Shakespeare's London

tains many words and phrases that he coined, among them "fascinate," "critical," "courtship," "dwindle," "primrose path," "flaming youth," "to catch a cold," and "hunchback."

The Globe (built in 1599) was the most important playhouse. It was patterned after the arrangement of tiered balconies overlooking an open courtyard, thus imitating the earlier practice of performing plays in the courtyards of inns. Little scenery was used and women did not act, so that the success of a play depended on vividness and the reality created by the spoken word. The acting company entertained a vast and varied audience: occasionally the monarch, always the "groundlings" who paid a penny to stand in the open floor of the playhouse before the stage, and the well-to-do who paid an extra penny to sit on stage—to see better and to be seen. Because all in the audience loved realism, an actor was expected to be an accomplished acrobat, wearing concealed bladders of red liquid which when pricked by a dueller's sword after a spirited fight on stage would graphically simulate death.

Renaissance London. The stage for Renaissance England was the burgeoning city of London, swollen in size from the 50,000 of Henry VII's time to 250,000 at Elizabeth's death. It was a glittering Renaissance city for the upper ranks of society, the home of the Court and the hub of the legal world and the center of a social season with plays and amusements. For the merchants it was a place of exceptional opportunity, the largest and most lucrative market in all of Europe and the center of a fast-growing world of commerce. London also attracted the less fortunate—the unemployed agricultural worker no longer needed on enclosed fields, the ne'er-do-wells who wished to escape the tedium of country life, and the criminal who saw a golden opportunity. Slums grew quickly, especially when unscrupulous builders subdivided buildings into small, dark tenements into which the poor could be overcrowded. Plague and poverty were as much at home in Renaissance London as were opulence and entertainment.

London was still a city of half-timbered wooden buildings with thatched roofs along twisting and winding streets. There had always been much greenery in the city, and the countryside was not far away. The first growth was internal, filling up empty spaces and especially tearing down the former spacious monastic buildings to erect dwellings in their place. North of the walls the expansion was limited by poor soil and drainage, but the growth westward and eastward occurred for two reasons.

The movement westward was mostly residential. First there were the palatial buildings in the area between the river and the main road westward from the city gates to Westminster. The duke of Somerset, Edward's lord protector, had erected Somerset House on the river, and closer to Westminster Cardinal Wolsey rebuilt his archepiscopal London home, York Place, until he "donated" it to Henry VIII (along with his fashionable palace outside London, Hampton Court) in a vain attempt to keep the king's favor. New and more opulent buildings north of the road and closer to Westminster housed those of high rank who wished to be near the Court. Near the western walls of the city there were slum areas. The movement eastward was mostly commercial. Docks and warehouses were required by the new overseas trading companies; the East India Company eventually built moorings and warehouses on ten acres of river frontage.

South across the river, there were the Globe and many other places of amusement, such as the place for the baiting of bears by English bulldogs. There were other new buildings besides the playhouses. Elizabeth's financial agent, Sir Thomas Gresham, built the Royal Exchange, a mart in which businessmen could display the wares so important in England's expanding trade, and then he endowed Gresham College, where instruction in English was tailored to the practical needs of the merchant class and the expeditionary trading voyages on the seas.

The vast overcrowding made London life exciting—and dangerous as well. Crime was endemic, fire was a constant danger because the structures were so flammable, filth was everywhere because the crush of people

Map of London, 1593 *(Henry E. Huntington Library and Art Gallery)*.

placed impossible demands on the existing manifestly inadequate sanitary facilities, and sickness and the plague spread rapidly through the teeming population. Richness and poverty existed side by side in gargantuan proportions in this Renaissance city.

The War Years and the End of the Reign, 1585–1603

Conflict with Spain. A state of war between England and Spain existed from 1585 to 1603. Its causes were long-standing: Elizabeth helped the Protestant Dutch who were fighting for their independence from the Spanish Netherlands; English seamen tried (unsuccessfully) to intercept the treasure ships returning from the New World; English merchants attempted to break the Spanish monopoly on trade with America; and, most important, the Catholic king sought the triumph of his cause over the Protestant queen.

The major campaign of the war was the attempted invasion of England in 1588, when the Spanish Armada, a fleet of about 130 ships, left to rendezvous with soldiers under Spanish command in the Netherlands and then to ferry them across for the invasion. The plan was beyond the capabilities of the time: communications were inadequate, there was no deep water in which the Spanish ships could anchor to pick up the soldiers, and the prevailing winds from west to east were likely to prevent the westward attack even if the troops reached the ships. The English seized the initiative by moving upwind, and with the wind at their backs they could harry the Spanish fleet, let the English heavy guns wreak havoc, and then even send unmanned fire ships into the moored Spanish fleet. Unable to retreat westward, the Spanish had to turn northward and circle Scotland, returning past Ireland. Philip had trusted God to overcome the obstacles his commanders had pointed out; the English felt the "Protestant wind" was their best ally.

Although the Spanish never mounted another armada, the fear of hostilities and of the chance of an invasion colored English life in the last years of the queen's reign. The English knew that the likely route for another invasion would not be direct but would be from Ireland, where a native population hostile to Protestantism might eagerly contribute men to assist in an invasion of England. The queen therefore dispatched commanders to "pacify" Ireland, first the flashy and mercuric earl of Essex and then the more dependable Lord Mountjoy. Essex botched his chance, failed to handle the situation, and in childish pique mounted an unsuccessful rebellion in 1601 against the queen who chafed at his failures—Essex paid with his head. Mountjoy succeeded just before the queen's death in defeating decisively the Irish forces, and thus he laid the foundation for England's complete dominance of that island.

The End of the Reign. As the queen aged and was less interested in government, and as the psychological toll of threatened warfare haunted the realm, a certain political malaise gripped the nation. The giants of administration were gone: Dudley died in 1588 and Burghley in 1598, and the newer members of the Privy Council engaged in unseemly factional disputes. Although James VI of Scotland was the seeming heir, the queen refused to designate him so. Burghley's son, Sir Robert Cecil, had inherited the skills and mantle of his father and now as principal secretary began the secret correspondence with James which would assure, after the death of the aged queen, a smooth transition in government.

Queen Elizabeth in Parliament *(D'Ewes, Journal)*.

The Elizabethan Age. Although the political skirmishes left an unpleasant taste, the realities of the queen's reign could not be eclipsed. Her nation had avoided the religious wars which so decimated France, and Protestantism was safe for England. Political problems of greater magnitude she had simply left unattended, keeping her reign relatively peaceful but portending serious difficulties for James and his successors. The economic strife of the end of the century had been generally overcome and there was prosperity, although few realized the full extent of the social changes that the new economic realities had inaugurated. The first tentative forays on the sea were small: colonization had not worked and the new trading companies were not yet flourishing, but the foundations had been laid for an empire of trade and only four years into James' reign a successful colony would be planted in Virginia, named after the Virgin Queen.

The English had left genuine triumphs: a triumph of spirit, a triumph of cultural achievement, the expanding of horizons in the minds of English subjects. Militarily a small nation, prostrate and unimportant after the civil century before, England had stood off the mightiest nation in the world, the symbol of the Catholic Counter-Reformation. There could have been no greater boost to English self-esteem. The trials of battle had proved that early modern England was of age—flourishing, proud, successful. It was a remarkable heritage to pass on.

Suggestions for Further Reading

A book cited in Chapter 5 is the best introduction to political events in Elizabethan England: G. R. Elton, *England Under the Tudors* (2nd edition, 1974). J. E. Neale's biography *Elizabeth I* (1934) is overly romantic and favorable but still the best; his *Elizabethan House of Commons* (1949) and two volumes of *Elizabeth I and her Parliaments* (1953, 1957) are the principal works on Parliament. A brief sketch of the institutions of government is A. G. R. Smith's brief and useful *The Government of Elizabethan England* (1967). Conyers Read's two-volume treatment of Sir William Cecil is also a good guide to domestic and foreign affairs: *Mr. Secretary Cecil and Queen Elizabeth* (1955) and *Lord Burghley and Queen Elizabeth* (1960). The best survey of foreign affairs is in R. B. Wernham, *Before the Armada, The Emergence of the English Nation, 1485–1588* (1966).

The best guide to the Elizabethan religious opposition is Patrick McGrath's *Papists and Puritans under Elizabeth I* (1967). An excellent further study of Puritanism, especially of the Presbyterian movement, is Patrick Collinson's *The Elizabethan Puritan Movement* (1967). The social teachings of Puritans and Anglicans are surveyed masterfully in Richard L. Greaves, *Society and Religion in Elizabethan England* (1981). The troubles of Catholics since Elizabeth are recounted in John Bossy, *The English Catholic Community, 1570–1850* (1976).

The best survey of social and economic affairs has been cited earlier: Joyce

Youings, *Sixteenth-Century England* (in the series The Pelican Social History of Britain, 1984). An older survey with penetrating insights is A. L. Rowse's *The England of Elizabeth, The Structure of Society* (1950). The workaday world of rural England is reflected in the essays in John Thirsk, ed., *The Agrarian History of England and Wales,* Vol. IV, *1500–1640* (1967).

The new awareness of the sea is reflected generally in J. A. Williamson's *The Age of Drake* (3rd edition, 1952), in economic studies such as G. D. Ramsay, *English Overseas Trade in the Century of Emergence* (1957), and in many editions of Richard Hakluyt's writings, such as Irwin R. Blacker, *The Portable Hakluyt's Voyages* (1967). The Renaissance in England is shown in Arthur B. Ferguson's *The Articulate Citizen and the English Renaissance* (1965). Imminently readable word-pictures of the leading literary figures and their times are M. Chute, *Shakespeare's London* (1949) and *Ben Jonson* (1949).

7

Conflict in Claims:
The Stuart Kings and
Parliament

1603–1660

The death of Elizabeth and the accession of James marks one of the great turning points in the history of England. It was more than a dynastic change. The mores and conventions of the sixteenth century were being displaced by a whole new set of attitudes toward authority, religion, and the rights of the individual. Those attitudes, which James brought to England, were not shared by his new subjects; the conflicts between the people, represented by Parliament, and the crown, which had been suppressed in deference to the aged queen, now came out into the open. These conflicts were initially carried on verbally—in Parliament, in the councils of the king, and in the law courts. As the essential disagreement between ruler and subject became ever more evident, and apparently irreconcilable, the conflict eventually took a new and more deadly form when the opposing sides took to arms. This struggle, between two philosophies and two camps, is the most significant feature of the Stuart century in English history. Its resolution, through two royal depositions and the emergence of parliamentary supremacy, is the principal theme of unfolding events for the seventeenth century.

For the new king who succeeded Elizabeth I in 1603, his inheritance must have seemed providential after his years of purgatory in the bleak, poor, contentious kingdom of the north. James Stuart had become king of Scotland at the age of nine months when the Protestant Scottish lords banished his Catholic mother, Mary Queen of Scots. His learned but stern Presbyterian tutors had developed the precocious youth into an accomplished intellectual who was particularly learned in theology. But the Scottish church claimed a total independence in ecclesiastical matters, and, as the self-styled voice of God, freely interfered in James's government. The Scottish lords at first dominated the young king and even later, as feudal magnates, were often able to resist his authority. James fought back with reason and with force. In his book *The True Law of Free Monarchies* (1598) he set forth the theory of the divine right of kings, demanding obedience as a religious duty from all men including the clergy. Gradually his military successes allowed him to assert his authority over many of the lords, but his flaws of character became known and compromised his reputation. Moreover, he never ceased to fear for his personal safety in Scotland, where even the privacy of his own bedchamber was not guaranteed.

James I of England

His entrance into his new kingdom was hardly auspicious. As king of Scotland he was so poor he had to raise a loan from the city of Edinburgh to finance his journey south. Even that sufficed to cover the costs of only half the progress, and he had to send ahead to his English council for money to enable him to complete the journey. His first appearance before his new ministers and subjects can hardly have been impressive. As revealed by a contemporary,

> He was of a middle stature, more corpulent through his clothes than in his body, yet fat enough; his clothes ever being made large and easy the doublets quilted for stiletto-proof; his breeches in great plaits, and full stuffed. He was naturally of a timid disposition, which was the greatest reason of his quilted doublets. His eyes large, ever rolling after any stranger came in his presence, inasmuch as many for shame have left the room, being out of countenance. His beard was very thin; his tongue too large for his mouth, which ever made him speak full in the mouth, and made him drink very uncomely, as if eating his drink, which came out into the cup on each side of his mouth. His skin was as soft as taffeta sarcenet, which felt so because he never washed his hands—only rubbed his finger-ends slightly with the wet end of a napkin. His legs were very weak, having had, as was thought, some foul play in his youth, or rather before he was born, that he was not able to stand at seven years of age—that weakness made him ever leaning on other men's shoulders. His walk was ever circular, his fingers ever in that walk fiddling about his codpiece.

His homosexual preferences were morally offensive to many and often led him to prefer attractiveness in a governmental minister rather than ability. He could be lazy and indolent, preferring horse races and hunting to the business of state.

James's Religious Problems. Early in his reign the new king received a petition, supposedly signed by many Puritan clergymen, which sought specific and some general reforms in the church. James presided at the Hampton

James I from a contemporary engraving *(The Bettmann Archive)*.

Court conference in 1604 to hear the ministers. When a spokesman used the word "presbytery," the king's memories of his Scottish experiences provoked him to argue that those who would reform the church's leadership would move on to meddle with the state's leadership, or, as he put it succinctly, "no bishop, no king." Thenceforth James insisted on religious conformity, and many Puritan ministers were removed from their livings (a benefice or position with income in the church). James's early tolerance for Catholics who attended the Anglican services alarmed many Protestants, and under intense pressure from them he reimposed the full rigor of the penal laws against Catholics. In response, one Guy Fawkes planted gunpowder in the basement of Parliament, to be ignited when James opened the session in 1605. The "Gunpowder Plot" was discovered (some argue that it was contrived from within the government to discredit the Catholics), and Fawkes and other Catholic conspirators were executed.

James became increasingly pleased with the Anglican church, which naturally championed the rights of its supreme head—the wood of the pulpit and of the council table came from one tree, as some put it. Under his auspices a new translation of the Bible was begun, the strikingly beautiful King James Version of 1611 which would rank as a masterpiece of the English language. But his intolerance of Puritanism alienated many reformers, and since many of them sat in the House of Commons the relations between king and Parliament increasingly soured.

King and Parliament: Claim and Counterclaim. James often called Parliament into session because he needed taxes to offset the annual deficits and to service the debts from Elizabeth's Spanish and Irish wars. He had none of her talents for conciliation and parliamentary management. By raising Privy Council members to the ranks of the nobility, he automatically transferred them from the important House of Commons to the House of Lords. With few adept spokesmen in the lower House, reform-minded Puritans often seized the initiative, acting with an intemperance and unwillingness to compromise that often matched that of the king. Rather than be opposed or lectured by the Commons, James usually dissolved a session before taxes had been granted, and thus his financial problems worsened.

The Commons responded by making many theoretical claims which would deny the king many rights long exercised by the crown. They reacted to his anti-Puritan statements at the Hampton Court conference by asserting that Parliament's consent was needed to alter religion. In 1610 they attacked impositions, a surcharge on customs rates which James had levied earlier without Parliament's approval but which a court decision had affirmed to be within his rights. By 1610 James was so short of funds that his ministers proposed a Great Contract, offering to give up impositions and other offensive revenues if Parliament would "buy out" his rights with a large lump-sum cash settlement. Not only was this proposal unsuccessful, but the Commons passed a resolution which argued that king-in-Parliament was superior to king-outside-Parliament and thus could review and control royal powers, impositions included. While none of these claims had the force of law, they showed quite clearly the growing estrangement of the two most important parts of the English government.

James's most formidable opponent was a judge, Sir Edward Coke. As attorney general under Elizabeth and James, Coke was a staunch defender of the royal prerogative. Upon his appointment as chief justice of Common Pleas in 1606 and subsequently King's Bench in 1613, he took up the cause of the common law and the independence of the judiciary with equal ferocity. Coke argued against royal absolutism, asserting, for example, that the king did not have the right to legislate temporarily in royal proclamations when an urgent need could not wait for Parliament to meet, and that the king could not remove judges from office. In his zeal to champion the law and attack James he used both his learning and the shady practice of inventing precedents when he needed to clinch an argument. Dismissed from his judgeship in 1616, Coke was elected to the House of Commons in 1620 where his learning served to raise occasional opposition into a principled cause.

The Duke of Buckingham and the Spanish War. James's problems were aggravated by his choice of ministers. His affections were dominated by George Villiers whom the doting king made duke of Buckingham, and the minister set out to grasp all patronage into his own hands. James also fancied himself the Protestant king who could maintain peace with Catholic rulers. His wife was a Catholic, and he sought to marry his surviving son Charles to a Spanish princess. But James's son-in-law Frederick was elected king of Bohemia in 1619 and thus became the head of continental Europe's Protestant forces, the last hope of stopping the military successes of the Catholic Counter-Reformation. In the Thirty Years' War which began in 1618, Frederick badly needed his father-in-law's assistance. James seemed paralyzed by inaction, the pacifist temperamentally unwilling to go to war, financially unable to assist.

In the parliamentary session of 1621 the Commons began to argue for war with Spain and for the support of Frederick, but by initiating a debate on foreign policy it was encroaching on the exclusive right of the king. James dissolved the session, but just before its end the Commons escalated its theoretical claims in a protestation that Parliament had the right not only to discuss but even to "treat, reason and bring to conclusion" matters concerning the liberties of Englishmen. In a fit of rage, James tore the page from the Commons' journal. As the tempo of hostilities abroad in-

Royalist portrayal of Charles I as a martyr *(The Works of Charles I with His Life and Martyrdom)*.

creased, Buckingham and Prince Charles made a romantically foolish secret trip to Spain to woo the princess, and were ill-treated. In the Parliament of 1624, James allowed a free discussion of foreign policy, and when he died the following year England was at war with Spain and was assisting Frederick.

Charles I: The Early Years

Charles I and Parliament. Charles was at once intensely strong and weak. As a child he had learned late to walk and speak and felt very insecure when faced with his father's learning and wit. Although he overcame these problems during his young adulthood and reign (1625–1649) he appreciated neither the sincere passion for individual rights which animated the Parliamentarian nor the intense religious zeal of the Puritan. Yet he was governed by passion and was a creature of obsession. He needed strong advisors upon whom to rely, but if any man deceived him, the king felt no moral constraint to keep his own word. He proved to be as artful and duplicitous as any of his enemies, yet lacked the tact and charm to win them over. In short, Charles was a tragic but ultimately unsympathetic figure.

The war that Charles inherited led him into actions which were so grievous to Parliament that those of his father's reign were as naught. Charles and Buckingham, now responsible for a war which Parliament had urged but was unwilling to finance properly, were inept managers, and even in success they were unpopular. A seaborne strike against Spain in late 1625 was a complete fiasco. Faced with the lack of adequate war funding, the government began to "borrow" from lenders who knew they would not be repaid and to imprison without charges those who refused. Decent citizens were ordered to board in their homes soldiers, often the dregs of society, and refusals could lead to a declaration of martial law. In 1628 Parliament framed a Petition of Right, demanding that the king cease these improper measures. Charles agreed but continued to protect Buckingham whose impeachment Parliament sought. An assassin's knife took Buckingham's life in 1628, but Charles had more problems to face.

When he had first become king, Parliament refused to grant Charles the customs duties for his life as was traditional, but doled them out in periods of years and months. After 1628 Charles began to collect the customs as if they had been granted, and Parliament saw that the Petition of Right was no protection. The militancy of Parliament in 1629 was so great that the king decided quickly to dissolve it. While the royal messenger was barred from entering the Commons, the angered Parliamentarians held the speaker in his chair to prevent the dissolution and then passed three resolutions that branded as a traitor to the state anyone who would support the alterations which Charles had introduced. The infuriated king stated that Parliament would not be called again until it learned its rightful, respectful place in the kingdom.

The King Rules Alone. Without calling a Parliament for eleven years of "personal rule" (1629–1640), Charles ended the wars and balanced his budget. Two ministers especially made his policies successful. Thomas Wentworth brought efficiency to areas heretofore very difficult to control, first as lord president in the North and then as lord deputy of Ireland, in reward for which he was raised to the peerage as earl of Strafford. Archbishop William Laud removed Puritan ministers from office and strengthened the Church of England in anti-Puritan and anti-Calvinistic attitudes. The spirit of these achievements frightened some more than the specific details. Strafford and Laud called their insistence on efficiency and compliance with the king's wishes a policy of "thorough," and, even though their activities were limited and often far from thorough, the king's opponents feared that any spread of "thoroughness" to other aspects of English life would spell the end of individual rights. Laud placed great emphasis on the continuity of Anglicanism with pre-Reformation Catholicism. The revival of ancient Catholic ceremonies was intended to bring the "beauty of holiness" to Protestantism, not to supplant it with Catholicism, but to the Puritans who emphasized the simple, unadorned preaching of the word it seemed to threaten the Reformation.

Much of what Laud accomplished was of permanent benefit to the church. Moreover, up to the time of the Civil Wars the quality of the clergy continued to show the steady improvement which began with the Reformation. The sacramental priesthood of the pre-Reformation church was transformed into a pastoral ministry. Clerical standards were raised in a variety of ways. The expansion of the universities meant more aspirants to the ministry received greater formal education. More careful examination of candidates for ordination, the insistence of bishops on consistent standards of conduct, and continuing education resulted in a more homogeneous and professional clergy. The continuing erosion of church wealth was a less happy complement and put the parish clergy too often at the mercy of lay patrons. But the church did retain its independent jurisdiction, and this independence and a better-trained and dedicated clergy, managed by the indefatigable Laud, made the church a more formidable challenge than its easy-going, tolerant predecessor.

During the period of personal rule, Charles and his French queen also created an atmosphere and style in the court that was equally as personal. The French influence was certainly not negligible, and a new grandeur was in evidence that was much more characteristic of Paris than London. Statues of the sovereign became an accustomed form of decoration in public places. The architecture of the Caroline Age was continental in origin, its models Italian rather than French, and official architecture was more prominent than private buildings. A fashionable Flemish painter, Sir Anthony van Dyck, captured the beauty, elegance, and formality of the age in his portraits, representations which have left an indelible impression of the court both then and on all succeeding times. Charles's own taste was impeccable, whether in dress, in furniture, or in paintings. Masques presented at the court and the great houses of the nobility, designed by Inigo Jones, the foremost designer and architect of his age, reinforced a new, elevated, celebratory though not frivolous concept of kingship. The air both of formality and artificiality that they presented was as much a part of the daily life of the court as it was of the entertainments. The ceremonial aspect which the king most valued was paralleled in the character of the Anglican church as administered by Laud.

What Charles called success his opponents branded as "tyranny"; to them "thorough" was a form of despotism, the "beauty of holiness" noth-

Ceiling by Peter Paul Rubens in the Banqueting Hall, Whitehall, designed by Inigo Jones *(The Bettmann Archive/BBC Hulton)*.

ing but popery. They objected to the king's raising revenue without Parliament's consent by arbitrarily extending the boundaries of royal forests and then fining people within the new limits for unlicensed dwelling or by transferring cases to the Star Chamber so that huge fines could be levied. The greatest problem was Charles's levy of ship money. Monarchs had an undisputed right to ask residents in the coastal shires to contribute money in time of war for the building of new ships which would provide an added and immediate means of defense. Charles began to levy ship money on inland counties and in times of peace. When John Hampden, a prosperous gentleman, out of principle refused to pay a small sum levied on him, he lost the case by a 7 to 5 verdict but won a moral victory from the dissent of so many royal judges.

It was religion that brought matters to a head. Charles tried to impose an episcopate and the English *Book of Common Prayer* on his kingdom of Scotland, but the General Assembly of the established Presbyterian church strongly resisted. Charles mounted an ill-conceived and inadequately financed invasion, but his armies fled without fighting when they saw the Scots. The king realized that he could put an effective army in the field

Equestrian portrait of Charles I by Anthony van Dyck *(The National Portrait Gallery, London)*.

only if it were adequately funded, and that required calling a Parliament. The session that began on April 13, 1640, ended the eleven years during which a wide range of issues had become crystallized and the sides polarized. Once again Charles was revealed as inept in his efforts to make Parliament cooperate in making war with an administrative machine and finances unequal to the task. It was but a short time until the Civil War broke out in 1642, but it was the product of more than disputes in politics and religion.

Ideas and the Challenge to Authority

Science and Practical Learning. Medieval thought was characterized by deductive reasoning that used logic to draw particular conclusions from general truths. Sir Francis Bacon, a royal official to James I, wrote to urge a reorientation: man should begin with the particular, and by repeated and extensive observation form a hypothesis expressing a general truth, capable of proof by experimentation. Bacon was sure that this scientific method would expand knowledge and produce many practical applications. Obviously the old was not instantly displaced (Oxford and Cambridge continued to teach the traditional curricula in Latin and many were suspicious of change), but the ideas of Bacon and many like-minded Europeans found fertile ground in the English emphasis on the practical. At Gresham College in London the instruction was conducted in English and emphasized scientific matters and applications in the business world, such as in navigation and shipbuilding. When Sir John Napier published his discovery of logarithms in 1614, a professor of astronomy popularized it and provided useful tables.

Scientific reasoning captured the imagination of the learned. In 1628 William Harvey set forth his theory that the blood circulated through the body, a major anatomical discovery. Navigational instruments like the telescope were widely produced, and the emphasis on mathematics awakened an interest in statistics and resulted in more reliable and accurate maps. By midcentury many of the upper classes had laboratories in their homes, even if just to be fashionable. An indirect result of the scientific method was to make authority and tradition less important and to emphasize the things of this world. When scientific discoveries proved wrong some of the churchmen's scientific orthodoxy, it impugned their credibility in religious matters as well. The full impact of all of this was felt fully only toward the end of the century, but seeds of disruption had been sown alongside those of scientific advances.

Alongside pioneering studies in science there were similar endeavors in the humanities. The Society of Antiquaries was founded near the close of Elizabeth's reign in 1586. In the Jacobean period, the Society could count a number of distinguished members whose studies in the primary materials of manuscripts were essentially the introduction of scientific method into historical studies. Much of what they wrote was polemical. But the desire to discover historical precedents to support political arguments, a practice raised to a fine art by Coke, also advanced knowledge about the past and the evolution of English society. Foremost among the antiquaries was Sir Robert Cotton, because his famous library was made freely available to all applicants and provided the stuff from which the tracts and books were made. In the next century the library was acquired by Parliament for the nation and became one of the cornerstones of the British Museum. Bolton, Camden, Speed, Ussher, and D'Ewes were among the more important of his friends and fellow scholars, historians whose work still has value today.

The Social Ethic of Puritanism. Puritanism was important in politics and religion but it also became a social ethic, a set of attitudes which became a lasting part of English society independently of religion. Preaching was all-important to the Puritans, not only stressing religious truths but also inculcating discipline and industriousness. The Puritan was taught that God rewarded His elect with material success in this world as well as with bliss in the next. Labor thus became a social duty and idleness a religious evil. This teaching appealed to artisans and merchants who lived in towns and ports, for whom frugality and hard work were necessary to get ahead. The profits of the industrious Puritan became capital ready for investing, and the business contacts they formed across England meant the creation of a network of economic interests. Puritans tended to be distrustful of agricultural society with its periods of inactivity and resentful of nonproductive persons, both of the poor and of the nobility and gentry whose social status exempted them from toil. Unwilling to accept the teaching in the parish churches, the Puritans placed great emphasis on Bible reading and spiritual formation in the home, a deemphasis on the Church's role which had social as well as religious consequences.

Capitalism and Trade. Most Englishmen continued to work in agriculture, but, although landowners paid greater attention to scientific ways of increasing production, it was in industry and trade that the seeds for England's future economic growth were sown. Increases in the scale of operation were often more important than innovation and invention at this stage, and thus vast supplies of capital for investment were required. In particular it was realized that England's vast coal resources were exceptionally valuable as the supply of timber for fuel and building dwindled. Seams near the surface had long been mined, but capital was needed for digging deep shafts and for the pumps to clear gasses, to remove water, and to help raise the coal. As production grew eightfold in a century, the coal from centers in the northeast such as Newcastle upon Tyne came to be valued as important for England as Peru's silver had been for Spain a century earlier. The iron industry grew apace, and the huge increase in the production of iron benefited both older industries, foundries making cannons and nails, and newer fabricating trades.

Traditionally, wool and unfinished cloth had been England's principal exports, shipped almost exclusively from London to a few continental markets such as Antwerp, and thus subject to vicissitudes outside England's control. Attempts were made to produce newer types of cloth such as worsteds and to finish cloths before export, but neither succeeded, and trading depressions continued into the seventeenth century. The opening of non-European trade revived English commerce. The highly capitalized trading companies traded with the new colonies in America and with parts of Asia and Africa. More ships were needed, and a new rivalry was thus created with the Dutch, a powerful maritime nation determined to dominate the seaborne carrying trade.

Capitalists became important in domestic trading also. Middlemen were needed to bring foodstuffs from distant counties to feed London's burgeoning population, and to put out the wool to spinners and weavers and then bring the finished cloth to the market. The increased demand for food encouraged a vast engineering project, the draining of the marshy fens of eastern England. Before the end of the seventeenth century nearly 400,000 acres had been made fit for farming.

The crown supported many of these ventures—the manufacture of gunpowder was important militarily, the new trading companies had royal charters, and Charles invested in draining the fens. But the more common royal attitude was indifference and even hostility. Capitalism was feared because of the new concentrations of wealth it created, for the social unrest which often followed, and because it was often unregulated. The Stuarts sought to control trade, as the Tudors had earlier, and they often exploited the wealth of the trading companies. The monopolies so freely granted to increase royal revenues often stifled economic development. Although most Englishmen were untouched by the new economic activities, the new economic entrepreneur came to resent the crown's attitude.

A distinction may be made between the merchants whose main interest was in foreign trade and those who managed domestic concessions—internal monopolies, patents, licenses, and the like. It was those dealing in foreign trade who were most estranged by the failure to protect shipping, the compromising of charters, and the increasing financial demands of the Court. The domestic concessionaires also had cause for disquiet from the Londonderry Plantation, incorporation of suburbs, royal commissioners, and arbitrary taxation. The latter received even worse treatment at the hands of the Long Parliament and were drawn back into the support of the crown in 1641 to 1642. A good deal of the military geography of the coming civil war was determined by the degree to which merchants and traders had welcomed or resisted royal interference in the economy.

Colonization and Trading Companies

Colonization

The English colonized near to home, sending Protestant settlers to Ulster in the north of Ireland, and though there were many difficulties in settling in Ireland there were few surprises. The "planting" of colonies in America was considerably more difficult, primarily because the difficulties could not be foreseen when the enterprises were launched. Religion motivated some colonizing efforts, the hope of economic profits spurred others, but in every case the impetus was private and not royal. The desire for profit led the London Company to send settlers to Virginia, where the first to arrive in 1607 named their colony Jamestown after the king. Half of the settlers were gentlemen, who in proper English fashion did not intend to work but rather sought to find precious metals or the route to the orient. There was no room in the harsh and hostile new land for such an attitude, and not many survived the early years of starvation and Indian massacres; success came only when tobacco cultivation became the colony's economic mainstay.

The landing of religiously motivated "Pilgrims" at Plymouth in 1620 was an indirect result of James I's anti-Puritan sentiments. A congregation in Scrooby, Nottinghamshire, left England for Holland to practice their religion freely, then relocated in the New World. They had no legal authority for the move, but as a close-knit community in a relatively unimportant location they were able to practice their religion without interference. In later years a great level of maturity in appreciating the difficulties of colonization was manifested by the Massachusetts Bay Company whose settlers first arrived at Boston in 1630. Everyone was equipped to be self-sufficient through early lean years, and the insistence on living in towns gave a degree of success and independence not to be found in England. The settlement in Maryland, which began in 1634, had yet a different authority and motivation. Charles I granted Lord Baltimore and his fellow Catholics the territory as a proprietary colony to be held by feudal tenure. As important as these mainland settlements were, the English colonies in the Caribbean islands such as Bermuda and Barbados were more beneficial economically to England.

In each of these instances the actual management of affairs proceeded independently of the king. If abuses arose and the aggrieved petitioned the king, then James or Charles might revoke a concession and nominally take control, but this was more theoretical than actual. The Stuarts had neither a plan for encouraging colonization nor a policy of political management of those which others began. The substantially larger migrations in the 1630s arose from the royal anti-Puritan policies. Only in 1651, when the Commonwealth and not the crown ruled, did an imperial commercial policy begin. The Navigation Act of 1651 required colonists to ship their produce exclusively to England, on English ships manned by English sailors, so that the mother country might monopolize the fruits of its colonies. The full implications of the measure would become clear in the next century.

Conflict at Arms: The Civil Wars and Cromwell

The Long Parliament. Charles called Parliament in April 1640 to demand taxes for fighting the Scots, and as soon as the session opened the able parliamentary leader John Pym rose in the Commons to list years of grievances against the Stuarts and to win approval for debating the issues first. After three weeks and no grant of taxes, Charles angrily dissolved Parliament (later to be called the Short Parliament); but that summer the Scots invaded and occupied two northern English counties and to meet the crisis Charles had to call a new session in November (the Long Parliament). Pym realized that even though two-thirds of the Commons was bent on reform, the proper tactic to keep together the majority was first to focus on removing hated royal officials. Accordingly he sought to remove from office Strafford and Laud, the ministers of "thorough" best able to rally the king's supporters. Strafford was the key figure, and Pym tried to remove him first through the process of impeachment, a trial before the House of Lords. When that faltered he resurrected the ancient process of attainder by which, through simple majorities, Parliament could legislate Strafford's death, thus ignoring the rules of equity and justice. Pym's intimidating tactics succeeded, and the king was persuaded to give his consent, thus sealing Strafford's death sentence. His trial, attainder, and execution on May 12 had a profoundly and permanently divisive effect on the realm and its leaders. Thereafter there could be no trust, no accommodation.

Even as Strafford was condemned to death, both Houses passed a bill in May 1641 which stated that Parliament could not be dissolved without its own consent. Then Parliament passed bill after bill to be rid of many institutions and practices that it despised. It abolished the Court of Star Chamber, which had coercively enforced questionable royal policies; the Court of High Commission, which had stripped Puritans from church offices; and the two regional councils in the North and in Wales. It granted the king customs for two-month renewable periods only, declared ship money illegal, and ended financial expedients such as enlarging the royal forests. It passed a Triennial Act, which required Parliament to meet once every three years, so that the king could not once again refuse to call it into session. Charles gave his assent to every bill. His subjects began to wonder why he had allowed his faithful ministers to be executed, his government to be stripped of crucial powers, and Parliament to gain a potential permanence. Late in 1641 Charles began to rally his supporters, claiming that he alone was able to save the Church of England from a minority who would displace it. He requested an army to put down a fresh rebellion in Ireland, and many Parliamentarians feared to accede lest an army under royal control would become the instrument to reverse the hard-won reforms.

Fears about the king's sincerity were heightened when on January 4, 1642, he burst into the House of Commons to arrest Pym and four other leaders, but they had been forewarned and had escaped. Soon Charles left the hostile mobs of London for the more loyal north. Long months proved that an accommodation was not possible, so in August 1642 war broke out between the king and Parliament. Each side justified its actions: Charles claimed to fight to preserve the balance of the constitution and to keep the Commons from assuming all powers; Parliament insisted on a distinction between the office of kingship and the person of the king, asserting that it sought to preserve the office from the unworthy Stuart tyrant.

The Civil Wars. The king's forces, the Royalists or Cavaliers, advanced in 1642 to the outskirts of London and won a major engagement at Edgehill, but neither then nor in the proposed triple offensive of 1643 were the royal forces able to convert occasional successes into a conclusive victory.

In the interim Parliament had to learn to govern the areas under its control. In such a novel situation there was much freedom in discarding traditional but inefficient practices, and gradually Parliament developed effective administrative and taxing procedures.

The war's turning point was Parliament's reorganization of the army made up of Parliamentarians, or Roundheads, in 1644. By passing a Self-denying Ordinance, Parliament excluded its own members from military offices, thus removing men for whom rank and birth and not ability had meant leadership. The result was the creation of the New Model Army which was open to Puritans with military skills, an innovation as novel for Europe as were the striking new red coats in which all the soldiers were uniformed. An exception was made for an extremely capable Parliamentarian, Oliver Cromwell, a member of the gentry powerfully motivated by his Puritan faith and a man who kept himself ready to serve God by diligent prayer and self-examination. Cromwell was a major proponent of the role of cavalry in battle, and the flair with which he led his mounted soldiers to rout the enemy in disciplined and perfected charges soon made him one of the highest ranking generals and an inspiration for the soldiers. In 1644 the military tide began to shift in Parliament's favor, and at Marston Moor that year and at Naseby in 1645 the Royalist forces were soundly defeated.

From the time that Charles surrendered in 1646 the central political issue was the terms of negotiation. Two factions in Parliament were seriously divided by religious and constitutional attitudes. The majority party, the Presbyterians, wished to make the long-delayed religious settlement along the Scottish Calvinistic lines while the Independents wanted to allow a great deal of doctrinal latitude to each individual congregation and to restrict the national church to matters of public policy such as repressing blasphemy. The Presbyterians were constitutionally more moderate, wanting to place no restrictions on the monarch beyond those enacted in the Long Parliament, while the Independents felt that further restraints were absolutely necessary.

The Presbyterians would prevail if it came to a vote, but a powerful force outside Parliament also claimed a role in determining England's political future. Refusing to be disbanded, as the Parliamentary Presbyterians wished, the army asserted it had been called "to the defense of our own and the people's just rights and liberties." Its officers prepared a plan of negotiations that strongly supported the Parliamentary Independents, and the soldiers, through elected spokesmen, presented their own scheme based heavily on the philosophy of the Levellers, a radical faction comprised mainly of Londoners of lower social ranks. The Levellers went beyond an insistence on religious equality to demand a "levelling" in economic and political life as well. This was to be won in great part by allowing all male heads of households to vote.

Oliver Cromwell. By R. Walker c. 1649 *(The National Portrait Gallery, London)*.

Meanwhile Charles escaped, and the Parliament and army buried their differences; within a year they would fight and defeat him. But when negotiations were resumed, the Presbyterians did not budge from their earlier "moderate" position which the Independents now judged folly in the light of the actions of the "perfidious king." Colonel Pride led an army contingent into Parliament to purge the Presbyterian members, and the fifty to sixty Independents remaining immediately set up a court to try the king for his crimes. Charles rose to true nobility in his last days, arguing strongly and persuasively in his own behalf, but his conviction was a foregone conclusion. On January 30, 1649, a few hours after the office of the monarch was abolished, he was beheaded, and then the small remnant of Independents, now called the Rump Parliament, also abolished the House of Lords and the office of bishop. James I's "no bishop, no king" had come true. Thus began an eleven-year period called the interregnum (1649–1660), a time of constitutional experimentation to find an alternative to England's traditional form of government.

The Commonwealth. The earliest experiment was the Commonwealth (1649–1653), in which the Rump was the legislature and the executive functions were shared by a forty-member Council of State composed of thirty-one Parliamentarians and some generals. The psychological wrench of abandoning so many traditional practices was a severe problem. The army was kept busy suppressing Royalist uprisings and crushing rebellions in Ireland and Scotland; the navy was kept busy fighting the Dutch in a mercantile war over the supremacy of the sea and the control of colonies. Little progress was made in the issue of religion, still unsolved since 1642. A diluted form of Presbyterianism was enacted but found little support outside of London. In default of an enforceable plan, all forms of worship were allowed except Anglicanism and Catholicism.

The most important political tension was between the Rump and the army. The latter wished old grievances settled and insisted that the Rump keep its promise to dissolve itself and call new elections. Cromwell had become the leading general as others died or retired, but he was unwilling to dispense with the Rump lest the last link to the traditional form of representation be broken. When in April 1653 the Rump declared itself permanent, Cromwell finally intervened to dissolve the Rump. He then tried an utterly novel and totally unsuccessful experiment. The army asked the Independent congregations to nominate God-fearing Puritans to enact reforms. The 129 members of the Nominated Assembly proved so radical that it acquired unpleasant nicknames such as the "Assembly of the Saints" and the "Barebones Parliament." The latter nickname was a word play on its member, Praise-God Barbon or Barebone, whose low social rank seemed to epitomize the perceived danger of entrusting government to others than the wellborn elite. Cromwell quickly ended the experiment.

The Protectorate and the End of the Interregnum. Cromwell and the army were ready with another plan, a written constitution called the Instrument of Government. As Lord Protector, Cromwell assumed executive control with sweeping powers such as the right to issue ordinances which were to have the force of law until Parliament should meet. It was the exercise of these powers that caused unrest. Cromwell realized that the army's power had to be reduced and civilian control extended, and this attitude dissatisfied the army, while Parliament was stunned by his use of ordinances to collect money and even settle religious matters. No Stuart king had ever enjoyed such power and independence.

To correct some of these problems, in 1657 Parliament drafted a new written constitution, the Humble Petition and Advice. Cromwell rejected that part of the proposal which offered him the title of king yet accepted most of the rest, including the right to name his successor. But the constitutional dilemma continued, and only the extraordinary skills of Oliver Cromwell kept the political state together. Even that had its limitations. The war against Spain was an expensive failure. It further alienated the merchant and financial interests of London, who were vital to the survival of the Commonwealth. When he died on September 3, 1658, and was succeeded by his son Richard, the interregnum was near collapse.

Richard Cromwell was ineffective—his nickname was "Tumble-Down Dick"—and many of the army's leaders grew increasingly arbitrary in opposition. The commander in Scotland, General George Monck, took the initiative to end the stalemate by marching his army southward and capitalizing on the public sentiment which called for a permanent solution. Monck was well suited to the task. He shared the conservative views of the gentry from which he sprang. These included the belief that the army should be the servant and not the master of the civil authority. First he called back the Rump Parliament, then he added all the others purged in 1648. The restored Long Parliament called for new elections and dissolved itself, and the newly elected body issued an invitation to the son of Charles I to return as king. In May 1660 Charles II arrived back from exile to inaugurate the Restoration—a restoration of the monarchy, of the Church of England, and of traditional government.

A Stocktaking: England in 1660

Society and the Economy. The size of the aristocracy had grown greatly in the seventeenth century, but its importance had diminished. The twin pillars of aristocratic preeminence in the Middle Ages had been military service and the nobility's wealth and influence. Most of the military responsibilities had been lost in the sixteenth century, and the eclipse of the House of Lords temporarily by the Commons had diminished their political role. More important, the aristocrats' land ownership was severely curtailed by the Civil Wars. Most had fought for the king and, although those whose estates had been confiscated were entitled to sue at law for recovery, the nobles who sold their estates for any reason whatsoever were not able to regain them.

The early modern state had opened up great opportunities for the gentry. What the dissolution of the monasteries had done to enlarge the land market of the sixteenth century the confiscation of the nobles' and bishops' lands had done in the seventeenth. Many became newly landed gentry in time to rise to the new nobility. The merchants who formed a nonagricultural middle class and the professionals such as lawyers had all grown in importance. Success in any endeavor produced capital ready for investment in myriad new economic adventures at home and in trade.

The economic restraints imposed by the monarchy were removed. Gone were regulations governing the quality of manufactures and the rates of wages; gone were feudal tenures which had disinclined landowners to invest to improve their crop yield; gone were the royal monopolies and the Star Chamber which hindered the free marketplace. The removal of restrictions primarily benefited the well-to-do. But many of the "lesser sort" had been politicized, allowed to speculate freely along with others in a time of constitutional experimentation and allowed to have access to printing presses to propagate sincere reform ideas such as the Levellers or the outlandish ideas of religious fanatics. Many of these movements had been suppressed either in the interregnum or at the Restoration, but politics was not likely to remain the close precinct of the upper classes alone.

Religion and Ideas. Sixteenth-century religion was based on the premise that truth was certain and discoverable and that dissent and diversity were literally intolerable. By 1660, Catholicism was effectively eradicated, but Puritanism had temporarily come to supplant Anglicanism. The varieties of religious dissent had multiplied, and no longer was it possible to substitute one set of practices and form of church government for another. Although Anglicanism in the Restoration would bring an end to the period of practical toleration, the memory endured. Puritanism had indeed triumphed in many urban settings as a social ethic. Long after the specific religious teachings had been lost, the lessons of industriousness and discipline in work remained to influence many in the middle ranks of society. New directions in thought emerged, especially the humanism of the sixteenth century and the scientific inquiry of the seventeenth. The how-to orientation of many books reflected the practical, this-worldly bent of Englishmen. Many of the old orthodoxies were crumbling as much in the world of religion and ideas as in society and politics; the next quarter century gave a firmer shape to the new.

Suggestions for Further Reading

An overview for the seventeenth century is Christopher Hill's *The Century of Revolution* (1961). David Harris Willson's *King James VI and I* (1956) is a good biography; the best treatment of Charles I is to be found in Pauline Gregg, *King*

Charles I (1981). Charles Carlton's, *Charles I, The Personal Monarch* (1983), an example of pyschobiography, provides suggestive insights. The favorite of both is treated in rich detail in Roger Lockyer, *The Life and Political Career of George Villiers, First Duke of Buckingham, 1592–1628* (1981). The man responsible for the restoration of the Stuart monarchy is well treated in Maurice Ashley, *General Monck* (1977). A chronological survey of the constitution is J. R. Tanner's *English Constitutional Conflicts of the Seventeenth Century, 1603–1689* (1928).

There is a spirited debate on the origins of the Civil Wars, to which a useful guide can be found in Philip A. M. Taylor's *The Origins of the English Civil War. Conspiracy, Crusade, or Class Conflict?* (1960). Conrad Russell, *The Origins of the English Civil War* (1973) and Anthony Fletcher, *The Outbreak of the Civil War* (1981) are excellent modern treatments. Narrative histories of the troubled 1630s and 1640s are in C. V. Wedgwood, *The King's Peace, 1637–1641* (1955), *The King's War, 1641–1647* (1958), and *The Trial of Charles I* (1964). The astute maneuvers of the reformers are described in J. H. Hexter, *The Reign of King Pym* (1941), while the growth of radicalism is treated by Hill in *The World Turned Upside Down, Radical Ideas during the English Revolution* (1972). David Underdown in *Pride's Purge* (1971) and Blair Worden in *The Rump Parliament* (1974) provide illuminating studies of parliamentary politics. Underdown, *Royalist Conspiracy in England, 1646–1660* (1960) explains the reasons for the failure of the schemes of the supporters to restore the monarchy.

Mark Kishlansky, *The Rise of the New Model Army* (1979) and Peter Young and Richard Holmes, *The English Civil War, A Military History of the Three Civil Wars, 1642–1651* (1974) examine the development and employment of the army raised by the Parliament, an innovative and important phase in the evolution of warfare. Among useful studies of Cromwell are Hill's *God's Englishman: Oliver Cromwell and the English Revolution* (1970), which stresses ideas, and A. A. Hillary's *Oliver Cromwell and the Challenge to the Monarchy* (1969), which is briefer but with a fuller context. The historiographical debate over Cromwell is introduced in Richard E. Boyer, *Oliver Cromwell and the Puritan Revolt, Failure of a Man or a Faith?* (1966).

Religious issues are briefly introduced by William M. Lamont, *Godly Rule. Politics and Religion, 1603–60* (1969). The literary aspects of Puritanism are stressed in William Haller, *The Rise of Puritanism, 1570–1643* (1938), the formation of the social ethic in Christopher Hill, *Society and Puritanism in Pre-Revolutionary England* (1964), the instructional side in Paul Seaver, *The Puritan Lectureships, the Politics of Religious Dissent, 1560–1662* (1970), and the many sects in George Yule, *The Independents in the English Civil War* (1958). For a consideration of dissent over a longer period one can consult Michael R. Watts' excellent *The Dissenters. Vol. I: From the Reformation to the French Revolution* (1978). A sympathetic account of the Anglican clergy is to be found in Rosemary O'Day, *The English Clergy. The Emergence and Transformation of a Profession (1558–1642)* (1979).

Useful social surveys are Wallace Notestein, *The English People on the Eve of Colonization, 1603–1630* (1954) and David Mathew, *The Age of Charles I* (1951). The political aspects of society are discussed in Perez Zagorin's *The Court and the Country* (1970), and the upper classes are discussed in Lawrence Stone's *The Crisis of the Aristocracy, 1558–1641* (1965); a provocative study of less spectacular Englishmen is in Peter Laslett, *The World We Have Lost* (2nd edition, 1971). There is a debate over the political and economic "rise" of the gentry and their role in precipitating the Civil War; a guide to the protagonists with penetrating critiques is in J. H. Hexter's *Reappraisals in History* (1961).

Economic developments are surveyed in Charles Wilson's *England's Apprenticeship, 1603–1763* (1965). The broad range of new avenues of thought are studied in Christopher Hill's *The Intellectual Origins of the English Revolution* (1965), and science is emphasized in the European context in Alan G. R. Smith, *Science and Society in the Sixteenth and Seventeenth Centuries* (1972) and in H. Butterfield, *The Origins of Modern Science* (new edition, 1957). A leading antiquary and his circle are treated in Kevin Sharpe, *Sir Robert Cotton, 1586–1631. History and Politics in Early Modern England* (1979). The importance of London in politics is studied in Valerie Pearl's *London and the Outbreak of the Puritan Revolution* (1961), which should be read in conjunction with Robert Ashton, *The City and the Court, 1603–1643* (1979). For urban centers elsewhere in the country one may consult P. Clark and P. Slack, *Crisis and Order in English Towns, 1500–1700* (1972) and *English Towns in Transition, 1500–1700* (1976), and John T. Evans, *Seventeenth-Century Norwich: Politics, Religion, and Government, 1620–1690* (1979).

8

Restoration England

1660–1688

When Charles II (1660–1685) set foot on English soil at Dover on May 25, 1660, he returned amidst general rejoicing and relief. Charles II appeared to be well cast for his role. He was dark and swarthy, not handsome; his young, athletic appearance, his stature (he was six feet, four inches tall), and his easy manner, sharp wit, and shrewd intelligence made him an instant success. His faults, though evident to his close associates and advisors, took longer to be revealed. Indolent, with little interest for business (though he unquestionably had the ability), insincere and gifted at dissembling (a trait he had been forced to acquire in his struggle for life and throne), overly fond of pleasure, women, and gambling, he cut the figure of a king but lacked the substance. Perhaps his most important trait, if hardly the most admirable, was an instinct for survival.

The Reestablishment of the Monarchy

The Restoration Settlement. Charles left to the Parliament the settling of such vexatious and difficult matters as the arrears of pay of the army, a general pardon, and the forfeited estates of the Royalists. Parliament rather than the king thus bore the odium of the disappointed. The Cromwellian army was reduced to a few regiments; the rest of the troops were paid what was owed them and retired from active duty. The Act of Indemnity which forgave all but fifty named individuals was a gracious and healing measure. The land problem was a more complex one, and any solution was bound to create opposition. The compromise was sensible if not wholly equitable. Crown lands and those of the church, together with confiscated estates, were returned to the original owners. Those properties sold by private individals during the Civil Wars could only be repossessed

155

through court action and then only in the case of abuses of the law not exempted by the Act of Indemnity.

The Political Settlement. The nature of the king's own authority had perhaps the most important long-range considerations. It seemed clear to most people that a return to the old constitution, shorn of the Commonwealth innovations, was the common desire. The Long Parliament, which called for the election of the Convention Parliament, had itself shown the way by resolving that the House of Lords "had and have to be a part of the parliament of England." When the new Parliament assembled the Lords participated fully and equally without any reference to their dissolution in 1649. Their presence and that of a substantial number of Royalists insured that the prerogatives of the monarchy would be preserved. The restoration was not complete. The acts passed by the Short Parliament and the Long Parliament until 1642 that had received the assent of the king remained on the statute books, including the acts which had abolished the prerogative courts. The most important changes were left unstated. Parliament had executed one king, now it had restored another to the throne. Though it supported Charles II by restoring the bishops to the upper House, by vesting sole command of all the armed forces in the king, and by repeal of the Triennial Act of 1641, the fact that these measures were done on the authority of Parliament and king and not the king alone was not lost on the participants.

The Financial Settlement. The adequacy of the financial settlement made to support the king's honor and government has long been a subject of debate. The radical innovations enacted by the Long Parliament in the 1640s had substituted a whole new series of internal taxes to maintain the army and navy and to replace those hereditary sources which had been abolished. These new taxes, especially the excise, an internal tax levied on commodities in general and on liquor in particular, were not popular with the general populace. For some months the Convention Parliament attempted to establish a tax on land to replace the feudal revenues that had been taken from the king. Direct taxes were regarded as an extraordinary rather than a regular source of revenue. When the Commons failed to agree on a land tax, an excise tax on liquor was successfully moved by court members in the Commons. The usefulness of this tax, which could be expanded to innumerable other commodities, was evident to the government. The most recent estimate of various taxes voted by the Parliament at the beginning of the reign show that they yielded approximately £980,000 per annum, short of the £1,200,000 which the Parliament projected. Additional taxes voted during the course of the reign brought the average up to £1,170,000, and if the king had managed his affairs wisely

Charles II. After Sir Peter Lely *(The National Portrait Gallery, London)*.

they should have sufficed. That they did not is an indictment of the king, not the Parliament.

The Religious Settlement. The religious settlement, like so many other aspects of the Restoration, proved to be an interim arrangement. While still in exile, Charles II had promised liberty of conscience to his subjects. During the Commonwealth, Presbyterians and Independents had been introduced into church livings, and both groups had expectations of remaining in an established church. The Anglicans were hardly unanimous in their attitude. That party identified as Laudian or high-church strenuously opposed any relaxation of the forms of the church to please the Presbyterians and showed little sympathy in general for Nonconformists. Others were disposed to define the church broadly so that it would be possible at least to comprehend the Presbyterians. The king and Clarendon were both disposed to moderation, though for differing reasons. The king was most interested in toleration for the benefit of the Catholics. Clarendon favored a church that was national and Protestant, and to achieve that he was prepared to and did incorporate many of the clergy who had accepted the Cromwellian settlement.

A conference was held in the spring of 1661 to reach an accommodation between the Presbyterians and the Anglicans. Unable to agree among themselves, the Presbyterians, who were poorly led and overconfident, prolonged the proceedings with the consequence that the Cavalier Parliament, which met on May 8, took the matter into its own hands. In league with the bishops, the Parliament ruled against an accommodation with the Presbyterians. The Anglicans now employed the same tactics of prohibition and persecution against the Nonconformists that had been used against them in the previous two decades. By the Act of Uniformity nearly 1,000 incumbents were purged from the church in 1662 for their refusal to accept the restored church's liturgy and doctrines. The Corporation Act denied Nonconformists the right to hold office even at the local level, though the Act was never completely implemented. The Five Mile Act of 1665 and the Conventicle Acts of 1664 and 1670 placed penalties on Nonconformist meetings and ministers. An intermittent and not always effective persecution lasted until the Glorious Revolution of 1688, but the civil disabilities under which the Nonconformists suffered were not removed until the nineteenth century.

The Diplomatic Settlement. Peace was an essential prerequisite to buy time to consolidate and secure the king's government in Britain. The fear of a Puritan insurrection made essential an alliance with a strong continental power who could supply troops in time of need. There were not many choices. Portugal, anxious to obtain allies to confirm her independence of Spain, was the most eager to conclude an alliance with England and offered Charles a bride—Catherine of Braganza—a handsome dowry, and the cities of Bombay and Tangier. Although the offer of Portugal was accepted, the most important link was forged with France. In part Charles was impelled by the ties of family. His French mother lived in retirement in her native country, and his sister Henrietta was married to the brother of Louis XIV. The views of Louis XIV on the nature of kingship were congenial to his English counterpart. Above all it was the offer of French gold that persuaded Charles to conclude a treaty for the sale of Dunkirk in 1662.

Restoration England. The social structure of Stuart England was a well stratified one. One can identify hierarchies in the cities and in the country; the two are roughly parallel though not identical. The whole was characterized by a very small upper layer with family incomes well above £1,000 a year, and middling groups with incomes ranging from £100 to £1,000 a year. These families controlled the wealth and political power. They and their immediate dependents totalled less than 10 percent of the population. All the rest fell below this level. The principal basis for wealth and political power was property, as in the House of Lords, whose members' titles and affluence reflected landed estates; the House of Commons, the majority of whose members were landowners; the law courts, where both the English common law and the litigation arising from it were all based on matters involving real property; the electorate both in cities and in the country, where the franchise was generally based on a property qualification; or the principal commodities of English commerce, especially wool. The society was firmly tied to the land.

An analysis by the pioneer statistician Gregory King, made at the end of the Restoration period, estimates the total population of England at 5,500,000 people. It is now known that his calculations were based on very limited and fragmentary sources. Moreover, King—a conservative, a divine right Tory working in the mid-1690s—projected his estimates back to 1688 to demonstrate the disastrous impact on the economy of William III's continental involvements. But even if his figures are deliberately conservative underestimates, his social categories are valuable for the manner in which one traditional but perceptive Englishman conceived of the social order of his country.

At the head were the nobility, some 160 lay lords and 26 spiritual lords, who were the leaders of the society, both because of their great wealth and their social status. Next in rank were the gentry, also possessing great landed wealth and often holding minor honors, baronets or knights. These were the men who filled the House of Commons and acted as the justices of peace in their counties. Gradations must be recognized within this class. The wealthiest rivaled the loftiest peers in holdings and political power. The lesser gentry were barely distinguishable from the small freeholders or farmers. Though numbered in the thousands, they still formed a small and discrete class. Small freeholders and farmers comprised the largest number in the country, according to King, and nearly six times that when their families were counted. They inherited the role of the yeomen of former times, though reduced in importance. They were distinguished by good husbandry and their economic independence. The lowest orders were the cottagers and paupers, who eked out a bare subsistence living by tilling small parcels of soil, grazing on the common, and hiring out as day and seasonal laborers while their families supplemented their income by making thread and by weaving. Some 20 percent of the population, essentially this group, received some form of public assistance or relief.

The leading residents of the cities were the wealthier merchants who controlled the moveable wealth of the kingdom and accounted for much of England's growing prosperity. Below them one found the shopkeepers, tradesmen, artisans, and craftsmen, which included some 5,000 substantial innkeepers. The middle and upper classes were sustained by a vast army of more than 300,000 laboring people and outservants, nearly 90 percent of them in rural employment, who with their families comprised some 1,275,000.

London: The Great Plague and Fire, 1665–1666. England was visited by two great natural disasters in the early years of the Restoration. The great plague struck England in 1665 for the last time. It lasted into the next year, and before it was over some 70,000 had lost their lives out of 460,000 in London alone. The court and the Parliament fled to Oxford in hopes of escaping the pestilence. In order to maintain communication with those left behind in the capital and to allay fears throughout the country, the secretaries of state inaugurated a newspaper, the *Oxford Gazette*, to be renamed the *London Gazette* upon the return of the Court. For twelve years it was the sole newspaper permitted in the country, and though rivals began to appear in 1679 the paper itself has continued down to the present day, a unique publication record.

London had not recovered from the plague when it was struck by a second disaster, the great fire. In the space of four days in September 1666, the fire destroyed 40 percent of the old city within the walls. The city of London was a maze of wooden buildings and houses, each story built further out into the narrow street so that the roofs almost touched those opposite. The city was dank, crowded, dirty, and fetid, and land in it was dear. Merchants and artisans wanted to live close to their businesses if, indeed, both home and shop were not on the same premises. Restrictions on new construction outside the walls tended to retard development in the suburbs and concentrate the population within the walls. To the west the upper classes were building their houses; the earl of Clarendon, the lord chancellor, put his up in Piccadilly shortly before his impeachment in 1667. But in the city proper and in East London living conditions were poor and crowded, with a density as high as 40.3 households per acre. Brick and stone were rarely used in construction until required by proclamation in 1661. The rapidity with which houses were put up is one

The Great Fire of London, 1666. Painting by an eyewitness *(The Bettmann Archive/BBC Hulton)*.

testimony to the poor quality; some houses were built in a night. Frontages were narrow, as little as eleven or twelve feet, and buildings were deep with the consequence that there was little light. The average house was a small, two-storied dwelling with a square footage of about 1,200 in the poorer parishes, on the average with four to six rooms each. Bed, chairs, and tables were the staple furnishings. After the fire, standards improved and the density of housing declined as some of the people moved out of the city to avoid the congestion and the high costs.

So much of the old city was swept away that an opportunity for a whole new start could be made, and the heart of the commercial capital could be laid out on a scale and plan that befitted one of the great centers of Europe. But the hurry to restore the business and commerce of the trading center, a necessity doubly important with the losses in revenue suffered because of the plague and the war, and the reluctance to trade building space for broader avenues and parks, limited the planners. The network of streets at least was regularized to some degree, and new building codes reduced the fire hazard for the future. But the main consequence was the opportunity given to Sir Christopher Wren and his assistants and successors to design and build a new cathedral of St. Paul and a series of parish churches that still survive as the great glory of the city of London.

The development that marked London, economic and material, intellectual and artistic, was not exclusive to the metropolis. The Restoration ush-

ered in a sustained period of general urban prosperity. Initially the growth
was not so much in population as it was in commerce. Trade and social
traffic burgeoned, perhaps in part as a reaction to the restrictions and so-
briety of the Commonwealth. Industrial growth was an essential component. Many towns developed specialized industries, fueled by the rise of
real wages in the countryside. Middle-rank towns not only served as market centers but also as the focus of occupational regions. The stocking
trade, with its heart at Leicester, or the metalware trade, with its epicenter
at Sheffield, are two examples. The growth of overseas trade was also an
important spur. But the sustained growth depended as much on the expansion of the home market for manufactured goods, and migration to
the towns, though at a lower level than earlier in the century, provided
labor, especially women who sought employment in the growing service
and market trades.

A notable example of the renewed vitality of the provincial towns after
the Revolution was Norwich. By 1700 it was the second largest city in
England, growing during the century from about 12,000 to 30,000
people. Atypical in terms of its demographic record, its achievement was
the more remarkable as it was the largest inland town in the country (it
was also atypical in the strength of Dissent in the city). External trade and
ports were characteristics of its competitors. Immigration, mainly of individuals or families from Norfolk and Suffolk, was the basis for its increase. The principal employment was in textile manufacturing. By the end
of the century the weavers jostled the merchants for power and prestige.
The mayor elected in 1693, reputedly the wealthiest man in the city, came
from the former rather than the latter group, heretofore dominant in the
town. The market for the cloth was mainly domestic, and the product was
mostly light and brightly colored textiles. The cloth was bought variously
for apparel, linings for more expensive fabrics, and home furnishings.
Competing chiefly with imported goods, the Norwich weavers shrewdly
devised and introduced innovations in finish and design to maintain their
competitive edge, especially in London, their principal market. Increases
in duties on foreign cloth and periodic bans on French goods also proved
important stimuli. In addition to its role as a principal market town, one
with an increasing number of permanent retail outlets, and as a center for
wholesale trade and distribution, Norwich waxed so prosperous that by
the end of the century it began to emulate London in its winter season
with theaters, shows and assemblies, the summer assize, and other entertainments.

The Royal Society and the New Science. The later seventeenth century was a
pivotal time in the intellectual and technological history of western Europe. England was at the heart of what is now recognized as the scientific

frozen Thames, Feb: 1684

Foot Ball

rious Sports behold here in this Piece,
ich for Six weeks were seen upon the Ice;
the Thames the great variety
Plays and Booths is here brought to your eye.
hes, as in Cheap-side, run on wheels:
(out-tipling of the Fishes) reels.
Waves that us'd to beat the shoar,
's they bait, till loudly they do roar.
do slide, where Boats were wont to row.
ips did sail, the Sailers do them tow.
ngers in Boats the River crost,
ne Price as 'twas before the frost,
Printing-Booth, of wondrous Fame,
at each Man there did Print his Name;
former Ages, ne're was found,
Print, where Men so oft were dround.
Booths, that sit at no ground-Rent,
in Beef and Brandy there is spent.

8. The Dutch-men here in nimble cutting Scates,
   To please the Croud, do show their Tricks and Feats.
9. The Rabble here in Chariots run a round.
10. Coffee and Tea and Mum doth here abound.
11. The Tinkers here do march at sound of Kettle;
    And all Men know, that they are Men of Mettle.
12. Here roasted was an Ox before the Court,
    Which to much Folks afforded Meat and Sport.
13. At Nine-Pins here they play, as in Moor-fields.
14. This place the Pass-time us of Foot Ball yields.
15. The Common-Hunt here, makes another show,
    As he to hunt an Hare is wont to go:
    But though no Woods are here, or Hares so fleet,
    Yet Men do often Foxes catch and meet.
16. Into an hole here one by chance doth fall,
    At which the Water-men began to bawl,
    When he, alas, poor man, no harm did think.

17. Here Men well mounted do
18. Here they do throw at Cock;
19. A Chariot here so cunningly
    That it did move it self, witho
    Of Horse or Rope, by vertue of
    That Vulcan did contrive, wh
20. The Rooks at Nine-holes here
    As they are wont to do in Sum
21. Three Ha'perth for a Penny,
    of Ginger-bread, come, who w
22. This is the Booth, where Me
    For Crape and Ribbons that the
    But in Six Hours this great and R
    Of Booths and Pass-times, all

London: Printed by G. Croom at
street, over against Barnar

Frost Fair on the Thames, 1684. A contemporary engraving *(Pepys Library, Magdalene College, Cambridge)*.

revolution. The country was alive with a ferment of ideas, artistic, philosophical, religious, political, and scientific. The Royal Society, founded in 1662, was one focal point for the interchange, discussion, and development of these ideas. A circle of virtuosos, dilettantes, practical men of business, wealthy aristocrats, and new professional men was formed, all inquisitive and interested in keeping abreast of the new developments in the natural sciences. Sir Christopher Wren typified this new breed of men.

A student of great brilliance, he shone both as a Latin versifier and a mathematician of distinction. Praised by no less an authority than Sir Isaac Newton as a geometrician, Wren was a professor of astronomy and engaged in scientific experiment and study until he became assistant to the surveyor-general of works and devoted the greater part of his life to architecture, a field in which he was largely self-taught. Newton, who joined the Royal Society in 1672, was the greatest mathematician of his time and made contributions to mathematics, physics, astronomy, and optics. Associated with Wren and Newton was Robert Boyle who made important contributions in chemical analysis. His work is remembered to this day by the law to which he gave his name on the relation between the volume, density, and pressure of gases. Yet one must not make the mistake of assuming a too sudden and complete modernity by the standards of our own time. We must also remember that both magical and apocalyptic ideas continued to hold great currency, even in the circles of the Royal Society. Throughout his life Newton displayed a strong interest in biblical chronology and a consuming commitment to alchemy.

The fellow of the Royal Society who has given us the most vivid picture of London in the 1660s when it passed through the two great catastrophes was the diarist, Samuel Pepys. As a key civilian official in the navy from the Restoration to the Revolution he was the perfect bureaucrat—industrious, knowledgeable, always protecting the interests of his office and the navy. He illustrated how a young man of ability and connections, though lacking a large fortune, could rise to a position of great responsibility. He lived a rich and varied life. An indefatigable worker, he put in long hours at his office or in attendance on his superiors. As a young man he already had cultivated tastes, was a competent musician, and was an ardent book collector. He was also a man of pleasure, enjoying the many divertissements of the metropolis, the taverns, women, musicals, and the stage. London was the center of his life and he rarely left it.

Political Theory and Literature. One of the founders of the Royal Society, Sir William Petty, pioneered in yet another branch of knowledge, political economy. He came to the field after a term as a professor of anatomy and then physician-general to the army in Ireland. He undertook to make a survey of Ireland for the Commonwealth government in order to map the forfeited estates. He went on to make a complete map of the whole island, a task not finished until 1673. His skill and accuracy set new standards. After the Restoration he wrote a pioneer work on vital statistics and treatises on finance, the growth of the city of London, taxes, the origins of wealth, and a host of related topics. Another physician, John Locke, the most important political philosopher of the age, did not see his magnum opus published until after the Revolution. Locke joined the entourage of the earl of Shaftesbury and employed his pen in defending his patron and his political views. In the early 1680s he wrote his classic *Two Treatises of Government* to refute the *Patriarcha* of Sir Robert Filmer, the latter published posthumously by the Tories in 1680 to support the king's authority. Hounded into exile with Shaftesbury, Locke published his *Treatises* in 1689 as a justification of the Glorious Revolution. Such was the conservatism of his countrymen that his view was not accepted until decades after his death.

The reopening of the theaters in 1660 made possible a rebirth of English drama. The theater was heavily patronized by the court, the men of letters establishing that connection with the great aristocrats and politicians which was to reach its fullest flower in Queen Anne's reign. However, the greatest products of English writers were in forms other than drama. John Milton, a vestige of the Commonwealth, blind and out of favor, ennobled the English language with his great epic poems *Paradise Lost* and *Paradise Regained*. Another Puritan, John Bunyan, who found only adversity in the Restoration, wrote the *Pilgrim's Progress* while in prison. The finest literary representative of the Restoration and the poet laureate to the royal brothers, Charles II and James II, was John Dryden. Though a prolific contributor to the Restoration theater, he is best remembered for his poetry, his translation of Vergil, and his satires. It is not surprising that the prolonged political heats of the Restoration spawned a profusion of polemical works. Dryden's *Absalom and Achitophel,* a satire on the duke of Monmouth and the earl of Shaftesbury, was the supreme example and was singularly effective in reducing the Whig cause to ridicule. The full flower of this literary outpouring was to be found in the Augustan Age which followed the Revolution. While the circle of educated readers these writings reached was limited, literacy itself was not limited to the upper classes. Husbandmen and laborers had gained elementary reading skills even before the Civil War. Popular educational improvement continued into the Restoration period and beyond as the abundance of cheap printed literature—primarily ballads and chapbooks—attests.

England, France, and the Dutch Republic

Clarendon and the Second Dutch War, 1665–1667. The first ministry of the reign was nominally headed by Edward Hyde, raised to the peerage as earl of Clarendon and made lord chancellor. Its record was not a happy one. Clarendon refused to act as a chief minister in the traditional sense by coordinating and supervising the other ministers, and he lacked the suppleness and flexibility to manage the Parliament successfully. He lasted in office until 1667 when he was brought down by the failure of his foreign policy and by discontent arising from the two great natural disasters at home, the plague and the fire of London. Relations with the Dutch, never good since the first Dutch War (1652–1654), had steadily deteriorated until war broke out again in 1665. Trading disputes had already led to armed conflict between the two nations in India and Africa. The war finally reached America in 1664 when an expedition from New England seized New Amsterdam and renamed it New York in honor of the king's brother, the duke of York. The war in Europe opened with an English attack on a Dutch convoy at Bergen the next year. In the European area, the English were able at first to withstand the challenge of the Dutch who were supported by an alliance with France. By 1667, however, their diplomatic isolation told against them. The low estate of the English military and naval power was revealed in that year when a Dutch fleet sailed up the Thames, destroyed half the English navy, and towed away the flagship, the Royal Charles. The ignominious failure of English diplomacy and arms toppled Clarendon from his post. Made the scapegoat for the disasters, he was impeached by the Parliament and forced into exile to France, where he lived until his death in 1674. The king and his other advisors negotiated the two treaties that brought hostilities with the French and the Dutch to an end. By the Treaties of Breda (1667), England regained the islands in the West Indies taken by France but ceded all rights to Acadia in North America. England kept the Dutch colonies in North America but gave up Guinea and most of the outposts in West Africa, except for Cape Coast Castle on the Gold Coast.

The Cabal. The ministers who succeeded Clarendon in the main offices and authority in the cabal, or inner circle, government were an ill-matched group. The fact that the combination of initial letters from their last names—Clifford, Arlington, Buckingham, Ashley, and Lauderdale—spelled CABAL was accidental, but the appellation when defined as a small body of persons engaged in private machination or intrigue is not inappropriate. Arlington alone seems to have demonstrated both a consistent and well-considered policy in his field of expertise, foreign affairs. All the ministers were overshadowed by the king, who now undertook the principal direction of affairs of state.

Even as the negotiations for peace at Breda were being concluded, Louis XIV undertook a new diplomatic initiative. Through his ambassador he suggested a defensive league or a joint expedition against the Spanish West Indies. He further implied that if hostilities were to break out again between the Dutch and England, France would no longer intervene on behalf of the Dutch. While negotiations dragged on, Arlington and his supporters sought to achieve the opposite, an alliance with Holland against France. Jan De Witt, the grand pensionary of Holland and chief official in the United Provinces, responded positively to the English overtures. The French seizure of a series of fortresses along the Spanish Netherlands had impressed upon him his nation's vulnerability to French military might and the need for allies. The Triple Alliance (1668) negotiated by Sir William Temple was the consequence, a treaty to which Sweden was also a signatory. In addition to mutual support in case of an attack by a third party, the Protestant powers hoped to lay the foundation for a larger alliance to prevent further French aggression. The alliance met with a positive reception in England. Parliament voted the improvident king a new tax on wine and spirits. More important, it marked the first stage in the rapprochement with Holland that was ultimately to unite the two great Protestant powers in arms against the ambitions of a Catholic France.

Despite a shared concern by England and Holland over the growth of French power, the Anglo-Dutch rivalry for colonial trade and European markets continued. Charles, chafing from the tedious and irksome necessity of having to persuade a recalcitrant and obstreperous Parliament to give him sorely needed funds, was encouraged to acept a French subsidy. His response to the French overtures was further encouraged in 1669 when his brother and heir, the duke of York, decided to avow Roman Catholicism. Charles was also inclined to embrace the Roman Catholic faith as one in harmony with his notion of the monarchy and the state. Urged on by his sister Henrietta, by his mother, by Buckingham, and, belatedly, by Arlington, Charles broached the terms of a new alliance to France. He would announce his own public conversion to Catholicism and the instigation of war against Holland if France in turn would provide him with the financial support he so desperately needed.

The Secret Treaty of Dover, 1670. Charles II's financial resources were so depleted that he could not await the results of the inevitably protracted negotiations required for the alliance. He recalled Parliament in October 1669 to seek additional subsidies. Instead of granting him a supply, the Commons proceeded to investigate the king's ministers in England and in Ireland and even threatened impeachment. Angrily the king prorogued the Parliament in December; when the members reassembled in February, the needed supplies were forthcoming and the threats against his ministers were dropped. The king now concluded the secret Treaty of Dover with France on May 22, 1670, in which he subordinated his country to France in order to satisfy his own needs. In so doing he put his country's independence and constitution in jeopardy. In order to ally the suspicions of Buckingham and his other Protestant ministers, the king openly negotiated a second "bogus" treaty which was identical to the first, except that it omitted the king's avowal of Catholicism. Though the cynicism of the king's designs has left an indelible stain on his record, the treaty made it possible for the English to win commercial advantages over their Dutch rivals in the important trade with France. Even the Parliament seems to have recognized this advantage in the articles made public; when they were recalled in October they provided an additional subsidy estimated to be worth £800,000 in new taxes for the king's support.

In April 1671, Charles prorogued the Parliament and embarked on a disastrous course of personal monarchy. Although he did not announce his conversion to Catholicism, he made a bold demonstration in favor of both Roman Catholics and Dissenters on March 15, 1672, when he issued his Declaration of Indulgence, which suspended the execution of all penal laws against noncommunicants of the Church of England. It was an audacious move, a resumption of regal authority that if followed successfully in other areas would have changed the nature of the English constitution. It did not succeed because Charles was undone by his own ineptness in the field of finance and by his misadventures in diplomacy. On January 20, 1672, his acute financial distress resulted in another more desperate gamble, the stop of the exchequer. Unable to meet his obligations he called a moratorium on all repayments of sums owed by the crown. He consigned his fortunes and those of his government to the long-planned war with Holland which he declared on March 17, two days after the Declaration of Indulgence.

The Third Dutch War, 1672–1674. Only success in war could save his plans. But the Dutch seized the initiative and inflicted a defeat on the English fleet, and the French pushed to the Rhine and into the Dutch Republic itself with nothing to prevent their advance. De Witt was overthrown and executed by his own people. They installed the young William of Orange, Charles II's nephew, in the long-vacant stadtholdership of their country as their last hope to preserve their independence from the French. With Charles's gamble having failed and the Protestant strongholds of Europe in mortal danger because of his surrender to France, the king was forced to recall Parliament. Meeting in February 1673 they withheld supplies until the king cancelled the Indulgence. Not content, Parliament passed a Test Act that required officeholders to take communion in the Anglican church and to disavow the doctrine of transubstantiation, a clause inserted specifically to eliminate Catholics. The duke of York was forced to resign the admiralty. He was followed into retirement by Clifford, another convert to Catholicism, and was replaced by a staunch Protestant, Sir Thomas Osborne, best known by his later title, earl of Danby. A second disastrous campaign abroad in 1673 only added further to the king's troubles. When Parliament reconvened in winter it criticized the Treaty of Dover, the war, and the duke of York's recent marriage to a Catholic princess, Mary of

Modena. Parliament refused any funds until peace was made. Charles quickly concluded a peace with the Dutch that restored the status quo, and he left control of domestic affairs for the most part to Danby for the next four years.

Danby and the Exclusion Parliaments

Danby as Lord High Treasurer. Danby proved equal to his task. He provided a personal direction and control to the ministry that was without parallel in the reign. Assuming the office of lord high treasurer from Clifford in 1673, Danby was faced with substantial debts, weak public credit, and mounting war expenses. By maximizing income sources and by curbing government expenditures he turned around the Treasury's near insolvency and slowly restored public confidence. He was aided during his ministry by the rise in customs receipts following England's withdrawal from the war on the continent in 1674. As a neutral and active trading nation England enjoyed commercial advantages. These advantages continued until anti-French sentiment in Parliament forced Danby to place an embargo on trade with France in 1678. Charles vacillated between his pro-French advisors and Danby, accepting French subsidies in 1675 and 1677 in exchange for prorogations of the Parliament. Danby pressed the king to make common cause against France with his nephew, William of Orange. In November 1677, Charles agreed to the marriage of James's eldest daughter Mary with William, hoping thereby to propitiate Parliament and to encourage Louis XIV to make peace with Holland. When Louis resisted, Charles recalled Parliament in 1678 and signed an offensive alliance with Holland. His initiative failed when the Parliament turned against him and Louis came to terms with Holland. Danby's Protestant, anti-French policy enabled him to convince Parliament to grant further subsidies in 1677. But all his efforts were nullified by his inability to curb royal expenditures. A renewed mobilization for a potential war against France in 1678 resulted in a growth once again of the floating debt. On his retirement he bequeathed to his successor a debt more than twice that he had inherited.

When Danby assumed the direction of the king's affairs, he realized that cooperation with Parliament was essential and that the grant of additional taxes was a necessity. To insure a compliant Commons he began to organize a government party in that house through a careful and judicious use of all the means of persuasion available to him—offices, pensions, and bribes. He introduced a new kind of professional management in recruiting and then directing the king's party in the lower house. Danby's efforts resulted in the foundation of what came to be known in 1679 as the Tory party (after the name for Irish Catholic outlaws). The Tory party is the beginning of the party system. But party loyalties were uncertain and fickle. The unpopularity of the king's policies and a well-founded suspicion of his intentions were too much for the lord treasurer. The efforts of the opposition led by Shaftesbury, which was given the name of Whigs (after truculent Scottish Presbyterians) in 1679 to distinguish them from Danby's Tories, gained an unexpected assist from the exposure of the "Popish Plot" in 1678.

The Popish Plot. This cruel hoax almost precipitated a revolution and kept the country in turmoil for the next three years. The "plot" was discovered by Titus Oates, a discredited Anglican clergyman, twice an apostate, who revealed a plan by Roman Catholics to murder the king after which James, with French support, would succeed to the throne. When the scheme was disclosed to the king and council, Charles immediately recognized the bogus nature of Oates's story. But Oates had unwittingly pointed to enough suspicious activities on the part of the English Jesuits and the duchess of York's secretary, who had been corresponding with French Catholics, that the alarm was raised. The death through misadventure of Sir Edmund Godfrey, the justice of the peace before whom Oates had sworn his story, provided further circumstantial evidence to confirm the validity of Oates's discovery.

Shaftesbury and his Whigs made the most of the opportunity. The king and his policies were discredited; thus the opposition-dominated Commons alone possessed popular confidence. Parliament stiffened the Test Act, removed Catholics from both houses, and attempted to disband the army and replace it with the loyal militia—all while it investigated unceasingly countless wild stories about a Catholic coup centering on the duke of York. Many innocent Catholics, including the queen herself, came under suspicion. More than a few peers, priests, and commoners who were so unlucky as to be incriminated were executed. The king was dangerously isolated and lost almost all power to protect himself. Not the least important consequence of the plot and its aftermath was the impact on the press. The censorship laws were allowed to lapse, and the court was powerless to curb the press. Newspapers, pamphlets, tracts, and books were published in wild profusion. The role of the press in influencing public opinion and in making the average Englishman aware of the torments his country was undergoing was one of the most important phenomena of these years.

The First Exclusion Parliament. The next two years were dominated by the struggle between the king and the opposition for supremacy and the attempt to exclude the duke of York from the succession. To appease his enemies Charles ordered his brother into exile at Brussels and remodeled his council by making places for the opposition, including Shaftesbury and the great moderating statesman George Savile, marquis of Halifax. The closest advisors included the new secretary of state, Robert Spencer, earl of Sunderland, who soon earned a reputation for industry and ability as well as deviousness and subservience. The election in February 1679 of a new Parliament was the first in which the two new parties of Whig and Tory contested for supremacy. The tone of conciliation employed by the king in his welcoming address to the new Parliament failed to appease his auditors. They took up the investigation of the plot again, ignored the king's pardon of Danby, and tried to pass an act of attainder to cut the Gordian knot of the pardon granted by the king to stop impeachment proceedings. Danby surrendered to the Lords and was incarcerated in the Tower for five years, narrowly escaping with his life. The main thrust of the Commons was to bar the Catholic duke of York from the succession. Charles responded that he was willing to give his assent to bills guaranteeing the Protestant religion and the laws of property; but he was indissolubly wed to the principle of hereditary succession. After passing a bill to further secure the right of habeas corpus, the Commons began work on an exclusion bill, and it was only halted by the king's prorogation and then dissolution of Parliament. A sudden and serious illness of the king resulted in the return of James and revealed the precarious state of the realm. If the king had died the Whigs would undoubtedly have precipitated a revolution rather than submit to James's rule. After Charles recovered, James was persuaded to exile himself once more from the court, though now to the more congenial climes of Scotland. There he had the opportunity as high commissioner to give proof to the fears of his opponents about his rigid and uncompromising attitudes. The quid pro quo was the exile of the duke of Monmouth, the illegitimate son of Charles II who was the hero of the Whigs and the pawn of Shaftesbury. Monmouth was removed from the office of commander in chief and was sent to Holland.

The Second Exclusion Parliament. The king delayed summoning the new Parliament for an entire year while he regained some control over the government, allowing opposition passions to be expended in demonstrations, investigations, and condemnations. The ministry was again remodelled and more compliant officers were appointed, drawn from the Tory or king's party. The chiefs were Sunderland and two new treasury commissioners, James's brother-in-law by his first wife, Lawrence Hyde, and Sidney Godolphin. Rochester (as Hyde later became known) has never received full credit for his achievements at the Treasury. He and his fellow commissioners were able to commit the king to retrenchment in expenditures with such success that a surplus in income was achieved to apply toward the debt. Moreover, the new commission, also with Charles's acquiescence, was able for the first time to exercise some control over departmental expenditures, thus establishing a new pattern of government that was to be carefully exploited by their successors. Foreign affairs were also part of Charles's strategy to wrest the initiative back from Parliament. France or its opponents were again the choice. Charles's own principles and his financial need made France the preferred alternative, and still another subsidy treaty was concluded in March 1681.

When the new Parliament assembled in October 1680, it joined the press wars by ordering its resolutions to be published daily as the *Votes*. A second exclusion bill that not only denied James the succession but also threatened him with the charge of high treason if he returned to England was only defeated in the Lords. Frustrated in this effort the Commons proceeded to address the king to remove Halifax for advising the dissolution of the previous Parliament, and then the Commons criticized or impeached ministers and judges who supported the king. The king responded to their precipitate actions by yet another dissolution in January.

The Third Exclusion Parliament. One last time the king tried to come to terms with Parliament. The location was changed to Oxford where the staunchly Tory and conservative church-dominated atmosphere would encourage a more tractable attitude than the Whig mobs of London and Westminster. At the same time the king made careful military preparations to protect his person and the capital. Five troops of the Royal Horse Guards were stationed along the Oxford road to escort the royal party. The garrison in London, the center of Whig support and organization, was doubled to prevent trouble in the king's absence. The parties were now experienced in election battles, and Shaftesbury employed all his energy and experience to secure control of the new lower House. He succeeded all too well. Meeting on March 21, 1681, the Commons devoted the first week to dredging up the old hostilities and platforms. Though Charles had indicated beforehand and in his opening speech a willingness to make major concessions to guarantee that the government would remain in Protestant hands during the reign of his brother, the Commons dismissed his proposals. Even the offer of a regency by the prince and princess of Orange, and after them the Princess Anne, would not satisfy them. Shaftesbury made a public offer to Charles to name Monmouth as his successor, which the king summarily refused. When the Commons rejected all compromise, Charles dissolved the Parliament on March 28. It would not meet again in his lifetime.

The Attempt to Establish Despotism in England

The Last Years of Charles II. Determined to rule without Parliament and to ensure his brother's succession, Charles was equally determined to bring all elements of government under his control. Diplomats who favored the French alliance were employed in the major English posts abroad. A scrutiny of the lists of justices of the peace was followed by a remodelling of local governments throughout the country to obtain Tory officers and, in the event a Parliament had to be called, a more sympathetic membership. The chief weapons of the crown, however, were directed against the Whig leaders. The Rye House Plot, revealed in June 1682, was hardly more credible than the Popish Plot, but the Court was able to exploit it with something like the same impact. Two radical Whigs, William Russell and Algernon Sidney, were executed as an example to the others. Shaftesbury was hounded into exile, his party broken. The process of calling in the borough charters was accelerated after London failed to win a stay, and with it the bastions of Whig power in local government were eliminated. When Charles died on February 6, 1685, his authoritarian policy had substantially strengthened his successor's hand.

The Accession of James II. James II (1685–1688) was fifty-two years old, an advanced age in the seventeenth century, when he became king. Increasing age had intensified his essential rigidity of thinking. Intolerant of Charles's vices, though he had often shared them, he demonstrated a firmness and a sense of moral rectitude that in other individuals would have been admired. But wedded to these were a devotion tò Roman Catholicism and a disdain for the hard-won and still vulnerable constitutional guarantees protecting the liberty of the subject and the inviolability of property. The new king immediately summoned a Parliament to meet in May. The Parliament that met was the most tractable since 1661, the consequence of the careful remodelling of the corporations under Charles II and Sunderland's assiduity in managing the elections. It confirmed James for life in the taxes he had already begun collecting. Responding to the king's assertions that he required additional income to satisfy the debts of his brother and the obligations of the services, they voted additional duties which gave him a combined income estimated at £1,900,000, almost double that awarded Charles in 1660.

In the midst of the Parliament's deliberations two invasions were mounted to unseat James, one by the duke of Monmouth in the southwest and another by the earl of Argyle in Scotland. Both invasions were poorly managed by their leaders, and the disciplined response of the king's troops put a quick end to them. Though able to outmaneuver the ill-trained militia, Monmouth was defeated at Sedgemoor on July 6, where the young

James II. By Sir Peter Lely *(The National Portrait Gallery, London)*.

John Churchill demonstrated his prowess for the first time with an English army. The manner in which the rebels were treated by the king and his minions was cruel and heartless. In England, Lord Chief Justice George Jeffreys dealt so harshly and punitively with those unlucky enough to be charged with complicity, whether innocent or not, that his court sessions have gone down in history as the "Bloody Assizes."

When Parliament reassembled in November the king used the failure of the militia in the recent crisis as a basis for requesting still more funds in order to support a standing army—a permanent, professional, active military force. The Parliament, stirred by a few old hands, demonstrated once again its unpredictability and resourcefulness by outspoken debates. Several members questioned the use to which the army might be put and warned that the king's introduction of Catholic officers made inadvisable this strengthening which the king sought. The Lords were even more independent and forthright than the Commons in their distrust of royal policies. The king, notoriously sensitive to criticism, prorogued the Parliament even before it concluded action on a bill to provide him with yet another £700,000, which it would undoubtedly have granted. Dissolved in 1687, it never met again during his reign.

James lost no time in placing Roman Catholics in positions of trust and importance in the army, in the ministry, and in the church. From a few thousand men and officers in 1685 James increased the army to 13,000 in 1686 and to more than 53,000 in 1688. Accompanying the introduction of Roman Catholics into the army, a deliberate policy was introduced to isolate the army from society, to improve its discipline, and to make it totally subservient to the crown; it became an unquestioning force to impose royal policy. The king came dangerously close to his goal of creating a professional military force. One consequence of this policy was the transformation of the government of Ireland. With the expansion of the army there was a complementary neglect of the militia, a force less amenable to royal will. The law courts were an early target, and James removed four of the judges in the spring of 1686 when they refused to recognize his right to dispense with the test and penal acts. When the king placed Roman Catholics in benefices in the church, the attorney and solicitor generals quickly found themselves out of office when they refused to issue the necessary warrants. In July 1686 James created a panel of ecclesiastical commissioners to act in his name as supreme governor of the church in all its concerns. Though not a court—it was not granted the power to impose fines and penalties and its jurisdiction did not extend to laymen—the unconscious parallel to the twice-proscribed early Stuart Court of High Commission was indeed ominous. Exercising its visitatorial authority, the panel first suspended Bishop Compton of London for refusing to remove a preacher who had offended the king. It then intervened in the affairs of the universities, removing the vice-chancellor of Cambridge from his office as well as removing him from his headship of a college for refusing to admit a Benedictine monk to the degree of master of arts. Oxford was even more abused when the king replaced the fellows of Magdalen College with Roman Catholics and then capped this audacity by placing one of his favorite priests in the presidency. James's threats to disturb the quiet possession of property were even more evident in the inquisitorial nature of his administration in Scotland. There opponents were hunted out, tortured, tried, and sentenced to heavy fines, transportation (shipment to the colonies), or death.

Determined not only to restore the Catholics to an active if not predominant role in public life but also to guarantee this restoration after his own reign, James decided in the summer of 1687 to summon another Parliament. Its charge would be to give legislative confirmation to a second Declaration of Indulgence which he intended to issue in 1688. His first Declaration, issued in April 1687, had been grudgingly accepted in England and in an earlier version promulgated in Scotland. Now a committee directed by Sunderland sent out a questionnaire in October 1687 to the lord lieutenants with instructions to obtain replies from their deputies, the sheriffs, and the justices of their counties. There were three questions. Will you, if returned to Parliament, vote for the repeal of the penal laws and the test? Will you support candidates who are in favor of such a measure? Will you live neighborly and friendly with those of a contrary religion? An unexpectedly large number of lieutenants resigned rather than carry out the instructions. Many loyal Tories who had demonstrated extraordinary tolerance in their acceptance of the king's arbitrary actions were turned into active opponents by these measures.

The second Declaration of Indulgence issued on April 27, 1688, was one of the two immediate causes of the Revolution of 1688. James ordered it to be read from every pulpit for the next two Sundays. Many faithful clergy refused, and the primate himself, William Sancroft, archbishop of Canterbury, together with six of his fellow ecclesiastics, petitioned the king not to insist upon his order. The king was outraged by this show of resistance and was determined to set an example by prosecuting the offenders, not by a summons to the High Commission but rather by a trial for seditious libel in the Court of the King's Bench. The trial which began on June 29 was one of the most famous and critical in English history. The judges abandoned their neutral role and risked the king's displeasure (two were subsequently removed) by supporting the defendants. The jury acquitted the defendants who were triumphantly escorted out of the court and back to Lambeth Palace amid great public displays of attention and joy. Even before the trial started the die had already been cast for a rebellion when Queen Mary of Modena gave birth to a son on June 10. With the prospect of a Catholic succession even the most loyal Anglicans now realized that the threat to the liberties of the church could allow for no further delay. The means of their deliverance was at hand: the Prince of Orange.

William of Orange and Revolution. Since assuming the leadership of the Dutch Republic in 1672, William had been watching the conduct of his royal uncles with the closest interest and concern. In the aftermath of the Popish Plot and even before, his small nation had become a refuge for both Scottish and English opponents of the royal brothers. His tacit support of the Monmouth and Argyle invasions in 1685 did not further the cause of family harmony. On every suitable ceremonial occasion he had sent emissaries to James mainly to conduct reconnaissance and to test the loyalty and strength of his English friends. Moreover, William had finally succeeded in constructing an imposing new coalition of European states against France, and he wanted to be sure of English support or neutrality. Most important, the birth of a son to James in 1688 meant that William's wife Mary was no longer the heir to the English throne. William sent a minister to congratulate his uncle on the birth of a male heir, but the minister's real mission was to secure an invitation for William to come to England. He fulfilled his instructions. On June 30, Edward Russell, cousin to William Russell who was one of the Whig martyrs of 1682, made his way over to Holland with a document signed by himself and six other prominent leaders: Bishop Compton, Danby, three other peers, Devonshire, Shrewsbury, and Lumley, and Henry Sidney, brother of the other martyr, Sidney. William was invited to come to England with his troops to save the English constitution and the Protestant religion.

Meanwhile James, who was urged on by the aged Sancroft and other moderate advisors, began to take tardy steps to regain the support of his countrymen. Early in October he abolished the ecclesiastical commission. He then restored the old charters to London and to the other corporations which had been forced to give them up. Unlike his royal predecessor, James could not be brought to renounce his Declarations of Indulgence, so that his good faith was still suspect, and he refused to summon a Parliament at this time. Moreover, when he attempted to restore the natural leaders of local government to their posts, he found that the majority were unwilling to serve on his terms. This left the government in the hands of men who had been repudiated by their compatriots; the government was without the means to support the king in his troubles.

The imminence of William's descent was known to all, but the intended landing place was a well-guarded secret. James relied on his fleet under the Protestant Dartmouth to prevent a landing, but the fleet proved a broken reed. Dartmouth's own loyalty is doubtful, and the fleet had been subjected to a constant stream of propaganda to support Prince William rather than King James. Whether due to the accident of the winds or to deliberate inaction, Dartmouth's fleet allowed William to land unopposed at Torbay on November 5. Announcing his mission to preserve the liberties and religion of England, William slowly moved toward London, gathering supporters along the way. The king summoned a new Parliament for January and sent commissioners to meet with the prince. But the successive desertions of his nephew, Viscount Cornbury, of John, Lord Churchill, who was his most trusted general and long-time advisor, of his son-in-law, Prince George of Denmark, and then of his Protestant daughter Anne, escorted by Bishop Compton, reduced the king to a state of total despair and helplessness. Having previously arranged for the passage of his son and wife to France, he embarked for France on the night of December 11. Caught by the tide, his ship was boarded by suspicious fishermen who forced the king to return to shore. James was returned to London briefly, but his presence was now only an embarrassment and an unwelcome bar to a speedy settlement. He was allowed to slip away again on December 23, never to return to England. The time for decision was now at hand.

Suggestions for Further Reading

For the later Stuarts the best modern survey is J. R. Jones, *Country and Court: England, 1658–1714* (1978). The fullest treatment is to be found in David Ogg's rich and reflective *England in the Reign of Charles II* (2nd edition, 2 vols., 1956) and *England in the Reigns of James II and William III* (1955). Thomas B. Macaulay, *History of England from the Accession of James the Second* (best edition, ed. C. H. Firth, 6 vols., 1913) is still valuable. Standard biographies include Andrew Browning, *Danby* (3 vols., 1944–1951); K. D. H. Haley, *Shaftesbury* (1968) and his essay *Charles II* (1966); J. P. Kenyon, *Sunderland* (1958); H. C. Foxcroft, *Halifax* (1946); John Miller, *James II: A Study in Kingship* (1978); and Maurice Cranston, *Locke* (1957). For studies of particular topics one may consult Keith G. Feiling, *The Tory Party, 1640–1714* (1924), J. R. Jones, *The First Whigs* (1961), Max Beloff, *Public Order and Popular Disturbances, 1660–1714* (1938), Godfrey Davies, *Essays on the Later Stuarts* (1958), Peter Fraser, *The Intelligence of the Secretaries of State and their Monopoly of Licensed News* (1956), Clayton Roberts, *The Growth of Responsible Government in Stuart England* (1966), and J. P. Kenyon, *The Popish Plot* (1972). J. R. Jones, *The Revolution of 1688* (1972) is the best analysis of that celebrated event. Betty Kemp, *King and Commons, 1660–1832* (1957) is a lucid explanation of the shift in political power.

Charles Wilson, *England's Apprenticeship, 1603–1763* (1965) is a stimulating economic history. C. D. Chandaman has provided a basic piece of historical revision in his *English Public Revenue, 1660–1688* (1975). Also important is Stephen Baxter, *The Development of the Treasury, 1660–1702* (1957). Other works of value are Lawrence Harper, *The English Navigation Laws* (1939), Louis Cullen, *Anglo-Irish Trade, 1660–1800* (1968), Phyllis Lachs, *The Diplomatic Service of Charles II and James II* (1964) and John Childs, *The Army of Charles II* (1976) and *The Army, James II and the Glorious Revolution* (1980). For the church and the Dissenters see Norman Sykes, *From Sheldon to Secker, 1660–1768* (1959), I. M. Green, *The Reestablishment of the Church of England, 1660–1663* (1977), G. R. Cragg, *Puritanism in the Period of the Great Persecution* (1957), and Douglas Lacey, *Dissent and Parliamentary Politics in England, 1661–1689* (1969).

Two classic diaries give an insight into contemporary life: *Samuel Pepys* (ed. R. Latham and W. Matthews, 11 vols., 1970–1978) and *John Evelyn* (ed. Esmond deBeer, 6 vols., 1955). For London see N. G. Brett-James, *The Growth of Stuart London* (1935), W. G. Bell, *The Great Plague in London in 1665* (1951) and *The Great Fire of London in 1666* (1951), and T. F. Reddaway, *The Rebuilding of London after the Great Fire* (1940). Gladys Scott Thomson, *Life in a Noble Household* (1937) and *The Russells in Bloomsbury, 1669–1771* (1940), David Owen, *English Philanthropy, 1660–1960* (1964), and Joan Parkes, *Travel in England in the Seventeenth Century* (1925) provide many insights into English society. Margery Purver, *The Royal Society* (1967), Richard S. Westfall, *Science and Religion in Seventeenth-Century England* (1958), Ray Frantz, *The English Traveller and the Movement of Ideas, 1660–1732* (1967), and David G. James, *The Life of Reason: Hobbes, Locke, Bolingbroke* (1949) are useful introductions to intellectual and scientific developments. A key figure may be studied in Richard S. Westfall, *Never at Rest. A Biography of Isaac Newton* (1980).

9

Revolution and Succession

1689–1714

The Revolution of 1688, the "Glorious Revolution," is one of the great landmarks in English history, yet it was no more a revolution than previous accessions except for the manner of James's going. The Revolution was inspired and controlled by the aristocracy and landed gentry to preserve the constitution in its traditional state, so the Revolution settlement itself was conservative and limited in character. There is a European dimension to the Revolution that cannot be disregarded. It could not have occurred without William and his army; William could not afford to let England remain in the French camp. Furthermore, William III (1689–1702) was by any standard the most effective and most active chief executive of any Stuart sovereign. Finally, the legacy that he left in terms of England's new-found prestige and importance in Europe and the commitments he made for continued participation in the coalition against Louis XIV and the succession of the Electress Sophia of Hanover and her heirs all transformed the status and character of England and its dependencies.

The Revolution of 1688

But as important as these considerations are for an explanation of *how* the Revolution occurred, we must not lose sight of the fact that the reasons *why* it occurred were wholly domestic and internal. William's new subjects, preoccupied with domestic matters, were loath to heed the European situation or to accept England's critical role in it. Part of the disillusionment and ultimately the opposition of the Tories to William was the consequence of their realization of William's true motives and interests. The other part of their disillusionment came with the recognition that he was as forceful and domineering as any of his predecessors. The control that

William III. Miniature by Sir Godfrey Kneller *(Victoria & Albert Museum)*.

this forbidding, cold foreigner soon obtained over the agencies of English government and the commitments he made of English men and English gold to European causes revived the traditional hostilities of the aristocracy and gentry to autocratic monarchs. This was the fate of William's ambition and reputation.

The Settlement of the Crown. The question of William's promotion to the kingship of England was never much in doubt, but the matter of securing the Revolution and his rule was far less certain. On the collapse of James's government the peers in and about London had met and had taken the government into their hands. Although the country was remarkably quiet, rioting in London and the burning of the chapels and homes of prominent Catholics required speedy action to preserve public order. The lords were soon joined by the surviving members of the Parliaments of Charles II. The assembled leaders requested the prince to assume the civil administration as he had already assumed control over the remnants of the military forces of the crown. A convention summoned by the prince met on January 22, 1689. This body divided essentially on the basis of attitudes toward the succession. Most Tories favored a regency to preserve a semblance of constitutionality and to honor their oaths to James as anointed sovereign. Only the most conservative element favored James's return under carefully controlled limitations. The Whigs were more united in their determination to assert the principles of parliamentary sovereignty by acknowledging a break in the hereditary succession. Most men recognized, albeit reluctantly, that English security was dependent on William's exercise of the executive authority. The question of the legal basis for this exercise was resolved by Mary's refusal to act as queen regnant and by William's equally positive assertion that he would not remain in England unless all executive authority was awarded to him for life. The activities of James II's supporters in the other two kingdoms cut short the discussion of constitutional safeguards in the convention, but before the crown was offered to William and Mary (with all authority vested in William) a Declaration of Rights was passed and was accepted by the new sovereigns; this was subsequently enacted into law to embody the essence of the Revolution.

The Declaration fundamentally changed the character of English kingship. The monarch was subordinated to the common law, the suspending and dispensing powers of the crown were severely restricted, prerogative courts were declared illegal, and the king was prohibited from levying taxes without parliamentary consent. A Whig document it passed because the Tories supported it to embarrass William and hopefully to create a climate for a regency or rule by Mary alone. The result of their compliance was to enshrine in the constitution what for them was repugnant, a victorious Whig ideology. For the first year and even longer the fate of the Revolution was in doubt. William had only limited financial resources of his own, and they were exhausted by the expedition. Although he requested the same revenues that James II had, he was granted the customs for life but the excise for only four years. These and other revenues were not sufficient to supply the extraordinary requirements of a nation at war.

The Revolution in Scotland and Ireland. Preoccupied with the situations in England and in Ireland, the new king gave Scotland little attention, and consequently that kingdom worked out its own destiny with little interference. The Jacobites, as James's supporters were called, were made up of the Episcopalians in the Scottish Lowlands and the Roman Catholics in the Highlands and were thus more active and stronger in the northern kingdom than in England. William was only able to send part of the Scottish regiments in the Dutch service to Edinburgh to buttress his supporters. Before they arrived, a convention had met, and the crown was offered to William and his consort on April 11. Yet even as the convention sat, Edinburgh castle was in the hands of Jacobites, and forces were raised in behalf of James in Stirling. Fortunately the rebels obtained no reinforcements from abroad. By the end of the summer all the Jacobite troops had capitulated. Because the new government was little beholden to William it was also independent of his influence. The Scots were determined to remove the shackles that James had used to restrain them. The crown-controlled Committee of the Articles that dominated the Scottish Parliament was abolished, and the episcopal government of the church, a useful instrument for insuring royal control, was dismantled. Scotland now embarked on a collision course with England that was only deflected by the passage of a parliamentary union in 1707.

Ireland was the more immediate problem. Lord Lieutenant Tyrconnel, a Roman Catholic, was one of the most able and determined of James's supporters. He and his coreligionists planned to use this opportunity to secure full control of their own country for themselves. James II came to Ireland in March 1689 planning to use a loyal Ireland as a base for the conquest of England and Scotland. The Irish nationalists refused to submit to his plans, and so James soon found himself in the midst of a war to drive the English and Protestants out of Ireland, a war he pursued with ferocity and determination. With funds provided by the new Parliament, William sailed for Ireland in June 1690. The critical stage of the campaign was soon over. At the River Boyne, William routed James's forces on the last day of the month. The mopping-up took another year, but William's attention was now directed to the continent.

The Nine Years' War and the Partition Treaties. The Nine Years' War, King William's War, the War of the League of Augsburg—it is known by all three names—had broken out in the fall of 1688 when Louis XIV laid siege to Phillipsburg and the Dutch took possession of towns on the lower Rhine belonging to the archbishop of Cologne. William had wasted no time in bringing his new kingdom into the war. Even before James II had left London for France, William had given orders to the English navy to attack French ships. The Nine Years' War is not one of the great European conflicts if measured in terms of notable battles or of major territorial transfers through the treaty which closed it. For England, the war served as a training session. The most seasoned officers in James's army were the Roman Catholics, and the remaining cadre of English officers and men were mainly raw, unseasoned troops. This fact, coupled with their dubious loyalty, caused William to employ foreign officers—Dutch, Germans, and Huguenots—in the commands. It was this apprenticeship that permitted the army to perform so well in the next war.

William personally commanded his armies in Europe from 1691 to the end of the war. He was not a great general, but he excelled in terms of organization, discipline, and care for his troops. The major sieges, with one exception, were won by the French. In part this was because the king was given inadequate financial support by the Parliament, except in 1690 and 1694. The French were always amazed at William's ability to regroup his forces after a defeat and to return to the field of battle more determined and stronger than ever. It was this war of attrition that eventually persuaded Louis XIV to agree to a peace. By the treaty of Ryswick that brought the war to an end in 1697, the French king was forced to recognize William as king of England, thus recognizing the Protestant succession, a major war aim of the English.

William III, King and Diplomat

War Finance—The Bank of England. The extraordinary cost of maintaining both a large army overseas and an expanded navy wrought a revolution in English public finance. The changes that took place in William's reign in this sphere are among the most important consequences of the Revolution of 1688. After a year's delay Parliament granted William the customs for only short terms. A portion of these were reserved for the support of the king's household and the ordinary functions of government, a new system to be known as the Civil List. The king's recurring need for funds during the war required that Parliament be called into session each year. Because of the need for funds to maintain the army and to pay off debts, the regular meeting of Parliament was guaranteed. Determined this time to exercise greater control over royal finances, Parliament now resorted to the expedient of appropriating funds for specific uses, and an accounting was required each year. The vast sums of money required resulted in new taxes, notably the land tax, a temporary expedient that became the basis for governmental income until it was transmuted by Pitt at the end of the eighteenth century. Because of this tax, landowners paid a greater proportion of taxes than at any other time in the eighteenth century. Other taxes were proposed, notably a general excise (a sales tax), but that was found to be intolerable politically, though the excise was extended on specific items.

The most important impact of the war was the new system developed to raise the enormous sums of money required. Formerly the king had to raise loans on the security of his name alone. Now Parliament, assured of its existence through the system of annual appropriations, itself undertook to guarantee the loans that were required to finance the war. With this kind of security the crown was able to secure funds much more readily and at much lower interest rates. The parliamentary guarantee of the king's credit was the basis for the new system of a national debt, a land-mark in public finance. A body of trained civil servants was created to continue to carry the system throughout the violent alternation of party administrations which characterized the quarter century that followed the Revolution. The traditional sources of credit used by the crown proved inadequate to the huge demands placed upon them during the war. To compensate for this deficiency the Bank of England was created, a joint-stock, limited liability corporation authorized by act of Parliament in 1694. With seasoned officials at the Treasury—the veteran Lord Godolphin, the Secretary Henry Guy, and the brilliant young chancellor of the exchequer, Charles Montagu—working in collaboration with the predominantly Whig financiers who composed the Bank's board of directors, England was able to produce the funds needed to sustain her and her allies in the struggle with France. The capture of Namur in 1695 can be directly attributed to the success of the new banking establishment.

The Parties and the Cabinet. William's success in securing his three king-doms, in restoring the strength and credit of the English army and navy, and in fighting Louis XIV to a standstill was not matched in his dealings with the parties and parliament. To begin with, the qualified support for his invasion and succession inclined many politicians to reinsure themselves with the exiled James in case of a Stuart restoration. William's refusal to give his confidence to any of his English ministers and his obvious partiality for his Dutch and other foreign aides created jealousy and resentment. William never really understood or accepted the party structure in England. His first ministries included representatives of all the major party groups as he endeavored to secure broad support for his program while keeping out of the clutches of one particular faction. Initially, he found the Tories most sympathetic to his views on government and the role of monarchy. In the early years of the reign the Whigs' desire to limit the power of the crown was ample reason to keep that party from dominating the ministry. But the setbacks in the land campaign in 1692 convinced the Tories that further expenditures on the army were wasted. William was forced to choose between fighting a war in Flanders with Whig support or pursuing the "blue water policy"—the reliance on the navy and not the army—favored by the Tories. He chose the former. By the end of 1693 the Whigs were in the ascendancy. Their promotion was advocated by Sunderland, who had emerged as the king's political broker or "manager," a practice necessitated by the rise of parties.

One of the most important constitutional innovations of the post-Revolution period was the Cabinet. The Privy Council had declined in authority as the Stuart kings expanded its membership to suit the vanity of the many courtiers who pressed to be included. Its work consequently fell into the hands of standing committees, of which the most important was the committee on foreign affairs. Managed by the senior secretary of state, it had developed into the principal advisory body of the crown. William III preferred the departmental style of government where he met separately with each minister. Circumstances dictated otherwise. When he went to Ireland in 1690 he left Mary as regent and instructed her to consult a committee of nine privy councillors who were given the designation of Cabinet Council. Continuing to meet during the king's absences, the Cabinet also met with the king during the winter of 1691 to 1692, though less frequently. William's attempt to replace it in 1694 with a smaller, less formal body failed. There were regular meetings in the winter of 1694 to 1695, and the members acted as lords justices for William after Mary's death when he was on the continent. The continuous history of the Cabinet, an informal body unknown to the law, dates from this time.

The Succession in Spain and England. Throughout his reign William III was preoccupied with the problem of the succession to the throne in both Spain and England. Louis XIV showed his concern for his own reasons. The Treaty of Ryswick was concluded in part so both monarchs could turn their attention to the disposition of the Spanish Empire upon the imminent death of the long-suffering Carlos II. Louis and the Austrian emperor, Leopold I, were each sons and husbands of Spanish princesses. The brides of the French kings in each case were senior but had renounced their claims to the Spanish throne both for themselves and their heirs. The other European powers did not want the crown of Spain to go either to the Bourbons or to the Habsburgs. Louis and William finally agreed that the throne would go to Leopold's grandson by his first wife, the son of the elector of Bavaria. The first partition treaty, concluded in 1699, provided for this settlement, but even as the treaty was being signed the young prince died. Louis and William, both anxious to avoid a major war over Spain, reopened their negotiations. A second partition treaty signed early in 1700 assigned the bulk of the Spanish inheritance to Archduke Charles, Leopold's second son by his third wife.

The death of another young prince, Princess Anne's only surviving child, the duke of Gloucester, meant that the Protestant succession in England was now in jeopardy. William had long favored vesting the succession in the Electress Sophia of Hanover, granddaughter of James I, and Sophia's heirs. But to do so required the assent of Parliament, and a majority of country members had been elected in 1698, many of whom were hostile to the king's continental interests and concerns. The Tory Parliament delivered a series of attacks on the ageing king, sending home his Dutch guards and taking back the large grants of Irish land he had made to his favorites. The king seriously considered abdication. But though his health was failing his will remained strong and his ambition constant. These qualities were put to their greatest test at the end of 1700 when Carlos II died. He bequeathed his empire to the younger grandson of Louis XIV, Philip, duke of Anjou, and Louis accepted the inheritance in the name of Philip. A new English Parliament elected in the beginning of 1701 was slightly more Whiggish in composition, and it confirmed the succession of the crown to the Electress Sophia, though the Commons included a number of limitations upon the crown which reflected their dislike of William's foreign advisors.

The Legacy of William III. Though the Dutch were cowed into accepting Philip V's accession in Spain, England was not. The Tories found their public stock falling as a result of their vindictive measures, so to restore confidence and regain the king's favor they passed a resolution asking him to take steps to curb the exorbitant power of France. The king responded promptly, appointing John Churchill, earl of Marlborough, who was the principal advisor to the Princess Anne, as his agent to negotiate a new alliance with the Dutch and the emperor. Fortunately for William, Louis XIV now entered into measures guaranteed to provoke English hostility. He sent French troops into the Spanish Netherlands to shut off English commerce to the continent and sent other contingents into Milan and its dependencies, thus enraging the Austrian emperor who claimed that territory for his family. Finally, Louis acknowledged the young son of James II as king of England when the old monarch died in exile in September 1701. Armed with a new grand alliance among England, the Dutch Republic, and the Austrian emperor, William returned to England in the fall of 1701, dissolved the Parliament, and began to transfer power once again to the Whigs, the party dedicated to support his continental policies. Though the election returns gave neither faction a real majority, he had the satisfaction of knowing that England would honor its commitments. The king died on March 8, 1702, after a fall from his horse. William died respected but unloved. His adopted country had been well schooled in the arts of war, diplomacy, and government but had not undertaken its tutelage willingly. Now, however, the benefits of William's rule were to be seen, and his successor was able to enjoy the fruits of his labors.

The Early Years of Anne's Reign

The Accession of Queen Anne. The new queen (1702–1714) was hardly a prepossessing figure for the newly emerging power of England. Although Anne was only thirty-five years old, the toll of seventeen pregnancies, chronic ill health, and the gout had already made her old before her time

Queen Anne. An engraving, c. 1750 *(Kenneth Spencer Research Library)*.

Married to William II

and rendered her a semi-invalid. After the death of her sister, Mary, and her father, James II, she could be accepted as the rightful and legal heir to the throne. A true daughter of the church, her devotion to her people and her country enabled her to draw upon a reserve of affection and loyalty that united at least for a time most of the influential elements in society behind her government.

Anne was a woman who was wholehearted in her loyalties once they were fixed. She immediately turned over her affairs to her most trusted advisors and friends, a triumvirate remarkable in English history. Sarah, Countess of Marlborough, had been Anne's constant companion and closest friend for a score of years. She was given control of the queen's entourage and access to her person by the grant of the offices of Mistress of the Robes, Groom of the Stole, and Keeper of the Privy Purse. Her husband, Marlborough, was named captain-general of the English army in Flanders and ambassador to the Dutch Republic, with command of the armies of the maritime powers in the Low Countries. The final member of this close-knit circle was another lifelong friend, Sidney, Lord Godolphin. While Marlborough took over the principal direction of foreign affairs and the conduct of the war, Godolphin acted as prime minister at home, with sole responsibility for the Treasury and supervision of the executive. He was also the liaison between the ministry, the queen, and Parliament. If Marlborough as general and diplomat was the architect of England's greatness abroad, it was Godolphin as prime minister who made Marlborough's successes possible by the firm support he provided from home.

The queen's predilection and the long associations with Marlborough and Godolphin meant that the ministry was initially composed almost entirely of Tories. No eighteenth-century ministry ever lost an election, and the new Parliament that was returned in the summer of 1702 followed the traditional pattern by containing a Tory majority. Although possessing the complete backing of the queen, Marlborough and Godolphin had to share power at first with the principal Tory leaders, Nottingham and Rochester, who returned to office respectively as secretary of state and lord lieutenant of Ireland. Both favored the now traditional Tory blue water policy which ran counter to the Williamite policies adopted by Marlborough.

The War of the Spanish Succession—The First Phase. When England entered the war in 1702, campaigns were conducted by the French on three fronts: in Italy, on the Rhine, and in the Spanish Netherlands against the maritime powers. Spain was dynastically linked to France. The Grand Alliance—England, the Netherlands and the Habsburg domains, Austria and Hungary—had only a few German princes in league with them initially. In 1703 Bavaria and Cologne joined France while Savoy and Portugal joined the Grand Alliance. As a condition to enter the alliance, Portugal insisted that the maritime powers open another front in Spain and endeavor to place the Habsburg candidate on the throne. Savoy brought some reinforcements to the Austrians in Italy, but the defection of Bavaria and Cologne laid the Rhineland and southern Germany open to French occupation and made an advance on Vienna a practical reality.

Marlborough had already shown superior tactical ability and generalship in the campaign of 1702. Contrary to the prevailing traditions of the time, which favored long and essentially static campaigns devoted mainly to sieges, he preferred to seek out the enemy's army in the field and destroy it, believing thereby that the fortresses would be cut off from resupply and would fall into his hands. The Dutch, whose political representatives at the field headquarters had to give their consent before their troops could be employed, regarded the army as a defensive weapon, as all that stood between them and a French invasion, and so they were loath to risk it in battle. Determined not to return to the field in 1704 unless he was given greater authority, Marlborough persuaded the Dutch to let him take part of the troops for a daring march up the Rhine to save the Empire. At the Danube, Marlborough joined the two imperial commanders, Prince Eugene of Savoy and Prince Lewis of Baden, and they laid waste to much of upper Bavaria. Marlborough and Eugene dispatched Lewis, a general of questionable loyalty, and, thus freed of his conservative influence, they deliberately provoked a battle with the Franco-Bavarian army. In one of the decisive battles of European history, they defeated the flower of the French army at the little village of Blenheim on the Danube. The victory saved the Empire from French control and provided Godolphin with the means to fight off the attacks of the parties at home.

The Revolution Church Settlement and Occasional Conformity. After the Revolution of 1688 it was expected that the Dissenters would be rewarded with a relaxation of the laws which were designed to suppress them as a consequence of their refusal to cooperate with James II against the Anglicans. William III, a Calvinist, was fully committed to religious toleration and was even prepared to go further and remodel the church so that it would be acceptable to Presbyterians if not most of the Dissenters. He was frustrated in his efforts because of the means he used to try to force the Tories to consent. They in turn were opposed to concessions, motivated not only by conscience but also by a desire to protect an Anglican monopoly of political offices. A compromise measure, the Toleration Act, was passed, though its terms were hardly very generous. It was the refusal of the crown to implement the more punitive measures still in force that really gave the Dissenters a measure of peace. Public office, both in the central government and at the local level, was restricted to communicants of the Church of England. Many Dissenters, however, would take communion in the established church once a year to qualify themselves for office and then return to their chapels. The high church party, synonymous with the Tories, was outraged at this behavior. After the dismissal of Rochester in 1703 and Nottingham and his colleagues from the ministry in 1704, the Tories seized upon the issue of occasional conformity to try and break the ministry. Two previous bills designed to eradicate this practice had been defeated in the Lords in 1702 and 1703. Now the Tories in the Commoms moved to add the provision to a money bill in late 1704, intending to force its acceptance on both the Lords (who had earlier given up the right to alter money bills) and the queen. The motion to tack the provision onto a bill was defeated but only after a most desperate effort by both sides to garner the necessary votes. The man principally responsible for its defeat was the speaker and new secretary of state, Robert Harley.

Robert Harley versus the Whigs. Robert Harley was one of the most interesting, important, and yet enigmatic statesmen of the early eighteenth century. Born into a Dissenting family, he became the leader of the church

The Battle of Blenheim, 1704. An engraving, c. 1735 *(Kenneth Spencer Research Library)*.

party or Tories after starting his political career in Parliament as a country Whig. Elected speaker in 1701 and again in 1702, he proved to be one of the most successful managers of the Commons in English history. Godolphin and Marlborough came to rely on him heavily; by 1704 the three jointly managed affairs. Harley was persuaded to take high office as a secretary of state, though he retained the speakership until the dissolution of the Parliament in 1705. A man of the middle, he was suspicious of the extremists of either party. When Godolphin made an opening to the Whigs in late 1704 to save his majority, Harley was opposed and resisted all efforts to increase the Whig presence in the ministry. In December 1706 the earl of Sunderland, Marlborough's son-in-law and one of the Whig junto or ruling clique of that party, was made secretary of state. Harley was unwilling to accept Sunderland as a colleague and now began to undermine Godolphin. In February 1708 he advised the queen to remove Godolphin and to remodel the ministry. Marlborough refused to support this move and without his prestige Harley could not hope to achieve his aims, so he voluntarily resigned. Just when the Cabinet crisis reached its height, word reached London that the "Old Pretender," Prince James Edward, the son born to James II in 1688, was now on the sea with a French fleet, determined to invade Britain and regain the crown. His landing was thwarted, but the threat and excitement tended to reinforce the Whigs. When parliamentary elections were held later in the spring, the Whigs were returned with a solid majority.

The Later Years of Queen Anne's Reign

The War of the Spanish Succession—The Second Phase. After an abortive advance along the Moselle, Marlborough returned to the battlefield in Flanders in 1705 for another year of frustration. Only the successful landing of an allied fleet with Archduke Charles in Catalonia and the capture of Barcelona provided any relief from the dismal dispatches from the other theaters. The year 1706 proved to be the annus mirabilis of the war. Marlborough was able to engage the French in battle at Ramillies, south of Brussels, and the resulting victory put most of Flanders into his hands. The English and their allies won a number of important engagements early in the war, but soon the war situation began to deteriorate for the allies. In 1707 the Austrians concluded a truce with the French in Italy, which freed French troops for employment elsewhere. A severe defeat in Spain lost that country for the allies, though the war dragged on there for another four years. Marlborough cleared the rest of the Netherlands, but the Battle of Malplaquet in 1709 was so bloody that it sickened the civilians on both sides. The turn of events at home made Marlborough afraid to risk another major engagement. In spite of two further impressive successes against the French, Marlborough was dismissed from all his offices at the end of 1711, defeated not as a general but as Marlborough the diplomat and the husband.

During the first part of the war Marlborough had practically singlehandedly held the Grand Alliance together. For several successive years he set out on exhausting trips around the capitals of Europe after the campaign to persuade the allied princes to contribute troops to the armies in the several theaters. In 1706 when the French first sued for peace, he was firm in his refusal to accept anything less than unconditional terms. When peace negotiations were undertaken in earnest in 1709, however, he insisted on a collaborator, the young Viscount Townshend, and Marlborough left the negotiating to him. It was the same in 1710 when the negotiations were again taken up after Louis XIV's rejection of the preliminaries the previous year. Marlborough's increasing caution and refusal to accept responsibility for anything but his own army was the consequence of political changes at home.

The Decline and Fall of the Godolphin Ministry. The duchess of Marlborough is often credited with almost complete control over the queen for the first half of her reign. Yet, in fact, she had lost whatever influence she possessed even before Anne's accession. The duchess, a convert to Whig principles, held views which were unpalatable to the queen. Disagreeing on politics as early as 1702, their relationship became more distant after 1703 when the duchess went into semiseclusion following the death of her only surviving son. Though placed in the queen's bedchamber by her cousin the duchess, the queen's dresser, Abigail Hill, later Mrs. Masham, worked to advance the interests and projects of another relation, Robert Harley. The duchess became increasingly outspoken and strident in forcing her unwanted advice on the queen. The queen turned increasingly to Masham and others, so that by 1710 all communication between the two former friends had ceased. At the end of 1710 the duchess was dismissed from all her offices. This estrangement was an important factor in the fall of Marlborough, Godolphin, and the Whigs.

The Godolphin ministry had fully earned the appreciation of the nation by its impressive accomplishments both at home and abroad. Besides maintaining English naval supremacy, a preeminence dramatized by the scuttling of the French fleet at Toulon in 1707, it had made possible the great victories of Marlborough in Flanders and Germany and had subsidized other allied victories in Italy and Spain. One must add to these accomplishments the taking of Gibraltar in 1704 and Port Mahon in 1708. At home the greatest achievement was the passage of the Act of Union in 1707. Precipitated by the Scottish threat to elect a sovereign other than the one to rule England after Anne's death, the English Parliament in 1705 had moved the queen to appoint commissioners to treat for a union. The Scots were encouraged to participate by the threat of the loss of their privileges in England as subjects of a common sovereign and by the promise of full participation in the lucrative colonial trade. The sixty-two commissioners (thirty-one from each nation) chosen by the queen did their work well. Completing their deliberations in July 1705, they recommended a parliamentary union in which 16 elected Scottish peers would join the House of Lords and 45 Scottish members would be added to the 513 members of the English Commons. After a stormy passage in the Scots Parliament, the recommendations were accepted without qualification, and the union came into being on May 1, 1707.

The increasing and irksome burden of taxation that fell heaviest on the landowners, the jealousy of those excluded from political power, and the growing frustration over the ministry's apparent inability to bring the war to an end, when combined with the estrangement of the queen, eventually brought down Godolphin and his colleagues. The instrument of the change was an unlikely object—an inflammatory, ultraconservative Tory parson. The high church clergy were among the most vociferous and influential opponents of the Godolphin ministry and were a key element in

Others would Swell with Pride, if thus carés'd,
But he bears humble Thoughts within his Breast.

Dr. Henry Sacheverell riding in coach. Detail from set
of playing cards, c. 1710 *(The Bettmann Archive/BBC
Hulton)*.

the strength of the Tories. In order to reduce the clergy to subservience,
one of the most notorious members, Dr. Henry Sacheverell, a fellow of
Magdalen College, Oxford, and a popular preacher in London, was impeached by the Commons before the High Court of Parliament in December 1709. This effort to muzzle the Tory churchman backfired on the
Whigs. The martyr cleric became a symbol of Whig oppression and tyranny. All those dissatisfied with ministerial policies of every kind now used
the parson to demonstrate their true feelings. Emboldened by the reaction
and counseled by Harley, the queen removed her servants one by one so
that by the end of the year Harley and the Tories were in control of the
executive. An election held in September returned an overwhelming Tory
majority.

The End of Anne's Reign. Ignoring Britain's commitments to its allies, Harley opened secret negotiations with the French. By the winter of 1711 to 1712 the preliminaries were sufficiently far advanced that Harley, now raised to the peerage as earl of Oxford, felt confident enough to dismiss Marlborough and to make public the negotiations. The abandonment of Britain's allies on the battlefield aroused powerful protest at home and on the continent, but Oxford, now assisted by his principal colleague and rival for authority, Henry St. John (created Viscount Bolingbroke in 1713), proceeded to confirm his arrangements with Louis XIV in the Treaty of Utrecht. The gains won by England were the most impressive since the Cromwellian wars and were not to be equalled again in the eighteenth century, except by the Treaty of Paris in 1763. In addition to Gibraltar and Minorca, Nova Scotia was ceded to England, marking the beginning to a retreat for the French in North America. The fortifications at Dunkirk were to be razed. Important commercial concessions were granted in Spain and the Spanish Empire, and France recognized the Protestant succession in England. The success of Oxford in turning out the Whigs and in restoring the Tories to power was ultimately his undoing. He found himself the prisoner of the newly dominant party, unable to play them off against the Whigs and thus retain control; the sickly queen began to repent the abandonment of her old friends and advisors. With the queen's health failing, Oxford and Bolingbroke looked to the heir to the crown to shore up their positions. But George, Elector of Hanover, loyal to the imperial cause, could never forgive the ministers who betrayed England's allies in the late war. Oxford and Bolingbroke then sought, independently, to ingratiate themselves with the "Pretender," the son of the late James II. When he refused unequivocally to change his religion for the crown of England they realized his cause was hopeless. Thus when Queen Anne fell mortally ill at the end of July, the Tories were unprepared to manage the succession. The Whigs, on the other hand, were fully prepared to launch a coup if necessary to secure the Protestant succession and had secretly arranged a takeover of the army if this eventuality proved necessary. It was not. When Anne died peacefully on August 1, 1714, George I was proclaimed king without any challenge.

Journalism and Trade: Growth and Change under the Later Stuarts

The Press and the Parties. The fall of the Godolphin ministry, the rapprochement with France, and the renewed attack on the Dissenters by the triumphant Tories, which was shown by the passage of the occasional conformity bill in 1711, all inspired political and press battles in England that exceeded even those of the exclusion controversy in their magnitude and ferocity. The party lines had hardened into a clear Whig-Tory split by the beginning of the reign. The successive replacements and then transformation of the ministry had changed its composition from Tory to Whig and back to Tory. The frequent parliamentary elections—1702, 1705, 1708, 1710, and 1713—were all fought on strict party lines. Though the parties lacked a formal national organization (that did not emerge until the mid-nineteenth century), the continuity of leadership and principles and the presence of some centralized management, both for elections and control of parliamentary sessions, are clear evidence of the existence of party in Anne's reign. These divisions are particularly well exemplified by the press.

With the lapse of the censorship laws in 1695 a steady increase in publications becomes evident. Newspapers and monthlies began to proliferate, and the first daily newspaper, the *Daily Courant*, made its appearance in 1702. In spite of a parliamentary prohibition, accounts of parliamentary debates appeared in annual histories at the turn of the century. The expanded activity of the press in Anne's reign, culminating in the great battles that dominated the last four years, is one of the most important phenomena of modern English history. By 1714 nearly all the features we have come to expect in modern newspapers—the editorial, the news, the advice to the lovelorn, the periodical essay—had all made their appearance. Newspapers began and ended in startling profusion. Press battles, such as those between Defoe's *Review*, Tutchin's *Observator*, and Leslie's *Rehearsal*, were the order of the day. By 1712 between 50,000 and 60,000 copies of newspapers were sold in London each week, in spite of a stamp tax imposed by Parliament to curb the Whig press. Nearly all the most celebrated writers of the day were drawn into the press wars. Joseph Addison, Jonathan Swift, Richard Steele, and Daniel Defoe were only the best known and the most active. A polemical tract could inspire literally dozens of answers. The most successful and influential tracts, such as Swift's *The Conduct of the Allies* (1711), were sold by the tens of thousands of copies and could swing the opinion of the whole country behind a change in policy. The attacks of Tory writers on Marlborough were sufficient to compromise his reputation for many decades.

The general election of 1710 was fought and won in the press as much as it was on the hustings. Even all the means of a powerful ministry were unable to save the French commerce bill in 1713 thanks to the efforts of the opposition. The electorate represented a surprisingly high proportion of the adult male population, although in many boroughs the right to return representatives was vested in a small number of individuals, often under the influence of a local patron. Nevertheless, recent studies of poll books have suggested the presence of a swing vote, beyond the control of borough-mongers and responsive to changing public opinion. The success of the Revolution of 1688 and the preservation of English liberties are no better illustrated than in the vigor of its press and the strength of its political parties.

Mercantilism. England's rise to great power status at the end of the wars against Louis XIV was the consequence of English arms backed by English industry and finance. The exploitation of this new eminence was the province of the merchants. The impact of the wars on England and the other European countries has been hotly debated. The depredations of the French privateers on English merchant shipping were tremendous. Yet the English gained as well as lost, and thousands of French ships were taken as prizes during the same period and incorporated into the English fleet. Though the English merchant marine may have been only marginally larger at the end of the period, and little more than it had been a century ago, the contrast with the situation in France and the Dutch Republic was more important and ultimately was decisive. Prior to 1688 Dutch ships carried much of the bulk cargo required by England. The Dutch navy also suffered at the hands of the French, and the great burden of war expense took its toll on this small nation; it never recovered from the drain of men, ships, and gold. France, though blessed with far greater resources, both human and material, likewise lost out in the competition with England. England emerged from the war unquestionably the strongest in terms of its fleet.

Some share of this economic success must be attributed to the mercantilist system that was developed in the Commonwealth period and reinforced during the Restoration. Given its classic statement in 1664 in Thomas Mun's *Discourse on England's Treasure by Forraign Trade*, mercantilism simply stressed the importance of a favorable balance of trade. If England exported more than she imported the consequence would be a steady flow of specie into the country and increased prosperity. The navigation laws, first passed in 1651 and reenacted 1660 to 1663, restricted the colonial trade and imports generally to English bottoms (ships), thus laying the foundation for the growth of the English merchant marine. As the colonies grew in size and the value of their exports increased, English merchants and the king's tax collectors were the beneficiaries. The colonies, restricted to England as a single trading partner, became a principal market for English goods just as they were an essential source of raw materials. The wars were fought to protect old markets as well as create new ones. When Philip V inherited Spain he excluded English and Dutch shipping from trading with the Spanish colonies—a trade which was regarded as vital to English prosperity. So, too, the Levant and Mediterranean trade was assured by the capture of Minorca and Gibraltar and the scuttling of the French fleet at Toulon in 1707.

The demand in unprecedented quantities for supplies for the services, clothing, sail cloth, armaments, and ships gave a stimulus to industry and larger commercial organizations. The lot of the lower classes, whether urban or rural, was not materially altered. But in general it seems that the trading and mercantile community and landowners benefited as well from the war. The unprecedented demand for money sired the Bank of England, encouraged the union of the old and new East India Companies in 1709, created the South Sea Company, and thus established a pattern of large-scale increases in capital formation. The more effective mobilization of resources made England's advance to great power status possible. This was a legacy of William and Anne.

Foreign Immigration into England

One of the many elements that fired the economic expansion and development that characterized the reigns of William III and Anne was the influx of refugees from the continent. There were two major groups. The second of these was comprised of Germans, largely from the Palatine along the upper Rhine. Driven from their homes by the depredations of the French army during the two wars, they made their way down the Rhine to Amsterdam. From thence many went on to England. William Penn was active in recruiting the Germans for his new colony of Pennsylvania in North America. They were the progenitors of those who came to be called the Pennsylvania Dutch (actually "deutsch" or German). From the sacking of Heidelberg in 1692 down through the first decade of the eighteenth century this migration continued. The severe winter of 1708 to 1709 increased the flow. The Whigs, then in power in England, welcomed the refugees with an eye to settling them in Ireland to reinforce the Protestant population. They were artisans and merchants for the most part, rather than farmers, and the plantation concept failed. But the "poor Palatines," as they were called, continued on to join their predecessors in the New World.

The more important refugee group was the Huguenots. From the time of the revocation of the Edict of Nantes in France by Louis XIV in 1675, there was a steady exodus of Huguenots from that country. Fearful of losing the right to worship as Protestants in their own churches they fled to the security of more hospitable, Protestant countries, notably the Netherlands and England. They were educated, professional people. Many joined the world of letters or the more prosaic field of journalism and became important middlemen in translating continental literature for the

English and in performing a like service for English writings for the continent where English political theorists were widely read. From their mercantile and banking experiences a network of Huguenots developed around the periphery of France, from Switzerland and Savoy in the south of Europe to England, the Netherlands, and Prussia in the north. They became essential in the rapidly expanding system of public credit and the transmittal of funds, critical to the financing of the French wars on both sides. A number of Huguenots came over with William III—generals like the earl of Galway and journalists like Guillaume de Lamberty and Abel Boyer. Huguenot bankers were instrumental in the establishment of the Bank of England. Others brought new trades and skills such as hatmaking, silversmithing, glassblowing, and silk weaving. Architecture, gardening, and furniture and cabinetmaking also were positively impacted. They were an invigorating and valuable new addition to England's resources, and their loss to France was a grave one.

The Growth of the Professions

The innovation, boldness, and expansiveness that marked the post-Revolution period is exemplified by yet another phenomenon—the rise of a new professional class. To be sure, it was not all new. There already existed lawyers, physicians, clergy, and military and naval officers. But in this period they took on a new kind of importance, increased substantially in number, and improved in expertise and training. Furthermore, they were joined by budding new professions: architects, landscape gardeners, musicians, and, above all, civil servants. The lawyers first came to prominence in the long struggle between crown and Parliament that led to the civil wars. The Revolution brought stability and independence to the judiciary. The rise in commercial and political activity, and thus the new prosperity, also meant a rise in litigation. The senior members of the bar, the barristers who alone were permitted to plea before the courts, reaped great profit from their practices. The number of lawyers in the Parliament steadily increased after the Revolution, and that meant greater access to places, capped by lucrative and prestigious posts both in the executive and judicial branches of government. The junior members, the attorneys, found increased demand for their services in the creation and management of great landed estates as well as the inevitable preparation and analysis of documents essential to the conduct of business. In all, the emoluments derived from the legal profession accounted for greater accumulations of wealth for this profession than any other during the period.

The late seventeenth century also saw the emergence of the practice of medicine as a respectable and lucrative profession. The latter character is amply testified to by the sharp rise in the size of fees. In part the improvement in professional status was the consequence of a gradual consolidation of the separate callings of physicians, apothecaries, and surgeons. The first determined the cause of illness and prescribed treatment; the second provided the medicines; the third treated external afflictions. By the mid-eighteenth century the three heretofore distinct classes merged loosely into what were now called "doctors." The loss of control by the College of Physicians over its profession was one factor, as apothecaries and then surgeons gained new respectability and the right to prescribe and administer treatment to the sick. Professional training and education was another factor. The graduates of Oxford and Cambridge licensed by the College were augmented by doctors trained in the provinces through apprenticeship and licensed by the bishops. In the late seventeenth century they were augmented by foreign-trained physicians, notably of Leyden. After the turn of the century the Leyden contingent was composed increasingly of Englishmen. In the Georgian period it was the Scottish universities that took the lead, both in the number and quality of doctors produced. The third factor, allied to the second, was the grudging acceptance of the surgeon-barbers into the profession. The two great French wars were the impetus; the surgeons gained substantially in numbers, expertise, and prestige through the heavy demand for their services in the army and navy. After the wars they returned to civilian life and found a ready market for their talents. The surgeons, too, increased the rigor and standards of their training through the development of Surgeons' Hall in London as a training center. Moreover, all branches of the profession of medicine benefited from the proliferation of hospitals that came in the eighteenth century. These provided training sites and the opportunity to learn and test skills.

The origins of the civil service can be traced back to the clerics who provided the secretariat or scriptorium for the crown from before the Conquest, then to the expanded, more specialized bureaucrats assembled by the early Tudors to administer their new taxes and to manage the secularization of church lands. The next great development came with the assumption by the crown of the collection and management of taxes beginning with the tenure of Danby as lord treasurer. It was completed by the great expansion of business generated by the French wars, wars which also greatly expanded the need for a large number of army and naval officers. By the death of Queen Anne one can see the presence of a proficient, indispensable body of civil servants in the treasury, at the court, in the offices of the secretaries of state, and in the army and navy and their support services. Their expertise and experience were so essential to the operation of the government that they were able to remain in office, secure in their tenure, in spite of the frequent alterations of ministers in the major

Hampton Court Palace. The south front designed by Sir Christopher Wren *(The Bettmann Archive/BBC Hulton)*.

posts and parties in control of Parliament in the two decades after the Revolution. If Samuel Pepys was the Restoration prototype of civil servant, the later officials who typified the new and enduring model included: the apolitical William Lowndes, employed at the treasury from 1679 and secretary from 1695 to 1724; Josiah Burchett, who commenced his career at the navy office as a clerk to Pepys in 1680 and eventually succeeded to the office of secretary in 1695, a post he held until his death in 1742; and Sir Christopher Wren, who began as a surveyor-general to Charles II's works in 1661, succeeded to the charge of all royal works in 1670, and remained in office until his removal in 1718 (at the age of 86). Nor should one forget that Sir Isaac Newton, in addition to his more celebrated accomplishments, was first warden and then master of the mint from 1696 until his death in 1727.

Suggestions for Further Reading

In addition to Jones, Ogg, and Macaulay mentioned in the readings suggested in the previous chapter, one may consult Lois G. Schwoerer, *The Declaration of*

Rights, 1689 (1981), Henry Horwitz, *Parliament, Policy and Politics in the Reign of William III* (1977), and George M. Trevelyan, *England under Queen Anne* (3 vols., 1932–1934). *The Marlborough-Godolphin Correspondence* (ed. H. L. Snyder, 3 vols., 1975) is a basic source. Geoffrey Holmes has contributed a number of important studies to the period, including his *Britain after the Glorious Revolution* (1969), *British Politics in the Age of Anne* (1967), and *The Trial of Doctor Sacheverell* (1973). For foreign policy consult Ragnhild Hatton and J. S. Bromley, eds., *William III and Louis XIV: Essays 1680–1720 By and For Mark A. Thomson* (1968); Hatton and M. S. Anderson, eds., *Studies in Diplomatic History* (1970); D. B. Horn, *The British Diplomatic Service, 1689–1789* (1961); Douglas Coombs, *The Conduct of the Dutch; British Opinion and the Dutch Alliance during the War of the Spanish Succession* (1958); Roderick Geikie and Isabel A. Montgomery, *The Dutch Barrier, 1705–1719* (1930); and A. David Francis, *The First Peninsular War* (1975) and *The Methuens and Portugal* (1966). Major biographies include Stephen Baxter, *William III* (1966); Edward Gregg, *Queen Anne* (1980); Horwitz, *Revolution Politics* (1968); Winston S. Churchill, *Marlborough, His Life and Times* (2 vols., 1947); and David Chandler, *Marlborough as Military Commander* (1973). Bishop Burnet's *History of His Own Time* (edited by M. Routh, 6 vols., 1833) is a rich contemporary source. The country is graphically described in Zacharias Conrad von Uffenbach, *London in 1710* (1934); *The Journeys of Celia Fiennes* (edited by C. Morris, 1949); and Daniel Defoe, *Tour thro' the whole island of Great Britain* (best edition, ed. G. D. H. Cole, 2 vols., 1927).

Other useful studies include Angus McInnes, *Robert Harley* (1970); H. T. Dickinson, *Bolingbroke* (1970); and William Speck, *Tory and Whig, the Struggle in the Constituencies* (1970). G. V. Bennett, *The Tory Crisis in Church and State, 1688–1730* (1975) and Norman Sykes, *Church and State in England in the Eighteenth Century* (1934) are fundamental to an understanding of the dilemma of the Anglican church. Scotland and the union are well treated in T. C. Smout, *Scottish Trade on the Eve of the Union* (1963); P. Hume Brown, *The Legislative Union of England and Scotland* (1914); and P. W. J. Riley, *The English Ministers and Scotland, 1707–1727* (1964). For Ireland consult J. G. Simms, *Jacobite Ireland* (1969); J. C. Beckett, *Protestant Dissent in Ireland, 1687–1780* (1948); and F. G. James, *Ireland in the Empire, 1688–1770* (1973). Specialized studies of value are Ian K. Steele, *Politics of Colonial Policy, 1696–1720* (1968); Lois G. Schwoerer, *"No standing armies"* (1974); John Ehrman, *The Navy in the War of William III* (1953); J. H. Owen, *War at Sea under Queen Anne* (1938); and G. H. Jones, *The Mainstream of Jacobitism* (1954). P. M. G. Dickson, *The Financial Revolution in England, A Study in the Development of Public Credit, 1688–1756* (1967) is a work of major importance.

10

Augustan England

1714–1754

The half century ushered in by the Hanoverian succession has traditionally been regarded as a somnolent one in England. The motto of its most famous politician, Sir Robert Walpole, who dominated the government for virtually half the period, was said to be *quieta no movere*, "let sleeping dogs lie." It has been regarded as a stretch of time singularly devoid of interest and excitement when compared with the reigns of William III and Anne, which preceded it, or the reign of George III, highlighted by the American Revolution, the French Revolution, and the Napoleonic Wars. Its sovereigns, the first two Georges, are regarded as dullards. Yet, as we shall see, it was a far more dynamic and interesting period than the stereotype suggests. Culturally, diplomatically, politically, the gains of the previous quarter century were preserved and extended, and the foundation was laid for the great expansion of England simplistically styled the Industrial Revolution, which embraces the whole of the reign of George III.

The New King

George I (1714–1727), a homely, stout, fifty-three-year-old German, was hardly the popular image of a king. Though king of Great Britain, he also remained ruler of Hanover; his continuing interest in the latter and apparent lack of concern for the former upset the British, who habitually resented foreigners and particularly feared their influence on British foreign policy. George was set in his ways, accustomed to complete mastery over his territories and subjects, and unfamiliar with Parliament and parties. George I dined in public once or twice a week but initially could discourse only with persons who spoke German or French. He preferred to spend his days quietly in his chamber, giving audiences to his ministers.

He took his supper with one or both grotesque German ladies in his household; the tall, spindly, middle-aged duchess of Kendal, George's morganatic wife, and the fat, rouge-cheeked countess of Darlington, George's half sister, who were respectively but irreverently known as The Maypole and The Elephant. His entourage also included two German advisors and a Huguenot secretary who managed the king's Hanoverian concerns. The most popular members of the family were the prince and princess of Wales who spoke excellent English and were as affable as the king was reserved.

George I proved to be the most able of the Hanoverian sovereigns of Great Britain. Trained for the army in his youth he was an experienced officer and field commander. He had successfully managed his electorate for more than a quarter of a century and was an equally shrewd and intelligent governor of his new domains. Though he may have deferred to his ministers in domestic policy, his knowledge of foreign affairs was unrivaled in England and the equal to any of his fellow European sovereigns. In following up the Treaty of Utrecht, in making a rapprochement with France, in negotiating the Quadruple Alliance, and in working to end the Great Northern War this proved an invaluable asset to England. Finally, he was not only a warm and benevolent paterfamilias but also a cultured European gentleman, an early patron of Handel. He was eminently worthy to occupy his new throne.

The Settling of the Hanoverian Dynasty

Even before George's arrival in England there was a shuffling of political leaders in readiness for the new order. Bolingbroke was sacked, and the Whigs repossessed all of the great offices of state. The greatest authority was granted to the two secretaries of state—Charles, Viscount Townshend, and James Stanhope. Townshend took the lead in domestic affairs, especially after his brother-in-law, Robert Walpole, succeeded Halifax at the Treasury in 1716; Stanhope was dominant in foreign affairs.

The Elections of 1715. The new ministers sought to consolidate their political gains by calling for the election of a new Parliament. Proclaiming their loyalty to the Protestant succession and denouncing the Treaty of Utrecht, the Whigs triumphed and were returned with a solid majority of 150 seats. When the Whig leaders proceeded to impeach the former ministers, Bolingbroke, who thought his life was in danger, fled to France and entered the service of James Edward Stuart, the Pretender to the British throne. The vindictiveness of the Whigs, the influence of the foreigners in the king's entourage, and the affront offered even to those Tories who had

George I. An engraving, c. 1750 *(Kenneth Spencer Research Library)*.

supported the Hanoverian succession, coupled with the fears of the church, turned popular opinion to the Tories. At the height of this reaction the earl of Mar slipped away from court to raise the standard of James Edward Stuart in Scotland on September 6, 1715.

The Jacobite Uprising of 1715. The Jacobite uprising of 1715 was a badly conceived, poorly concerted movement. The Pretender's only hope for success depended on the support of France. The aged French king, Louis XIV, died, however, on September 1, and the duke of Orleans, who became regent for the minor successor, Louis XV, adopted a policy of watchful neutrality—disastrous to the Jacobite cause—because the regent himself was a candidate for the French throne and support from Britain might spell the difference in his ambitions. The Jacobites, nevertheless, pressed on; they had the initial advantage because, as poorly prepared as they were, the government had even fewer forces at its command. The Jacobites' initial successes were short-lived, however. After an indecisive battle at Sheriffmuir, Mar and the Jacobite forces no longer had the means to undertake another engagement. The belated arrival of the Pretender in January, without reinforcements or supplies, was anticlimactic. He returned to France, leaving his unsuccessful supporters to be hunted down in Scotland.

The Diplomacy of Stanhope. The Jacobite rebellion only reinforced Britain's pressing need for allies. James Stanhope moved immediately to rebuild the old alliances. As both envoy and general in Spain in the late war, Stanhope had formed an intimate acquaintance with Archduke Charles, who had succeeded his brother as emperor in 1711. This friendship now became the hinge of Britain's foreign policy. In June 1715 Stanhope made a personal trip to Vienna to persuade Emperor Charles to permit the Dutch to maintain fortresses in the Netherlands as a barrier against French aggression. Following a treaty of alliance with the Dutch in February 1716, Britain signed the Treaty of Westminster in June 1716 by which Austria guaranteed the Protestant succession. Stanhope's most remarkable achievement was an alliance with France, so recently England's enemy. The resulting treaty, which provided for a guarantee of the succession of the British and French thrones, was concluded in November and approved by the Dutch in February 1717.

The haste with which the treaty was drafted reflected George I's concern for his Hanoverian dominions. In the Baltic area the Great Northern War (1700–1721), which had begun as a conflict between Sweden and Denmark, had now grown to include Russia, Poland, and Prussia. Though Sweden was the aggressor, her defeat by Russia in 1709 put her permanently on the defensive. Prussia, Denmark, Hanover, and Russia all hoped to secure additions to their territories at Sweden's expense. George I employed the British fleet in the contest, first against Sweden and then later against Russia after the death of Sweden's King Charles XII in 1718. With Stanhope's connivance, British forces were used to secure advantages for Hanover, an action that had adverse political repercussions in England. Finally, Britain regained its favorable commercial position with Spain in a treaty negotiated late in 1715.

The Whig Split and the Triumph of Walpole. The sweep of offices the Whigs enjoyed on George I's accession had still not satisfied all of them. Sunderland was disgruntled as he watched Townshend and Stanhope take charge of offices to which he had pretensions. Townshend and Walpole came to resent the influence of the Hanoverian advisors with whom Stanhope was still influential. This division was exacerbated by the ill feeling that existed between the king and his heir. When George determined to visit Hanover in 1716, Sunderland used the pretext of a visit to Aix for health reasons as an excuse to follow the king to the continent. There he heightened the suspicions of the king and Stanhope that Townshend and Walpole were in league with the prince of Wales. On his return the king dismissed Townshend and Walpole, and others resigned in sympathy. When the king banished the prince and his wife from his presence soon after, the opposition established itself around the prince.

Because the Septennial Act (1716) extended the maximum life of a Parliament from three to seven years, it would have seemed that the Whig ministers could be assured of lengthy control of government, yet the split in the Whig party made the survival of the ministry tenuous. The dissident Whigs capitalized on popular fears to charge that English interests were subordinated to Hanoverian goals, and after several legislative defeats Stanhope and Sunderland realized they would have to join forces with Townshend, Walpole, and other dissident Whigs. The reunion of all Whig factions was capped by a reconciliation of the king and the prince and a banishment of the Hanoverian advisors in 1720. The consolidation was timely, for the ministry suddenly found itself faced with a grave crisis.

The late wars had saddled England with a substantial public debt. The South Sea Company, organized by Robert Harley in 1711, managed part of the debt in return for the exclusive trading rights in Spain and the Spanish empire, which had been confirmed at the peace table. Offering lower interest rates, the South Sea Company took over the remaining part of the debt not earlier funded by the chartered companies, making a series of stock offerings to finance this undertaking. To create a demand for the stock issues, it paid handsome dividends out of capital—a fraudulent practice—and tendered bribes that may have reached the king himself. The shares rose from £130 to £1,050 in the space of a few months, but as the South Sea bubble burst suddenly, along with other speculative enterprises in the summer of 1720, financial ruin was brought to countless individuals. The crown itself was in danger because the court was deeply implicated, and only the masterly defense by Walpole in the Commons' investigation saved it. Stanhope, who was free from personal guilt, died suddenly during the investigation. As the price of his acquittal, Sunderland had to surrender his office of first lord of the Treasury to Walpole in 1721. Sunderland's unexpected death a year later left the field clear to Walpole.

The Age of Walpole

Walpole's Political System. In 1721 Walpole was in a position to assert his political leadership. He had emerged from the South Sea Company crisis

Sir Robert Walpole and the Speaker of the House of Commons. A contemporary engraving *(BBC Hulton Picture Library)*.

without direct taint of corruption, the champion of the investors, and defender of stability. More, however, was needed. He made himself indispensable to the king by shielding George and his friends from the investigation. Sir Robert made himself master of the king's ministers by driving independent or contrary ones out of office. In 1724, for example, he forced Carteret, Stanhope's successor as secretary and Sunderland's polit-

George II. An engraving, c. 1750 *(Kenneth Spencer Research Library)*.

ical heir, to resign and then removed him from Westminster by making him lord lieutenant of Ireland. When the exiled Bolingbroke engineered his return by a sizeable gift to the duchess of Kendal, Walpole was able to exclude him from his seat in the House of Lords. In the Commons and in the constituencies, Walpole built up his support by a pacific policy abroad and low taxes at home. Even the death of George I in 1727 did little to shake Walpole's grasp because he could count on the support of Queen Caroline, the brilliant consort of George II (1727–1760). She and Walpole concerted plans for the government, and it was her job to persuade the king to give his assent. It was not easy for her to subordinate herself to her intellectual inferior, but she handled the part well. Her early death in 1737 was a serious blow to Walpole.

Walpole created a new model for a prime minister. He developed patronage to a fine art. By the judicious use of positions in the gift of the crown, whether in the military services, the church, the civil administration, or the court, he built a stable majority in the Commons. Secret service funds were generously disbursed to control votes in the Parliament and win elections in the constituencies. In the House of Lords the votes of the sixteen representative peers of Scotland, who were chosen from a government-selected list, and of the bishops ensured him a working majority. Walpole's success rested on a combination of royal support, on his ability in finance, on his skill in forging parliamentary majorities out of the many interests and factions, and, above all, on his remaining in the House of Commons and resisting the temptation of a peerage and his consequent removal to the upper house.

The Opposition and the Excise Crisis. Walpole utilized a solid core of the court's supporters for votes in the Commons, but without the votes of independent, landed members of Parliament, he could not forge majorities. Power was concentrated in the hands of the landed gentry and the aristocracy—great landowners, many of whom controlled one or more seats in Parliament and whose collective interest exceeded that of the government. It was important to the landowners that the taxes remain low, even though taxes levied on land were the most reliable sources from which to raise funds. The other principal sources of government revenue were customs duties and the excise, a tax levied on selected commodities— a tax best controlled and least abused and the most easily enforced. In 1733, Walpole proposed the introduction of an excise tax on wine and tobacco coupled with a lowering of the land tax to one shilling in the pound (a rate of 5 percent). He expected that it would be warmly welcomed by the landed gentry. For once Walpole misstepped. Dr. Samuel Johnson reflected a widespread attitude when he described it as "a hateful tax levied upon commodities, and adjudged not by the common judges of property, but wretches hired by those to whom excise is paid." Initially attacked by the merchants and shopkeepers, who saw that its efficient collection would affect their commerce in contrast to the easily evaded customs, the issue was quickly seized on by the opposition and ballooned into an issue out of all proportion. Walpole was forced to abandon his scheme, in the greatest defeat of his career. The power of the press is emphatically illustrated by its role in the uproar.

The main credit for the defeat of the excise went to the resurgent parliamentary opposition. The Tories, discredited and disorganized, had been out of office since 1714. By 1716 they began to join forces with disaffected Whigs. William Pulteney, once considered Walpole's protégé, had not been returned to office in 1720 when the Whig split was healed; soon after he began to concert measures with the Tories. The weeding out of Sunderland's followers and any other Whig who showed signs of independence gradually swelled the ranks of the opposition over the next decade.

Europe in the Eighteenth Century

In 1727, under the inspiration of Bolingbroke, they launched *The Crafts-man*, which became their principal organ, and developed a program that gave them an aura of respectability. The opposition writers adopted the Roman orator Cato of Utica as their model with which to castigate the ministry. The court Whigs responded in kind, though with less brilliance, settling on Cicero as the one who epitomized their virtues. The basis of the opposition program was the perennial issues of the danger of a standing army and the undue influence of the crown in Parliament by the presence of placemen—political appointees to seats in Parliament—and pensioners. By espousing these sacrosanct themes, the very essence of Whig ideology, Bolingbroke could appeal to the patriotism of the voters. Brilliant writers such as Henry Fielding and Alexander Pope lent their pens. John Gay's *The Beggar's Opera* was only the most successful of numerous stage works sponsored by the opposition. They bore down so heavily upon the embattled Walpole that he introduced censorship for all theatrical productions—a code of censorship which survives even to the present and has been extended to motion pictures.

British Diplomacy under Townshend and Walpole. Walpole's policy of stability at home required peace abroad. Townshend, who had returned to the ministry as lord president in 1720, set out to forge a series of alliances that would forward both Britain's and Hanover's interests. By allying Britain with France and Prussia, he sought a coalition designed at once to build a German coalition against Austria and to prevent Russian domination in the Baltic. By providing new security for Hanover, Townshend was in fact following much the same practice as his predecessor. Spain not only rebuffed Townshend's offer of an alliance but also concluded a treaty with Austria, giving more to the Habsburgs than it received. Britain then became more belligerent toward Spain, and British trade with the Spanish colonies deteriorated, reflecting how Spain had ignored its obligations under the Treaty of Utrecht. Walpole became increasingly concerned both for the effect of this hostility on trade and hence revenue. In 1730 Townshend was forced to resign, and Walpole took over the direction of foreign affairs.

Walpole concluded a treaty with Spain that restored the rights of British merchants to trade in Spanish America, promising in return Britain's support for Spanish dynastic ambitions in Italy. In spite of Walpole's show of goodwill, Spain had never really reconciled its basic hostility to England and its resentment of England's predominance in her colonial trade. The grievances over the loss of Gibraltar, border disputes in America, and the regulation of trading concessions were problem enough. But the real bone of contention was the lucrative and flourishing contraband trade carried on by English merchants in Spanish America. The Spanish authorities retaliated by seizing British ships and torturing British seamen. The clamor of the public to obtain satisfaction for Spanish atrocities committed against British seamen, the agitation of the merchants for protection, and opposition charges that British honor was at stake finally pushed Walpole into the War of Jenkins' Ear with Spain in 1739.

The Fall of Walpole. In 1740 Emperor Charles VI of Austria died, and his daughter and heir, Maria Theresa, succeeded to her father's possessions. Frederick II ("the Great") of Prussia used this opportunity to snatch the province of Silesia from the young queen, thereby launching the War of the Austrian Succession (1740–1748). France, Spain, and Bavaria could not resist the opportunity to join Frederick in his dismemberment of the Habsburg domains, with Bavaria wresting the imperial title away from Maria Theresa's husband. Walpole had no choice but to come to the aid of the beleaguered Austria. The spectre of a hostile Prussia to the east of Hanover and threatening French armies on the southwest only added to Walpole's predicament. When George II, as elector of Hanover, concluded a convention of neutrality to save Hanover (1741) and cast his ballot as elector for the French candidate for emperor, Charles Albert of Bavaria, Walpole's humiliation was complete. The aged (sixty-six) prime minister was finally forced to retire in 1742 after an embarrassing reversal in the parliamentary elections of 1742 and a series of defeats in the session that followed. By accepting a peerage he escaped the wrath of the opposition in the Commons.

The Pelhams

The New Ministry. When Walpole had sacked Carteret in 1724 he had replaced him with the inoffensive but industrious duke of Newcastle, a man who had inherited great wealth and unparalleled electoral influence. Newcastle's political apprenticeship began when Walpole made him Carteret's successor as secretary of state in 1724. He learned well from Walpole the management of patronage; in time he engrossed control over crown appointments in the church, the colonies, and many other places. Because he and his astute brother but junior colleague, Henry Pelham, had favored the Spanish war and acquiesced in George II's capitulation in Germany, Newcastle did not share his patron's fall. William Pulteney, long Walpole's bête noire and now finally restored to office, was nominally the ministry's leader, but he committed himself to political oblivion by taking a peerage as earl of Bath. Moreover, he allowed the Treasury to go to Spencer Compton, who also took refuge in the Lords, as earl of Wilmington. Carteret, who returned to a secretaryship, proved the one really vigorous new addition to the cabinet, where his skill in languages and intimate knowledge of European affairs made him a royal favorite.

The War of the Austrian Succession and the "'45." So far as England was concerned, the middle years of the War of the Austrian Succession were as much a scene of battle at home as they were abroad. Indeed Britain was hardly more successful in Europe than the king was in promoting Carteret. The war largely favored France and its ally, Prussia. England and her allies, especially Austria which was important for supporting Hanoverian claims, did win a victory at Dettingen in 1743 on which occasion George II personally took command of the troops. Though the French were the opponents, war was not officially opened between the two countries until 1744. The confusion in motives and goals that characterized this conflict is indicated by the several sets of overlapping belligerencies. They included not only the war with Spain but a separate and parallel conflict in the colonies between France and England known as King George's War. Though the real focus of competition lay in the Americas and beyond, the ostensible struggle was in Europe. The critical role of Hanover obscured the real interests of both parties. Carteret, with his preoccupation with European affairs and his disdain for the business of parliamentary management, was forced to give way completely to the Pelhams in 1745, two years after Henry Pelham had been promoted to first lord of the Treasury upon the death of Wilmington.

The newly united ministry faced its most immediate challenge from still another source. Yet another (and final) Jacobite invasion was launched in 1745 by France to neutralize Britain. Led by the Pretender's son, "Bonnie" Prince Charlie, the uprising began in Scotland in July, and by September Edinburgh had fallen. But Charles misstepped and pressed into England where his local support soon evaporated. He advanced as far as Derby in December but was then forced by his officers to retreat to Scotland. The king's favorite son, the duke of Cumberland, aggressively pursued him, and the superior resources of the English government soon told. In April Cumberland routed Charles's army, then he mercilessly hunted down the survivors, earning the epithet "the Butcher."

At about the same time, the king precipitated a crisis in London. In February 1746, the king informed Pelham of his decision to reinstate Carteret, now the earl of Granville, and the earl of Bath, to head the ministry. Pelham responded by resigning, and the entire cabinet resigned en bloc in sympathy. The king was undone because Granville had not heeded Walpole's lesson and had not built a base of support in Parliament. Unable to draft a new Cabinet, he and the king were forced to surrender; Pelham and his colleagues returned on their own terms. Seeking to pull the teeth of the opposition, Pelham constructed his ministry on a "broad bottom"

The First British Empire

basis, including as many factions as possible to gain the widest possible support. The only major group left out of the ministry was the faction around the heir to the throne, the prince of Wales.

The Conclusion of the War. Pelham's first responsibility was to bring the war to an end. While England had been putting down an internal revolt, the war had gone badly for the country and its allies on the continent. The French capitalized on early victories and occupied Brussels and the Austrian Netherlands, while Britain's allies, Austria and Sardinia, suffered defeat in southern Europe. Only the death of the Emperor Charles VII (Charles Albert of Bavaria) early in 1745 offered any hope for a negotiated settlement by opening the imperial throne once more to a Habsburg candidate, Maria Theresa's husband, Francis of Lorraine. Indeed English success in arms existed only in one theater, but one prophetically important— North America. The heavy continental military obligations in the wars against Louis XIV and again in the present war had prevented the commitment of substantial forces against Spain in the western hemisphere. Although early disappointments led the British to abandon campaigns in the West Indies, the war went well in the north when, in June 1745, a small expedition of New England colonists supported by British naval forces captured Louisburg, the great French fortress on Cape Breton Island, which was the key to control of the St. Lawrence River, the gateway to French Canada. The capture of Louisburg was more of an embarrassment than an asset; it retarded peace efforts, for the French could not rest until it was retaken. The British public on the other hand was so overjoyed at this victory that its retention became obligatory. In 1747 Pelham suddenly called parliamentary elections to take advantage of his newly found support. The solid majority he won made it possible for him to risk an unpopular peace settlement. French successes in the Low Countries and elsewhere gave little prospect of military success in Europe, though the naval victories of Anson and Hawke in the New World did reassert British supremacy on the seas. France, too, saw reason to negotiate a peace, not least because of a serious famine and a major fiscal crisis in 1747. The peace of Aix-la-Chapelle that followed in 1748 was essentially a recognition of the exhaustion of the belligerents. British ambitions for Canada were temporarily abandoned as Louisburg was returned to France. Both countries recognized that the surcease was not permanent.

Pelham and Leicester House. For the remaining years of his ministry, Pelham strove to maintain his political strength in Parliament while restoring stability to the king's finances and prosperity to the economy. His first effort was to reduce taxes. He did so by drastically reducing the size of the fleet and the army. In the political sphere, the coalition of parties Pelham had put together proved effective. The main threat to his regime came from the men who gathered around the king's son, Frederick, the prince of Wales and heir apparent to the throne; they met at the prince's residence, Leicester House. Ever since he had broken with his father, George II, in 1736, the prince of Wales had sought to maintain an independent political base. In spite of financial difficulties, he had built up a formidable circle of advisors in the late years of the Walpole regime. Pelham had weaned most of them back in building his coalition ministry in 1746. But the advancing age of the king (who was sixty-three in 1746) made Frederick's succession inevitable, and Pelham patiently negotiated through intermediaries to prepare himself for this eventuality. The unexpected death of the prince in 1751 dramatically altered the situation. A resumption of Walpolean tranquillity characterized England in the early 1750s until another early death—that of Henry Pelham in March 1754—brought it all to an end. George II was perhaps the most sincere and realistic mourner when he commented, "I shall have no more peace."

The Intellectual and Religious Milieu of the Hanoverians

The Age of Reason. At the same time that Britain's stature in European affairs grew, the country participated fully in another European phenomenon, the Enlightenment. As the old religious controversies subsided and the ideological contests abated, a new tone and confident spirit characterized the publications of the major British literary figures. The periodical essay spawned by Joseph Addison and Richard Steele in the *Spectator* (1711) had countless imitators well into the middle of the century when it inspired Samuel Johnson's *Rambler* (1750) and *Idler* (1758). Elegant, devastating satire reached its peak in the mock epics of Alexander Pope. Elegiac pastoral verse glorified the serenity and natural beauty of the countryside, a retreat from the glamour and artificiality of the city.

History as a guide and means of instruction took on new importance as a subject for laborious tomes and learned essays. It reached its peak in the phenomenally popular six-volume *History of England* (1754–1762) by the eminent Scottish philosopher David Hume, who set a standard not to be challenged for a century to come. Hume also epitomized another aspect of the intellectual life of the Age of Reason. His several philosophical treatises made all knowledge empirical and struck at the very foundation of religion. Seeking to create a moral philosophy that would accomplish for the world of ideas what Newton had accomplished for the world of science, Hume stands at the intellectual watershed of the eighteenth century.

The refined elegance of Pope and Hume were not the only models for eighteenth-century writers. The savage irony of Jonathan Swift in *Gulliver's Travels* (1726) attracted a wide audience as did the more conventional but nonetheless compelling imagination of Daniel Defoe in *Robinson Crusoe* (1719). Skill in expression was not limited to one political faction. The dominant Whig propagandists of the Hanoverian period found their match in the powerful Toryism of the most celebrated literary figure of the mid-eighteenth century, Samuel Johnson.

The new quest for knowledge, the growth of a leisured class, and the general increase in prosperity all resulted in a vast and sustained growth in publishing. Whether practical manuals for farmers or justices of the peace, the newly developed novel aimed at readers of both sexes, books catering to hobbies and diversions of the most heterogeneous kind, or treatises on topics such as economics, raising fish, or guides for the grand tour, the emphasis was on novelty and practicality. The most notable omission was the emphasis on religion that had been so characteristic of the preceding century.

The Church in the Early Hanoverian Period. The vehement efforts of the clergy and the high church party to preserve their monopoly of political offices and representation in Parliament, their unrelenting efforts to inhibit and restrict the Dissenters, their churches and schools, their strenuous support of the Tories, and their equivocal attitude to the Revolution and the Protestant succession all were liabilities for the church with the new regime. Only the Whigs' patent weakness in the Parliament and in the country had prevented them from completing the repeal of the Test and Corporation Acts in 1718 and the reduction of the universities to a place of complete subservience. The opposition of the Anglican archbishop to the proposed statutory repeals condemned him to twenty years of political neglect and isolation. In 1717 Benjamin Hoadly, who had been made a bishop for his services as a political pamphleteer, delivered a famous sermon before the king in which he attacked the very basis of the church's authority by denying its institutional significance and the role of the priest as intermediary between God and worshipper. The furor that resulted both in Convocation and the press gave the crown the excuse to prorogue the Convocation, which was not permitted to meet again until 1855. The hiatus removed the potential vehicle for badly needed church reforms.

The geographical distribution and size of the dioceses were woefully uneven, but the income to support the bishops and their offices was even more unequal. In countless parishes the income was insufficient to maintain a clergyman, and the consequence was that many pulpits lay vacant. Not infrequently the incumbents were pluralists, holding several benefices at once. In 1704 Queen Anne gave back to the church the fee exacted from each cleric as he entered into his benefice, for use by commissioners

to raise the income of the poorest positions. This did something to mitigate the most pressing cases, but the essential inequities remained, especially among the bishops whose annual incomes ranged from a low of
£450 at Bristol to a high of £7,000 at Canterbury. Many of the duties of
the see fell personally on the bishop who was not authorized to employ
deputies or suffragans. The requirement for bishops to attend the House
of Lords kept most of them absent from their dioceses for much of the
year. Some of the bishops, either because of infirmity or neglect, did not
return to their dioceses as often or stay as long as they should have. The
uneven size of the dioceses created exceptional burdens for some bishops.
Lincoln, the largest diocese, had 1,312 parishes—a marked difference
from Carlisle which had only 100. Edmund Gibson, bishop of London
and Walpole's ecclesiastical advisor, proposed a number of schemes to correct the worst abuses and to enable the church to carry out its duties. But
they all foundered either on the Scylla of ministerial indifference or the
Charybdis of lay hostility. Although the civil disabilities of the Dissenters
were not removed until 1828 they managed to participate in the political
process because a series of indemnity acts relieved them of the statutory
penalties. This was the Hanoverian modus vivendi, a compromise that
satisfied few but was tolerable to most.

Wesley and the Methodist Revival. The church had fallen into such a state of
lassitude that it was unable to meet the spiritual needs of the people. Sermons were cold and formal and did little to evoke enthusiasm and religious fervor. The writings of latitudinarian clergymen such as Benjamin
Hoadly, the Deists, and mystical writers such as the nonjuror William Law
did little to reinforce a devotion to the established church. Methodism
arose within the church to fill this void. The founder and leader was John
Wesley. Ordained in the Church of England and a graduate of Oxford, a
member there of a severe, ascetic society, he went with James Oglethorpe,
the founder of Georgia, to that colony in 1735. On the voyage he became
acquainted with the Moravians. On his return to England he was deeply
influenced by an eminent member of that sect, Peter Boehler, and embraced those tenets which became the foundation of Methodism: the doctrine of justification by faith, the belief that every man existed in a state of
damnation until the moment of illumination, and the recognition that
Christ had expiated man's sins. Wesley and the band of followers he attracted from the regular clergy preached the new doctrine with fervor and
success. Their objective was to create Methodist societies as churches
within the church to rekindle religious enthusiasm and commitment
among Anglicans. Denied a hearing from the pulpits of the established
church, the Methodists turned to preaching in fields and any place where
they could gain a hearing. In 1739 they created their own chapels, and in

1741 Wesley instituted lay preachers. Those new missionaries were dedicated to saving souls and found an enthusiastic reception among the lower classes, especially in those places where the established church did not reach. In Wales, for example, the great majority of the population joined their chapels.

Though Wesley did his best to keep the societies within the Anglican tradition, he finally broke with the Anglican church in 1783 by appointing a bishop to supervise the Methodists in America. In 1784 he began ordaining clergy for Scotland. The Methodists offered the hope of salvation to those whose lot was most unfortunate and miserable. They were responsible for a general revival of religious feeling in England, both within the Church of England where Anglicans were revitalized and reinvigorated and outside the established church as well.

Local Government in England

The local government structure in England was and is unique in the western world. Essentially, it was in the hands of the ubiquitous justice of the peace, an unpaid administrator drawn from the local gentry or gentlemen. This office, whose origins go back to the early Middle Ages, began to take shape in the fifteenth century, and in the Tudor period the office became the center of local government. Until the civil wars it was regulated by the lord chancellor, reviewed and instructed by the Privy Council, and disciplined by Star Chamber. When the prerogative jurisdiction was abolished, the justices of the peace became virtually independent. The Privy Council could still issue directives but did so only in emergencies. The judges in the semiannual assizes had a larger role. They heard criminal cases with which the justices could not or chose not to deal, and they also heard appeals from the justices and rendered decisions on disputes about rights to property. In conjunction with the justices they issued orders concerning local administration. But any supervisory authority had lapsed by the eighteenth century.

The justices singly issued licenses for inns and taverns, heard minor civil cases, and performed other local administrative functions. Acting in twos or more they had much greater authority. Furthermore, all justices were automatically appointed to the commissions for the land and window taxes. It was through these commissions and the petty sessions that they wielded their power. Their administrative authority and their ability to affect taxes gave them substantial political influence. Those over whom they held sway were often empowered to vote in parliamentary elections, hence the justices of the peace had a critical if not deciding voice in elections.

The Tower of London. From an engraving, c. 1720 *(Kenneth Spencer Research Library)*.

Because of their political influence it followed that the political parties, as they evolved, tried to control the county bench. Charles II and even more notoriously his brother James II made wholesale replacements on the bench in an effort to insure the return of members of Parliament favorable to their policies. As Whigs and Tories alternated in control of the government after the Revolution it has been widely assumed by historians that the same policy prevailed. Strictly speaking, this is known to be incorrect. The power of appointment rested ostensibly and exclusively with the lord chancellor. Recent examination of the records shows that Lord Somers and Sir Nathan Wright under William III and Wright and Lord Harcourt under Anne did try to pack the bench. They did so by adding new members, not turning out old. The result was that they ran out of appropriate candidates who had the income and position to support their appointment, and men of lesser quality were added. When Lord Cowper returned to the great seal after the Hanoverian succession he realized that the number was unwieldy and began to reduce the size of the county benches, but did so by rooting out Tories. His policy was continued by his successor, Lord Macclesfield, so that by the accession of George II most county benches had Whig majorities.

The reason that a majority of like-minded justices was necessary was the fact that they acted in concert in the quarter sessions. Here and at the assizes the bench as a whole had the power to discipline individual justices and overturn their decisions. Consequently political control demanded the majority to insure that individual justices would not be impeded in their zeal. When Philip Yorke, Lord Hardwicke, began his long (20 years) tenure at the great seal in 1737, he found the Whig domination virtually complete. However, many Tories had made their peace with the government and for some years in the 1740s actually supported and served in a coalition government. It was not deemed proper to disenfranchise good Protestant gentry, so that Tories only gradually began to appear once more on the lists. Though he took nominations from lords lieutenants, members of Parliament, and other individuals of importance, the final decision was his, and the lord chancellor wielded that authority fully. Once appointed, justices were rarely dismissed, except for the period between 1685 and 1725. Secure in their power, conscious of their responsibility, the justices of the peace functioned successfully and well. Whether licensing taverns, supervising road and bridge construction and repair, attending to the poor, assessing taxes, hearing cases, or performing a myriad of local administrative chores, they provided a sound, intelligent, generally knowledgeable, and remarkably vigilant and cooperative local administration for the country. With little supervision by crown or Parliament they reached the peak of their power in the 150 years after the Glorious Revolution. The duties they performed they performed because they wanted to. Those matters that did not interest them or to which they objected were ignored. Such was the nature of local government in England in the eighteenth century.

The Urban Centers in Johnson's England

London and Westminster. The jewel of a revitalized Britain was London. When Samuel Johnson, the great lexicographer and pundit and archetype devotee of London first saw the great metropolis in 1737 he must have found much to impress him. The great city of more than one-half million people, it was ten times larger than Bristol, which was England's second largest city. The eastern-most part was notable for the bustling Pool of London, the inner harbor which was then the main port for commerce. Rising above it stood the Tower of London, imposing in its Norman splendor, a prominent landmark from the river. If Johnson made his way west from the Tower the next object to command his attention was old London Bridge, located opposite the splendid new cathedral of St. Paul's, Wren's masterpiece that dominated the city skyline. The bridge, the only

Old London Bridge. An engraving, c. 1720 *(Kenneth Spencer Research Library)*.

span across the lower Thames until Westminster Bridge was constructed in 1750, had been built over completely. It presented a quaint sight of ramshackle old buildings of varying heights and style, stuck fast together and hanging perilously over the water, with a bustling traffic crowded into the narrow passage remaining between the houses.

Below the bridge, to the east, scores of tenements, warehouses, and wharves crowded the river's edge. Above the bridge there were most impressive structures to behold. The palaces and great houses of the nobility and wealthy on the north bank extended westward to a bend in the Thames where one found Whitehall Palace and the Palace of Westminster. After the bridge, Johnson would have made his way through Stockmarket to St. Paul's churchyard, past the church "already so black with coal-smoke that it has lost half its elegance," then down Ludgate Hill to the Fleet out of the City at Temple Bar. The streets of London were reckoned by a German writer as "the finest in Europe," full of taverns, houses, and shops "where the choicest merchandise from the four quarters of the globe is exposed to the sight of the passers-by [and] a stranger might spend whole days, without ever feeling bored, examining these wonderful goods." This was the part of London Johnson especially loved, where he lived, worked, and drank and passed his hours in memorable conversation. The book-shops and printers and the attendant writers were so numerous in this district that one short passage called Grub Street gave its name to a whole genre and period of the English press. North of the Strand the area was filled with mansions and was especially marked by Covent Garden, the square laid out by Inigo Jones a century earlier and, even in Johnson's time, a market for flowers, fruits, and vegetables.

Passing into Charing Cross Johnson could have seen the Admiralty and the famous Banqueting Hall, which was all that remained of the old Whitehall Palace after it burned in 1698. Ahead lay the Palace of West-minster, seat of the Parliament and law courts—a conglomeration of buildings, chapels, houses, meeting halls, and offices adapted to a multi-plicity of uses over many centuries. The most impressive was Westminster Hall, which dated to the time of William Rufus, but it was so hedged about with small structures that only the upper portion and roof were exposed to view. Even Westminster Abbey and the parish church of St. Margaret were crowded about, though the lofty towers and the exquisite tracery of Henry VII's chapel were a sight to delight the eye.

Life in London. The appearance of the king's principal London residence, St. James's Palace, was not attractive; a squat, drab structure that dated from the time of Henry VIII, it lies about a quarter of a mile northwest of the Abbey, adjacent to Pall Mall. A series of parks to the south and west furnished an attractive prospect and a popular place for relaxation and recreation for the inhabitants who lived nearby. The most impressive house in the park was that of the duke of Buckingham. To the west, at the end of Hyde Park, lay Kensington Palace, acquired by William III in order to escape the damp and fog of the river. Villages and estates generally occupied the land west and north of Westminster, and these areas re-mained predominantly rural into the next century. The streets of the town were of all sorts, some "dirty, narrow, and badly built; others again are wide and straight, bordered with fine houses [and] most of the streets are wonderfully well lighted." The parks were not well lit, and the public that thronged them on Sundays tried to be back in the town before dark to avoid becoming a target for the highwaymen who frequented the lanes, one of whom, at least on one occasion, held up the king at pistol point in his own garden.

Beyond the great houses and royal parks, especially in the city, there was squalor, poverty, and filth. Some of those who flocked to London for

Johnson's London

employment found seasonal work only, serving the needs of the great families when they came into town for the winter season. Much of the year these less fortunate migrants were unemployed and lived by their wits. Robbery and petty thievery were commonplace. Living conditions were wretched; the water was foul taken straight out of the river at the bridge by "a curious machine which turns in either direction, according to the tide, so that it is always in use." The consequence was regular epidemics of cholera and other waterborne diseases until the middle of the nineteenth century. Life expectancy was short. A survey made in 1716 showed that of 1,200 children born in a parish, three-fourths were dead within the year. Parish officials consigned the poor to workhouses where conditions were abominable. In midcentury another survey revealed that of 2,239 children who passed through the workhouse only 168 were alive at the end of five years. The large criminal class and the ever-present press gangs used to provide recruits for the navy and colonists for the Americas made life so dangerous that the young James Watt, who lived in London in 1783, hardly left his house during the entire time of his residence there. Bullbaiting, cockfighting, and public hangings were the favorite entertainments; beer and gin were the standard beverages. Gin was so cheap and unlicensed dramshops were so numerous—by 1736, 6,000 to 7,000 in London alone—that consumption rose to unprecedented heights. The city was in literal danger of extinction as the oppressed lower classes drowned their sorrows and forgot their miseries in alcohol.

Bristol, the Capital of the West. Although no city approached London in size and scope, the increase in population over the century necessarily affected major provincial centers. The city that benefited most from this expansion in the first half of the century was Bristol. It displaced Norwich as the second largest city in England after the turn of the century, with a population of more than 20,000 people. Its status was the result of trade. Bristol was the unofficial capital of the west. It aggrandized the overseas trade at the expense of its neighbors. Its geographical position on the Bristol Channel, dominating the coast, and its function as the gateway to the river and canal network of the Severn and Wye gave it a commanding position. The number of ships leaving Bristol doubled from 1700 to 1750 and doubled again by the 1770s, to more than 1,700 ships a year. Bristol consumed the bulk of the agricultural products produced in the region. It was a major entrepôt for raw materials, many reshipped for London. Local manufacturers—metalworks, soap, glass, sugar refining—accounted for a considerable portion of the trade. Timber from the Baltic, linen from Germany, agricultural products from such diverse places as the Mediterranean, Africa, the West Indies, and North America all were brought to Bristol. The mining and metal industries of Wales that prospered in the eighteenth century were financed and controlled by Bristol merchants. The heavy commerce in turn generated banks and insurance companies, so much so that Bristol was second only to London in the number of underwriters it supported. By the end of the century it began to decline. The American trade, of primary importance, never regained its strength after the Revolution. Liverpool and other western ports gradually took over its position. Its heyday, then, coincided with the expansion of the American colonies and passed with their independence.

The Country

Country Life. The rest of England was rural. Few towns had more than 10,000 people; most towns were much smaller—in reality mere villages and marketplaces. The leading families of provincial towns were professional men and merchants whose scale of living was comfortable rather than ostentatious. Rural (landed) wealth was centered in the aristocracy and gentry whose great country houses rose in stark contrast to the humble, often squalid homes of the rural agricultural laborers and the

Blenheim Palace, constructed for the first Duke of Marlborough *(The Bettmann Archive/BBC Hulton)*.

working poor in the towns. The cottagers who found work were fortunate. Often the only support for a family was that of carding and spinning wool, an employment chiefly reserved for women and children. Until the mid-eighteenth century poor families could eke out a living from the commons, cutting wood, raising geese and perhaps some livestock, taking odd jobs, and poaching. The great series of enclosure acts in the latter century deprived them of these means of subsistence.

The artisan class flourished in the towns. Cabinetmakers, shoemakers, tailors, butchers, cobblers, smiths, and drapers populated the shops. The market towns were specially engaged in serving the local landowners and providing for their amusement and comfort. In the west and the northeast of England the wool trade was their main support. Marked by the absence of paved streets, police, and good water and other amenities, the towns were not improved until the second half of the century. In the smaller towns, the parish was often the unit of government, with the church responsible for what little education the lower and middle classes received. As roads and communications improved and the nation increased in wealth and population, the county centers began to take on some of the attributes of the metropolis. Newspapers were founded, theaters opened, booksellers established, and concert assembly rooms erected for the entertainment of local society. But even to the end of the century the scale of towns remained small, their diversions limited.

The Country House. London always remained the social center without rival, especially during the social season, coinciding with the meeting of Parliament, which extended from late fall to early spring. For the gentry the summer assizes provided the excuse for social interchanges after they had returned to their estates. Apart from London, there remained yet another social center, indeed hundreds of them—the country house of the wealthy. The country house may have reached its apogee in England in the first half of the eighteenth century. That span, the period of the first two Georges, may well contain its finest examples, although fine examples exist from the times before and after. Hardwicke Hall epitomized the great Elizabethan house, as does Hatfield House the Jacobean. Boughton House, rebuilt and extended by the first duke of Montagu in the 1690s, impresses one by its magnificence and its purity, for it remains essentially unaltered from the time it was completed until the present day. Moreover, its mansard roofs and interior designs evoke Versailles and the French chateaux the duke admired while ambassador to Louis XIV in the 1670s. Boughton House foreshadowed the strong French influence on the English baroque style that emerged after the Revolution. But the increasing prosperity of the country in the century after the Glorious Revolution, and the stability that accompanied it, made the great houses flourish. The more frequent travel on the continent, notably the grand tour that was a part of every gentleman's education, provided the models and the inspiration.

In the period leading up to the Hanoverian succession a new distinctive English baroque emerged, dominated by the genius and incredible productivity of Sir Christopher Wren. As Master of the King's Works from 1670 to 1718 Wren made extraordinary contributions in state buildings— the west end of Hampton Court, St. Paul's, and the Royal Hospital at Greenwich. He also trained several generations of architects who served under him. Of these architects, two stand out—John Vanbrugh and Nicholas Hawksmoor. Vanbrugh was the more creative and flamboyant. Regrettably, few of his houses remain essentially as he designed them, but those that do—Blenheim Palace, Castle Howard, and Seaton Deleval—are masterpieces. Moving from the standard blocklike, rectangular model to the French model typified by Vaux-le-Vicomte outside Paris, the model for Versailles, he built great central halls with dual flanking staircases and then extended quadrant corridors from the center block to wings that projected to form a large forecourt. The monumental nature was his alone. Hawksmoor, working in the shadow of Wren and then Vanbrugh, does not have the individual credits, though the splendors of Queen's College, Oxford, ought to be sufficient for any man.

The heavy ornamentation of the exterior of the baroque houses was outdone by greater magnificence within. Each house had a series of great rooms, apartments of state, reserved for display and the rare, extraordinary royal guest or noble of great distinction. The rooms usually constituted the first floor (English style, above the ground floor reserved for services); the second was used for the family. One finds splendid staircases, entrance walls and ceilings painted with mythological scenes, ornate wood carvings and gilded plaster composing the doors, windows, and rails, and great tapestries, woven with gold and silver thread, alternating with large oil paintings to cover the walls. The furniture, covered in needlework or velvet, was as massive as the house. The formal gardens were equally as ornate, as regular, and as splendid.

The Tory glory of the baroque was succeeded after 1714 by the Whig splendor of the Palladian. There was a transitional period, roughly from 1715 to 1730, when a modified Georgian baroque emerged. The grandest house of the period, Cannons, lasted barely thirty years. Worked on by a series of architects, including several baroque authorities, its extravagant scale put it in a class apart. Made possible by the war profiteering of James Brydges, whose wealth won him the noble title of duke of Chandos, its enormous long front gave way to a miniature city whose entertainments and guests included the great Handel. The Whig grandees who dominated the state for the next half century had lofty visions of an England evoking the best attributes of the Greco-Roman world—political, moral, artistic. Reacting against the Tory exponents of the baroque they chose Andrea Palladio of Vicenza as their model and inspiration. His treatise of 1570 was not only a rich source of classical designs but also espoused the classic virtues and harmony that the Augustans wished to emulate. The amateur architect and patron Charles, earl of Burlington, not only sponsored an English edition of Palladio's work, but himself designed a model Palladian villa, Chiswick House in Middlesex, modelled on Palladio's Rotunda at Vicenza. In contrast to the projected wings of the baroque house, the great Palladian house used the wings to enlarge the house itself. The professional architects, led by Colen Campbell and William Kent, lacked the glamor of their amateur colleagues or the ostentation of their baroque predecessors. The interiors of Campbell's Houghton Hall, built for Sir Robert Walpole, the prime minister, or Kent's rooms at Hampton Court, built for George I and George II, hardly match the splendor and color of

The Palladian Bridge, Wilton House, c. 1737 *(The Bettmann Archive/BBC Hulton)*.

Wren's royal apartments or Vanbrugh's Blenheim Palace. White modelled stucco replaced the painted scenes of Verrio and Laguerre or the elegant woodwork of the seventeenth-century house. Sculptures by Rysbrach replaced the wood carvings of Grinling Gibbons. Chasteness rather than voluptuousness was more in favor. The great Whig houses of Wilton (Burlington) and the remodelled Chatsworth, Claremont, Wentworth Woodhouse, and Holkham Hall triumphantly enshrined the classical austerity and virtues of the ancients espoused by the Augustans.

The later Georgian period, completing the eighteenth century, is dominated by neoclassical styles, Greek rather than Roman. Its exemplars are the Adams—John, James, William, and especially Robert—who succeeded their father William in his Scottish practice. Robert moved on to England where he led the family firm to preeminence in their profession. The ubiquitous Robert left his mark on countless houses throughout the United Kingdom, sometimes only a room or two, as in the Anglo-Norman Chirk Castle, but more often not only the house but the furniture, the wall coverings, and even the gardens. Robert Adam, very sensitive to contemporary tastes, incorporated the latest fashions and crazes in his designs. The Pompei room at Osterly Park or the Wedgewood room at Mellerstain are particularly fine examples. But above all one admires the care for detail, the consistency with which he conceived and carried out his ideas. The tapestry and Etruscan rooms at Osterly Park, with their designs carried out in plaster, in wall coverings, and in upholstery for the furniture and the carpets, are breathtaking in their beauty and symmetry.

The state apartments, music rooms, orangeries, theaters, numerous

The Etruscan Room by Robert Adam, Osterly Park.

guest rooms, and large staffs made these homes great public spectacles and social centers. The collections of paintings, sculptures, ancient marbles, glass, and porcelain resulted in a whole series of local museums that were on display for the edification and diversion of gentle folk throughout England. The increasing size of the estates, the essential importance of the wealth derived from the land, and the need to maintain residence in the county to assert one's political influence meant that these houses were occupied by the owners for the greater part of the year, only empty during the London season, and not always then. As a symbol of power and affluence, as a place of entertainment and education, and as a social and economic center, the eighteenth-century country house was one of the period's most distinctive features.

Suggestions for Further Reading

Dorothy Marshall, *Eighteenth Century England* (2nd edition, 1974) and John B. Owen, *The Eighteenth Century* (1973) are reliable surveys. The most comprehensive is Wolfgang Michael, *Englische Geschichte im achtzehnten Jahrhundert* (5 vols., 1896–1945), of which the first two volumes have been translated as *England under George I* (1936–1939). Still useful and containing essays on many aspects of English life is A. S. Turberville, ed., *Johnson's England* (2 vols., 1933). Many excellent surveys of various aspects of the nation have been published, including Dorothy Marshall, *The English Poor in the Eighteenth Century* (1926) and *English People in the Eighteenth Century* (1956); M. Dorothy George, *London Life in the Eighteenth Century* (1951); John Rule, *The Experience of Labour in Eighteenth-Century English Industry* (1981); T. S. Ashton, *An Economic History of England: The Eighteenth Century* (1959) and *Economic Fluctuations in England, 1700–1800* (1959); Gordon Mingay, *English Landed Society in the Eighteenth Century* (1963) and *The Gentry* (1976); and Edward Hughes, *North Country Life in the Eighteenth Century* (2 vols., 1952–1965). In *The Population History of England, 1541–1871* (1981), E. A. Wrigley and R. S. Schofield provide a convincing answer to the mechanisms for English demographic growth in the eighteenth century. Peter D. G. Thomas, *The House of Commons in the Eighteenth Century* (1971) and Sheila Lambert, *Bills and Acts* (1971) report on aspects of parliamentary history.

Politics and political parties have undergone intensive investigation in recent years. Essential are Linda Colley, *In Defiance of Oligarchy. The Tory Party, 1714–60* (1982) and J. C. D. Clark, *The Dynamics of Change. The Crisis of the 1750's and English Party Systems* (1982). The spokesmen for the ministry are discussed in Reed Browning, *Political and Constitutional Ideas of the Court Whigs* (1982). Jacobitism continues to excite controversy; useful statements can be found in Eveline Cruickshanks, ed., *Ideology and Conspiracy: Aspects of Jacobitism, 1689–1759* (1982). Political biography is noticeably rich. J. H. Plumb's, *Sir Robert Walpole* (2 vols., 1956), though incomplete, is a good beginning. The great crisis of Walpole's ministry is admirably analyzed by Paul Langford in *The Excise Crisis: Society and Politics in the Age of Walpole* (1975). Ragnhild Hatton's *George I: Elector and King* (1978) is a magisterial work, a fascinating, revisionist account. One may also consult Owen, *The Rise of the Pelhams* (1957); Basil Williams, *Stanhope* (1932) and *Carteret and Newcastle* (1943); Ray Kelch, *Newcastle. A Duke Without Money* (1974); Browning, *The Duke of Newcastle* (1975); Robert Halsband, *Lord Hervey* (1973); and John Wilkes, *A Whig in Power: the Political Career of Henry Pelham* (1964). Valuable for both military and political history is W. A. Speck, *The Butcher: The Duke of Cumberland and the Suppression of the '45* (1981). For the development of Scotland after the '45 there is a good survey in Bruce Lenman, *Integration, Enlightenment, and Industrialization: Scotland (1746–1832)* (1981).

Specialized monographs of value include Archibald S. Foord, *His Majesty's Opposition, 1714–1830* (1964), Isaac Kramnick, *Bolingbroke and His Circle* (1968), Robert Robson, *The Attorney in Eighteenth Century England* (1959), Kenneth Ellis, *The Post Office in the Eighteenth Century* (1958), Ralph Davis, *The Rise of the English Shipping Industry in the Seventeenth and Eighteenth Centuries* (1962), W. R. Ward, *The English Land Tax in the Eighteenth Century* (1953), and Norma Landau, *The Justices of the Peace, 1679–1760* (1984), which should be read with Lionel Glassey, *Politics and the Appointment of Justices of the Peace (1657–1720)* (1984). Also useful are W. R. Ward, *Georgian Oxford* (1958), R. J. B. Walker, *Old Westminster Bridge: The Bridge of Fools* (1979), Red Ruddock, *Arch Bridges and their Builders, 1735–1835* (1979), P. J. Corfield, *The Impact of English Towns: 1700–1800* (1982), and Mark Girouard, *Life in the English Country House: A Social and Architectural History* (1978). For intellectual life one may note Basil Willey, *The Eighteenth Century Background* (1957), Gerald R. Cragg, *Reason and Authority in the*

Eighteenth Century (1964), A. R. Humphreys, *The Augustan World: Life and Letters in the Eighteenth Century* (1954), and Caroline Robbins, *The Eighteenth Century Commonwealthman* (1959).

John M. Beattie, *The English Court in the Reign of George I* (1967) is a definitive study. For a contemporary account of court life one should read John, Lord Hervey, *Some Materials Towards Memoirs of the Reign of King George II* (ed. Romney Sedgwick, 3 vols., 1931), *The Political Journal of George Bubb Dodington* (ed. J. Carswell and L. A. Dralle, 1965), *The Complete Letters of Lady Mary Wortley Montague* (ed. R. Halsband, 3 vols., 1965–1967), and Horace Walpole, *Memoirs of the Last Ten Years of the Reign of George the Second* (3 vols., 1847). The new emphasis on marriage, family, and demography has produced two valuable studies in Lawrence Stone, *The Family, Sex and Marriage in England, 1500–1800* (1977) and Randolph Trumbach, *The Rise of the Egalitarian Family: Aristocratic Kinship and Domestic Relations in Eighteenth-Century England* (1978).

11

The Problem of
the Americas

1754–1783

*T*he three decades that span the years from the death of Henry Pelham in 1754 and end with American independence may be viewed as transitional in several important respects. George III's predecessor and grandfather was a child of the seventeenth century and foreign-born. His views on the nature of government and England's role in Europe looked back to William III. The Seven Years' War reflected his Hanoverian preoccupations. At the same time, the peace treaty that concluded the Seven Years' War marked a significant gain for Britain in its contest with France for colonial and economic interests. The contest was waged with its cross-channel rival throughout the century. North America and India were now British preserves. The war of American independence was focussed in a different hemisphere, and the British army and government were introduced to a whole new range of problems and attitudes to which it was unable to adapt. Although the reigns of George I and George II were not devoid of political unrest, the new challenges to the authority of the crown exemplified by the Wilkes' disputes and the protests over the employment of general warrants began a long process of agitation for parliamentary and governmental reform that did not come to fruition until 1832 and the Great Reform Act. The American rebellion and the disturbances in Ireland all served to intensify the debate. With all the political ferment, England continued to prosper, and the beginnings of industrialism only served to heighten the sense of well-being and achievement that characterized those who controlled the nation's power structure and economy.

The Marks of Affluence

Great houses in the neoclassical Palladian style sprang up around the country; most of them were based upon landed wealth, frequently increased in not a few cases by advantageous marriages with wealthy merchant or banking families. Sculptures, paintings, and tapestries acquired by the young men of fashion as they made the grand tour on the continent adorned the salons and dining rooms. Princely libraries were often an important feature in the mansions that dotted the countryside. In some cases they were the result of the expertise and interest of the owner, such as the earl of Sunderland's incomparable collection of incunabula (books printed before 1500) that found its way to the duke of Marlborough's Blenheim Palace. Equally important was the vast collection of 14,000 documents, 7,500 volumes of manuscripts, 50,000 books, 41,000 prints, and 350,000 pamphlets collected by Sunderland's political and bibliophile rivals, the earl of Oxford and his son.

The tastes and acquisitions of the aristocracy were copied on a grander scale by George III, as evidenced by the 54 paintings and 142 drawings by Canaletto in the royal art collection and his impressive library, which was given later by George IV to the British Museum. Exotic birds and rare plants adorned the stately houses; citrus trees blossomed and bore fruit in the orangeries. Britain's increasing traffic with the Orient made Chinese motifs one of the dominant design elements in decorating throughout the century. Chinese wallpaper, furniture, and objets d'art were universally admired; porcelain dinnerware specially made in China, often in patterns bearing the family crest or coat of arms, graced the great dining tables. Even when the art of making fine china spread to England in the later eighteenth century the Chinese models were often the basis for the patterns created by English designers.

The manners and fashions of the wealthy were copied at the lower social levels insofar as incomes permitted. The libraries might not have contained so many rare books but they were generally stuffed with row after row of devotional works, sermons, and political pamphlets, usually bound and titled in the same "house" binding. If porcelain could be had only by the greater families, the introduction of a fine cream-colored earthenware by Josiah Wedgwood about 1765 and high-grade stoneware by Josiah Spode a little later—both usually decorated in Chinese-style patterns— gave a new refinement and quality to English tables. The engravings of Hogarth and Rowlandson and the mezzotint reproductions of well-known paintings adorned the walls of more modest homes. Brussells lace, French silk, and Italian velvet were much appreciated in London. Clothing was ornate and full and was increased in sumptuousness with embroidery on the sleeves and coats of the gentlemen and on the dresses of the ladies. By mid-eighteenth century men wore elaborate wigs often tied or knotted at the nape of the neck with the side hair in horizontal roll curls lying one above the other and covering the ears. The lower classes wore wool or linen, and the men frequently wore leather breeches. Often they did not possess a change of clothing and wore what they owned until it literally disintegrated. The diet was a heavy one for the wealthy: an exhausting succession of meat dishes and pastries with fruit when in season. For the poor, the daily fare was only bread or gruel or soup, with a little meat once or twice a week. The lower classes drank beer or ale and the upper classes drank wine. French claret had been displaced by port and sherry after the Methuen treaties with Portugal in 1703, though French brandy continued to be enjoyed by the wealthy. These tastes and customs were not unique to England. Increasingly they were replicated, with some local modifications, in the English colonies of North America.

The Seven Years' War

The North American Colonies and the Problem of Imperial Defense. In the mid-eighteenth century the rivalry of England and France dominated both Europe and the colonial areas that were under their influence. France possessed important holdings in the Caribbean, Africa, India, and, above all, North America, from Quebec and the St. Lawrence, through the Great Lakes, and down the Mississippi to Louisiana. These possessions and the competition for trade in these areas, in Europe, and in the Spanish colonies brought England and France into frequent conflict. In North America the English colonies were undergoing growing pains. The population of the British colonies grew from 250,000 in 1700 to perhaps 1,500,000 in 1750; the settlers penetrated further west, across the Alleghenies into the river valleys of the Ohio and Mississippi. The French had similar ambitions, and, though their number was not so great, they had visions of linking their two colonies of Quebec and Louisiana and forming a great empire in the mid-North American Continent. The expansion of the two empires created friction in Acadia (later Novia Scotia), along the St. Lawrence, around the Great Lakes, along the Ohio, and at isolated points on the Mississippi. Georgia found itself in frequent dispute with Spanish Florida.

The importance of the colonies to the economy and welfare of England and the importance of England to the economy and welfare of the colonies was mutually acknowledged. North American exports just to England were estimated to be worth over £5,000,000 by the 1740s and employed as many as 3,000 ships, of which half belonged to the colonists. The management of the colonies was the responsibility of the Secretary for the Southern Department and of the Board of Trade and Plantations. As Newcastle held the former office for a record thirty years, he had an increasingly preponderant influence and also a considerable knowledge of the situation in the North Americas. He concentrated on patronage matters, hamstrung the Board, and yet gave little attention to maintaining a tight control over colonial governments. The result was a laissez-faire attitude, which encouraged the growing colonial independence. Newcastle, who had succeeded his brother Henry Pelham at the Treasury in 1754, was not unmindful of the colonists' demands to curb French expansion in America but was reluctant to engage England so soon in another expensive war. Events in America, however, soon took the initiative out of his hands. In 1753 the French governor of Canada began the construction of a series of forts to control the Ohio River, including Fort Duquesne at the present-day site of Pittsburgh. When in 1754 the French repulsed an attack led by the young colonial officer George Washington, an English response was needed. Two regiments were sent from England under the command of Edward Braddock early in 1755, only to be repulsed again by the French near the same fort. When the French acted to reinforce their troops in Canada the English sent a fleet to intercept the French transports in the spring of 1755. The fleet failed in the attempt but set up a blockade of the French Canadian ports. This effort and the expulsion of the French colonists in Acadia were the only accomplishments of the year to balance heavy losses. Nevertheless England had laid down the gauntlet, and a formal declaration of war was now only a question of time.

The Diplomatic Revolution and the Advancement of Pitt. In Europe the situation was unstable. Austria, England's traditional ally, still smarted at the loss of Silesia to Prussia and was anxious to obtain satisfaction. England and, even more, Holland were bent on keeping the peace, a goal which was clearly not in harmony with Austrian ambitions. George II feared that if war were to break out Hanover would be caught in a vise between Prussia and France, and thus he sought Austria's continuing support to counter this threat. In an effort to garner more allies, England signed a subsidy treaty with Hesse-Cassel in 1755 and a defensive alliance with Russia to counter the threat of Prussia. The Anglo-Russian treaty neutralized Prussia and made that country less useful to France as an ally. Austria meantime had been making tenders to France in order to build up sufficient strength to defeat Prussia. France, whose continental ambitions had waned in the face of her increasing imperial interests, no longer viewed the Habsburgs as rivals but now saw them as potential allies. When Frederick II of Prussia was persuaded to sign the Convention of Westminster with England in January 1756, the allies of both countries, France and Russia, were understandably annoyed. In the case of Russia, it was because Empress Elizabeth had seen the Anglo-Russian treaty as a preliminary to an attack on Prussia. France reacted by acceding to Austria's invitation for a defensive alliance in May 1756. When the Dutch promised France their neutrality in any conflict, the alliance of England, Austria, and Holland, which dated back to William III, was at an end.

Hostilities in Europe began in May when the French threatened to cross the Channel and then seized Minorca. This disaster was followed by the loss of Oswego in America, which opened the way for further French advances into the middle of the continent. The attack by Frederick II on Saxony turned the war in Europe into a general conflict, the prospect of which Newcastle and George II had so ardently tried to prevent. The atrocities perpetrated by the French in India in the infamous Black Hole of Calcutta were the last straw. This series of humiliating defeats had precipitated the fall of Newcastle and brought about the formation of a new ministry to prosecute the war under the joint direction of William Pitt and Newcastle in May 1757.

The Conduct of the War. Pitt was not able to influence the conduct of the war (also known as the French and Indian War) in 1757 materially, and the advantage that year lay with France. British attacks on Rochefort in France and on the French fortress of Louisbourg in Canada both failed. England's ally, Frederick II, suffered a disastrous defeat at the hands of the Austrians; George II's son, the duke of Cumberland, surrendered Hanover and its adjoining territories to the French. Everything now hinged on the campaign of 1758. Intent on America, Pitt was yet persuaded of the necessity for providing some succor for Frederick II in Germany. A major treaty with Prussia was signed in April 1758 under which England subsidized a new army in northern Germany that drove the French out of Hanover and Westphalia. This cover at Prussia's rear enabled Frederick II to withstand the combined onslaughts of Austria and Russia and to retain possession of Saxony and Silesia. Pitt's main concern was in North America. There he planned a three-pronged attack: on Louisbourg, on Montreal or Quebec from New York, and on Fort Duquesne from Philadelphia. Though the second attack miscarried, Bradstreet's attack on Frontenac gave the English the control of Lake Ontario and thus the possession of a ring of French fortresses around Canada.

The great year of the war was 1759. This "year of victories" was the consequence of Pitt's great stress on the revitalization of the navy so that England was able to establish naval superiority in virtually every theater. This was particularly crucial in Canada because Quebec was weak in foodstuffs and materials, and any lack of resupply rendered the city more vulnerable to attack. A thrust through New York resulted in the taking of Niagara, Ticonderoga, and finally the control of Lake Champlain. An expedition along the St. Lawrence under the dashing General Wolfe ended in the celebrated capture of Quebec in September. Another expedition took Guadeloupe in the West Indies. The taking of Goree in West Africa at the end of 1758 had cut off the main source of slaves for the French islands in the West Indies. In Europe the defeat of French fleets off Gibraltar and Brest averted the threat of a French invasion of England. The year 1760 was anticlimactic, notable only for the capture of Montreal, which placed all of French Canada in English hands. In a more distant theater, India, successes in 1760 capped a series of confrontations with the French dating back to 1756. India was now virtually an English preserve.

King George III and His Ministers

The Accession of George III. The death of George II in 1760 and the accession of his grandson George III (1760–1820) undercut Pitt's position. The new king placed his confidence in the earl of Bute, long a member of the entourage of his father and mother. Pitt wanted to continue the war to ensure that England had all the bargaining power she needed at the peace table. He even proposed a preemptive attack on Spain in anticipation of her entry into the war on the side of France. But George III and his advisors were anxious to bring the war to an end, and public opinion and the Cabinet supported their view. Pitt resigned angrily and, though Spain did enter the war as he had guessed, Bute was able to conclude a peace with France and Spain at Paris in November 1762. Though Bute won less than Pitt had demanded, the fruits were still considerable. All of French Canada and the lands west of the North American colonies were granted to England together with the return of Minorca, with its strategic importance in the Mediterranean, Senegal in Africa, and four additional islands in the West Indies. From Spain England received Florida, thus securing the southern border of the colonies; England gave up Havana, captured in 1762, in exchange. France was allowed to retain her rich sugar islands in the West Indies and fishing rights off Newfoundland and in the Gulf of St. Lawrence, concessions that were to remain a bone of contention between the two countries until 1904.

The accession of George III, only twenty-two years of age, caused a great change in English politics and introduced a period of turmoil and instability that was to last in some respects to 1784. George III was the first native-born sovereign since Queen Anne. He gloried in the fact that his heart was truly English. Raised in the circle of Leicester House, long the center of opposition to George II and his ministers, he saw the late king as the prisoner of the Whigs who had dominated the ministries of his two predecessors. George III was determined to free the crown from the Whig's corrupt influences and to rule without regard for party or clique. In these aims he was encouraged and advised by a Scottish peer, the earl of Bute, his closest confidant, but unfortunately a man without

George III at the time of his coronation. By Sir Joshua Reynolds *(Royal Academy of Arts)*.

either the strength or the wisdom to implement his ideas. Pressed by the king, Bute took office and ultimately served for a short time as first lord of the Treasury. Working to eliminate first Pitt and then Newcastle and their followers, he bought the services of the unscrupulous Henry Fox to shepherd the peace through Parliament. Finding himself beset on all sides he made a hasty resignation in April 1763, leaving the king alone to face the politicians.

Party Politics in the Mid-Eighteenth Century. The situation with which the young, inexperienced king had to contend in the 1760s was far different from that which his great grandfather, George I, faced in 1714. The forty-five years of Whig dominance had broken and, to a large extent, destroyed the old Tory party. The Whigs in turn, contesting each other for office, had broken up into a series of factions, none of which could be dignified with the title of "party." The majority of the Commons was made up of unaffiliated country gentlemen. Traditionally supporters of the king's government, the gentry were, if anything, more Tory than Whig in sympathy and refused to be organized into a disciplined party. A smaller group consisted of the civil servants, officers, pensioners, and other placeholders whose livelihood depended on the favor of the king. They could be relied on to support whatever politicians were in office. The other members were clustered around a few great men, aristocratic grandees of substantial wealth and electoral influence, who led the factions that jostled for the direction of the king's affairs. It was from among these last groupings that the king was forced to choose his ministers. George III found them almost uniformly repugnant.

Although the old parties no longer existed as they had in the early eighteenth century, the names Whig and Tory survived, and many families and individuals identified themselves with one or the other. To a considerable extent the survival of the names had meaning because each stood for an attachment to a certain set of principles. The old Tory loyalties to the crown, church, and established social order were strong. In a similar fashion the association with the city and mercantile interests, the sympathy for the Dissenters, and the support for land campaigns in Europe were regarded as Whig doctrines. With the stigma of Jacobitism finally erased after the failure of the rebellion of 1745 and the end of the Whig supremacy, a new Toryism evolved once again under George III. Some historians saw its origin in the following attracted by the elder Pitt, its formal founding in "the king's friends," or placemen, organized to support the ministry of Lord North, and its full emergence under the younger Pitt.

The Uncertainty of the 1760s. George III had to contend with a situation where old parties were crumbling and new political alignments were emerging. He has often been accused of trying to act as his own chief minister in the manner of the later Stuarts, reversing the trend toward parliamentary government that had been evolving since the death of William III. Most historians now believe that he was faced with a power vacuum; the Whig leadership was old and discredited, and there was no viable, organized party to supplant it and govern the Parliament. George stepped into the breech, but never with the intention of subverting the constitution. He was a man of unimpeachable integrity and was dedicated to the interests of his country and his people. He gave every possible support to those ministers who gained his confidence. However, until a new system of political management was created to supplant that employed by Walpole and the Pelhams, the government was too often weak, uncertain, and in confusion. The king required a prime minister whom he could trust. This minister in turn should be able to lead the Commons, should possess the financial expertise of a Walpole, and should be able to command the allegiance of more than one faction. In the 1760s no one filled these criteria completely.

After the resignation of Bute, the king reluctantly gave the leadership of the ministry to George Grenville, an earnest, knowledgeable administrator with considerable expertise in finance and a man devoted to the Commons. But Grenville was cold and tactless and soon so affronted the king and influential politicians that his removal became imperative. Using his uncle, the duke of Cumberland, as his political broker the king turned in 1765 to the young marquis of Rockingham, who claimed to inherit the mantle of the Whig party. Rockingham, whose greatest contribution was his promotion of his young Irish secretary, Edmund Burke, lacked the ability and the experience to guide the ministry and to manage the Parliament. His following was limited, and too many influential leaders were alienated and hostile. The king withheld his full confidence and as soon as he found a convenient excuse, which came in 1766 after the ministry had barely a year in office, he dismissed them.

George had some time earlier become reconciled to Pitt, a man who had been very close to Leicester House in the 1750s. The two had many things in common—both prided themselves on being true patriots, both disdained the pettiness and self-serving of faction, and both believed that government should be above party. Pitt accepted the charge to form a government on his own terms and proceeded to put together a ministry that amazed and confounded his contemporaries. With ministers acting independently of each other, indeed virtually unknown to each other, only a very strong leader could have made a coherent whole of it. Pitt took a peerage as the earl of Chatham, thereby removing himself from the Commons, the seat of his power. Moreover, his health was broken, and he lacked the stamina to direct this curious assemblage. Even worse, he fell into a state of profound depression and retired to his country house where he remained incommunicado for more than a year. The young duke of Grafton gradually assumed nominal control, though he was unequal to the task. But out of duty to the king and an obligation to see through certain projects the ministry had initiated—notably a renewal of the East India Company's charter—Grafton somehow held the government together until 1770. In that year his chancellor of the exchequer and George's childhood friend, Frederick, Lord North, took command and restored order to the king's government.

The Beginnings of Radical Agitation for Reform. The succession of weak ministries in the 1760s had to contend with unusually agitated times in the body politic. The dislocations caused by the war had to be mended. The war left a heavy burden of debt and a continuing need for imperial protection. Grenville, who pursued a severe policy of economy and retrenchment, was determined to shift the burden of imperial defense onto the colonists who benefited from it. He first tried to close certain loopholes in the customs duties that enabled the colonists to trade freely with the French West Indies. This alone was sufficient to raise a strong outcry in America. When he imposed a stamp duty on newspapers and legal documents, he provoked active opposition in the colonies—petitions, a refusal to pay debts owing to British merchants, and a general boycott of British goods. Riots occurred in the colonies, and colonial leaders even considered joint action in protest. Rockingham, on succeeding Grenville, repealed the stamp tax but reaffirmed Parliament's right to tax the colonies. Charles Townshend, the chancellor of the exchequer under Chatham, tried to tax the colonies again in 1767, with duties at the ports on glass, lead, paper, paint, and tea. This action provoked further protests across the Atlantic, answered by the suspension of the New York legislature and the employment of troops in Boston.

The claim by the colonists that Parliament had no right to tax them without their consent evoked a sympathetic response in England. Aside from occasional riots in times of stress, the British public was docile and accepting. Harsh laws and brutal punishments were used to impose order on the lower classes. But the unrepresentative character of the Commons, the widespread use of patronage or corruption to lubricate and manage the political machine, and occasional arbitrary actions of the crown began to stir thinking men to champion the cause of reform. In 1763 the thinly veiled attack on the king by John Wilkes in number forty-five of his newspaper, *The North Briton,* so outraged the government that a decision was made to apprehend Wilkes and suppress his paper, on a charge of seditious libel. The Secretaries of State issued a general warrant, an instrument that gave the messengers license to seize any or all persons suspected of a part in the paper, the printing press, and the offending issues themselves. The legality of general warrants was doubtful, though they had been long employed. When Wilkes sued successfully in court, the bench held the instrument illegal, and its future use was condemned by the Commons in 1766.

The government was not yet through with Wilkes. Exposing him as the author of a salacious satire, *An Essay on Women*, the government had the strength in the Commons to expel him from the House. Wilkes, already a cause célèbre was now at the center of radical agitation for a decade, first over the issue of general warrants and then over his right to sit in the House. He returned from self-imposed exile in France in 1768 to run for Parliament. Four times new elections were held for his seat, and four times the voters of Middlesex, the county around London that felt greatly underrepresented in the Commons, returned him or his proxy by an overwhelming majority. On the fourth occasion, in 1769, the Commons finally voided his candidacy and seated the runner-up. But the government was not rid of Wilkes. His friends organized the Society of the Supporters of the Bill of Rights to defend his interests. The ministers and Wilkes's opponents in the Commons were frequently the victims of well-directed mob action. The London populace, in assemblies, petitions, riots, demonstrations, and a host of public displays, continually championed his interests while challenging the crown. In 1770 Wilkes was elected an alderman of London; the city with rare unanimity was mobilized against the government. Wilkes was then elected lord mayor of London in 1774, the year in which he was finally permitted to reenter the Commons. Before this he was involved in still another issue—the unrestricted publication of parliamentary debates in the daily press, a practice long banned by the Commons. John Almon, a printer closely connected with the radicals and Wilkes, successfully challenged the ban of the Commons and won his case with the support of Wilkes and the city officials when the Commons found it wiser to abandon the claim in 1771.

The First Years of Lord North's Ministry, 1770–1776. When Lord North accepted the Treasury on January 27, 1770, no one could foresee that he would continue as prime minister for a dozen years. The opposition in Parliament was formidable, composed of both the Rockinghamites and Chatham. Through their oratory in the two chambers and their even more effective attacks in the press, the opposition sought to force George III to come to terms with them. Edmund Burke, in his *Thoughts on the Present Discontents* (1770), had charged that a secret cabal dominated by Bute possessed the king and hence controlled the ministry. Though this was a fabrication, Burke and his party seemed to have given some credence to this interpretation in order to explain their own inability to gain acceptance. The government was still on the defensive from the onslaughts of

The Wiremaster and His Puppets, 1767. The Earl of Bute as the power behind the scenes *(Kenneth Spencer Research Library)*.

Wilkes and the demands for reform. The final burden was the unrest in the American colonies. North took this all in stride. Though an unprepossessing figure and an overtolerant and weak prime minister, he showed remarkable ability in managing the Commons. With the firm support of the king, the power of the Treasury behind him, and his sure touch with the Parliament, he proved invulnerable to opposition efforts to unseat him. His early years in office were much taken up with financial matters. He proved to be an expert in financial management and genuinely concerned with the reform of the revenue system. Aside from America, the most pressing problem was that of the East India Company.

The supremacy in India gained by the British East India Company at the end of the Seven Years' War brought a new train of problems. The East India Company was a commercial enterprise, organized to earn a profit for its backers and ill-equipped to carry the responsibility of governing nonwestern people. The enormous power and influence that the Company's managers possessed in India provided unprecedented opportunities for personal gain and, at the same time, for corruption. Mismanagement of the Company's affairs at home and the substantial new financial burdens caused by the assumption of governmental responsibilities in India drained the Company of its profits. The government looked to the Company whose wealth might alleviate the government's pressing financial needs. At the same time, the heavy commitments the Company had in the east and their importance to the economy meant that the state might have to insure the integrity of the Company's possessions. This could mean the provision of troops and ships to be used against the French. Temporary settlements in 1767 and 1769 only postponed the day of reckoning while yet acknowledging the government's responsibility and interest. North's Regulating Act of 1773 was a compromise measure intended to introduce some measure of stability and integrity into the Company's operations until the renewal of its charter in 1780. In addition to subjecting the dividend rate to the review of Parliament, a governor-general and council were appointed to manage the area of Bengal in India. The Treasury or Secretary of State was given the right to review all correspondence from India. That these arrangements did not prove satisfactory was due as much to the persons appointed to serve on the council as to the methods employed.

The Trouble with the Colonies. The events that led to rebellion were sometimes small in themselves and often unconnected. But each in turn furthered the breach between the colonies and the mother country, created suspicion on the side of the colonists, and provoked English defiance, anger, and then retaliation. The Stamp Act, the closing of the frontiers, and the Townshend duties, which were taxation by indirect means, and, even more insidious, the suspension of the New York and Massachusetts assemblies, the closing of Boston harbor, and the firing on the Boston mob—all were seen by the colonists as provocative. The Stamp Act Congress, the circular letter sent by the Massachusetts Assembly, the evasion of customs duties and illegal trade with the French West Indies, the boycott of British goods, and the attacks on royal troops—these were equally as offensive to the British. Throughout all this the basic issue became clarified and refined. The colonies were bent upon extirpating all direct English control over their governments and finances though retaining the link of the crown. English political leaders in Parliament were unprepared to surrender English sovereignty to the colonists though they might be sympathetic to their concerns. Rockinghamites were opposed to a grant of independence and resisted all such claims until well after the rebellion broke out in 1776. It was North's unhappy lot to precipitate this final rupture.

The East India Company, plagued increasingly with financial troubles, had a surplus of tea. To help it reduce the surplus North proposed to let the Company import the tea directly into the colonies. The colonial merchants now saw their price undercut and saw the prospect of financial ruin as the Company's direct import would deprive them of their market. In most colonial ports a simple boycott was enough, but in Boston the colonists were more aggressive and, disguised as Indians, stole aboard the ships in the harbor and dumped the offending merchandise in the bay— the "Boston Tea Party." Once the news of the incident reached England the government responded by passing a bill through the Parliament to close the port of Boston. Subsequent legislation strengthened the control of the crown over the Massachusetts government. The Quebec Act of the same year, which created an appointive rather than elective legislative council for the French-speaking provinces, was regarded as a still more ominous sign or portent of future retaliation, particularly as it was to extend the Canadian system into the Ohio and Illinois territories. Massachusetts responded by calling a General Congress of the British colonies to deal with these threats to their liberties. Even before the Congress met in September in Philadelphia, fighting had begun at Lexington in April 1775. The American rebellion was underway.

The American Revolution and Its Aftermath

The American Rebellion, 1775–1783. England was ill-prepared for the war; the geographical considerations alone made victory doubtful, and the nature of the leadership of the ministry was a further liability. Given these constraints one may ask why England prosecuted war against its colonies.

The challenge to the imperial constitution was almost unanimously accepted at home, given the unacceptable alternative—independence for the colonies. The ease with which Britain had fought overseas campaigns in the last war was a misleading example. Now her major European rivals were free of continental operations, had stronger navies, and thus could effectively challenge her in the American theater and upon the high seas. Lord North was no match for Pitt. Refusing to take full responsibility for the direction of the ministry and the war, he left a vacuum that was only partly filled by the king. Lord George Germain, who as Secretary of State for the American colonies had the prime responsibility for the conduct of the war, was an experienced and able officer, but he did not have the authority, the genius, or the good fortune of Pitt.

Britain faced war not only in the thirteen colonies but also in India, the West Indies, and Canada. To blockade the whole North American coastline against a skilled and intrepid civilian navy that knew all the innumerable indents and turnings of the coastline was impossible for any navy of that day, no matter how large or proficient. But the disorders at home and the weakness of the commanders in America simply compounded the problem. Though the years 1775 and 1776 appeared favorable to the English—Boston was evacuated but New York was occupied—1777 was a disaster, climaxed by the surrender of General Burgoyne at Saratoga. The success of the colonists impelled France, which had supported them covertly since 1776, to conclude a formal alliance with America in 1778. The following year Spain entered the lists against England. The year 1780 crowned the series of diplomatic reverses. Led by Russia, the other nations of Europe declared a state of armed neutrality in which they refused to accept English inspection of neutral cargoes; Holland joined those waged in active hostilities against England. The surrender of Cornwallis at Yorktown in 1781 only acknowledged the inevitable outcome of the struggle.

The Impact of the Rebellion in England and Ireland. The demand for parliamentary reform had not died with Wilkes's readmission to the Commons in 1774. The opposition had charged the ministry with handling of the American colonies in an arbitrary and coercive manner, which in turn encouraged complaints of autocratic and corrupt practices in the government in England. The forces of Chatham and Rockingham in the two houses were small and little able to stem the overwhelming support for the ministry and the prosecution of the war—against the colonists. But they kept alive the issues through their contributions in the debates in Parliament, which were duly noted in the daily press. In tracts and journals they influenced an increasing number of thoughtful citizens against the government as the tide of war and diplomacy turned against England. The natural turbulence and lawlessness of the London mobs, combined with disaffection and economic misery caused by the war, were sufficient to incite the lower orders to violent attacks on property and on prominent citizens. The introduction of a bill to relieve the Catholics of civil disabilities imposed on them sparked an outburst of anti-Catholicism that began in Scotland and eventually reached the metropolis in June 1780 under the leadership of Lord George Gordon. Catholic chapels were raided, houses were burned, the Parliament itself was besieged, and Newgate prison was demolished, the prisoners let free. Only the personal intervention of the king and the employment of royal troops restored order. With the surrender at Yorktown and the collapse of the government's war effort, even the independent members who were traditionally loyal to the crown turned against the king's ministry. North was forced to resign in June 1782.

One of the contributing factors to the ministry's demise and one of the problems that confronted North's successors was the situation in Ireland. Though that country was composed of an oppressed and destitute Roman Catholic majority, ruled by a tiny but omnipotent Protestant minority, which in turn was subjugated to an indifferent if not hostile English government, Ireland had remained calm and loyal during the great eighteenth-century wars. Its economy had been depressed and to some extent impoverished or strangled by the English who were hostile to any competition from their subject neighbor. Yet the country had experienced a slow but steady recovery since the Revolution of 1688. As transatlantic trade increased Ireland profitted from the provisioning trade for the sailing vessels that stopped in route to and from America. Dublin, the seat of government, developed into what remains to this day the finest and most handsome eighteenth-century city in the British Isles.

The government was controlled by the Protestant landed class, many of fairly recent English origin. Supported by an extremely narrow franchise and controlled by the great Protestant landowners, the Irish Parliament dutifully followed the dictates of the ministry in England. By the mid-eighteenth century these "undertakers" were alarmed at how Irish wealth was being used to line English pockets. Even loyal Protestants were suffering at the expense of their English neighbors. The Irish Parliament's refusal in the 1760s to submit to further English demands for revenues led to the imposition of a resident English lord-lieutenant who ran the government under direct orders from London. It is remarkable that the inhabitants, both Protestant and Catholic, remained loyal during the American rebellion. When Irish troops were withdrawn to fight in America, the Irish gentry raised volunteer regiments at their own expense to defend their country against possible foreign invasion. The increasing concern about the depredations the country suffered at the hand of England combined with the new-found strength and unity the gentry gained from the volunteer movement led them to demand home rule and the abolition

Rowlandson's cartoon of Fox and North as "The Right Honourable Catch Singers," 1783 (*Personal collection of Henry L. Snyder*).

of the several constraints by which the Irish executive and Parliament were bound to the British Parliament and Privy Council. These demands were presented in 1782 just at the moment the English government, beset with difficulties of its own at home and abroad, was least able to resist them.

The Ministries of Shelburne and Fox, 1782–1783. Lord North's resignation left George III no choice but to turn to Rockingham and the opposition members whom he disliked intensely and whose efforts to storm the Cabinet he had so long and so strenuously resisted. The government that succeeded was a weak coalition, half controlled by Rockingham and Charles

James Fox and the other half controlled by William Petty, earl of Shelburne, and Lord Camden, the heirs of the earl of Chatham. Initially they had no choice but to act in harmony. The demands of the Irish were met almost without exception, and Ireland enjoyed a brief period of almost unhampered political independence, the sole link remaining the crown, but with that the vital power to appoint the executive. The new leaders also moved quickly to pass a series of reform measures that they had long been championing, though the impact was limited. The main features were to prevent government contractors from sitting in the Commons, to disenfranchise thousands of Treasury officers, and to curtail the places available to the king and hence to his ministers for patronage. The early death of Rockingham at age 52 in July 1782 resulted in a competition between the two factions in the ministry for his place. The result was the resignation of Fox and the other Whig leaders and the emergence of Shelburne as prime minister.

Shelburne had served in a junior capacity in Chatham's ministry in the 1760s and had many of his mentor's better qualities combined with an equanimity and consistency that the elder statesman lacked. His attitude toward the American colonies was notably liberal and magnanimous and one which served English interests well. The peace settlement that he negotiated gained more for England than she had reason to expect. He decided that the best course was to be conciliatory toward the colonies in hopes of splitting America off from France and ensuring favorable commercial relations between England and America for the future. In this he was eminently successful, aided by English naval victories in the West Indies and at Gibraltar and by the just suspicions of the Americans as to French designs in North America. By the Treaty of Versailles concluded in 1783 the Americans were granted their independence and obtained the lands between the Appalachians and the Mississippi River. France made modest imperial gains, and Spain regained Minorca and Florida. Although other minor concessions were made, the British Empire remained essentially intact except for the crucial loss of the thirteen American colonies.

Shelburne had negotiated a peace which was wise and generous, but he fell victim to the political factionalism that divided the Parliament even though he still retained the confidence of the king. The former followers of Rockingham, now led by Fox, resented the means by which Shelburne had come to power. The followers of North were bitter at the peace settlement that he had made. Furthermore, despite his many good qualities, Shelburne was a man who evoked suspicion and mistrust. In 1783 Fox and North came together in a political coalition which led Shelburne to resign. George III hated and felt betrayed by North. Desperately the king looked for an alternative while Shelburne's chancellor of the exchequer, the young William Pitt, younger son of the earl of Chatham, headed a caretaker administration. On March 31 Pitt resigned. George III, left with no other alternative, was compelled to accept Fox and North as leaders of a coalition ministry headed nominally by a respected nobleman, the duke of Portland. Fox and North completed the peace settlement and then turned to the explosive question of India. When Fox's India Bill, presented in the fall of 1783, aroused bitter controversy, George III seized his opportunity and dismissed the coalition, naming Pitt to head a minority government. Supported by the king, Pitt held his ground despite the bitter opposition of the Fox-North majority in the House of Commons. When Pitt held firm, the independent members of the Commons began to drift back to their usual support of the king and his ministers, until, in March 1784, Pitt found a majority of one supporting him. At this point, according to plan, the king dissolved Parliament and called an election in which the full resources of the crown were deployed in support of the young (24-year-old) prime minister. The result was a stunning electoral victory. Pitt found himself leader of a government with a secure majority, and George III savored the downfall of men who had sought so often to thwart the king's plans.

The Emergence of Leisure

In spite of the upheavals brought about by the American Revolution, England was an increasingly prosperous as well as populous country. Just as in the wars against Louis XIV, armed conflict could well be coupled with economic prosperity and even new opportunities for personal gain. The prosperity was particularly marked in the increased affluence of the middle class. The affluence was manifested by what one eminent historian has termed the commercialization of leisure, a peculiarly eighteenth-century phenomenon in England. The fashions, the entertainments, the diversions, and the increased variety of goods on the market were first adopted by the upper classes but increasingly became available to those below them on the social and economic scale. Moreover, by the mid-eighteenth century the variety of leisure activities was totally unprecedented. One example of a new industry resulting from this phenomenon was horse racing. Stables, professional trainers, and jockeys date to the late Stuart period. By the 1750s there were major races conducted throughout the country. Arabian horses, popularized by Lord Treasurer Godolphin, improved the quality of the breed and the excitement of the contests. The Jockey Club brought order to the rules of racing and betting firms institutionalized the gambling.

With more leisure and more money there was more demand for cultural and popular entertainments. The theater, restored by Charles II, continued to grow in quality and variety. Added to Drury Lane and Covent Garden, rival establishments provided a rich range of offerings to the public and a livelihood to a host of playwrights, actors, and support personnel. Theaters were also established in the provinces, and town after town erected assembly rooms and theaters to accommodate the throngs. Professional musicians found new opportunities for work with the introduction of Italian opera in Anne's reign. George Frederick Handel was only the most prominent of countless performers and composers who were brought over from the continent to perform for English audiences. Through the genius of Handel, England introduced a major new art form, the oratorio, to European audiences; in *The Messiah,* Handel created a lasting monument. Not all the entertainments were so edifying. Sideshows and freaks, bearded ladies and siamese twins, vied with Westminster Abbey, Covent Garden, Cox's Great Room, Merlin's Cave, and Wylde's Great Globe for public attention.

The development of the newspaper at the beginning of the century was not simply for news but was also important for advertisements. This new medium for marketing goods encouraged a whole new range of commerce responding to the leisure and new wealth that abounded. The newspaper was critical in attracting customers. It advertised exotic birds for aviaries for the wealthy and cages for the middle classes; exotic plants for orangeries for the grandees and ornamentals for middle-class gardens; and paintings and art objects for the nobs and prints for the upward mobile. Books, tracts, pamphlets, and broadsides abounded. Classics and the new novel were offered in cheap versions, and handsomely printed and bound volumes were offered for show, the coffee-table equivalents of the eighteenth century. For the more prurient, sexually oriented material, "how to" manuals, fiction, and prints were all offered for sale.

One of the most famous and visible manifestations of this new dedication to pleasure was the development of the resort town, spas, and baths. Of these the quintessential center was the city of Bath. Bath had been renowned for its hot springs since Roman times, but its distance from London (107 miles), the lack of suitable lodgings and other entertainments, and the expense and difficulty of travel meant they were little exploited until the eighteenth century. The visits of Queen Anne in 1702 and 1703 gave the baths the necessary social éclat. But even then development was slow. "Beau Nash," appointed master of ceremonies in 1705, did much in his long term of office (until his death in 1761) to create the fashionable resort that Bath became. In charge of the entertainments, he created a highly organized and formal social life that made Bath a popular resort for the aristocracy in the first half of the century. His improvements—the concerts, the erection of the assembly rooms, and the encouragement of gambling—were all major attractions. The baths themselves were quite primitive and public, used indiscriminately for drinking and bathing initially.

But it was in the third quarter of the century that Bath began to achieve the beauty and appearance that set it apart from other spas. A necessary preliminary was the improvement of access. A series of turnpike acts transformed the road from London to Bristol with the branch to Bath by 1750. The improvement of the river to enable barges to come from Bristol to Bath was accomplished by 1727, thus providing building materials and opening a market for easy transport of goods to London. But it was the great building projects of the Woods, father and son, carried out between the 1740s and 1780s, that transformed the town into a European showplace. The Parades by the river, the Circus to the north, the Royal Crescent dominating the west, the Pulteney Bridge opening up the land across the river for expansion, together constituted an early example of town planning, often to be copied. The improvements to the baths themselves, the erection of more public rooms, and an ample supply of lodgings all combined to change the nature of Bath from a center for the elite to one which accommodated the larger numbers of the middle classes. By the end of the century its heyday was past. Too large to be bound within the one society Nash had dominated, increasingly a residential as opposed to a resort town, its expansion curtailed by the Napoleonic Wars, Bath became a backwater after the turn of the century when travellers could visit the more fashionable spas and cities of the continent.

A Stocktaking: England in 1783

The year 1783, which marked the formal close of the war with America and was to usher in the great ministry of the younger Pitt, marked a significant stage in the evolution of England. The decade of the 1780s closed what historians call the "classical age of the constitution." The balance of political power between the monarchy and the Parliament now begins to shift decisively and irrevocably in the direction of the Parliament. Radical agitation—for a more representative House of Commons, an enlarged electorate, freedom of the press, relief for Dissenters and Roman Catholics—entered a new, more violent phase at the end of the decade. Traditional, hierarchal English society headed by the landed aristocracy was soon to be challenged by an urban, industrial, and commercial managerial class and a working class. This phenomenon in the social and economic spheres was the consequence of a number of factors discussed at length below. They may be summarized here as increased sophistication and experience in large-scale commercial enterprises; the series of inventions that

The Royal Crescent, Bath *(The Bettmann Archive/BBC Hulton)*.

ushered in the industrial revolution; a rapidly increasing population attended by a shift in concentration from the country to the city; and gradual improvements in the field of agriculture.

Though shaken by the loss of the American colonies and by displays of political unrest at home and in Ireland, England was still a remarkably stable and progressive country by any European standard. Though a class-conscious nation, there were still ample opportunities for social mobility given the right combinations of intelligence, perseverance, and good fortune. The signs of prosperity were all around. London epitomized this level of enterprise and activity that the country had achieved. It was the intellectual and commercial capital of Europe. A lively press, relatively unfettered by government restraints, was paralleled by a bustling commercial world of manufacturers, bankers, merchants, and traders. Theaters, museums, concert halls, pleasure gardens, stately parks, and well-attended coffee houses and pubs attest to the range of diversions beloved by Samuel Johnson, who remarked, "He who is tired of London is tired of life." The erudite and pungent wit of Johnson, the worldly plays of Richard Sheridan, the new economics of Adam Smith, the refined elegance of the portraits by Reynolds and Gainsborough, the technological mastery and revolutionary inventions revealed by James Watt in his development of the steam engine, the urbane wisdom of David Hume, and the brilliant prose of Edmund Burke are evidence for a creativity that made England a leader among nations.

With the loss of the American colonies England had lost one empire. But based upon what remained to her in Canada, the Caribbean, Africa, India, and the Far East, she was to build a larger and even greater empire. Her fleet was already supreme on the seas of the world. The duel for markets and colonies with France had ended in victory for England in 1763, and even the setback suffered in 1783 did not force her from her dominant position. In the long familiar world of small professional armies and impressed navies, England had good reason for satisfaction, complacency, and pride. A relaxed, but conscientious attention to reform and improvement in all spheres without sacrificing the essential nature and constitution of the nation was the goal of the best intentioned and most enlightened leaders in the intellectual, political, and economic circles of the nation. What these leaders could not know was that the country was on the brink of the greatest challenge—economically, diplomatically, and politically— that the country had yet faced. This challenge was that of the Industrial Revolution and the Napoleonic Wars.

Suggestions for Further Reading

In addition to the general works noted in the preceding chapter, the reader should consult J. Steven Watson, *The Reign of George III* (1960) and Asa Briggs, *The Age of Improvement* (1959). The imposing chef d'oeuvre of Lawrence H. Gipson, *The British Empire before the American Revolution* in 15 volumes is an invaluable reference work for the British Isles and the other colonial possessions as well as the Americas. Volume XIV contains a massive *Bibliographical Guide*; volume XV, *A Guide to Manuscripts*. The most influential of twentieth-century historians was Sir Lewis Namier. In addition to his seminal *Structure of Politics at the Accession of George III* (2nd edition, 1957), which should be read with John Brewer, *Party Ideology and Popular Politics at the Accession of George III* (1976) and with Namier's essays reprinted in *Crossroads of Power* (1962), he began a survey of the period from 1760 to 1782. He only completed the first volume, *England in the Age of the American Revolution* (2nd edition, 1961), which bears the subtitle *Government and Parliament under the Duke of Newcastle*. His students John Brooke, *The Chatham Administration* (1956), Bernard Donoughue, *British Politics and the American Revolution. The Path to War 1773–75* (1964), and Ian Christie, *The End of North's Ministry* (1958) have continued Namier's work. This may be filled in with Herbert Butterfield, *George III, Lord North and the People, 1779–1780* (1949) and followed with John Cannon, *The Fox-North Coalition* (1971).

Excellent works on politics abound for this period. Richard Pares, *King George III and the Politicians* (1953) is indispensable. Also valuable are Ian Christie, *Wilkes, Wyvill and Reform* (1962), George Rude, *Wilkes and Liberty* (1962), Lucy

Sutherland, *The East India Company in Eighteenth Century Politics* (1952), and Erich Eyck, *Pitt versus Fox: Father and Son, 1735–1806* (1950). The corpus of one of the most celebrated political writers has been edited superbly by John Cannon, *The Letters of Junius* (1978). There are many excellent biographies to choose from, among them are John Brooke, *King George III* (1972), Stanley Ayling, *George III* (1972) and *The Elder Pitt* (1976), Sir Lewis Namier and John Brooke, *Charles Townshend* (1964), John Derry, *Charles James Fox* (1972), and John Norris, *Shelburne and Reform* (1963). Ida McAlpine and Richard Hunter in *George III and the Mad Business* (1969) suggest that the king suffered from a rare hereditary disease, while Butterfield in *George III and the Historians* (1957) surveys changing historical interpretation about the king. The American revolt has been covered exhaustively. From the standpoint of England one should note Lawrence H. Gipson's summary, *The Coming of the Revolution* (1954), P. D. G. Thomas, *British Politics and the Stamp Act Crisis* (1975), Charles Ritcheson, *British Politics and the American Revolution* (1954), Piers Mackesy, *The War for America* (1965), and Ian Christie, *Crisis of Empire* (1966) and (with Benjamin Labaree), *Empire or Independence 1760–1776* (1976).

Some specialized monographs of interest are John Derry, *The Regency Crisis and the Whigs* (1963), J. E. D. Binney, *British Public Finance and Administration* (1958), and John Brooke and Sir Lewis Namier, *The House of Commons 1754–1790* (3 vols., 1964). Edmund Burke has yet to receive a definitive biography but one may read with profit Philip Magnus, *Edmund Burke* (1939), Carl Cone, *Burke and the Nature of Politics* (2 vols., 1957), Alfred Cobban, *Edmund Burke and the Revolt against the Eighteenth Century* (1929), and Charles Parkin, *The Moral Basis of Burke's Political Thought* (1956). Richard D. Altick, *The Shows of London* (1978) discusses popular entertainment. Aspects of Bath's history are treated in R. S. Neale, *Bath: A Social History 1680–1850, or A Valley of Pleasure, yet a Sink of Iniquity* (1981).

12

The Revolutionary Age

1783–1815

*H*istorians can argue about the use of the word "revolutionary" as opposed to "evolutionary" to describe the period that falls between the terminations of two great wars—the American War of Independence and the series of Napoleonic Wars. Yet, the changes whose origins have already been discussed began to accelerate so rapidly that "revolutionary" is not inappropriate. Politically, the changes were less dramatic than might be expected. Historians still puzzle as to why England did not experience a true revolution in government at the end of the eighteenth century. At the same time the changes wrought by the younger Pitt in the nature of the executive—the increasing agitation that eventually resulted in the Great Reform Act—the decline in the power of the crown resulting from the illness and later senility of George III and the inadequacy of George IV and, above all, the changes resulting from the rise of modern industry created a revolutionary atmosphere. Together these changes ended forever the structured, traditional, comfortable environment that characterized the eighteenth-century world for one far more adventuresome though uncertain.

George III and William Pitt

In 1783 to 1784 George III demonstrated the decisive role that a determined monarch could play in eighteenth-century politics, but those exciting events marked the high point of the personal power of the king. Once George III had placed Pitt in office, he had no choice but to keep him there because the alternative, the restoration of those he had turned out, was unacceptable to the king. Pitt proved to be so competent, and at the same time so sensitive to the king's concerns, that the arrangement was an enormous success. Pitt's precocious ministry was unique in British parliamentary history. The lone commoner in an aristocratic ministry, he took cabinet government a step further by insisting on being the sole intermediary between the king and his ministers. He was as fully prepared for the problems and challenges that he faced as the king was unprepared. In 1787 to 1788 George III suffered an attack of mental illness that lasted for about four months. Thereafter, he was concerned about his health and reduced his involvement in public business. When war broke out with France in 1793 the king gained stature as a symbol of national unity, but the needs of war thrust the real responsibility on Pitt and his cabinet. In 1801 a political crisis in which Pitt resigned was followed by another of the king's mental breakdowns. Although the king recovered, he was now advanced in years and his political involvement had to be further curtailed. By 1811 his sanity was permanently lost, and when he died in 1820 he was little more than a memory. The long reign of the king who had taken the throne determined to restore the royal power proved to be the reign in which the British monarchy was irretrievably set in the direction toward the parliamentary monarchy of today.

William Pitt and Charles James Fox. Throughout the eighteenth century, British government worked best when the king had the services of a strong, capable prime minister who could lead the Cabinet, supervise finance and administration, and win parliamentary support for his policies. William Pitt was such a man. From the beginning of his ministry he showed himself to be a masterful person, despite his youth, and he never ceased to be the dominant figure in his ministry, even as he drew other powerful leaders to his side. He was a superb administrator, using his post as first lord of the Treasury to extend Treasury supervision into many facets of government. In the House of Commons, where oratory could have a powerful effect, Pitt was inferior to none. He was responsive to new ideas, quick to see how they could be applied to the improvement of government, and also sensitive to humanitarian concerns such as prison reform and the abolition of the slave trade. His ministry, however, depended on a conservative king and a body of supporters in Parliament who were content to leave well enough alone. Thus his achievements fell short of his aspirations.

One of the important features of eighteenth-century politics was the development of a "loyal opposition." The opposition led by Lord Rockingham had eventually brought about the downfall of North's ministry and the end of the American Revolution. When Rockingham died in 1782, his place was taken by Charles James Fox. It was Fox who was dismissed by George III in December 1783 when young William Pitt was installed in power. For the remainder of their lives, Pitt and Fox were

William Pitt, the Younger. By J. Hoppner *(National Portrait Gallery, London)*.

political rivals. Like Pitt, Fox was a superb orator and debater, and in his few brief periods in office he showed himself to be a capable administrator. With the prince of Wales as his patron in what had become a tradition for the Hanoverians, Fox became the leader of those who now styled themselves Whigs. The foundation of Fox's programs was his concern for the independence of Parliament and the rights of individuals. The foundation was extended to encompass parliamentary reform, the reduction of royal patronage, freedom of the press, religious toleration, and the abolition of the slave trade. By taking his stand in opposition to royal power, Fox condemned himself to political frustration, but he won a place in the hearts of his contemporaries as a powerful defender of liberty.

Pitt and Reform. It was Pitt's task to restore confidence and unity to a nation torn by partisan strife and shaken by defeat in the American Revolution. Britain had emerged from the war in desperate financial straits, and Pitt, as first lord of the Treasury, had primary responsibility for restoring the finances of the government. It was in this area that Pitt's rationality, efficiency, and openness to new ideas were most effectively displayed. He improved financial management by refinancing the national debt, consolidating and simplifying the revenues, reducing smuggling and other evasions of taxes, and improving the management and audit of public money. Another important concern was to improve the revenue by encouraging trade through a series of trade treaties with other nations. Pitt's goal was a surplus of revenue over expenditure, which could be used to begin reduction of the national debt. When the necessary surplus was achieved in 1786, he created a sinking fund to be earmarked for debt reduction. Although Pitt's surplus was soon to be consumed by new wars, Pitt's sinking fund had an important psychological effect, for it demonstrated that Britain was again financially strong.

Stealing the thunder from the opposition, Pitt also took the lead in the reform of Parliament. In the previous decade, complaints had frequently been made that the House of Commons was dominated by the crown and failed to represent the views of the public. The influence of the crown was thought to be derived from small boroughs controlled by local magnates, while the growing electorates of the shires and populous towns were underrepresented. In 1785 Pitt proposed a moderate measure of reform that would disfranchise thirty-six small boroughs (with compensation) and distribute the seats to London and the larger counties. Because he was unable to carry George III, and even many of his own supporters, the measure was soundly defeated—and with it, Pitt's attempt at parliamentary reform. Thereafter, Fox and his friends raised the issue in 1793 and again in 1797, but without success. The electorate and its political representatives were not yet ready for even a modest change.

Ireland, which had received legislative independence in 1782, was another problem with which Pitt had to contend. Pitt tried to counteract the weakening of British political control by strengthening the economic ties that bound Britain and Ireland. In 1785 he presented his Irish Commercial Resolutions, in which he proposed to institute free trade between Britain and Ireland in exchange for an Irish contribution to the cost of the navy. Again a statesman-like policy failed. British economic interests that feared Irish competition mounted a powerful lobby against Pitt's proposals, and the Irish resented Pitt's insistence on support for the navy.

Pitt and the Empire. When Pitt came to power in December 1783, the British Empire had been rocked by the loss of the American colonies. The immediate problem facing the young minister was the restoration of commercial relations between Britain and her former American colonies. Pitt's mentor, Lord Shelburne, had favored a generous arrangement, but strong opposition developed in Parliament and the nation, based on the contention that the Americans, having chosen to leave the Empire, should no longer enjoy its advantages. When Pitt came into office, Orders in Council had already been issued which declared that American ships would be considered as foreign ships and thus subject to the restrictions of the Navigation Acts, a policy that was not modified until 1795. Pitt was able to encourage good relations with the new American states, and in 1785 John Adams was received as the first American ambassador to the court of St. James. Relations with the American states in turn had an important bearing on the British West Indies, for the American states were an important market for West Indian products and supplied the West Indies with grain, fish, barrel staves, and other necessities. The new trade regulations meant that this trade could not legally be conducted in American ships. The West Indies interest in London protested this policy vigorously, but to no effect. The British government expected that Canadian colonies could supply food and timber products, and that imperial trade would benefit if West Indian products went directly to Britain. Despite their cries of alarm, the British West Indies continued to be profitable. With the outbreak of war with France in 1793 the British government now found it expedient to reactivate trade relations between the West Indies and the United States. In 1795 Jay's Treaty gave American ships increased access to the West Indian market.

Pitt faced serious problems in dealing with the Canadian colonies that had been profoundly affected by the American Revolution. Prior to the war, Canada consisted principally of the French settlements along the St. Lawrence River. The American Revolution led to a large influx of Loyalists from the rebelling colonies into Canada. They demanded a representative assembly and English law. The French inhabitants, however, preferred to preserve their traditional laws and customs. Pitt's solution was the Canada Act of 1791, which divided Canada into two parts. Quebec (Lower Canada), which was primarily French, preserved French land tenure and the rights of the Roman Catholic church. Ontario (Upper Canada) had English land tenure and law. Both colonies had assemblies, but there was one royal governor for both and his power was dominant. Nova Scotia, New Brunswick, and Prince Edward Island were already separate colonies. Thus the Pitt ministry provided a system of government for the Canadian colonies which proved workable for the next half century.

Pitt's major imperial problem was the extent of the powers of the British East India Company in India, a bone of contention in Britain for the previous two decades. When the East India Company acquired authority over the great province of Bengal, the Company became involved in government and war, while its commercial activities fell upon evil days. Two other problems also emerged: the influence exercised by the East India Company upon British domestic politics, and notorious abuses of power by the Company in dealing with the native inhabitants of India. When Pitt took office the demand in Britain for legislation regulating the Company was overwhelming; the only question was the form it would take. Pitt's India Act of 1784 (amended in 1786) provided a compromise solution. The Company continued to govern its territories in India, but a Board of Control in London and a strong governor general in India established public authority over the Company. The first governor general was Lord Cornwallis, who atoned for his defeat at Yorktown by introducing a new standard of rectitude and efficiency into the government of India.

The Pitt ministry extended the Empire into a new area when it began British settlement in Australia. One of the common sentences passed upon convicted felons was transportation, ordinarily to America. With American independence, however, Britain lacked a place to send convicts, and for several years the government could only confine the convicts to derelict ships (hulks) anchored in the Thames. The Pitt ministry proposed to relieve the situation by settling the convicts in Australia, which had been discovered by Captain Cook in 1770. The first shipload of convicts arrived in 1788, and Sydney was established as a penal colony governed by a military commander and a garrison. After considerable hardship, discharged soldiers and freed convicts began to settle the region, and the new colony took root.

The Beginnings of Industrialism

Economic Growth. The eighteenth century was a period of remarkable economic growth in Britain. These economic changes were so far-reaching in

The Industrial Revolution

their effects that historians have called them "The Industrial Revolution." There are many reasons why Britain became the first industrial nation. The government of Britain combined political stability, individual freedom, and security of property in a mix conducive to enterprise and investment. Britain's institutions of banking and credit were well developed, and her far-flung trade and Empire provided capital, raw materials, and markets for industry. Strong domestic demand, fueled by wealth derived from trade and agriculture, stimulated new methods for increased production of goods. The availability of coal, iron, and waterpower was an important factor. A growing population provided labor for factories and mines; a prosperous agriculture produced the food and fiber needed to sustain an industrial economy. Thus in the later half of the eighteenth century a unique set of circumstances, brought together by a generation of unusual inventiveness and enterprise, made Britain the leader in a movement that has transformed the world—the Industrial Revolution.

Iron, Steam, Coal. One important feature of the early industrial age was the manufacture of cheaper and more abundant iron. Prior to the eighteenth century, iron was smelted with charcoal, which made it necessary to locate most iron works in forests to obtain fuel. In the eighteenth century a family of iron makers located in the Severn Valley, the Darbys, developed a method of smelting iron with coal by first converting the coal to coke. The most striking of the new industrial ironmasters of Britain was John Wilkinson, who built an ironworks across the river from the Darbys. His cannon boring machine greatly improved the range and accuracy of his cannon and could also be adapted to make cylinders for steam engines. He promoted iron products in a variety of ways: he built iron barges, installed an iron pulpit in the local church, and was buried in an iron coffin. Wilkinson was a strong-willed, hard-driving person who could take advantage of new processes and transform iron making from a small family enterprise into a large-scale industry. As a result of these new processes, iron production in Britain more than doubled from 1760 to 1788, and quadrupled again in the next seventeen years.

Another feature of industrialism was the development of a vital new source of power—the steam engine. Engines powered by steam had been in use since the later seventeenth century, but they were highly inefficient and were used mainly to pump water out of coal mines. In the 1760s a Scottish instrument maker, James Watt, began developing a more efficient type of steam engine. He also invented a device to convert steam power to a rotary motion. In 1774 Watt went into partnership with Matthew Boulton, a Birmingham businessman, to manufacture steam engines. Watt's engines were first used for coal mines, smelting, and forges and were later adapted to textile manufactures, rail transport, and ships.

Double-Action Sun-and-planet Engine designed by James Watt, 1788 *(The Science Museum, London)*.

Iron smelting and the steam engine made necessary a larger supply of coal. Britain possessed abundant coal, much of it near the surface, and coal had been an important product since Tudor times. Until the industrial age coal was used principally for home heating. By the eighteenth century the coal trade from Newcastle to London was extensive and was also an important source of revenue for the crown. The development of the coal industry was a harbinger, a foundation, and a catalyst for the Industrial

Revolution. It began with technical advances in pumping, ventilation, and lighting. The steam engine created a new demand for coal and made it possible to supply that demand by providing power to raise coal and to pump water out of mines. Horse hauling (as opposed to human) and steam-powered hoists to raise the coal to the surface were important innovations. Wagon ways and canals to transport the coal were also put to other uses. New industrial uses followed—gas supply, for example, in addition to iron and steam power. By 1800 coal mines were being opened up in Scotland, Wales, and the west of England. In the 1830s the railroad created a new demand for coal and also lowered the cost of bringing it to markets, thus making coal more practical as a source of energy for industry. The coal industry was also important as a model for large-scale investment and management. Continuing improvements in the efficiency of the industry resulted in ever lower prices that, in turn, helped other industries. The wages of the hewers rose considerably ahead of prices in the period 1700 to 1810, which stimulated the economy.

Textiles. In some respects the textile industry was the spearhead of British industrial growth. Textile manufacture was long established in England; ever since the later Middle Ages woolen textiles had been one of England's most important products. For centuries woolen cloth manufacture was a cottage industry in which artisans and their families worked in their own homes scattered throughout the towns, villages, and countryside. In the later eighteenth century a revolution took place in the manufacture of textiles, as machines were developed which were too large and expensive to be owned and operated by the workers in their homes. This revolution first took place in the process of spinning thread, where Richard Arkwright became the leader in development of the factory system. Arkwright came from humble beginnings and got his start in textile manufacture by developing a spinning machine driven by waterpower. Although his role as an inventor is dubious, there can be no question of his ability as an organizer of production. He built his first factory along an isolated river in Derbyshire and brought in pauper children to tend his machines, housing them in a dormitory near the factory. Arkwright was one of the first textile manufacturers to use steam power, thus freeing himself from the need to locate his mills in labor-short areas where waterpower was available. Like Wilkinson, he may be seen as typical of the new industrialists whose imagination and determination were transforming the production of goods in Britain.

Arkwright was engaged in spinning cotton, and it was in the cotton textile industry that the new methods were most rapidly developed. The American Eli Whitney's invention of the cotton gin greatly increased the supply of raw cotton. The introduction of the power loom after 1815

Iron bridge, Coalbrookdale *(E. A. Reitan)*.

brought the factory system to the weaving of cloth; this had disastrous effects upon the hand weavers, who had increased in numbers due to the abundance of cheap yarn. Although figures for productivity in the industry are sketchy, it is estimated that the value of manufactured cotton cloth increased from £4,000,000 in 1783 to £15,000,000 twenty years later. The value of cotton manufactures doubled again in the next twenty years, by which time cotton manufacture had passed the woolen textile industry, which was slower to change.

Pottery. Another old industry that was transformed by new industrial processes was the manufacture of pottery. Josiah Wedgwood, a Staffordshire potter, introduced the factory system in the manufacture of earthenware, not only to increase productivity but also to improve the quality and uniformity of his products. Wedgwood's superior product was due to excellent design, carefully controlled processes, and workers with more specialized skills resulting from the division of labor. His basic patterns could be afforded by the middle class, and when decorated by his superb artists they were fit for the crowned heads and aristocracy of Europe. He built a model town near the factory to house his employees, although not all of them appreciated the discipline and efforts at self-improvement that went with it. Since he needed reliable transportation to bring in clay and coal and to take out his products, he was an active investor in canals. When Pitt's Irish Commercial Resolutions (1785) threatened his industry with cheaper Irish products, he actively opposed them. A man of cultivated tastes and generous impulses, Wedgwood was a pioneer who presented the more attractive face of industrialism.

Transportation. Changes in the production of goods would have had limited effect without improvements in transportation. By the mid-eighteenth century turnpike roads had greatly improved the movement of people and goods by coach or wagon, and the growing size, speed, and reliability of ships contributed to the growth of trade. With her many rivers, England made important use of water transportation from the earliest times. In the later eighteenth century, canal building greatly improved water transportation, especially in the new industrial areas of the north and west of England. A remarkable nobleman, the duke of Bridgewater, led the building of canals. Bridgewater wanted to exploit the coal on his estates near Manchester; his answer was to build a canal to carry the coal to the Mersey River. In this task he benefited from the services of a talented engineer, James Brindley, who designed a complex canal which included tunnels, aqueducts, and levees to bring coal barges to their destination. In 1776 he finished his second canal, which gave access to the River Mersey and Liverpool. Bridgewater's canals encouraged a canal building boom that provided cheap transportation for coal, clay, bricks, farm products, and other bulky items necessary in an industrial society.

Agriculture. The role of agriculture in the Industrial Revolution is a matter of some debate. Certainly a distinctive feature of agriculture in England in the eighteenth century was its capacity to augment output while releasing labor for employment in industry and services. The growth in agricultural labor productivity developed from the substitution of animals for manpower and fertilizer for land. The critical factor in this process was the planting of fodder crops, which increased the capacity of farmland to raise more animals. This was an evolutionary rather than a revolutionary process, one going back to the seventeenth century, and one which owed much to practices learned from the Dutch. These practices included the rotations of crops, the use of clover and turnips to provide more winter fodder for cattle, improved breeds of animals, and new agricultural implements and machinery. The diffusion of the innovations was hastened by a marked upswing in the prices of food and raw material in the period from 1760 to 1815. This was especially true in the period of the French Revolution and Napoleonic Wars. Imports were cut off from the continent for long periods while the domestic economy was struggling to support large contingents of British forces overseas.

An increase in the supply of food was essential to support the increase in population that occurred during the century. Up until the mid-eighteenth century the increases in productivity kept pace with the increase in population. Thereafter, agriculture productivity fell behind. Instead of exporting agricultural products England became a net importer by the end of the century. The gap was closed primarily by imports from Ireland. By the later eighteenth century, the new methods of agriculture led to an extensive movement for enclosure of the open fields. In 1760 probably half the arable land was still farmed in large open fields that were allotted to local residents in successive strips of land. This resulted in non-contiguous holdings. The new methods, however, could not be introduced under the old communal system, and progressive landlords sought to enclose the open fields into smaller individual fields divided by fences or hedges. Enclosure usually required an act of Parliament and the agreement of the holders of three-fourths of the land. Commissioners were appointed to determine individual rights to the land and to divide the land into equitable shares.

The principal benefits of enclosures went to those with the largest amount of land. Those with small landholdings found it difficult to survive without the communal life of the former system. Villagers who did not have rights to land, but who had rights in the common pastures and woodlands, also found themselves at a disadvantage. The benefits of the increase in prices for agricultural products also went primarily to large landowners. In terms of the Industrial Revolution the changes in agriculture made their impact in several ways. Real incomes derived from agriculture rose 81 percent in the eighteenth century, and this meant an increase in purchasing power and a larger market for manufactures. The increase in productivity released workers, who went to the cities, worked in industry, improved their earnings, and, consequently, spent more. The adverse effect of the rise in prices was the increase in the cost of labor for industry as the cost of subsistence went up. The export market for manufactured articles was ultimately a far more important stimulus for the Industrial Revolution than the slow advances in agricultural productivity.

Society. The standard of living of the urban working class in the early industrial age is one of those questions that evokes conflicting opinions. Although historians disagree on this point, there can be no doubt of the sense of injury felt by industrial workers, and especially by craftsmen in long-established industries. The competition of factory-made goods destroyed the value of their skills, and machines that could be tended by children took away the dignity formerly possessed by skilled labor. The Luddite riots of 1811 and 1812 were an early example of the tensions emerging in the new industrial age. The Luddites were framework knitters

Factory scene, 1840 *(BBC Hulton Picture Library)*.

who made the long knitted stockings used by gentlemen in the eighteenth century. They found their position seriously eroded for a variety of reasons: extreme fluctuations in costs and markets due to wartime conditions, changing styles which reduced the demand for their product, and new machinery which produced cheaper stockings. They identified themselves as followers of a mythical "King Lud" and protested by issuing manifestos and breaking the new machines for making stockings. The Luddites were not a depressed industrial proletariat; they were from the aristocracy of labor, proud of their status and skill. Their expressions of outrage were not purely economic. They were a response to the loss of personal dignity and security which their craft and parliamentary regulation had formerly guaranteed. It was among such persons that protest against the new industrial system was most likely to be found.

Lurking over all was the sense of insecurity found in the depersonalized wage relationship of the new industrial system. The working people of England had always labored long and hard, but in turn they expected to be protected by their employers against short-term fluctuations in prices, wages, and employment and to be provided for by the parish if afflicted by long-term hardship arising from unemployment, disability, or old age. Many factory owners in the new industries, however, felt little responsibility for their workers. The concentration of industrial growth in certain areas and the distress resulting from war, inflation, poor crops, and economic fluctuations contributed to a breakdown of the old system of poor relief. The propertied classes who paid the rates (local taxes) for poor relief complained of an excessive burden, and the poor complained that they were not provided for as required by law. Sometimes the poor reacted with riots and destructiveness; sometimes they read Tom Paine and agitated for political power; sometimes they formed labor unions, in defiance of the Combination Acts. Much of the time they suffered in silence, but they grew increasingly conscious of their grievances. The revolution in production that had created the new industries had also produced a new social force—the industrial working class—which was thereafter an important factor in British life.

It would be unfair, however, to characterize all these changes as detrimental to the new urban working class. Indeed one of the positive features that accompanied the Industrial Revolution was a general improvement in what one historian has described as the "standards of comfort" in this period. Wheat had replaced courser grains as the basic ingredient of bread for all classes. The basic diet included a larger portion of fresh meat. The dramatic increase in the production of coal and the improved transportation that made it available to more areas of the country meant warmer homes and better-cooked food. The same transportation was used to increase the distribution of fruit produced in the south of England. Tea became the national beverage, displacing beer and harder spirits. As it was prepared by boiling water, the benefits to public health were not insubstantial, considering the lack of sanitation and protected water supplies. The consumption of soap and candles rose sharply in the 1790s to a rate double that during the beginning of the century. Cheap cotton cloth replaced leather, wool, and linen and permitted even the lower classes to have changes of clothing and laundering, which impacted positively on

Lott house, Flatford *(E. A. Reitan)*.

health. Even the unattractive housing of the cities had virtues. The construction of brick and stone with wood floors above the ground level and the use of glass windows was a considerable improvement over window-less cottages, often of wood and dried mud, with dirt floors and thatched roofs, unsanitary and unhealthy, however quaint and attractive they may appear to us now. Finally, the water closet began to come into general use, a humble but important innovation. These were all by-products of the Industrial Revolution.

Britain and the French Revolution

In 1789 the French crown was bankrupt. In desperation, King Louis XVI called the ancient Parliament of France, the Estates-General, for the first time since 1614. The impecunious king looked to the estates of the realm—the clergy (First Estate), the nobility (Second Estate), and the people (Third Estate)—to come to his aid. When the Estates-General met, the businessmen and lawyers who emerged as leaders of the Third Estate, joined by some of the nobility and clergy, demanded that the Estates-General be transformed into a National Assembly which would draw up a new constitution for France. The king yielded, and great excitement spread through France. The French Revolution had begun. At first the aspirations of the National Assembly were well received in Britain. British political ideas had been widely disseminated in France through the works of Locke and by French writers such as Voltaire and Montesquieu. The British felt a sense of pride that the haughty French had seen fit to follow their example. When Fox heard that the people of Paris had seized the Bastille, the hated symbol of arbitrary power, he declared: "How much the greatest event that has happened in the world and how much the best." Pitt was less enthusiastic about the new political currents in France but was relieved to think that internal difficulties would make France less a problem to British foreign policy. British reformers were encouraged by the ferment in France. The Revolution Society, formed to celebrate the centennial of the Glorious Revolution of 1688, praised the French for following the same course and looked for a revival of the reforming spirit at home.

The initial reaction in Britain soon turned to horror as the moderate leaders of the National Assembly were supplanted by radicals determined to overthrow the monarchy and the other forms of privilege in France and to establish a democratic republic. The domestic upheaval in France was complicated by foreign intervention as Austria and Prussia came to the aid of the French king. In 1793 the radical revolutionaries seized power, executed the king and queen, introduced mass conscription, and suppressed dissent with the guillotine. The revolutionary armies repulsed the Austrians and Prussians and then burst into the Netherlands, the Rhineland, and northern Italy. Soon, deposed princes, nobles, and churchmen were arriving in Britain as refuges, telling tales of atrocities and bewailing their loss of property and status. George III, the Pitt ministry, the aristocracy and gentry, the church, and most of the propertied middle class were shocked at the wreckage and were disturbed by the thought that British radicals might attempt a similar upheaval. British dislike of France as the national enemy was heightened by the view of France as the center of a revolution which, given an opportunity, would also destroy the balance of social relationships in Britain.

Conservatives and Radicals. The war with revolutionary France was, in one sense, a return to the long-standing conflict between Britain and France in Europe and overseas, but it had a new dimension—a conflict of ideologies. Revolutionary France was dedicated to the triumph of reason over tradition, secularism over religion, equality over privilege, and patriotic fervor over the cosmopolitan culture of eighteenth-century Europe. The dominant effect of the French Revolution in Britain was a strong reaction not only against French power but against French ideals and, by extension, against most forms of domestic discontent. The chief spokesman of the reaction against French ideology was Edmund Burke, whose *Reflec-*

tions on the Revolution in France (1790) first sounded the alarm. Burke had spent most of his political career in opposition, first as the chief parliamentary spokesman for the marquis of Rockingham and then as a follower of Fox. In 1790, however, Burke came forward as a defender of the status quo, arguing that the developments in France were not simply an attack on abuses but a revolution which would destroy the fundamental basis of society, leading eventually to conflict, chaos, and despotism. When Fox expressed sympathy with the French, Burke broke openly with his colleague and gave his support to Pitt. Burke's writings against the French Revolution became a classic exposition of a conservative philosophy still respected in our own time.

Replies to Burke were not long in coming. Tom Paine, whose *Common Sense* (1776) had encouraged the American colonists to seek independence, responded with *The Rights of Man* (1791). Paine's ideas were the conventional radicalism of the eighteenth century, but he possessed the gift of stating his views in a direct, pungent manner, which struck home to the ordinary man. He ridiculed Burke's high-flown reverence for institutions based on the injustices of the past and urged that they be replaced by institutions that would protect the rights and dignity of all men. The ideals of the French Revolution were expounded in more moderate form by William Godwin. Godwin was a doctrinaire rationalist, whose *Political Justice* (1793) held forth the prospect of human progress to perfection as a result of the triumph of reason over tradition and ignorance. Godwin was not a revolutionary who sought to destroy the past by force, but the results he anticipated from the march of reason were every bit as revolutionary as those urged by Paine. In 1792 Mary Wollstonecraft, a remarkable young woman who later married Godwin, penned her own reply to Burke, *A Vindication of the Rights of Woman*, in which she urged equality for women, especially in education and careers, which would enable them to develop their full potential as persons.

Britain at War. The political and ideological conflict engendered by the French Revolution was intensified by war. In 1793 France, already at war with Austria and Prussia, declared war on Britain, Spain, and the Dutch. By this time the British had come to believe that war was inevitable and necessary, and Pitt changed from the minister of peace and moderate reform to the leader of a European coalition against French power and French revolutionary ideals. He was not a great war minister. Moreover, his stubborn belief that the war would be short because of an imminent French collapse proved to be mistaken. Pitt's strategy was to rely principally on British sea power, using it in areas such as the Baltic, the Mediterranean, and the Caribbean which he regarded as vital to British trade. He preferred to leave the land war to allies subsidized by British gold. In

1797 a brilliant young French officer, Napoleon Bonaparte, won a startling victory over the Austrians in northern Italy. In 1798 he invaded Egypt. At this point British sea power struck a heavy blow as a bold naval officer, Horatio Nelson, destroyed the French fleet at the Battle of the Nile and trapped the French army in Egypt. Napoleon escaped and returned to France, where in 1799 he seized power with the title of first consul.

By 1800 both sides were ready for peace. Napoleon had defeated a coalition of European powers and was consolidating his control of France. Britain still ruled the seas but was desperate for relief from the costs and strains of war. High food prices and economic dislocations caused widespread distress. In 1797 mutinies broke out in the navy, and in 1798 revolt flared in Ireland. The Peace of Amiens (1802) was an uneasy truce, but nonetheless welcome to both Britain and France.

Political Consolidation. In the meantime, the need for resistance to France led to a consolidation of political forces behind the Pitt ministry. The prime minister strengthened his position by discrediting the radicals in Parliament while repressing their supporters. George III gained new popularity as the symbol of national unity against France, and he became more firm than ever in his defense of traditional institutions. In 1793 to 1794 the largest part of the Whigs, led by the duke of Portland, gave their support to Pitt. Fox was left the ineffectual leader of a small band of opposition Whigs, who were no longer a threat to the ministry or taken seriously by the public. In 1797 Fox's friend, Charles Grey, moved proposals for parliamentary reform. Pitt had never been more than lukewarm in his support of parliamentary reform, and he now used the war and radical agitation as an excuse to insure that the proposals were overwhelmingly defeated. The Pitt ministry possessed what appeared to be unshakable control of the government.

The triumph of conservatism in government was matched by public opinion. In general, Burke's point of view triumphed: the French Revolution was seen as a destructive force that must be contained in Europe, lest it infect Britain. Criticism of existing institutions was stigmatized as unpatriotic. Although Pitt was more moderate than many of his followers, political pressures led the Pitt ministry to take strong measures to suppress discontent. In 1794 the Habeas Corpus Act was suspended to permit imprisonment without trial of those persons suspected of political agitation. In 1795 the Treasonable Practices Act defined treason to include words as well as actions. The Seditious Meetings Act, passed the same year, prohibited meetings of more than fifty persons without license from the local magistrates. Food riots and naval mutinies led to further repressive measures in 1799: radical societies were dissolved, and the Combination Acts prohibited the formation of unions by workingmen to bargain with employers. The unity of the nation in the face of revolutionary France was primarily a matter of national feeling, but it was strongly reinforced by the use of the power of the state to suppress criticism and organized expressions of dissent. Yet one should not overstress the extent of repression. The machinery for this purpose was already in existence and little changed. The number of actual prosecutions was well below those that followed the 1715 and the 1745 rebellions. If the repressive measures taken by Pitt demonstrated the limits of traditional liberty and the powers the crown had at its disposal, one must also recognize that the concept of liberty advanced by the radicals in the 1790s was very different from that espoused earlier in the century. There was, rather, a new sensitivity to liberty, a result of the agitations that began with Wilkes and were given new prominence by the eloquent though sometimes raucous opposition led by Fox. If Pitt sometimes attacked these concepts he was also to be acknowledged for being aware of them.

Ireland. The problem of political control was most marked in Ireland. The Patriot movement of the early 1780s, coming at a time when the English were preoccupied with the American Revolution, had resulted in an unaccustomed degree of autonomy for the governing class. The ripple effect of the French Revolution had its inevitable impact in Ireland, which further reinforced the desire for de facto if not de jure independence bound only by the crown. An organization called the United Irishmen was created to realize this goal. Originally it was Protestant in the majority and was committed to a moderate policy of constitutional monarchy. The repressive measures introduced by the English, both at home and in Ireland, to control radical agitation had the opposite effect from that intended. The indigenous discontent was inflamed by French agitators and the prospect of French assistance. One consequence was that the United Irishmen now became predominantly Catholic in its membership, republican in its aims. Mobilizing those who embraced these sentiments, Theobald Wolfe Tone now launched the United Irishmen in a fight for independence from Britain.

By 1798 Britain's struggle against France had created the opportunity that Irish patriots were seeking, and the United Irishmen rose in a desperate insurrection. The uprising was doomed from the start: most leaders had been seized before it began; Protestant and Catholic malcontents had different ends in view; poorly armed artisans and peasants were no match for the Irish militia; and Wolfe Tone arrived from France with French aid too late to be of use. At this point Pitt decided that the political unity of the British Isles was essential, a project which could succeed only if the Irish were given a fair share in their government. He sent Lord Cornwallis, his favorite troubleshooter, to pacify Ireland. Cornwallis proposed an

Act of Union, similar to that which had successfully joined England and Scotland in 1707. The Irish Parliament would be abolished, and the Irish would send members to the British Parliament at Westminster—a group of elected peers and bishops and 100 members of the House of Commons. The formation of the United Kingdom would, of course, give the Irish free trade with Britain and the Empire. The Anglo-Irish ruling leadership class was totally dependent on British power in the face of French intrigues and domestic insurrection. With the further inducement of generous bribes, they were persuaded to agree to the Act of Union, and the new Parliament of the United Kingdom first met in 1801.

An important corollary to Pitt's Act of Union was his proposal for Catholic emancipation—the admission of Catholics to Parliament and political offices. Pitt recognized that the United Kingdom could not succeed without the support of the Irish Catholic population, but he did not allow fully for the resistance such a proposal would encounter in Britain. George III declared his unalterable opposition to the idea, which he saw as fatal to the position of the Church of England, and then he collapsed in another bout of mental illness. Pitt faced strong opposition in his Cabinet, in the House of Lords, and among many of his followers in the House of Commons. Realizing that he had overreached himself, he abandoned Catholic emancipation and resigned, being replaced by Henry Addington in 1801.

Britain and Napoleon

Pitt's resignation, and the Peace of Amiens which followed in 1802, marked a brief breathing space in the long struggle between Britain and revolutionary France. Napoleon needed time to consolidate his power which he had accomplished by 1804, when he assumed the title of emperor. After the Peace of Amiens he began building up an army and fleet, ostensibly for an invasion of Britain, and in 1803 the Addington ministry, upset by Napoleon's restless inability to adhere to the agreements he had made, again declared war. In 1804 Addington was replaced by Pitt, who returned to office to form one more coalition against Napoleon. Pitt was in ill health and had lost some of his former supporters, but his name and ability could still rally the nation. In 1806 he died, to be followed by a coalition ministry ("Ministry of All Talents") in which Fox played an important part until his death a few months later. Once again Britain was at war with France, but this time without the two leaders who had held the center of the political stage for almost twenty-five years.

The dominant fact of British history from 1804 to 1814 was the long struggle against Napoleonic France. When Pitt returned to power in 1804 he persuaded Austria and Russia to join with Britain in another coalition

Battle of Trafalgar by Stanfield *(BBC Hulton Picture Library)*.

that would be supported by British money and sea power. Abandoning his plans for an invasion of Britain (or perhaps they were a ruse), Napoleon marched quickly against the Austrians and Russians whom he defeated at Ulm and Austerlitz in 1805. The next year he defeated the Prussians at Jena, and in 1807 he made a favorable peace with the tsar of Russia. In 1808 he occupied Spain. Napoleon had defeated the major powers of Europe and was busy reorganizing the smaller states of Germany and Italy. As in 1940 when Hitler's armies dominated Europe, Britain stood alone.

Napoleon's dominance on the continent was offset by Britain's growing industrial power and by her command of the seas. In 1805 a British fleet under Nelson defeated a combined French-Spanish fleet off the coast of Spain near Cape Trafalgar. Thereafter France could not threaten Britain by sea, and British sea power could be used to destroy French shipping, blockade the Napoleonic Empire, support allies, encourage insurrections, and capture colonies. Since the conflict between British sea power and French power on land had created a stand off, the two antagonists turned to economic warfare. Napoleon scornfully dismissed the British as "a nation of shopkeepers" and tried to destroy the British economy by depriving Britain of her European market. His "Continental System" was an attempt to close the Napoleonic Empire to British goods. The British, in turn, reacted with the Orders in Council, which established a blockade of Napoleonic Europe. The British blockade affected neutral nations especially, and, along with impressment, contributed to the outbreak of the War of 1812 between Britain and the United States. Neither policy was entirely successful, although each nation imposed a considerable hardship on the other. Britain found new markets for her manufactured goods overseas and maintained some of her European customers through smuggling. Even Napoleon needed some British goods and permitted their entry through a system of licenses. The economic warfare had some effect, but the eventual decision was to be made on the field of battle.

Seeking an opportunity to engage Napoleon on land, the British turned to Portugal and Spain where French occupation had encountered strong national resistance. In 1808 Arthur Wellesley, later the duke of Wellington, was sent to Portugal to expel the French and to begin the process of driving them out of the Iberian Peninsula. Wellington was thoroughly patrician, a firm, dignified, and stern disciplinarian, a master of careful, systematic warfare. Faced by a hostile population and Wellington's methodical progress, the French slowly gave way. Wellington's Peninsular War was a secondary factor in the eventual defeat of Napoleon, but it gave the British the sense that they had found a way to get at "Boney" and a commander who could make the most of it.

Tory Control of Britain. In the meantime, the deaths of Pitt and Fox and the long struggle against Napoleon led to the emergence of new political leaders and a new party alignment in Britain. The name Tories was revived for the conservatives who had previously followed Pitt. The Tories were strong supporters of the monarchy, the church, and the status quo in social relationships. They adopted as their watchword Burke's veneration for traditional institutions, without his keen eye for the abuses to which any long-established ruling class is liable. But Pitt had not depended on Tories alone; it was, after all, the Tories who had abandoned him on the issue of Catholic emancipation, leading to his resignation in 1801. Pitt had also been supported by a strong contingent of Whigs led by the duke of Portland. The Portland Whigs continued their cooperation with the Tory government, but they still maintained some of the old Whig tradition of resistance to royal power and support for religious toleration. The opposition Whigs, formerly followers of Fox, were now led by Charles Grey. They continued in their belief that parliamentary government, religious toleration, and individual liberties were threatened by the power and influence of the crown, swollen by the needs of war. In the House of Commons there was a small group of radicals who continued to press for

The Napoleonic Wars

familiar radical goals, such as a more representative House of Commons and the reduction of political corruption. A large number of independent members who usually supported the Tories were also to be found in the House of Commons. In 1812 Lord Liverpool became leader of a reorganized Tory ministry, holding that position until incapacitated by a stroke in 1827. Liverpool was a poised, confident, capable aristocrat whose father had risen from humble beginnings to a position of great influence under Pitt. Addington (now Lord Sidmouth) became home secretary, thus assuring the Tories that domestic agitators and dissidents would be dealt with firmly.

Liverpool had the capacity to attract and utilize young men of talent who came forward as Tories because the Tories offered the only opportunity to hold office. One of Lord Liverpool's younger ministers was Lord Castlereagh, a handsome, intense Irish nobleman, who refused an English peerage so he could continue to sit in the House of Commons representing his Irish constituency. Castlereagh became foreign secretary under Liverpool, serving with distinction in that post until his death in 1822. Another brilliant young Tory was George Canning, whose intellect and oratorical ability made him a powerful force in the House of Commons. Liverpool admired Canning and wished to use him in his ministry, but

Castlereagh and Canning were bitter personal enemies, and this fact made it impossible to bring Canning into office. The third of the capable young Tories, with a long career of public service before him, was Robert Peel, the son of a prosperous Lancashire textile manufacturer. Peel made his mark as a protégé of Liverpool, first in the War Office and then when Liverpool became prime minister, as chief secretary in Ireland. The ability of Liverpool and the talented younger Tories, combined with the conservatism of the country, gave the Tories a grip on power which meant that parliamentary reform, Catholic emancipation, and other controversial issues would be postponed indefinitely.

Victory and Peace. As the Liverpool ministry settled into place, the tide of battle began to turn in Europe. Napoleon overreached himself in 1812 when he sent a powerful force against Russia. He defeated the Russians in battle and occupied Moscow, but he could not obtain a formal surrender from the tsar. Defeated later by the Russian army and by the Russian winter, Napoleon's soldiers were left to struggle back to France while their commander desperately tried to recruit another army. The Russians, Austrians, and Prussians all joined the war—the first time that all three powers had been included in one coalition. Britain served as paymaster to the coalition, and British gold flowed as never before. Nationalist uprisings against the French took place in Germany and Italy, and in Spain Wellington, supported by Spanish hatred of the French, continued his methodical advance. In 1813 Napoleon was decisively defeated at Leipzig, in eastern Germany, while Wellington crossed the Pyrenees Mountains and entered the south of France. In 1814 Napoleon surrendered and was exiled to the little Mediterranean island of Elba.

As the victorious allies advanced, they began to think of the peace settlement. Castlereagh, the British foreign secretary, was determined that the allies should act together in the peace negotiations and in the postwar period. He was also concerned that France be brought back into the community of nations, and thus he advocated a peace that would stabilize the French government, check French expansion, and be acceptable to most Frenchmen. The settlement made with France was along the lines advocated by Castlereagh: a Bourbon monarchy under Louis XVIII. The borders of France were restored as of 1792; Britain restored most of the captured French colonies; the allies abandoned claims for indemnities; and France, at British urging, agreed to abolish the slave trade. Considering the turmoil that France had brought to Europe in the previous twenty-five years, the peace with France was an enlightened one. Castlereagh's role in the settlement reasserted Britain's leadership role in European diplomacy.

The peace with France had gone easily in comparison with the problems and great power rivalries that complicated a settlement of Germany, Italy, and eastern Europe. Thus the decision was made to call a general conference at Vienna, which met in September 1814. The Austrian emperor provided lavish entertainment for a brilliant assemblage, but the important decisions were made by representatives of the four major powers, led by the Austrian chancellor, Metternich. When disputes arose concerning Poland and Saxony, Talleyrand, the astute representative of France, was able to obtain an important voice for his country. The conference was interrupted in March 1815 when Napoleon escaped from Elba, landed in France, and rallied his veterans to his standard. The duke of Wellington was put in command of a mixed army of British, Dutch, and German soldiers, which defeated Napoleon at the Battle of Waterloo (June 1815). Napoleon was then sent off to the island of St. Helena, an obscure British possession in the South Atlantic, where he spent his remaining years under British guardianship. The great struggle that had dominated Europe for more than twenty years was finally ended.

Shortly before the defeat of Napoleon at Waterloo, the Congress of Vienna completed a settlement for the territories that had been conquered by France. Each of the major powers had its own dynastic or territorial ambitions, but in general they were determined to restore the European balance of power and to prevent a renewal of revolutionary outbreaks. A strong buffer was placed to the north of France by the union of Holland and the Austrian Netherlands (Belgium) in the Kingdom of the Netherlands; Austria was made dominant in northern Italy by control of Lombardy and Venetia. The Bourbon monarchy was restored in Spain, but the Spanish colonists in the New World continued the struggle for independence that had begun during the Napoleonic period. Germany and Italy continued to be divided among small or medium-sized states, although no attempt was made to restore all the petty states of the prerevolutionary period. Britain was rewarded with colonies and naval bases. British power in the Mediterranean was confirmed by the retention of Gibraltar, the acquisition of Malta, and a protectorate over the Greek islands. The Cape Colony in South Africa, the island of Mauritius in the Indian Ocean, and Ceylon provided bases on the route to India. Britain also strengthened her possessions in the West Indies and Central America. Britain's policies regarding search and seizure on the high seas were left unchallenged, although these had been a cause of great complaint among neutral nations and a major factor in the War of 1812 with the United States. In short, the Vienna settlement confirmed the naval and imperial supremacy that Britain had gained during the Napoleonic Wars.

The dynastic and territorial provisions of the Vienna settlement appeared to be a return to the balance of power diplomacy of prerevolutionary Europe. But Castlereagh took Britain a step further by committing

Britain to cooperation with the major European states for the purpose of preserving peace. In the eighteenth century Britain had been involved in European alliances for specific purposes: to maintain the balance of power, to protect the Netherlands or Hanover, and to have a continental ally in the struggle with France and Spain for colonies and sea power. Many of these reasons still applied. But in the glow of the joint effort by which Napoleon had been destroyed, Castlereagh advocated a British commitment to Europe in a Quadruple Alliance, expanded to include France in 1818, which was designed to keep the major powers in harmony. "The Concert of Europe," as it was called, meant different things to Metternich and to Castlereagh. Metternich looked for cooperation among the crowned heads of Europe to put down revolutionary movements. Such a policy was less acceptable in Britain. The British already possessed constitutional government, representative institutions, civil liberties, religious toleration, and national unity. They could not, in good conscience, set themselves against movements on the continent that sought those same ideals. This was the dilemma that destroyed Castlereagh's foreign policy and, indeed, Castlereagh himself.

British Society in a Revolutionary Age

Stability and Change. The remarkable feature of British society in this age of political, economic, and intellectual change was its stability. To some extent social stability was artificial—a defensive posture adopted by a ruling class using the powers of government to bolster its position. But for the most part, the stability of British society was genuine. The traditional institutions and social relationships of Britain were accepted by the bulk of its population as good, to be defended against French ideologues or domestic radicals. A long period of war imposed new social stresses but also contributed to the sense of national unity that saw Britain through to victory. But in this age of conservatism, new ideas were taking root in Britain that were, in their own way, as revolutionary as the political and diplomatic upheavals taking place abroad. In France, dissatisfaction with existing institutions had created an ideology of revolution; in Britain, where existing institutions were more satisfactory, the goal was not revolution but reform. One approach to institutional change was philosophical or analytical, examining institutions rationally in terms of their function. The principal exponent of this approach was Jeremy Bentham, whose *Introduction to the Principles of Morals and Legislation* was published in 1789. Bentham believed that institutions should be judged by their utility—by their contribution to human happiness. He ridiculed Burke's mystical appeal to the accumulated wisdom of the past as nonsense designed to perpetuate privileges for which there was no reasonable justification. Bentham was especially interested in law and prisons, both of which were admirably designed to inflict vengeance but which had little effect on crime. In his view, the Poor Laws ran counter to human nature and thus were not a rational method to deal with poverty. By 1809, when he wrote his *Plan for Parliamentary Reform* (published in 1817), Bentham was convinced that other necessary reforms would not take place until Parliament itself was reformed to remove the unrepresentative franchises and distribution of seats which made the House of Commons unresponsive to the nation. Bentham was not a politician and did not sit in Parliament. His great contribution was to present an intellectual defense of reform, based upon reason and utility.

The rationalistic approach to reform advocated by Bentham and his followers was matched by reform movements based upon religious and humanitarian considerations. In 1777 John Howard, a man of independent means dedicated to prison reform, published a landmark work, *The State of Prisons in England and Wales*. At that time prisons were rarely used as places to serve sentences. They were used to hold accused persons until their trial, or for debtors who were imprisoned until their debts were paid. The prisons were a source of income to the jailers, who charged excessive fees while keeping their prisoners in the most wretched conditions. Sometimes debtors would pay their debts but be held indefinitely because they could not afford to pay the jailers' fees. Conditions were even more intolerable on the congested, disease-ridden hulks in which prisoners sentenced to transportation were confined. Howard campaigned ceaselessly for the improvement of prisons and obtained some legislation which was largely ineffective. In 1807 Sir Samuel Romilly, then solicitor-general, succeeded in obtaining passage of a Bankruptcy Act that provided a legal process by which debtors could settle their debts and be freed. The next year Romilly began a crusade to reduce the number of offenses that required capital punishments—for even such a minor crime as shoplifting by a child was punishable by death. Romilly was opposed by the full majesty of judges and lawyers, who thought in terms of punishments and fees; but Romilly's lifetime of dedicated labor began to bear fruit after his death.

Religion. The Church of England was part of the established apparatus of power and privilege and as such felt threatened by the secularism of the French Revolution and the scoffing of Tom Paine. Archbishops and bishops were appointed and promoted by the crown and they sat in the House of Lords, thus they had to be politicians as well as spiritual leaders. The church regarded the Test and Corporation Acts, which limited political offices to Anglicans, as the essential basis for its established position. The churchmen were strongly supported in this view by the king, the Tories, and most of the political class. The efforts of Nonconformists (non-Anglican Protestants) to obtain some relaxation of these laws failed repeatedly, and the controversy concerning political rights for Catholics (Catholic emancipation) brought the downfall of Pitt and continued to be one of the most divisive issues in politics.

While the church was struggling to preserve its political and legal privileges, it was being criticized from within for its lack of spiritual vitality. A group known as "Evangelicals" worked to bring about a revival of traditional Christian concepts of personal salvation and holiness and to imbue churchmen with a more dedicated approach to their calling. The most prominent of the Evangelicals was William Wilberforce, member of Parliament for Yorkshire, a personal friend of Pitt and other political leaders. As a young man Wilberforce experienced a "conversion" that made his Christian faith the center of his life. He joined with other Evangelicals in the encouragement of Bible reading, prayer, and good works. Wilberforce looked to the political and social leaders of the nation to support his cause. In his book, *A Practical View of the Prevailing Religious System of Professed Christians in the Higher and Middle Classes* (1797), he criticized nominal Christianity and urged a revival of religious and moral commitment.

Wilberforce and the Evangelicals devoted themselves to many good causes, but the most important was the abolition of the slave trade, in which they were supported by many humanitarians who did not share their religious convictions. Wilberforce agreed to take the lead in Parliament, and in 1788 a parliamentary committee was formed to take evidence. In 1792 Wilberforce, drawing upon evidence from the committee report, moved for abolition of the slave trade. His motion was supported by both Pitt and Fox, but neither wished to divide his supporters on the issue and Wilberforce's motion failed. Wilberforce continued to make an annual motion against the slave trade, but the measure was not passed until Fox put the government behind it in the "Talents" ministry of 1806 to 1807. The efforts of Wilberforce and others also bore fruit in an anti-slave trade clause in the Treaty of Vienna (1815) and eventually in the abolition of slavery itself.

Poverty. Public attention to the problem of poverty focussed on the Poor Laws, for the local authorities were confronted with an extent of poverty which the existing law had never been intended to handle. The Elizabethan Poor Laws were based on the assumption of a stable society where people spent their lives in one locality, where prices and wages varied little from year to year, and where the community (i.e., the parish) was responsible for providing a minimum subsistence for all its members. Such assumptions were invalidated by violent fluctuations of prices, wages, and employment in this revolutionary age. The problem was not just a matter of providing for the unemployed, although fluctuations in employment frequently placed large numbers of able-bodied workers into this category. Even employed workers were compelled to seek poor relief; as prices rose, wages based on traditional wage rates were inadequate to support the workers and their families. The employers who dominated the process by which wages were set strongly resisted increases in wages. Workers could not leave their parishes in search of better-paying work elsewhere, for to do so would forfeit their rightful claim to poor relief. The Poor Law authorities attempted to meet their responsibilities by supplementing wages with relief payments (the Speenhamland system). As a result, employers were enabled to keep wages low, for the rate payers (local taxpayers) subsidized their workers, while employed workers became dependent upon poor relief. The public was confused by the arguments among those who viewed poverty as the result of personal faults, those who advocated a free market in labor which would require both employers and workers to respond to economic fluctuations, and those who felt a sense of community responsibility for the poor. From any of these perspectives, the Poor Laws were inadequate.

One observer of the problem, an Anglican clergyman named Thomas Malthus, believed that there was nothing that public policy could do about poverty. In 1798 Malthus published *An Essay on the Principle of Population* (revised in 1803), in which he argued that population would always increase faster than food supply, and thus poverty, famine, war, and vice were inevitable. Malthus's main concern was to refute the views of William Godwin, who anticipated the steady advance of mankind to perfection, but the main influence of his book was in discussions of poverty and the Poor Laws. In Malthus's view, humanitarians and the Poor Laws only made the population problem worse, for they permitted the poor to have more children than they could provide for. The "dismal science" of Malthus appalled philanthropists and humanitarians, but its "tough-minded" realism had a powerful influence upon the social thought of the age.

A more typical reaction to these problems was presented by a journalist of genius, William Cobbett. A tough, John Bull patriot, Cobbett was angered by the fiscal demands of government and the luxury of the upper classes at a time when an inflated currency and rising prices were destroying the livings and self-respect of the British working class. Cobbett deplored the effects of industrialism in destroying the simple life and cottage industries of the old England he knew and loved. Cobbett excoriated the great politicians, aristocrats, bankers, and government contractors who profitted from public expenditures while the cost fell on those who toiled in fields and factories. He was a patriot who looked back, regretfully, to an England that would be no more, and who expressed, in angry but powerful words, the sense of loss felt by humble people.

Suggestions for Further Reading

General works include J. Steven Watson, *The Reign of George III, 1760–1815* (1960) and Asa Briggs, *The Age of Improvement, 1783–1867* (1959). Ian R. Christie in *Stress and Stability in Late Eighteenth-Century Britain: Reflections on the British Avoidance of Revolution* (1984) provides a fascinating gloss on the period and the results of a lifetime of study on this ever fascinating question. There are many good biographies of prominent persons. Among the most useful are John Brooke, *King George III* (1972); Stanley Ayling, *George the Third* (1972); Roger Fulford, *George the Fourth* (1949); John Ehrman, *The Younger Pitt, The Years of Acclaim* (1969); Derek Jarrett, *Pitt the Younger* (1974); John W. Derry, *Charles James Fox* (1972); Philip Ziegler, *Addington: A Life of Henry Addington, First Viscount Sidmouth* (1965); C. J. Bartlett, *Castlereagh* (1966); Derry, *Castlereagh* (1976); P. J. V. Rolo, *George Canning: Three Biographical Studies* (1965); Chester New, *The Life of Henry Brougham to 1830* (1967); and Elizabeth Longford, *Wellington* (2 vols., 1969–1972). For Ireland there is much of value in A. P. W. Malcolmson, *John Foster: The Politics of the Anglo-Irish Ascendancy* (1978). The negotiations that led to the peace settlement in 1814 to 1815 can be followed in J. G. Lockhart, *The Peacemakers, 1814–15* (1968) and Charles K. Webster, *The Foreign Policy of Castlereagh, 1812–1815* (1963, first pub. 1931).

The Industrial Revolution has produced a voluminous literature, but perhaps the best works for the beginning student are T. S. Ashton, *The Industrial Revolution, 1760–1830* (1948); Phyllis Deane, *The First Industrial Revolution* (1965); and M. W. Flinn, *The Origins of the Industrial Revolution* (1966). The agricultural changes that were an important factor in economic change are reviewed in Gordon Mingay and J. D. Chambers, *The Agricultural Revolution, 1750–1880* (1966); it is useful to compare Patrick O'Brien, "Agriculture and the Home Market," *English Historical Review*, C (1985), 773–799. Transportation is treated in E. Pawson, *Transport and Economy: The Turnpike Roads of Eighteenth Century Britain* (1977); W. Albert, *The Turnpike Road System in England 1663–1840* (1972); and Hugh Malet, *Bridgewater, the Canal Duke, 1736–1803* (1977). Good coverage of the effects of industrialism on ordinary people can be found in G. D. H. Cole and Raymond Postgate, *The British Common People, 1746–1946* (1947) and in an enormously learned and stimulating book by E. P. Thompson, *The Making of the English Working Class* (1964). For a broad interpretation of the social changes of this period see Harold Perkin, *The Origins of Modern English Society, 1780–1880* (1969). The impact of the Napoleonic Wars is treated in Clive Emsley, *British Society and the French Wars, 1793–1815* (1979). The reaction by one segment of society is chronicled in J. E. Cookson, *The Friends of Peace: Anti-War Liberalism in England 1793–1815* (1982). Important aspects of the evangelical movement are treated in T. W. Laqueur, *Religion and Respectability: Sunday Schools and Working Class Culture 1780–1850* (1976) and in Roger Anstey, *The Atlantic Slave Trade and British Abolition, 1760–1810* (1975).

13

Conservatism and Reform

1815–1850

*I*n 1815 Britain was compelled to face the profound changes that had taken place in the previous quarter of a century. Britain's involvement in the European wars had led to a commitment to share in the task of preserving peace. Her political institutions had held the nation together until victory, but now her leaders were required to deal with the sense of alienation that had grown up between those who shared in the political process and those who did not. The growth of industrialism had created new problems and social needs. Faced with this challenge, the British did not become revolutionary; their instinctive reaction was to cling to that which was time-tested and familiar. Yet new problems could not be dealt with without new ideas, and by 1815 a variety of new ideas had become available. The result was a period of intense political, economic, and social stress leading to a series of reforms that, by 1850, provided the institutional framework for the first industrial and urban nation.

Britain in 1815

Government. Britain faced these challenges with a political system that had withstood the challenge of Napoleon but that was ill-equipped to deal with the problems of peace. King George III was aged and insane, living out his last years (he died in 1820) in Windsor Castle. His son and heir, George, the regent for his father, who had once been a bright, lively, charming man-about-town, had become a fat, peevish, middle-aged voluptuary. His youthful attachment to Charles James Fox and the Whigs was forgotten, and as regent he continued the Tories in office. The regency possessed none of the dignity or mystique of monarchy, and the regent petulantly surrendered to his ministers those remnants of royal power that his father had struggled to preserve. He was separated from his wife, Princess Caroline, a coarse, eccentric woman who lived in Italy accompanied by a disreputable entourage. Their daughter Charlotte, heir to the throne, died in 1817, leaving the succession to the regent's brother. As he had all his life, George spent money freely on himself, his palaces, and the entertainment of his friends. In a period when difficult economic adjustments had to be made, he was not the kind of person who would strengthen public attachment to the principle of monarchy.

The Tory ministry of Lord Liverpool, which had seen Britain through to victory, was unready to grapple with the adjustment to peace. Liverpool was a capable, fair-minded man, but cautious in action and temperamentally unwilling to offer a strong lead. As foreign secretary, Lord Castlereagh was hardworking and willing to make decisions that would involve Britain in peacetime commitments to Europe. Lord Sidmouth (Henry Addington) was home secretary, a man frightened by dissidents and determined to hold the line against those who threatened the existing order of things. The Cabinet was overwhelmingly aristocratic and quite unsuited by education and experience to cope with the political and economic discontents that were suddenly unleashed when the war ended. The Tory party, which was the backbone of the ministry's support in Parliament, was conservative in outlook, was dominated by landed interests, and was opposed to reforms of Parliament or the Church which would threaten its grip on power. The Tories were supported by the independent gentlemen in the House of Commons, who shared their conservative social views but sometimes suspected that the Tory leaders and "placemen" (officeholders) were primarily interested in power for its own sake.

The desire for national unity in the face of French power and a revolutionary ideology had made political opposition during the war futile and, in the eyes of some, unpatriotic. The Whigs were led nominally by Charles Grey who, in 1797, had proposed parliamentary reform. Long exclusion from power had reduced their numbers and weakened their morale. To some extent their hopes for the future rested upon able, aggressive middle-class Whigs, such as the energetic lawyer and publicist, Henry Brougham. These middle-class Whigs had adopted some of the reform ideas of Bentham and the Radicals, criticizing especially the waste and inefficiency of government. A small band of Radicals kept alive the demand for reform of the House of Commons. In the later years of the war a spirit of restlessness and dissatisfaction had been evident in many sectors of the public. In 1815 the Liverpool ministry found that victory abroad had unleashed pent-up demands at home.

British Society. Although the Industrial Revolution had begun to transform British society, in 1815 Britain was not yet an industrial nation. Most of the population of 13 million lived in rural villages or hamlets, engaged in agriculture or handicraft industries. By 1851 the population had increased to 21 million, and slightly more than half the population lived in urban communities. Britain had become the first urban nation. The London metropolitan area continued its sprawling growth, but much of the population increase was in the new industrial towns such as Birmingham, Manchester, Leeds, and Sheffield. These towns were characterized by ugliness, grime, congestion, poorly built housing, lack of sanitary facilities and pure water, and an absence of civic amenities such as parks, playgrounds, schools, and libraries. Despite the long hours, low wages, and insecurity of employment characteristic of early industrialism, the towns continued to draw people from the countryside. Towns were also swelled by the natural increase of the urban population.

Although romantic poets found much to praise in rural England, the working people of this leafy realm found that industrialization was also changing their lives, in many instances not for the better. During the long wars with France agriculture prospered, and more land was plowed than at any other time. The new crops and methods of agriculture that had developed in the previous century and a half were rapidly introduced, and this process required a continuing extension of enclosure. Those who lost lands or customary rights without adequate compensation found employment in the rising industrial towns or remained to form a rural proletariat, employed at low wages which at times were supplemented by poor relief to enable them to survive. The landed aristocracy and gentry found that high wartime prices enabled them to live comfortably and to build splendid country homes which were elegantly furnished. With the end of the war this artificial prosperity came crashing down, with disastrous effects on all levels of rural society. Furthermore, rural England had depended for much of its livelihood on handicraft industries, now menaced or destroyed by industrialism and, after 1815, foreign competition. For some, rural England still provided an attractive and secure place to live. But many of its young people were compelled to leave for the industrial towns, and those who remained were often reduced to a poverty made no less distressing by quaint surroundings.

It is a common mistake to underestimate the importance of the Church in the life of early nineteenth-century England. The Church continued to fulfill an important spiritual and social role for the majority of Englishmen, and a new stimulus to religious feeling was provided by the Evangelical movement, with its emphasis on Christian piety, Bible reading, prayer, and personal morality. Methodism, which had begun as an effort to renew the spiritual vitality of the church, had now become a separate dissenting denomination which was strongly rooted in the lower middle class and working class of the towns. Nonconformity, primarily Presbyterians, Congregationalists, and Baptists, continued to hold a following of earnest, hard-working people. In whatever form, religion was still an important part of English life and would continue to be so for another century.

As Britain grew into an industrial and urban society, education was one of its weaknesses. The Scots, with their local schools and fine universities, were the best educated, which was an important advantage as many of them sought employment in England or the empire. In England the so-called "public schools" (Eton, Westminster, and others) had not gained the eminence which came to them later, and most boys of the upper and middle classes were educated at home by tutors or in the local grammar schools. The academies of the dissenting denominations offered a sound education with attention to useful skills such as bookkeeping, navigation, and surveying. A variety of privately operated schools, many with only one or two teachers, offered primary education for those who could pay modest fees, and Sunday schools were operated by religious bodies to provide the rudiments of literacy to the children of the poor. Oxford and Cambridge had magnificent buildings, libraries, and endowments, and their curricula retained the humanistic and clerical emphasis of the past. The two universities boasted some fine scholars, and some students took advantage of these resources to get an excellent education. But instructional standards were slack, and the universities fell far short of meeting the needs of the new industrial and urban society that was emerging.

Scotland and Ireland. The United Kingdom of Great Britain and Ireland was not as united as its name implied. The political union of England and Scotland in 1707 had been successful, but the Scots preserved their distinctive accent, administrative system, judicial system, and church. Edinburgh was the intellectual and social center of Scotland, and the development of the "New Town" was transforming Edinburgh into the attractive city it is today. Glasgow and its hinterland were emerging as a major center of trade and industry. A cluster of brilliant thinkers and scholars led "the Scottish renaissance," and Sir Walter Scott's novels gave Scots new pride in their national history and character. The visit of King George IV to Scotland in 1822 was seen as symbolic of the acceptance of Scotland as a respected part of the United Kingdom.

The Act of Union with Ireland (1801) was less successful. Ireland continued to be governed by a viceroy and secretary sent from England, and the Anglo-Irish ruling class continued to fill the Irish administration, judicial system, and seats in Parliament. Dublin, like Edinburgh, had become an attractive provincial capital, dominated socially by the Anglo-Irish. The Scots-Irish centered in the north of Ireland (Ulster) were Presbyterian and determined to uphold the Protestant ascendancy, although their own political role was modest. The Irish Catholic majority had received the vote in 1793 but were excluded by law from political office or election to Parliament. Many of the Irish Catholics were tenant farmers, increasingly dependent on the potato and undergoing a rapid rise in population. Their usual response to political and social exclusion was violence, a tactic that the Protestant authorities dealt with in the same manner. Encouraged by French ideas and their own second-class status, the Irish were ripe for revolt whenever the opportunity arose.

Tory Conservatism, 1815–1822

Foreign Policy. More than twenty years of war had convinced the Tories that stability at home required peace abroad. For this reason the Liverpool ministry, led by Lord Castlereagh, made an unprecedented commitment to European peace. In 1814 Britain joined with Austria, Prussia, and Russia in an alliance to complete the defeat of Napoleon and to keep the major powers working together in the peace settlement. At the Congress of Vienna, the Austrian chancellor, Metternich, advocated cooperation to preserve peace and stability ("The Concert of Europe"), a concept that Castlereagh strongly supported. The entrance of France into the alliance in 1818 was welcomed by Castlereagh as a further stabilizing force. The principal problem that the "Concert of Europe" offered to Britain was Metternich's determination to preserve the principle of monarchy and the existing social order throughout Europe. In 1820 revolutions broke out in Spain and several Italian states. Metternich reacted by calling a congress of the allied powers, which agreed to Austrian intervention in Italy to suppress the revolts. In 1822 another congress met to consider the revolution in Spain, and in 1823 the French sent an army to restore the despotic king of Spain to his throne. Intimations were raised that something might be done to restore Spanish control over the former Spanish colonies in Latin America.

Castlereagh protested strenuously against these actions, especially the French intervention in Spain. He held that the "Concert of Europe" had been formed to prevent general war and not to intervene in the internal affairs of the European states. Furthermore, the revolutionists were demanding constitutional government, representative institutions, and civil liberties—rights that the British already possessed and could not justifiably deny to others. Any attempt to restore Spanish control over the former colonies would threaten Britain's access to trade in Latin America. By 1822, when he committed suicide, Castlereagh realized that Britain's domestic institutions and overseas interests made it impossible to cooperate in any meaningful way with autocratic states such as Austria, Prussia, and Russia.

Castlereagh was succeeded at the foreign office by George Canning, a brilliant, individualistic, and highly nationalistic man whose boldness and independence stood in contrast to Castlereagh's painstaking diplomacy and search for cooperation among the European powers. Canning could not stop French intervention in Spain, but British sea power could and did block any attempt to restore Spanish authority over the former Spanish colonies in Latin America. The young United States, acting independently, took a similar position in the Monroe Doctrine. In 1826 Canning successfully supported constitutional monarchy in Portugal, where British sea power could be used.

The most difficult problem that faced Canning was a revolution that broke out in Greece in 1821 as the Greeks sought independence from the Ottoman Empire of the Turks. Metternich viewed the Greek revolt as another uprising that should be suppressed in the interests of stability. The Russians, however, prepared to aid the Greeks because they saw an opportunity to gain territory and influence in the Balkans. They had a special reason for helping the Greeks, since both Russians and Greeks were Eastern Orthodox Christians. Canning was faced with a dilemma: he wished to support the Ottoman Empire as an obstacle to Russian expansion into the Mediterranean, but he could not in good conscience support the Moslem Turks against the Christian Greeks, especially when the Greeks, fighting for freedom against an oppressive regime, evoked in the British memories of ancient Greek democracy. The colorful romantic poet, Lord Byron, further dramatized the Greek cause in 1824, when he died in Greece trying to aid the rebels.

Canning's approach to the Greek problem was to try to bring about Greek independence without leading to a breakup of the Ottoman Empire or to an extension of Russian influence in the area. He decided his goal could be achieved only by direct British involvement. Britain, France, and Russia entered the arena and destroyed the combined Turkish-Egyptian fleet at the Battle of Navarino (1827). The next year the Russians invaded the Balkans, and in 1829 the Turks were compelled to sign a peace agreeing to Greek independence. By that time Canning was dead and Metternich's concept of a "Concert of Europe" had broken down. Castlereagh's involvement of Britain as a continuing force in the European balance of power had come to a close.

Domestic Dissension. The Liverpool ministry also faced serious problems of postwar readjustment at home. One problem had nothing to do with the war; it was a series of bad crops, which was always an important factor in economic distress in the preindustrial age. The second problem was the result of inflated wartime rents at a time when there was a sharp fall in agricultural incomes. The problems of agriculture were compounded by a decline in foreign trade, as European competitors entered into markets formerly cut off by war, selling their goods at desperation prices. The demobilization of many soldiers and sailors, accompanied by shutdowns of industries as wartime demands ended, resulted in many bankruptcies and high unemployment. Relief was left to the justices of the peace and the parishes, as required by the Poor Laws, and the system broke down completely under the strain. Nevertheless, the costs of war continued, including the army of occupation in France, paying off the vast floating debt, and interest charges on the much-increased national debt. Victory came at a high price, and much of the cost had to be paid under conditions of economic distress.

The first requirement of the Liverpool ministry in 1815 was to deal with the problems of agriculture. The Tory party was, above all, the party of the landed interest. Faced with acute agricultural distress, the Liverpool ministry responded with a Corn Law intended to keep the price of wheat high by imposing a tariff on imports. This action satisfied landlords and farmers but aroused a torrent of protest from industrialists and urban workers who complained that the policy kept food prices high at their expense. The money supply was also an important factor in the adjustment to peace. During the war the Bank of England had suspended payments in gold for its bank notes; thereafter, the money supply was based on paper currency. Inflation did not become serious until the last years of the war. With the return of peace, financiers, merchants, and economists advocated a return to money backed by gold. This step was taken by the Liverpool ministry in the Bank Act of 1819. The immediate result was deflationary, accentuating the postwar depression, although it was probably beneficial in the long run. Those who suffered from business setbacks and unemployment accused the government of being more responsive to the wishes of landlords and financiers than to the needs of the nation.

Economic problems were made even more volatile by a backlog of political discontent. The distress of the time caused those who suffered most to strike out against the government, landlords, and employers. Some of the most serious problems were found in the new factory areas; much of the distress was in declining industries, such as the hand-loom weavers who could not compete with the new power looms. A government controlled by a small privileged class was held responsible for many of these problems and was criticized for failing to deal with them. The working class expressed their grievances in the only way they could: through mass meetings, violence and threats of violence, and attacks on the factories and machines that they thought took bread out of their mouths. The effect was to strike fear into the ruling class of the nation, who saw in social turmoil a threat to constitutional government, social stability, and private property. It seemed that Britain, having withstood the challenge of the French Revolution and Napoleon, might fall into internal strife herself.

The postwar turmoil brought a revival of Radicalism, a movement for fundamental reform that found support in both the middle class and the working class. Although Radicalism included a wide variety of goals, the key issues were those that affected the distribution of political power—the privileges of the crown and the aristocracy and the structure of the House of Commons. In Parliament the aristocratic Whig leaders favored reduction of the political influence of the king and his ministers, but they were dubious about changes in parliamentary representation and the franchise. The Whig party, however, attracted a number of middle-class reformers who had no such inhibitions. The most articulate of these was Henry Brougham, a talented Scot. Brougham's intellect and energy were devoted to a variety of radical causes: reform of the law and prisons, free trade, abolition of slavery, public education, the Poor Law, and parliamentary reform. The privileges of the Church of England also came under heavy attack, and in Ireland equal political rights for Catholics (Catholic emancipation), which would destroy the dominance of the Protestant ruling class, was a major issue. The disputes that had been shelved during the long period of war could be deferred no longer.

The agenda of reform was partially shaped by systematic thinkers through books, pamphlets, and periodicals. The ideas of Jeremy Bentham were expounded by "philosophic radicals" such as James Mill, who wrote extensively on politics, economics, education, the Poor Laws, prisons, colonial policy, and the history of India. Mill took a leading role in founding the University of London as a Benthamite counterweight to the genteel, clerical traditions of Oxford and Cambridge. The main contribution of philosophic radicalism was to develop the habit of rational analysis of political and social institutions in terms of their costs and benefits to society. Seen in this light, the ancient institutions that Burke had idealized as the product of some mysterious collective wisdom began to appear as unwarranted sources of power and income for a privileged minority.

Closely related to the rational analysis of the Benthamites was the new economics of a group known collectively as "the classical economists," who derived their ideas principally from Adam Smith's *Wealth of Nations*. The outstanding figure among the classical economists was David Ricardo, the son of a Dutch-Jewish speculator who had settled in London. Learning from his father, Ricardo took advantage of wartime finance to make a fortune. He married an English woman and was converted to the Church of England. In his *Principles of Political Economy and Taxation* (1817), Ricardo argued that political attempts to control the economy could only impede economic activity and reduce the level of national investment and wealth. In 1819 he became a member of Parliament, where he was regarded as an authority on economic questions. He was critical of the Corn Law, a pillar of the Tory creed, which he viewed as an unwarranted benefit to landlords at the expense of the productive part of the nation. He also opposed the Poor Laws, where he adopted a Malthusian approach, arguing that population would always fluctuate in proportion to productivity, with the result that wages for a substantial part of the population would inevitably hover around the subsistence level. The economics of Smith and Ricardo placed economic policy in an entirely new light. Gone was the concept of a stable community in which each element of society had its proper status and proper reward. In its place was "the invisible hand" of the market, governing rents, profits, wages, and interest rates and shaping the lives of individuals and nations. By destroying the older economic views, the classical economists left the field open to aggressive middle-class bankers, merchants, and industrialists who were confident they could succeed in a free market and were prepared to work themselves and their employees hard to do so.

Radicalism also found support among the growing working class of the towns, who were increasingly conscious of the effects of political decisions upon their lives. Francis Place, a London tailor, was a master at organizing the artisans and shopkeepers of London and Westminster. In 1793 Place gained prominence as leader of the London breeches makers in a strike. He also joined the London Corresponding Society and was active in spreading the works of Tom Paine. He became a friend of Bentham and Mill and established a library that eventually was a gathering place for Radicals. Place's views were those of the skilled artisans and small shopkeepers. An employer himself, Place was not an advocate of mass democracy, but he believed that the well-established workingman was entitled to a voice in the political process.

A similar movement developed in Birmingham, where the metal trades were organized in many small units and relations between masters and men were close. In Manchester, however, working-class discontent took a different direction, for Manchester was the center of the cotton textile industry, and the factory system had created strong antagonism between employers and factory workers. Yorkshire was different again, for there the emergence of the industrial system had left pockets of poverty in the old handicraft industries, such as the hand-loom weavers who struggled in vain to compete against the products of power looms. Despite these variations, three common themes can be seen running through working-class protest: the dignity of work was debased by the new industrial system; the wealth produced by labor was unfairly distributed; and the structure of authority was weighted against those who worked. The workers, feeling ignored by the aristocracy and gentry and oppressed by middle-class employers, developed a sense of alienation that has continued to the present.

Repression of Dissent. The reaction of the Liverpool ministry to Radicalism was repression. Drawn from a long-established political and social elite, it was difficult for the ministry, members of Parliament, and local magistrates to accept a challenge to their authority from persons whom they saw as far beneath them in the social scale. The rise of radical agitation in 1815 and 1816 led the government in 1817 to strengthen the powers of the local magistrates. In 1818 public expressions of discontent diminished, but in 1819 another economic slump provoked a new round of protests and mass meetings. Powerful orators such as Henry Hunt traversed the nation, demanding redistribution of parliamentary seats and a broadening of the franchise. The most striking confrontation took place in Manchester, where a great crowd assembled peacefully in St. Peter's Fields to listen to Hunt and other radical speakers. The Manchester magistrates, fearful of a riot, panicked and sent in the militia, assisted by soldiers, to arrest the speakers and to disperse the crowd. In the melee that followed 11 persons were killed and over 400 were wounded. The government was disturbed by the reaction of the Manchester magistrates but felt compelled to support their actions. The dissidents, in mocking reference to the Battle of Waterloo, referred to this "victory" of sabre-wielding soldiers over unarmed citizens as "Peterloo." When Hunt was brought to London for trial he was hailed as a hero. The government responded with the "Six Acts," which further restricted public meetings and the dissemination of inflammatory literature and placed heavier duties on newspapers. It appeared that more confrontations were imminent.

At this point an extraneous event drew public attention and served as an outlet for popular discontent. In 1820 George III died and his son, the regent, became king as George IV (1820–1830). To the dismay of George IV and the Liverpool ministry, the new king's estranged wife, Caroline, decided to return to Britain and claim her place as queen. George IV was determined not to accept her and demanded that his ministers obtain a divorce by act of Parliament. The public, however, supported Queen Caroline as a means of showing their detestation for the king and his ministers. The Whigs and Radicals came to the defense of the queen. The result was a parliamentary and public hubbub that thoroughly embarrassed the ministry and provided an outlet for discontent. Conveniently for George IV and the ministry, Queen Caroline died in 1821. By that time the worst problems of the postwar period had begun to ease. But the affair of Queen Caroline revealed the resentments and sense of alienation that had flourished in the previous six years.

Tory Liberalism, 1822–1829

Economic and Social Reform. By 1822 the worst of the postwar adjustment was over: the economy was improving, political tensions were declining, and the Liverpool ministry was ready to take a more liberal direction in its policies. The death of Castlereagh in 1822 made necessary a reorganization of the ministry, which enabled Lord Liverpool to bring forward Tories who had progressive views. George Canning replaced Castlereagh as foreign secretary, Robert Peel became home secretary, and William Huskisson entered the cabinet as president of the Board of Trade. It was agreed that the Tory ministry would continue to stand fast against parliamentary reform and Catholic emancipation. On matters of foreign policy, economic policy, and social reform the ministry took new directions that have been labelled "Tory liberalism."

Although conservative where the distribution of political power was concerned, the Tories showed themselves willing to respond to new economic and social needs. The Tories were heirs of a long tradition of upper-class responsibility for the welfare of the lower orders of society. As a party identified with the landed interest, they were not unwilling to use the power of government to interfere with urban or industrial elites. The key figure in giving the Tory party a concern for social reform was Robert Peel. Son of a Lancashire cotton manufacturer, Peel had been prepared at Harrow and Oxford for a political career. He was a man of great integrity and strength of character: he was conservative in that he did not act hastily; he was liberal in that he was willing to respond to needs that were clearly demonstrated. Peel became the leader of those Tories who recognized that an elite could hold power only if that power was used for the welfare of all. Thus he helped define a conservative philosophy rooted in the works of a devoted Whig, Edmund Burke.

At the Home Office Peel was primarily concerned with police, law, and prisons, problems that had become acute as a result of industrialization and urbanization. He took up the cause for which Romilly had worked and obtained legislation that greatly reduced the number of crimes that carried the death penalty. He also responded to the work of prison reformers, and legislation was passed to improve the conditions of prisons. Peel's most notable achievement was the establishment of the London metropolitan police. The government needed trained policemen to control riots, for calling in the army often made matters worse. Members of Parliament and visitors to London, as well as inhabitants, favored a police force, for they were victimized by London's huge criminal class. Headquartered at Scotland Yard in Westminster, the "bobbies" soon gained respect and provided a model for other towns.

The Tories also took steps toward a more liberal commercial policy, signalled by the appointment of William Huskisson to the Board of Trade. Picking up the legacy of Pitt, Huskisson led in a broad reduction and simplification of the customs duties, thereby improving the revenue. The Navigation Acts, which protected British shipping at the expense of trade, were modified to permit freer trade between the colonies and Europe. Huskisson also took a liberal attitude toward another major obstacle to trade, the Corn Law. This was a subject that was sacrosanct to Tories, and he made only modest progress. The Tories were prepared to be liberal with the economic privileges of others but not with the tariff protection given the landed interest. The repeal of the Combination Acts in 1824 showed that the Tories were aware of the problems of working men, although legislation the next year deprived trade unions of the right to strike.

The Breakdown of Tory Unity. In 1827 Lord Liverpool suffered a severe stroke, and it became necessary to reconstitute the ministry. The Tory party by this time had become deeply divided: the duke of Wellington spoke for conservative Tories, while George Canning was the recognized leader of those committed to the "Liberal Toryism" that had emerged during the period of 1822 to 1827. King George IV, recognizing Canning's ability, experience, and wide popularity, called on him to form a ministry. Wellington and Peel, uneasy with Canning's support of Catholic emancipation, refused to join, but some of the Whigs gave Canning their support. Later in the year Canning died, worn out by strain and overwork. After further dissensions Wellington, with Peel as his spokesman in the House of Commons, formed a ministry controlled by the conservative Tories; many of the Canningites refused to support Wellington. Thus the Tory party, which had controlled British government since the days of William Pitt, began to fall apart. It appeared that a new political alignment was emerging, which was likely to bring out into the open those constitutional issues that Lord Liverpool had avoided—parliamentary reform and the privileges of the Church of England.

Wellington and Peel were immediately confronted with the church question. The Test and Corporation Acts were regarded by the Church as essential to its privileged position, for in principle they permitted only Anglicans to hold office under the crown or in local government. The application of the acts to Protestant Nonconformists was riddled with exceptions, but the exclusion of Catholics was of some importance in Britain and was regarded as vital in Ireland. In 1828 Wellington and Peel were confronted with a demand from Nonconformists for relief from the Test and Corporation Acts. Needing the support of Nonconformity in the struggle against Catholic emancipation, they yielded, and the acts were repealed insofar as they applied to Protestants. In repealing the acts, Wellington and Peel found they had opened the floodgates.

While Wellington and Peel were wrestling with the problem of Nonconformity, a crisis blew up in Ireland. Daniel O'Connell, a Catholic, came forward as candidate for Parliament in an Irish by-election and won with a strong majority, although he was legally ineligible to sit in the House of Commons. Wellington and Peel were now confronted with the possibility of civil war in Ireland. Again they felt they had no choice but to give way, and in 1829 they declared themselves in favor of Catholic emancipation. George IV raged; the Church of England was aghast; the Tory party split wide open; the country squires, so long supporters of the Tories, felt betrayed. Catholic emancipation was passed by a combination of ministers, placemen, liberal Tories, Whigs, and Radicals. At that critical moment King George IV died, which made a new election necessary at a time of political ferment. A great crisis was at hand.

The Reform Bill Crisis, 1830–1832

Background of Reform. The movement for parliamentary reform that had begun in the 1780s had been halted by the French Revolution and the conservative reaction, but complaints concerning the unrepresentative character of the House of Commons had not ceased. By 1830 the desire for change was in the air, and the House of Commons was seen as the principal obstacle to essential reforms. The indictment of the House was varied: the dominance of the House by ministers and officeholders; the small boroughs controlled by aristocratic patrons or men of great wealth; the decayed towns that still sent two members to Parliament while new industrial towns were unrepresented; the manipulation of elections by interest groups; the disorder that accompanied voting in many constituencies. Despite these complaints the House of Commons had been accepted as broadly representative of, and responsive to, the national interest. By 1830 this sense of confidence had broken down. Conservative Tories had seen Tory ministers use their powers to pass Catholic emancipation. Industrial leaders resented the control of the House of Commons by the landed interest, who used their disproportionate weight to maintain the Corn Law. The working class had come to think of the House of Commons as a bastion of privilege that protected the interests of landlords or mill owners while leaving them at the mercy of economic forces. Humanitarians found that the House was the defender of atrocious criminal punishments and slavery. Whig politicians seemed to be excluded indefinitely from the sweets of office. Rather suddenly the election of 1830 brought these various forces together, and parliamentary reform became the overriding issue of the day.

The new king and his ministers little suspected the storm that was brewing. King William IV (1830–1837) was a bluff, straightforward man without strong political opinions apart from his desire to preserve what was left of monarchical power and the general dislike of change characteristic of the Hanoverians. Wellington and Peel continued in office; stung by Tory charges that they had betrayed the church, they were more determined than ever to hold the line. In the election of 1830 the aristocratic Whig leaders bided their time, and the cause of parliamentary reform was put forward by middle-class advocates: William Cobbett, the journalist, who attacked the reign of privilege; Francis Place and other London Radicals who stirred up popular demonstrations; Thomas Attwood, a Birmingham banker, who organized the Birmingham Political Union to agitate for parliamentary reform. In Yorkshire Henry Brougham, the Whig reformer, campaigned brilliantly on the issue. A revolution in France in July, which expelled a reactionary king, offered a lesson that William IV did not overlook, but it does not seem to have affected the election. In the south of England agricultural laborers rioted, burning haystacks and destroying threshing machines; although their concerns were economic, their actions added to the sense of emergency. When Parliament met in November 1830, Wellington made clear his determination to oppose any kind of parliamentary reform, and on the first important vote of the session the ministry was defeated by a combination of Whigs, liberal Tories, Radicals, and disgruntled country gentlemen. Wellington and Peel resigned, and William IV asked Earl Grey, leader of the Whigs, to form a government. The door to reform was ajar.

The Reform Bill. Earl Grey was sixty-six years old in 1830. He was a poised, confident aristocrat who had entered the House of Commons in 1786 as a follower of Charles James Fox. In 1797 he had presented an unsuccessful proposal for parliamentary reform; when he took office in 1830 his commitment to parliamentary reform was clear but unspecified. The leading spokesman for the ministry in the House of Commons was Lord John Russell, who had been an advocate of parliamentary reform for more than a decade. It was Russell who led in drawing up the Reform Bill and piloting it through the House of Commons.

The bill that Russell presented in March 1831 was more drastic than had been expected. The bill preserved the principle of separate county and borough constituencies, but it extended the franchise to those persons whose property was thought sufficient to guarantee a responsible use of the vote. The county franchise for freeholders remained the same (property worth forty shillings per year). Tenants with secure or long-term tenancies worth £10 per year would receive the right to vote, as would tenants with short-term leases (amended to include tenants-at-will) worth £50 per year. These provisions would greatly increase the number of

Earl Grey *(National Portrait Gallery)*.

county voters, but the landlord-tenant relationship was such that the new franchise would strengthen the influence of the aristocracy and gentry in the counties. In the boroughs the bill made two important changes: a redistribution of seats and the establishment of a uniform borough franchise. In its final form, the bill disfranchised fifty-six small boroughs and took 1 seat from thirty others, making available 143 seats for redistribution to populous counties and large towns such as Manchester, Birmingham, and Leeds. The borough franchise, which had varied widely, was made uniform: the owner or tenant of property with an annual rental of £10 per year and who met other qualifications—such as payment of rates (local taxes)—received the vote. In some boroughs the bill extended the franchise, and in others it reduced the number of voters. Open voting continued in the counties and boroughs, thus maintaining the influence of landlords and employers. Similar bills for Scotland and Ireland accompanied the main bill.

The struggle for passage of the Reform Bill was a great national crisis. Although historians may dispute the intentions of the reformers and the effects of the bill, there can be no doubt that those who lived through the events of 1831 to 1832 felt that decisions of fundamental importance to Britain were being made. In March 1831 the bill was approved by the House of Commons by one vote, but when it appeared that it might be whittled away by amendments Grey persuaded the reluctant William IV to call an election. The election of 1831 was a national referendum on the bill, supporters demanding "the bill, the whole bill, and nothing but the bill." Well-organized pressure groups held parades and mass meetings in London, Birmingham, and other major towns. The advocates of reform won a clear victory, and in the new House of Commons the bill passed, 367 to 231. In October the House of Lords rejected the bill, setting off a new round of mass meetings, protests, and riots. Russell introduced the bill again in December. It passed the Commons without difficulty, but in April 1832 the bill was blocked in the House of Lords by an amendment that the ministry refused to accept. Grey asked William IV to create enough new peers favorable to the bill to pass it, and when the king refused the Whig ministry resigned. Wellington tried to form a government, but this time public opinion had gained such irresistible force that he was compelled to withdraw. Grey and the Whigs returned to power, fortified by the king's promise to create peers if needed to pass the bill. Faced with defeat, Wellington and other Tory peers agreed not to vote against the bill, and it was passed in the House of Lords on June 4. Three days later the royal approval was given, although William IV refused to perform the ceremony personally, sending commissioners instead.

The passage of the Reform Bill of 1832 was a great triumph of public opinion and the House of Commons over the king and the House of

Noble Lords Opposing the Torrent of Reform *(BBC Hulton Picture Library)*.

Lords. Throughout the crisis William IV had shown his distaste for the bill, but when faced with what appeared to be a dangerous situation he twice used the royal power with great effect—calling an election in 1831 and agreeing to create peers in 1832. The aristocracy were also forced to yield. After the election of 1831 Wellington and the Tories were helpless in the House of Commons; they made the House of Lords the last defense against a bill that they saw as a serious blow to aristocratic power. Faced with the king's promise to create new peers, backed up by a majority in the House of Commons, and a determined public opinion, the Lords had no choice but to give way.

Throughout the two-year crisis Grey and the Whig ministers remained remarkably cool, balancing strong determination to preserve order with the need to gain the maximum political advantage from legitimate political agitation. One must not forget that it was the unreformed House of Commons that passed the bill and the unreformed electorate that produced the majority needed to do so. The Reform Bill of 1832 did not end the dominance of the aristocracy and gentry, politically or socially, but it gave more weight to the urban middle class and the rising industrial areas. Since the right to vote was defined in terms of property, growing prosperity increased the number of voters substantially by 1850. The urban working class, which had contributed to the public pressure that secured passage of the bill, gained little and lost the vote in some previously democratic constituencies.

The British people were the real heroes of the Reform Bill crisis. Middle-class and working-class leaders shared in a masterful organization and manipulation of public feeling. The political issues involved were thoroughly aired in books, periodicals, pamphlets, and other publications. The amount of violence was minimal but was enough to have a salutary effect. The public remained united in its determination to have the bill despite strong differences of opinion concerning many of its features. By their determination and steadiness during a two-year crisis the British people demonstrated that they were indeed ready for a constitutional change that broadened the base of political power.

Economic Expansion and Hard Times, 1830–1850

Economic Growth. By the time of the Great Reform Bill industrialization in Britain had proceeded from the initial stage, in which a few industries were involved, to the stage of broadly based development. In 1830 the factory system was well established in the cotton textile industry, and by 1850 the new industrial system dominated textile manufacture in both cottons and woolens. The growth of industry placed great new demands on the iron and coal industries, but until the 1850s expansion in these industries was more a matter of increases in scale than technological breakthroughs. Perhaps Britain's most important industrial advance from 1830 to 1850 was in engineering and the production of machinery. British engineers and skilled workmen led the world in designing and building steam engines, locomotives, steamships, factories, roads, bridges, docks, and cranes. The British were without rivals in using machine tools to make interchangeable parts manufactured to close tolerances. Many of these engineers, inventors, and machinists were men from humble families who found opportunities in an expanding economy that needed their talents.

The most characteristic feature of industrial expansion from 1830 to 1850 was the building of railways. For more than two decades inventors had been working to develop a steam locomotive and rails had long been in use for coal carts. It was George Stephenson, son of a Northumberland coal mine engineer, who first put the two together successfully. He served as engineer for the Stockton and Darlington Railway, opened in 1825. His greatest triumph was the Liverpool and Manchester Railway, opened in 1830, where he demonstrated the superiority of his steam locomotive over stationary steam engines. Stephenson directed construction of the thirty-one-mile railway, using cuts, bridges, and viaducts to produce a roadbed with gentle grades. Stephenson and his son, Robert, also a rail-

Stephenson's *Locomotion Number One* (E. A. Reitan).

way engineer, became leaders in a railway boom which by 1850 provided Britain with 5,000 miles of track and greatly stimulated related industries, such as coal, iron, and engineering. Although the railway companies had expected that their principal business would be carrying freight, initially most of their revenues came from passenger traffic, which also required building stations, waiting rooms, and buffets. The economic effects of railway building are obvious; the social and psychological effects of fast, cheap travel can only be conjectured.

In the public eye the chief rival of the two Stephensons was Isambard K. Brunel, also a son of an engineer. Brunel distinguished himself in the building of the Thames tunnel, the Great Western Railway, and many remarkable bridges and docks in which he made imaginative use of structural iron. His most notable efforts, however, were devoted to the application of steam power to oceangoing vessels. In 1838 his wooden paddle steamer, the *Great Western*, crossed the Atlantic under steam. Brunel used an iron hull and a screw propeller for his second oceangoing steamship, the *Great Britain*, which made several transatlantic crossings before she ran aground off Ireland in 1846. His most ambitious project was the *Great Eastern*, designed to be large enough to go all the way to India without recoaling. With a huge iron hull, ten boilers, eight engines, and paddle wheels and a screw propeller, the *Great Eastern* was one of the engineering marvels of the age and the largest ship built until 1901. She lost money for her owners every year until she was broken up for scrap, but she served a useful purpose in laying the transatlantic cable in the 1860s. Although steamships had their uses on inland waters, where refueling was simple, the quantity of coal needed by early steamships made them inefficient for ocean travel, and the bulk of the world's ocean traffic was carried by wooden sailing ships until 1870. By that time the powerful steamships pioneered by Brunel were replacing the graceful clipper ships with their billowing clouds of sail. Beauty's loss was efficiency's gain.

Economic Distress. The progress of British industry was much affected by periodic fluctuations, and the business cycle began to appear as the bane of industrial capitalism. An early speculative boom took place in 1825, followed by a business recession complicated by poor harvests. By 1835 an upswing was taking place that was aborted by the panic of 1837. By 1840 there was a full-scale depression, which reached its low point in 1842. From 1844 to 1846 the railway boom stimulated the economy, followed by another breakdown in 1846. By 1850 strong economic growth had begun, which continued with few setbacks to 1873. Not all of these problems should be attributed to industry. The banking system, based on gold, could not adjust money and credit to needs. Most industrial firms were owned by families or partnerships and lacked capital or reserves to withstand a momentary downturn. The domestic market was small and inelastic, and for that reason British industry depended on the vagaries of foreign trade and foreign exchange. Industrialism presented Britain with a new set of problems, but it also generated the growing wealth by which these problems could be resolved.

One of the results of economic fluctuations was unemployment and distress among the industrial working class. The classical economists, who followed the principles of Smith and Ricardo, held that economic fluctuations were the unavoidable consequences of economic laws and served a useful purpose in redirecting economic activity into the most profitable channels. This philosophy of economic individualism was strongly criticized by Thomas Carlyle, a product of a stern Scottish upbringing, who insisted in powerful, angry words that the new industrial world must adopt a faith more powerful than submission to economic laws—a faith which emphasized leadership, hard work, and concern for the moral and physical welfare of the community.

Despite the influence of laissez-faire ideas, humanitarianism and a sense of social responsibility led Parliament and the public to consider regulation of employment in factories. In 1832 Michael Sadler, a Tory member of Parliament from Yorkshire, led a parliamentary committee that investigated child labor in the factories and issued a remarkable report. Although Sadler lost his seat in Parliament in 1833, the Factory Act of that year responded to the abuses revealed in his report. The act prohibited employment of children under nine and limited the hours of work of children

Brunel's suspension bridge, Bristol *(E. A. Reitan).*

from ages nine to eighteen. Sadler's place as the conscience of Britain was taken by Lord Ashley, later earl of Shaftesbury, whose investigation into the labor of women and children in the coal mines shocked the nation and led to the Mines Act of 1842. For many years Shaftesbury worked for legislation to limit the employment of children to ten hours per day, which would also have the practical effect of a ten-hour day for adult workers in the same factory. Finally in 1847 legislation was passed limiting the working day of women and children to ten hours. Although Parliament was willing to regulate the labor of women and children, there was strong reluctance to interfere with the labor of adult males, who were considered to be free agents, responsible for making their own contracts with employers.

Politics and Reform, 1833–1841

Whig Reform. The Great Reform Bill was justified by its supporters, not as an end in itself but as the means to other reforms. The Parliament that met in 1833, the first elected under the new system, was, however, not much different in its leadership and membership from former Parliaments. The Whig leaders, Earl Grey and Lord John Russell, had won a great political and popular triumph and were not eager to assume new challenges. Because they had suffered a defeat, the Tories realized that unity was essential to block a flood of unwelcome legislation. For leadership they continued to look to Robert Peel, whose staunch opposition to the Reform Bill had restored some of the confidence he had lost by giving way on Catholic emancipation. The gentry were primarily concerned to get the country back to tranquillity, a view shared by many leaders and prosperous businessmen in the towns. The Radicals were enormously heartened by their achievement in the Reform Bill crisis, which convinced them of the value of public agitation in the pursuit of legislative goals. Their energy and conviction enabled them to push through Parliament some important legislation before the reform spirit evaporated.

Earl Grey, who had earned his niche in history, retired from office in 1834. After several months of Whig floundering, King William IV called on Peel to form a government. An election in 1835 strengthened the Tories, but an alliance of Whigs, Radicals, and Irish members made it necessary for Peel to resign a few months later. Once again a British monarch had learned that his right to appoint his own ministers and to provide them with a majority through an election was limited by political realities. The king turned again to the Whigs, and Lord Melbourne, a genial, easygoing aristocrat, became leader of a Whig ministry that lasted until 1841.

In 1837 King William IV died, to be succeeded by his niece, Queen Victoria (1837–1901), a sprightly eighteen-year-old girl. Victoria looked to Melbourne for advice, and he became her friendly father-confessor and advisor. In 1839, when Melbourne felt it necessary to resign, the young queen stubbornly showed her displeasure with Peel by refusing to add Tory ladies to her bedchamber. Peel, as always respectful toward monarchy, refused to take office, and Melbourne returned for another two years. In 1840 an important new influence entered Victoria's life when she married Albert of Saxe-Coburg-Gotha, a handsome, dignified, capable German whose serious purpose made him the most "Victorian" of her subjects. For Albert a new role was devised, that of prince consort. Victoria and Albert worked closely together, but the exclusive responsibility of the queen to exercise the royal power was never questioned. Under Queen Victoria the monarchy regained the respect it had lost under her two predecessors.

Despite the political weakness of ministries, some important reforms were implemented in the years following the passage of the Reform Bill. The Factory Act of 1833, which regulated the employment of children in factories, established an important precedent by providing for inspectors to enforce the act. In the same year slavery was abolished within the British Empire, legislation that affected primarily the British West Indies and the Cape Colony on the southern tip of Africa. The Municipal Corpora-

Queen Victoria and Albert, Prince Consort *(BBC Hulton Picture Library)*.

tions Act (1835) applied to incorporated towns the general principles of the Reform Bill. A uniform structure of municipal government was established, consisting of mayor, aldermen, and councillors, with the franchise extended to all resident householders who paid rates. Perhaps the most important feature of the act was authorization to impose rates for public purposes; as a result, municipal corporations began making improvements in streets, sewers, water supplies, police, and other local facilities although major advances of this kind did not come until the 1870s and after.

In addition to broadening the franchise, the reformers sought another major goal: the improvement of public administration. An example of this approach to reform was the Poor Law of 1834, which established central control of poor relief under a Poor Law Commission with extensive powers to reorganize administrative units, inspect local poor law practices, and prescribe standards for poor relief. The policies of the Poor Law Commission were aimed at economy and efficiency. Poor relief was to be less attractive than the worst-paid employment, and employers were forced to pay market wages by taking away relief payments to the employed. The key to the system was the elimination of "outdoor relief" by requiring indigent persons to live in poorhouses. The poor called the poorhouses "bastilles," and local opposition to the new poor law system was intense. Despite wide variations in enforcement, the Poor Law of 1834 introduced an element of uniformity and rigor that had been lacking under the old system without abandoning the principle of public responsibility for maintenance of the poor.

Political Pressure Groups. By 1837 the weak reforming spirit of the ministry had subsided as Lord Melbourne presided urbanely over a quarrelling coalition of Whigs, Radicals, and Irish. In the meantime new political issues had arisen, stimulated by the severe depression that began in 1837 and reached its depth in 1842. One of these issues was political democracy, frustrated in the Great Reform Bill and now brought into prominence by a working-class movement called Chartism. The goals of the Chartists were stated in The People's Charter: universal manhood suffrage, equal electoral districts, annual elections for Parliament, vote by secret ballot, abolition of property qualifications for Parliament, and the payment of salaries for members of Parliament. The first four would create a House of Commons that was democratically elected and subject to annual review, and last the two would make it possible for workingmen to sit in Parliament. The Chartists relied upon agitation through speeches, newspapers, pamphlets, and mass meetings to create the kind of working-class support that had been so important in the passage of the Reform Bill. The Charter was presented to the House of Commons in 1839, 1842, and 1848, each time supported by public demonstrations. The House of Commons refused to consider a document that would transfer political power from gentlemen and substantial property owners to "the great unwashed." Chartism was too narrowly based to succeed. Support for the movement was found almost exclusively among the urban working class. The movement lacked capable leaders and was torn between those who advocated violence and those who preferred orderly agitation through normal political channels. As the economy improved, the appeal of the movement waned, and workingmen found they could promote their interests more effectively through trade unions. Eventually, however, all but one of the Chartist goals (annual Parliaments) were achieved.

The depression also aggravated the growing conflict between the rising forces of industrialism and the established position of agriculture. The conflict was expressed in terms of free trade, which was advocated by industrialists, as opposed to protectionism, primarily embodied in the Corn Law, which the landed interest regarded as vital to its prosperity. In 1839 the Anti-Corn Law League was formed, which was led by Richard Cobden and John Bright and was supported primarily by middle-class businessmen. For the next seven years the League carried on a highly effective campaign of agitation and propaganda. The issue was an inflammatory one, pitting town against country and drawing upon strong antiaristocratic feeling. To manufacturers the League offered the prospect of lower food prices as a means of keeping wages low. Although suspicious of an organization dominated by factory owners, many workers were attracted by the promise of "cheap food." The issue was another example of the strong sense of injustice produced by economic distress. Chartism and the Anti-Corn Law League expressed the view of important segments of the British public that the reformed Parliament was still insufficiently responsive to their needs.

Religious Controversy. Another powerful issue during this age of political dissension was the privileged position of the Church of England and its Irish offshoot. Having lost its political privileges in 1828 and 1829, the Church was more determined than ever to preserve its other rights, which came under attack from Nonconformists, Catholics (mainly Irish), and secular Radicals. The Church was clearly out of step with the times, and its most loyal members were those who sought to set it on the path of autonomous reform by redistributing its incomes more equitably and by bringing its services to the new industrial areas. During his brief tenure of office in 1834 to 1835 Peel constituted an Ecclesiastical Commission, continued by the Whigs, which began a process of gradual reform and probably saved the Church of England as the national church. The major cause of religious controversy was education. As Parliament developed an interest in education, the Church claimed for itself the exclusive right to public funds for schools. This claim was disputed by Nonconformists, who maintained their own schools, and by Radicals, who advocated a secular school system free from control by denominational bodies. The combined determination of Anglicans and Nonconformists to preserve religious instruction in the schools was sufficient to block the advocates of secular education, and the combined efforts of Nonconformists and Radicals were sufficient to prevent an Anglican monopoly of public funds. The most that could be accomplished by 1850 was the establishment of a Committee on Education led by a dedicated reformer, Sir James Kay-Shuttleworth. In all of this agitation, Catholic influence was weak, except in Ireland where Daniel O'Connell led a powerful attack on the Anglican Church of Ireland. In 1838 the Irish peasants were relieved from paying tithes to a church that they did not attend, but, since the former tithes were merged in their rent, their economic position was no better than before.

The Ministry of Sir Robert Peel, 1841–1846

Political Parties. During these years of economic fluctuation, political controversy, and social discontent, the dominant political figure, in office or out, was Sir Robert Peel. During his brief tenure of office in 1834 to 1835 Peel found that the shattered fragments of the Tory party were insufficient to support a Tory ministry, despite gains in the election of 1835. Peel then set to work to build a broader base of support, relying on his Tory nucleus but seeking to attract others who believed reform had gone far enough. Peel proclaimed a political philosophy that was both conservative and constructive: preservation of existing institutions and values by timely reform where needed and redress of grievances when a strong case had been made. He addressed his appeal to "that class which is much less interested in the contentions of party, than in the maintenance of order and the cause of good government." In contrast to Peel's statement of principles, the Whig ministry of Lord Melbourne was a loose coalition of disparate groups, without coherent goals. In 1841 Melbourne called an election, in which Peel and the Conservatives won a clear majority.

Peel and Reform. As prime minister from 1841 to 1846, Peel brought to the office a degree of integrity and competence that marked him as one of the major political figures of the nineteenth century. His concerns were not narrowly partisan, nor was he the advocate of special interests; his purposes were truly national, on the assumption that competent conservatism was what the nation wanted and needed. He was a master of public finance, and in his budgets he restored the income tax and removed many of the customs and excise duties that hampered industrial growth and the flow of trade. By 1846 the only important tariff remaining was the Corn Law, which was sacrosanct to the Tories. The Railway Act of 1844 introduced some regulation of this important new industry. Other important legislation of Peel's ministry strengthened the role of the Bank of England in controlling the money supply and simplified the process of forming business corporations. In short, the Peel ministry was conservative in constitutional matters but responsive to the needs of a rapidly expanding industrial nation.

Despite his masterful leadership and unquestioned competence, Peel met his downfall when the two issues least susceptible to rational solution converged in a single crisis: Ireland and the Corn Law. In 1845 a potato blight struck Ireland, and that unhappy land, almost totally dependent on the potato for subsistence, was devastated. Neither the British government nor private charities were able to cope with the situation. In the next several years a million Irish emigrated, primarily to Britain or America, and another half million died. Confronted with a disaster of this magnitude, Peel could no longer support the tax on food embodied in the Corn Law, especially when faced with mass agitation by the Anti-Corn Law League. Despite his personal pledges to preserve the Corn Law, and the insistence of the landed interest that the Corn Law was vital to British agriculture, Peel bowed to what he considered pressing necessity. In 1846 he introduced proposals for sweeping tariff reform, including repeal of the Corn Law. In so doing he split his party. With the protectionist Tories (led by young Benjamin Disraeli) voting against him, the Corn Law was repealed with the support of Whigs and Radicals. Peel was forced to resign and never held office again.

The resignation of Peel, and his death in 1850, removed from British politics its most thoughtful and competent leader. But the time was passing when Britain needed leaders of the stature of Liverpool, Castlereagh, Canning, Grey, and Peel. The postwar adjustment had been made, and the worst problems of the early industrial age had been resolved. Britain had dealt with these challenges in a helter-skelter manner, but the decisions dictated by logic had been made and accepted. Britain was now entering a period of political calm, when the energies of the nation could be permitted to follow their own courses. Waiting in the wings were Peel's most talented pupil, William Gladstone, and his most ambitious rival, Benjamin Disraeli. Eventually their time would come.

Suggestions for Further Reading

The best general introduction to the scholarly literature on British history is *Recent Views on British History,* edited by Richard Schlatter (1984). Robert A. Smith, *Late Georgian and Regency England, 1760–1837* (1984) and Josef Altholz, *Victorian*

England, 1837–1901 (1970) are among the useful bibliographies published by the Conference on British Studies. For detailed textbook coverage of modern British history, with a good bibliography, see Walter L. Arnstein, *Britain Yesterday and Today: 1830 to the Present* (1983) and Robert K. Webb, *Modern England* (2nd edition, 1980).

Important studies of politics in the period covered by this chapter are J. E. Cookson, *Lord Liverpool's Administration: The Crucial Years, 1815–1822* (1975), W. R. Brock, *Lord Liverpool and Liberal Toryism, 1820–1827* (1967), Michael G. Brock, *The Great Reform Act* (1973), Geoffrey Finlayson, *Decade of Reform: England in the Eighteen Thirties* (1970), and Norman Gash, *Reaction and Reconstruction in English Politics, 1832–1852* (1965).

Foreign policy was a major concern of the Victorians. *The Cambridge History of British Foreign Policy, 1783–1919*, edited by G. P. Gooch and Adolphus W. Ward (3 vols., 1922–1923), is a good place to begin. A more recent work is Kenneth Bourne, *The Foreign Policy of Victorian England, 1830–1902* (1970).

Good surveys of British economic development are Phyllis Deane and W. A. Cole, *British Economic Growth, 1688–1959* (1967) and Peter Mathias, *The First Industrial Nation: An Economic History of Britain, 1700–1914* (1969). Works dealing with Victorian economic growth are J. D. Chambers, *The Workshop of the World: British Economic History from 1820 to 1880* (1961) and S. G. Checkland, *The Rise of Industrial Society in England, 1815–1885* (1964). The condition of the urban working class is reviewed in A. J. Taylor, *The Standard of Living in Britain during the Industrial Revolution* (1975).

Victorian studies are rich in social history. One of the most stimulating works is G. M. Young, *Victorian England: Portrait of an Age* (2nd edition, 1953). See also Harold Perkin, *The Origins of Modern English Society, 1780–1880* (1969) and J. F. C. Harrison, *The Early Victorians, 1832–1851* (1971). For urban growth see Francis Sheppard, *London, 1808–1870: The Infernal Wen* (1971) and Asa Briggs, *Victorian Cities* (1963). The growing interest in the history of women is seen in Duncan Crow, *The Victorian Woman* (1972).

Religion was an important part of Victorian life. Standard works are Robert Currie, *Churches and Churchgoers: Patterns of Church Growth in the British Isles since 1700* (1977) and Owen Chadwick, *The Victorian Church* (2 vols., 1979).

Books dealing with the rich intellectual life of Victorian Britain are Josef Altholz, *The Mind and Art of Victorian England* (1976), Richard Altick, *Victorian People and Ideas* (1973), Gertrude Himmelfarb, *Victorian Minds* (1972), and Walter Houghton, *The Victorian Frame of Mind* (1957).

A good survey of Scottish history is William Ferguson, *Scotland: 1689 to the Present* (1968). The best places to begin study of the Irish problem are J. C. Beckett, *The Making of Modern Ireland, 1603–1923* (3rd edition, 1966) and Lawrence McCaffrey, *The Irish Question, 1800–1922* (1968). Cecil Woodham-Smith tells the story of a turning point in Irish history in *The Great Hunger* (1963).

The Cambridge History of the British Empire (8 vols., edited by J. Holland Rose and others, 1929–1963) provides a great stockpile of information about the subject. A brief but incisive survey is Trevor Lloyd, *The British Empire, 1558–1982* (1984). An interesting social history is C. E. Carrington, *The British Overseas: Exploits of a Nation of Shopkeepers* (1950).

A representative selection of biographies for this chapter includes the following:

Christopher Hibbert, *George IV: Regent and King, 1811–1830* (1973), Philip Zie-gler, *King William IV* (1973), Woodham-Smith, *Queen Victoria, 1819–1861* (1972), Daphne Bennett, *King Without a Crown: Albert, Prince Consort of England, 1819–1861* (1977), Elizabeth Longford, *Wellington: Pillar of State* (1973), John Derry, *Castlereagh* (1976), Peter Dixon, *George Canning: Politician and Statesman* (1976), Gash, *Mr. Secretary Peel* (1961) and *Sir Robert Peel* (1972), George M. Trevelyan, *Lord Grey of the Reform Bill* (1920), John Prest, *Lord John Russell* (1972), David Cecil, *Melbourne* (1955), Donald Southgate, *"The Most English Minister": The Policies and Politics of Palmerston* (1966), and Donald Read, *Cobden and Bright: A Victorian Partnership* (1967).

14

Mid-Victorian Britain

1850–1886

*B*y 1850 Britain had reached a remarkable degree of political stability, economic prosperity, and social harmony. The wrenching changes of the early industrial age were finished, and Britain could enjoy the benefits of the increased productivity that industrialism brought. The political system in Britain rested on a broad base of public acceptance, in contrast to the situation on the continent, where the revolutions of 1848 to 1849 brought turmoil and disappointment with no resolution of the problems that had led to them. Overseas the British saw a strong and growing foreign trade, unchallenged by European competitors and unthreatened by local disorders. For the fortunate generation that came of age in 1850 the future was indeed promising.

Politics, Foreign Policy, and the Empire

Government. In *The English Constitution* (1867), Walter Bagehot, a perceptive journalist, described the British constitution as combining "a simple, efficient part" and "historical, complex, august, theatrical parts." At the time Bagehot wrote, the monarchy was the most important of the "theatrical" parts of the British government. In 1867 Queen Victoria was in semiseclusion, mourning the Prince Consort, Albert, who had died in 1861. Victoria still met with her ministers and read the dispatches, exercising the accepted functions of the monarch: "the right to be consulted, the right to encourage and the right to warn," as Bagehot put it. Earlier, with Albert at her side, she had carried out the role of monarch in a manner that won the approval and allegiance of her people. The high point of the royal family was reached in 1851 when Victoria and Albert presided proudly over the Great Exhibition (see page 000) displaying the indus-

319

trial, technological, and cultural achievements of Britain. When Albert died Victoria entered a prolonged period of mourning until encouraged to return to public view by a shrewd Conservative prime minister, Benjamin Disraeli, who realized the magic of monarchy identified by Bagehot in 1867.

Bagehot's "simple, efficient part" of the British constitution was the Cabinet, comprised of political leaders who were compatible enough to work together with some degree of harmony and who were supported by a majority in the House of Commons. At first glance a two-party system seemed to function in the ebb and flow of Cabinets. Cabinets that were predominantly Whig, led by Lord John Russell, Lord Aberdeen, or Lord Palmerston, alternated with Tory Cabinets led by Lord Derby and Benjamin Disraeli. In reality, however, the political process was a good deal more complex. Lord John Russell and other Whig leaders were uncomfortable in the role of reformers. In time a loose coalition called "Liberals" began to emerge, combining progressive Whigs, former followers of Sir Robert Peel, and Radicals. Those Tories who rejected Peel in 1846 were led by Lord Derby and the brilliant young politician, novelist, and dandy, Benjamin Disraeli. In this confused party situation the dominant political figure was Lord Palmerston, a man of strong character and personal independence, who was enormously popular in Parliament and the country. Palmerston was not bound by party ties. As prime minister from 1859 to 1865 he presided over a coalition of Whigs, Peelites, and Radicals who accepted his vigorous foreign policy in exchange for modest installments of institutional reform. With a weak party system, Cabinets were loose coalitions of political leaders, using personal or party groups as the core of their parliamentary followings but needing additional support from independent members of the House of Commons.

The Foreign Policy of Palmerston. The unstructured politics of the mid-Victorian period were possible because, to a considerable degree, a broad consensus existed within the nation and the political class. As domestic conflicts diminished foreign policy became the major topic of political controversy. In foreign policy the dominant minister was Lord Palmerston, who served as foreign secretary or prime minister for twenty-four of the thirty-five years from 1830 until his death in 1865. Jaunty, confident, ebullient, Palmerston communicated the John Bull patriotism of the British, who were proud of their nation: "a political, a commercial, and constitutional country," as Palmerston put it, which had reconciled individual freedom and the rule of law.

Although Palmerston gave a highly personal touch to British foreign policy, the national interests of Britain were generally recognized and accepted. As an island nation, it was important to Britain to preserve her naval and maritime supremacy and keep open the links with her Empire. Ever since Canning Britain had avoided close commitments to Europe, yet it was very much in Britain's interests to preserve the balance of power in Europe and to protect the Netherlands and Belgium from dominance by a great power. The British public felt strong sympathy with liberal and national movements on the continent, but practical realities made it unlikely that Britain could do much more than issue encouraging pronouncements and provide a refuge for exiles. The bête noire of Victorian Britain was Russia, that vast, autocratic, expanding state, which lurked on the verges of what the Victorians called the civilized world, threatening Britain's interests in the Baltic, the eastern Mediterranean, the Middle East, India, and the Far East. Britain was most likely to be stung into action when Russia threatened the Ottoman Empire, the decaying bulwark against Russian expansion into the Mediterranean and the Middle East. It was this foreign policy, consistently recognized but inconsistently applied, that occasioned most of the political crises of the period.

Palmerston's approach to foreign policy was seen in 1848 to 1849 when a series of revolutions rocked Europe. His major concern was to preserve peace and stability, and he especially feared a revolutionary government in France that would return to the warlike policies of the French Revolution and Napoleon. On the other hand, he hoped that the fulfillment of liberal and national aspirations in Italy and central Europe would be a stabilizing force. He was ready enough with pronouncements but short on action, which made him equally unpopular with threatened governments and disappointed revolutionaries. The reality of the situation was that Britain, secure in her strong government, expanding economy, and invincible fleet, could afford the luxury of such a foreign policy. Palmerston, despite his bluster, had not shed British blood or spent a significant amount of British money. Palmerston's bravado was again demonstrated in 1850 in a petty incident, the Don Pacifico affair. Pacifico was a Portuguese Jew who claimed British citizenship on the grounds that he had been born in Gibraltar. His house in Athens had been attacked by a mob, and Pacifico called on the British government to help him collect damages. Palmerston came vigorously to the aid of Pacifico, acting in such an independent manner that he humiliated the Greeks and thoroughly offended France and Russia, who were also concerned, as well as Queen Victoria, who was furious. When his political enemies attacked his conduct of foreign policy, Palmerston replied with a resounding speech in which he boldly proclaimed the British government's support of its citizens anywhere in the world: "As the Roman, in days of old," Palmerston concluded, "held himself free from indignity, when he could say *Civis Romanus sum*; so also a British subject, in whatever land he may be, shall feel confident that the watchful eye and strong arm of England, will protect him against injustice and wrong." The House of Commons and the British public loved it; the queen, the politicians, and the diplomats had no choice but to give way.

The less successful side of mid-Victorian foreign policy was seen in the Crimean War (1854–1856). In 1853 Russia and the Ottoman Empire entered into one of their periodic conflicts resulting from Russian ambitions in the Balkan peninsula and the Black Sea area. Although the prime minister, Lord Aberdeen, wanted to avoid war, hostility toward Russia in the press and public sentiment forced the government to come to the aid of the Ottoman Empire. The British were joined by France, whose emperor, Napoleon III, was eager to play an important role in European affairs, and by the Italian state of Sardinia. The war, fought in the Crimea, a peninsula on the north shore of the Black Sea, consisted primarily of a costly siege of the Russian fortress of Sevastopol. The allied generals managed the war with gross ineptitude, which was reported in full detail by war correspondents who accompanied the troops. The British public, which had initially supported the war, was appalled and infuriated by reports of needless deaths and hardships. The redeeming feature of the war was the dedicated work of the resourceful young Florence Nightingale, who brought a group of women to the Crimea to care for the wounded and thus helped establish nursing as a profession for women. To still the public outcry, Palmerston was made prime minister in 1855, and some prestige was salvaged when Sevastopol fell. The death of the Russian tsar also contributed to peace, which was made in 1856. The result was that Russian expansion in the area was checked, although the problem remained to fester for another two decades.

The moralistic streak in Palmerstonian foreign policy influenced Britain in dealing with two major conflicts, the War for Italian Unification (1859–1861) and the American Civil War (1861–1865). Palmerston and the British public sympathized with the aspirations of Italian patriots for national unity, even though achievement of that goal would require war against the Austrian Empire, which controlled the north Italian provinces of Lombardy and Venetia. In 1859 the king of Sardinia, aided by Napoleon III of France, provoked a war with the Austrians, which soon led to uprisings in other parts of Italy. Palmerston and Lord John Russell openly displayed their sympathy with the Italians, and British support contributed to the Sardinian victory that, by 1861, had brought most of Italy under the Sardinian crown. The issue was less clear for Britain in the American Civil War. The initial British view was that the Confederate states, like the Italians, had a right to independence if they wanted it; furthermore, the southern states were major suppliers of cotton to British industry. Palmerston's government at first took a firm tone with the Lincoln administration, especially on the issue of freedom of the seas. When the Civil War became a war against slavery, however, a more compelling moral issue replaced that of Confederate independence. Despite hardships in Britain due to the Union blockade of southern cotton, Confederate hopes for a British declaration of war were disappointed.

The Move Toward Democracy. The travail of the American republic was of considerable interest in Britain because the United States, for good or ill, was seen as the principal example of popular democracy, a topic that had become important in British politics. The idea of democracy had not died with Chartism. John Stuart Mill in his *Considerations on Representative Government* (1861) argued that democracy was the best form of government because it fostered creative and productive individuals and built a broad base of loyalty to the state. Through the democratic process, he contended, the general interest would be served since particular interests would cancel each other. Mill would exclude from the democratic process illiterates, nontaxpayers, bankrupts, and welfare recipients since they could not be regarded as capable of exercising the franchise responsibly. He saw merit in giving more than one vote to persons whose education or profession marked them as better qualified for the responsibilities of citizenship. He even went so far as propose the vote for eligible women. The victory of Lincoln and the Union in the United States Civil War strengthened the advocates of democracy in Britain, among them John Bright, a dedicated Radical, who argued that the success of democracy in the United States and the colonies showed that it would work in Britain too. The major opponent of an extension of the franchise was Lord Palmerston, the prime minister, whose death in 1865 removed the principal obstacle to reopening the question in Parliament. The conversion of William E. Gladstone, Palmerston's capable and energetic chancellor of the exchequer, gave the advocates of democracy a powerful new voice to plead their cause.

In 1867, the year of Bagehot's *The English Constitution*, the casual, unstructured character of mid-Victorian politics began to change as new leaders and new issues emerged after the death of Palmerston. Palmerston was succeeded as prime minister by the Whig leader, Lord John Russell, now in the twilight of his long and distinguished career. The most vigorous member of the Cabinet was Gladstone, who came forward as the leader of the political group known as Liberals. In 1866 Russell and Gladstone proposed a bill for reform of the House of Commons that called for a moderate extension of the franchise. Parliamentary reform, which had been in abeyance since the Reform Bill of 1832, suddenly gained enormous public popularity, and the politicians discovered they had aroused a sleeping giant.

The result was a series of debates of great intensity and bitterness as old political alignments were shattered. Russell and Gladstone, abandoned by the more conservative Whigs, resigned and were replaced by a Tory ministry led by Lord Derby and Benjamin Disraeli. Popular support for reform, as demonstrated in mass meetings and public demonstrations, persuaded Derby and Disraeli to bring forward their own bill, hoping to win support for their party from the newly enfranchised voters. In the ensuing debates Gladstone, Bright, and others succeeded in amending Disraeli's bill to extend its provisions more widely. The Reform Bill of 1867, as eventually passed, extended the franchise to urban workingmen, with a modest redistribution of seats to industrial areas. The electorate was almost doubled, and, although many adult males were still excluded from the vote (as were all women), the issue—clearly seen and debated—was a democratically chosen House of Commons as opposed to a political system that gave power to persons of property, education, and established social position. The hazards as well as the advantages of democracy were thoroughly aired, and when the bill was passed Lord Derby admitted that Britain had taken "a leap in the dark."

The British Overseas. Britain's overseas interests continued to be of the greatest importance, although the value of political control of colonies was diminished by the policy of free trade. In some respects people were Britain's most important export, as thousands of emigrants left the British Isles every year to seek new homes and opportunities in the United States, Canada, the Australian colonies, New Zealand, and the Cape Colony and Natal in southern Africa. British bankers and merchants pursued their business throughout the world, and the British merchant marine and whalers plied the seven seas. The principal value of British trade was in the sale of manufactured goods and the importation of basic commodities such as cotton, wool, tea, foodstuffs, fertilizers, jute, whale oil, palm oil, and tropical woods. In the age of free trade the British government had little to do with the activities of its nationals abroad. The British navy patrolled the seas from its bases at Nova Scotia, Bermuda, Gibraltar, Malta, the Falkland Islands, the Cape Colony, Mauritius, Aden, Ceylon, Bombay, Singapore, and Hong Kong. The consular service offered some help to British businessmen and travellers, and the Post Office extended its overseas services. Otherwise the British government preferred to let well enough alone, except in instances such as the Opium War with China (1839–1842) which opened that great empire to trade with Western nations.

The trend in those colonies where the British had settled in large numbers was toward greater self-government. In 1837 uprisings in Quebec (Lower Canada) and Ontario (Upper Canada) led the Melbourne government to send Lord Durham, a radical Whig nobleman, to visit the Canadian colonies and make recommendations. The *Durham Report* (1839) proposed unification of the two Canadas with "responsible government," that is, vesting the executive powers in a cabinet with the support of the majority of the assembly. The first of Durham's recommendations was adopted in 1840, although responsible government was not granted until 1847. In the next few years responsible government was extended to the Australian colonies (1855) and New Zealand (1856). In southern Africa the Cape Colony and Natal offered special problems, both in the relations of the two white peoples—British and the Dutch settlers known as Boers—and between the white peoples and the native black populations. After the abolition of slavery in 1833 many of the Boers had migrated into the interior and had established two frontier republics, the Orange Free State and the Transvaal. British claims in this area led to friction between the Cape Colony and the Boer republics, but in 1852 to 1854 the independence of the Boer republics was confirmed. In 1872 the Cape Colony and Natal received responsible government.

The most striking example of the extension of self-government within the empire was the British North America Act (1867), which formed the present federation of Canada. The economic advantages to be gained by union were considerable, and the lessons to be drawn from the American Civil War were fresh in mind when the proposal was made to join the two Canadas and the maritime provinces (Nova Scotia, New Brunswick, Prince Edward Island) in a federal union. The government of Canada established under the act preserved the governor-general as the link with the Empire and continued the imperial relationship in such matters as foreign policy and defense. The federal government, located in Ottawa, followed the cabinet model, with ministers responsible to Parliament. The federal government possessed power in all matters not specifically delegated to the provinces. Provincial governments were constituted on a similar pattern, and provision was made for the addition of new provinces as settlement proceeded westward. Thus the principles of self-government developed in the mother country were extended to her offshoots in various parts of the world.

India, with its complex political structure, its ancient and diverse cultures, its hereditary animosities, and its great value, was a special case. Pitt's India Act of 1784 had entrusted the government of the British territories in India to the British East India Company, under the supervision of a governor-general in India and a Board of Control in London. In 1833 the Company ceased to engage in trade and became exclusively a governing body. The Company developed its own civil service and an army with British officers and Indian soldiers called sepoys. From time to time wars broke out with Indian princes, which led to extensions of the Company's territories, but the Company never ruled more than two-thirds of India, with the rest continuing under native princes dominated in varying degrees by the British. British rule brought many modern advantages to

India: effective central government, a professional civil service (open to Indians in the lower ranks), railroads, postal and telegraph systems, a vast free trade area that stimulated economic development, peace between the Hindus and Moslems, famine control, and the English language—the only language common to all of India. On the other hand, the British rulers remained aloof from the Indian population, British manufactured goods destroyed native handicraft industries, and British rule interfered with many traditional customs and practices.

In 1857 a great crisis broke out in India when the sepoys in some regiments mutinied. For a time it appeared that the authority of the small cadre of British officials and military officers might collapse. After hard fighting, which included the dramatic rescue of a British garrison in Lucknow, the sepoy mutiny was suppressed by the British authorities using other Indian regiments. The result of the mutiny, however, was the dissolution of the East India Company and the establishment of direct British rule of India through a secretary of state for India. The civil service and army were continued as before, and British investment in railroads and industry was encouraged. But the new regime, while showing greater respect for Indian customs and beliefs, also contributed to a growing gulf between the British authorities and the Indian population.

A Stocktaking: Mid-Victorian Society

The Idea of Progress. As we have seen, by 1850 Britain had entered a period of political stability, economic growth, and social harmony. The British were proud of their achievements and compared their lives favorably with the despotisms, revolutions, and wars of Europe. Despite great problems of poverty, ignorance, and crime, the general attitude of the mid-Victorians was optimistic. The key concept of the age was "progress"— belief that the present was better than the past and confidence that the future would be better than the present. To some extent the Victorian concept of progress was materialistic, supported by statistics showing the increase of population, trade, industrial and agricultural production, and national wealth. But it was also idealistic, for the Victorians took pride in the advancement of scholarship, science, and technology; the material achievements of the age were valued as contributing to the spiritual and moral improvement of the nation. In view of the enormous social problems of the day, this mid-Victorian confidence may be derided as complacency, hypocrisy, or humbug. But the Victorian confidence may also be seen as the spirit of a people at their peak—proud of their achievements and ready for whatever the future might bring.

One example of the Victorian belief in progress was Thomas Babington

The Crystal Palace *(BBC Hulton Picture Library)*.

Macaulay's *History of England*, which began appearing in 1848. Macaulay's work dealt primarily with the Glorious Revolution of 1688 and its consequences, but he took the opportunity to remark on the advances—intellectual, material, spiritual—that had been made since that time. Macaulay was a staunch Whig and proud of the principles that he associated with Whiggism—constitutional and parliamentary government, economic individualism, intellectual and religious freedom, and national pride. Another notable symbol of progress was the Great Exhibition of 1851, presented in the Crystal Palace, an astonishing prefabricated structure of iron and glass. Prince Albert was the guiding spirit of the Exhibition; its purpose was to display the industrial, technological, scientific, and artistic achievements of the age. Although the Great Exhibition drew displays from all over the world, most of the exhibitors were British and it served as a showcase for Britain's industrial leadership. Cheap railway excursions brought thousands of visitors from all over Britain to observe and take pride in the achievements of their country.

The pride of the mid-Victorians in their economic progress was not unwarranted. From 1831 to 1851 the population of Great Britain increased from 24 million to 27 million, and from 1851 to 1871 it increased to 31.5 million. The factory system was by this time fully established in the textile industry, and production of textiles increased from £60 million in 1845 to £84.5 million in 1870. In 1856 Henry Bessemer patented a process for converting molten pig iron into steel, thus introducing the age of cheap, abundant steel. An important feature of the British economy was the technological industries, such as engineering and the manufacture of machine tools, where Britain led the world. The revolution in transportation and communications continued with the building of railroads, the development of the steamship, the improvement of domestic and overseas postal services, and the opening of the transatlantic cable in 1866. Jules Verne's novel *Around the World in Eighty Days* (1873) was science fiction verging on the possible. It is not surprising that this French author chose a resourceful English gentleman as his hero.

The Landed Class. Considering the cries of alarm raised by the repeal of the Corn Law, it is ironic to find that the years from 1850 to 1870 were the golden age of British agriculture. New methods increased productivity, a growing home market sustained prices, and the effects of foreign competition had not yet been felt. In addition to the profits of agriculture, landowners also benefited from the growing value of mineral rights and urban properties. Great aristocrats, such as the duke of Bedford, collected enormous incomes, lightly taxed, from both urban and agricultural land. Aristocrats dominated the royal court and the glittering social functions related to it. They entertained lavishly in their comfortable London townhouses or at their splendid country estates, provided with every comfort by swarms of domestic servants. Members of noble families were liberally sprinkled throughout Cabinets, the diplomatic service, and the army. The House of Lords was the special preserve of the aristocracy, including the bishops. Although most decisions of importance were made in the House of Commons, the House of Lords could delay, alter, or reject controversial legislation. The Lords also exercised great power as the supreme court of law. The country gentry prospered and maintained their domination of the government and society of the shires. The life of the landed gentleman continued to exert its fascination, and the aristocracy and gentry were strengthened by the influx of ability and wealth from men successful in government, business, and the professions or were strengthened by marriages of heirs to their daughters. The legal arrangements that guaranteed the transmission of the estate to one heir (usually the eldest son) continued; younger sons were provided for by careers in the law, the Church, the army, or the Empire. Long-established traditions of deference, and the continuing opportunity for successful business and professional men to enter the ranks of the gentry, meant that the landed class remained powerful and influential.

Urbanization. The most notable feature of mid-Victorian society was the transformation of Britain into an urban nation. The census of 1851 showed that, for the first time, the number of urban inhabitants exceeded those living in rural areas, and the proportion of the population living in

Victorian London

an urban setting continued to grow. The greatest urban center of all was London, the name commonly applied to the metropolitan area that included the city of London, Westminster, and the urban sprawl into the counties of Middlesex and Surrey. London grew because it served a variety of functions, all of which were growing. London was the capital of a dynamic nation and the heart of the world's greatest empire; London was one of the world's busiest seaports; it was the hub of international finance, insurance, and commodity trading; it was an important manufacturing city, principally conducted in small factories and shops; it was a center of communications, publications, fashion, entertainment, and polite society. London attracted many foreigners who came to visit or to settle, including notable political refugees such as the Austrian Chancellor Metternich, the French Emperor Napoleon III, the Italian nationalist leader Mazzini, and a stream of lesser exiles, agitators, and publicists, among them an obscure German named Karl Marx.

As a result of this rapid growth the older parts of London were changing: the city became increasingly a business district, losing population, and the centers of shopping, entertainment, and fashionable residence moved westward. The distinctively Victorian growth of London was seen

St. Pancras Station, London *(E. A. Reitan)*.

in its residential areas and suburbs, made possible by the underground and the commuter train. To the north the area called Bloomsbury, developed principally on land owned by the duke of Bedford, maintained the classical dignity of the early nineteenth century in its stately squares and tree-lined streets. The presence of the British Museum, the University of London, and various charitable and religious foundations gave it a somewhat intellectual tone. Kensington, to the west, displayed a Victorian air, with its tall rows of flats, often ornately decorated, and imitation Gothic churches. A cluster of museums, built on the site of the Great Exhibition of 1851, contributed to the dignity of Kensington. The true Victorian suburbia was found farther out, at places such as Wimbledon and Bethnal Green, where rows of brick houses with bay windows and tiny gardens, well supplied with schools, churches, and shops, provided homes for the growing white-collar class as well as the "respectable" working class. The suburbs represented a new element in the British social structure and exerted great influence upon Victorian politics, morality, family life, literature, domestic arts, and religion.

Even more dramatic than the growth of London was the rise of provincial towns, whose rapid growth was a counterbalance to the dominance of London. Although London was the largest seaport, other ports attracted an increasing trade. Bristol, for centuries the principal western port, continued to be important, although it was eclipsed by the rise of Liverpool and Glasgow, both of which served major industrial areas. On the east coast Newcastle and Hull flourished as ports, with special interest in shipbuilding and fisheries respectively. Old, well-established towns such as Norwich and Nottingham, which for centuries had served as market towns with domestic industries, added new industries while preserving much of their preindustrial character. The most notable provincial towns, however, were those that were the result of the Industrial Revolution. Manchester, center of the cotton textile industry, was dominated by an elite of landlords, bankers, and businessmen. Birmingham was famous for the metal trades and a strong sense of political involvement and civic responsibility. In Yorkshire, Leeds was the center of an important industrial complex, and another cluster of industries grew up in Scotland in the valley of the Clyde, with Glasgow as its principal city.

The pride of the industrial towns was most notably displayed in magnificent town halls and civic centers. Great Victorian railroad stations, accompanied by grandiose hotels, proclaimed by their size, opulence, and location the central importance of the railroad in Victorian life. Banks and insurance companies tried to match the dignity of the public buildings with ornate structures that exemplified in granite and marble their (presumed) financial solidity. Factories and working class housing were still located near the center of the city, but commuter trains and improved

Industrial Halifax *(E. A. Reitan)*.

roads made it possible for the middle class to leave the grime and noise of the central city for residential areas of brick houses, usually with a small garden, with churches, schools, and parks nearby. The provincial towns tried to emulate London as cultural centers too, with "red-brick universities" and civic libraries, museums, and art galleries, but in this respect London stood unchallenged. Politically the provincial towns had become a powerful new force. They were dominated by business leaders who were often antiaristocratic, and Nonconformity was strong. A literate working class that read newspapers and formed trade unions and "friendly societies" became an important factor in local and national politics. These towns were less influenced by the traditions of the past and were more inclined to seek rational justifications for political institutions or public policy. The political leader who could gain the allegiance of the provincial towns would unlock a powerful new force, especially after the Reform Bill of 1867.

Thought and Society

The Problem of Poverty. When the Victorians spoke of progress they meant not only the improvement of political institutions and material well-being but the "March of Mind"—the increasing ability of man to understand his world, control it for his benefit, and govern his personal and corporate conduct according to reasoned principles. The most intractable problem faced by Victorian thinkers was the problem of poverty, for the remarkable achievements of the time had also created vast areas of privation, ignorance, immorality, vice, and crime. Although a bewildering variety of answers was available, the question was usually the same: how could "two nations," the comfortable and the deprived, be justified, reconciled, and eventually brought together in a community of mutual well-being?

In the mid-Victorian period the rigorous doctrines of Utilitarianism and the classical economists were softened by a growing sense of humanity. John Stuart Mill, whose arguments for democracy have been mentioned earlier, demonstrated the changes that were taking place in social thought. A child prodigy, Mill was educated by his father, James Mill, in rigid Utilitarian doctrines. In young manhood he found his emotions touched by romantic poetry. He lived up to his father's expectations, writing extensively on political and economic questions, but he also recognized that strict logic must be bent to allow for human considerations. In his later years he continued to support the economics of laissez-faire as applied to production, but he conceded that some interference with economic laws was needed to secure a more equitable distribution of the wealth produced by industrial society. In his famous *Autobiography*, published in the last year of his life (1873), he wrote:

> The social problem of the future we considered to be, how to unite the greatest individual liberty of action, with a common ownership of the globe, and an equal participation of all in the benefits of combined labor.

In short, Mill had become what he and his contemporaries called "a socialist."

The most usual mid-Victorian answer to the problem of poverty was to trust in man's ability to master his destiny through the translation of knowledge into practical uses. The Victorians made popular heroes of great engineers, who had demonstrated their ability to understand nature and utilize natural forces to serve human needs. Samuel Smiles, a prolific writer, gained popularity with his *Life of George Stephenson* (1857) and his *Lives of the Engineers* (1861–1862). In Smiles's view, the successes of the engineers grew out of their knowledge, determination, and resourcefulness, qualities that he extolled in *Self-Help* (1859) and other works praising moral character, self-reliance, and hard work. Smiles's confidence that moral and technological advances could build a better world was shared by many, although his cheery optimism seemed scarcely warranted in view of the problems of the time.

Literature and the theater were also concerned with the problem of poverty in the midst of plenty. Charles Dickens, the foremost novelist of the age, had known poverty as a child and never lost his respect for the dignity of humble people. His novels dealt primarily with the middle class but he portrayed vividly the lives of the common people, lovingly cataloguing their simple virtues and their patience under circumstances over which they had no control. Dickens offered no political or economic nostrums; his response to the problem of poverty was reliance upon one's own intelligence and resourcefulness, a dose of good luck, and mutual helpfulness in adversity.

The leading Victorian poet, Alfred, Lord Tennyson, shared some of the Victorian confidence in progress and technology but was acutely sensitive to the losses, as well as the gains, that came with change. In *Locksley Hall* (1842) Tennyson foresaw savage war, as well as peaceful commerce, and he anticipated revolutionary changes of global scope. Nevertheless, he was optimistic. He was proud to be part of his dynamic new world. He looked forward to a time when "the war drums throbbed no longer, and the battle flags were furled, /In the Parliament of man, the Federation of the World."

The Victorian theater dealt with similar themes. As the middle class began to provide the bulk of the theater audience, the classic plays of the Elizabethan playwrights or the Restoration comedy lost popularity, to be replaced by the melodrama. The melodrama featured colorful spectacle, often drawing upon subjects that were in the news. But its primary appeal lay in a clear-cut struggle between right and wrong, often with a noble hero, an evil villain, and a sweet young girl, the pawn in their struggle. Financial distress frequently was the central factor in the plot. Action was constant as one crisis followed another, leading to the inevitable happy ending. Dion Boucicault, a talented Irishman who won and lost several fortunes as a playwright and impresario, was the master of this genre. His plays dealt with themes with which his audiences could identify: fear of mysterious danger (*The Vampire*), revolution (*The Reign of Terror*), current events (*The Relief of Lucknow*), slavery (*The Octoroon*), labor problems (*The Long Strike*), urban poverty (*The Streets of London*), and crime (*After Dark*). The naivete of the Victorian melodrama is ridiculed today, but its simple idealism was that of a people to whom right and wrong were quite clear. Its crises were real to middle-class audiences who knew how quickly they could pass from comfort to misery; and its happy ending reflected their faith in a just world where virtue and prudence flourished and wickedness and improvidence led inevitably to disaster.

The Impact of Science. In 1859 this generation of hopefulness and generous feelings received a severe blow. For several decades philosophers and scientists had been considering the effects of natural processes over time. Charles Lyell's *Principles of Geology* (1830–1833) explained geology as the result of gradual changes taking place over millennia as mountains were thrust up and worn down or as rivers cut valleys and built deltas. Lyell's account left little for the hand of God who, according to the Victorian understanding of the Scriptures, had created the land and seas, mountains and valleys in 4004 B.C. The idea of evolution was already in the air when Charles Darwin applied it to living things in his *On the Origin of Species by Means of Natural Selection* (1859). The key to Darwin's book was his doctrine of natural selection, which held that the world of nature was a struggle for existence in which life-forms with small advantages were able to survive and pass these advantages on to their offspring, while other life forms, less well endowed, fell by the wayside. In *The Descent of Man* (1871) Darwin applied his evolutionary doctrine to human origins. Darwin's concept changed God from a beneficent Providence to a creator who left his universe to struggle for survival; nature was found to be "red in tooth and claw." Man himself was seen to be a product of struggle, rising gradually to supremacy over the prostrate bodies of his rivals. The mild-mannered biologist with the bold thoughts had introduced a jarring note into the optimism and good feeling of mid-Victorian Britain.

The concept of evolution gave a new turn to discussions of the social problems of the age. The churches supported the traditional Scriptural doctrines of God as creator, governor, and sustainer of all things, including the loving God who provided the means of redemption and fulfillment for all his children, in this world and in the world to come. Advocates of science such as the brilliant biologist and controversialist, Thomas Henry Huxley, rejected traditional religious explanations, contending that human intelligence had found the key to understanding life and had liberated man from supernatural explanations and hopes. In Huxley's view, the doctrine of evolution was invigorating to man. While it left man to make himself through his own efforts, his previous achievements gave him reason to believe that he could make further progress up the evolutionary ladder. Herbert Spencer, a philosopher more popular in the United States than in Britain, formulated a philosophy of "Social Darwinism," in which he offered the view that human societies evolved in a manner similar to biological evolution, moving from simpler to more complex forms through the principle of natural selection. In his view, social evolution was to the advantage of mankind and should not be checked or distorted by legislation or ill-considered humanitarianism. The "tender-minded" sympathies of Mill, Dickens, and Tennyson were challenged by a new "tough-minded" realism that accepted conflict as a necessary part of all existence. Thus the "March of Mind" continued, but in directions little contemplated by an earlier generation.

Gladstone and Disraeli

Gladstone and the Liberal Party. Bagehot's analysis of the British constitution was published in 1867, the year that brought a new element into

British politics—the beginnings of political democracy. Like the Reform Bill of 1832, the long-range implications of the Reform Bill of 1867 were more important than the immediate changes. Cabinets and Parliaments continued to be comprised of the same kinds of people, and the two most prominent political leaders, Gladstone and Disraeli, had been in politics for a long time. Yet both of these leaders forged to the front because they were able to understand, accept, and take advantage of changed political circumstances. The new political scene was that of emerging democracy: leaders, parties, and platforms with national appeal and national constituencies.

Although Disraeli had proposed the legislation that became the Reform Bill of 1867, the expanded electorate turned in 1868 to Gladstone and those who had joined with him in giving the bill its dominant features. Gladstone was a man of great intellect, energy, administrative ability, and moral fervor. He was unquestionably the dominant figure in his ministry and the principal spokesman for the ministry in Parliament and the nation. Gladstone advocated caution in foreign policy, avoiding involvement in the Franco-Prussian War (1870–1871) and taking a conciliatory approach to Russian repudiation of restrictions on Russian naval power in the Black Sea. At considerable cost to his popularity he made a statesmanlike settlement of American claims for damages done by the *Alabama*, a Confederate warship built in Britain. Thus Gladstone minimized external involvements to concentrate on domestic reform.

Gladstone's major concern was to obtain economy and efficiency in government by removing privilege and waste. Adoption of the secret ballot (1872) was a major contribution to purity in elections and a blow to the influence of landlords and employers. Open competitive examinations were introduced for the civil service and the army was extensively reformed, including the abolition of the purchase of commissions. A major undertaking was revision of the tangled jurisdictions of the ancient courts of common law. The Forster Education Act (1870) sought to provide elementary education for every child by increasing government grants to existing schools, which were primarily operated by religious denominations, and by instituting local school boards to provide additional schools maintained by local taxes. One of Gladstone's major concerns was to remove the grievances of Ireland. His most important step in this ministry was disestablishment of the Anglican Church in Ireland. Gladstone dominated his ministry in administration, Parliament, and public debate and gave to the office of prime minister a degree of national leadership that looked forward to the twentieth-century concept of that office.

Gladstone was also important in the emergence of the Liberal party, a new kind of political party that supported its parliamentary contingent with organizations in the constituencies. Although many of the leaders of the Liberal party had worked together for some time, the Reform Bill crisis of 1866 to 1867, the election of 1868, and the reforms of Gladstone's first ministry welded them together. On the local level Liberal associations and clubs organized the voters and fought elections. The Liberal party appealed to business and professional men, clerks, shopkeepers, and skilled workmen, with a strong leavening of Nonconformity. The goals of the Liberal party were defined by Gladstone's first ministry: a conciliatory foreign policy, reduction of imperial commitments, economy in government, institutional reform, free trade, individual responsibility, and removal of Irish grievances. By 1874 those policies had created opponents and brought rankling discontents. The public had become tired of change and were upset by other aspects of Liberalism, such as the temperance movement, which worked to limit access to liquor through licensing pubs. In the election of 1874 Disraeli and the Conservative party won a decisive victory on a platform of saving the country from Gladstone's weak foreign policy and his restless urge to reform.

Disraeli and the Conservative Party. The Conservative party was, to some extent, the successor of the Tories, as the Liberal party was of the Whigs, but both of these parties were different in important respects from their predecessors. As leader of the Conservative party Disraeli's achievement was to develop a party that capitalized on the British desire for continuity and tradition while giving the party a mildly progressive program. The Conservatives also developed a network of local party organizations linked together by the Conservative Central Office and the National Union. Disraeli's ministry (1874–1880) avoided political and administrative reform of the Gladstonian type but brought forward measures of social reform designed to win working-class votes. Another Factory Act (1878) codified and extended earlier legislation dealing with working conditions in factories, and the Public Health Act (1875) established a sanitary code. The Artisans' Dwelling Act (1875) was the first important attempt by government to improve the wretched housing of the poor. The Merchant Shipping Act (1878) was passed to improve the safety and health of British seamen. Trade unions, which had been legalized under Gladstone, were given the right to picket. As a Conservative Disraeli sought to preserve the institutions of the past by making them serve national purposes. He persuaded Queen Victoria to abandon her seclusion, and in 1876 she was given the grandiloquent title, empress of India. He also showed deference to the House of Lords and the Church of England and made clear his determination to preserve British authority in Ireland. The Conservative party built by Disraeli was still dominated by the aristocracy and gentry, but he succeeded in winning a broad base of support among businessmen, urban workers, and people in small towns and villages. Like Gladstone,

Benjamin Disraeli *(National Portrait Gallery)*.

Disraeli was a superb publicist. The age of democratic leaders and parties was emerging.

Disraeli's Foreign and Imperial Policy. Disraeli's foreign policy earned national acclaim by flattering national patriotism. The defeat of France in the Franco-Prussian War and the unification of Germany and Italy changed the European balance of power and introduced a period of great power rivalries that eventually became threatening to Britain. Disraeli could do little to affect the European balance of power, but he could strengthen Britain's role in the world by attention to her overseas interests. In 1875 he scored a major success when he purchased 44 percent of the stock of the Suez Canal Company, thus gaining Britain a voice in the management of that vital waterway to the East. In 1877 a threat arose in the eastern Mediterranean when another war broke out between Russia and the moribund Ottoman Empire. The Russians had made extensive gains in the Balkans when Disraeli intervened to maintain the historic British policy of supporting the Turks to check Russian expansion into the Balkans and the Mediterranean. In addition to various warlike gestures, Disraeli was active at the Congress of Berlin (1878), called by the German chancellor, Otto von Bismarck, to resolve the problem. The Congress was a great success for Disraeli, who succeeded in obtaining modifications of Russia's Balkan gains; he also gained the island of Cyprus as a British base to guard the Eastern Mediterranean and the Suez Canal.

Another aspect of Disraeli's policy was to promote the Empire as essential to national greatness. The jewel of the Empire was India, and in 1876 Disraeli dramatized his imperialism with a magnificent ceremony in which Queen Victoria was crowned empress of India. Russia was seen as the principal threat to British power in India, and in 1878 British fear of Russian expansion led to an ill-advised expedition into Afghanistan, which was still causing trouble when Disraeli left office. Disraeli also tried to resolve the problems of southern Africa. Conflict was endemic on the borders separating the British colonies from the two Boer republics of the interior. In the 1870s these problems were aggravated by the discovery of diamonds in disputed territory. In 1877 Disraeli's government, seeking to unify the area, annexed the Orange Free State and the Transvaal. Two years later, with the Boers still smouldering as a result of this action, war broke out with the fierce Zulus. Disraeli left the problem of Boer resistance and the Zulu War to his successor. By the end of his ministry, Disraeli had found that the flowers of empire came with dangerous thorns.

Gladstone Again. In the meantime Gladstone had taken his attack on Disraeli's policies to the people. As Liberal candidate for Parliament from the Scottish county of Midlothian, he delivered a series of powerful speeches that were reported throughout the nation. Gladstone attacked Disraeli's opportunism and manipulation, holding before the British public the ideal of a foreign policy based on moral principles and international law. His words fell on responsive ears, for by that time Disraeli's showy foreign policy, dangerous imperial ventures, and lackluster domestic reforms had begun to pall. The election of 1880 gave a new mandate to Gladstone and the Liberals. Much to the dismay of Queen Victoria, who disliked his appeals to public opinion, Gladstone returned to office as leader of a Liberal ministry.

Gladstone soon found that the problems of the new decade did not lend themselves to clear solutions, especially those growing out of the imperial rivalries of the great powers. Gladstone had severely criticized Disraeli's involvements in Afghanistan and the Boer republics, and he was able to pull out of Afghanistan while maintaining appearances. The Boer republics offered a more difficult problem, for influential elements in the Liberal party were reluctant to bring British control to an end. While Gladstone temporized, the Boers of the Transvaal, led by Paul Kruger, rose in revolt and defeated a British detachment at Majuba Hill (1881). Faced with a difficult and costly war, Gladstone agreed to independence for the Transvaal but under circumstances that appeared to be a response to defeat. Gladstone also found that the rising tide of imperialism drew him into unwanted involvements in Egypt and Sudan. In 1882 disorders broke out in Egypt, and foreign involvement appeared inevitable. Since Egypt was important to the safety of the Suez Canal, Gladstone proposed joint intervention with France. When the French refused Gladstone sent a British force to restore order. Gladstone was left with a protectorate he did not want, but at that point he saw no alternative but to bring solvency and good government to Egypt through British rule. The problem was further complicated by an uprising in the Sudan led by a religious fanatic known as the Mahdi. Gladstone had no desire to become involved in the Sudan, but he did agree to send a British detachment under General Charles Gordon to evacuate the Egyptian garrisons there. Gordon, a strong-willed individualist with his own opinions of what should be done, tried to form a counterforce to check the Mahdi and found himself trapped in Khartoum. After considerable discussion and delay Gladstone sent an expedition to rescue Gordon, which arrived too late—Gordon and his men had been massacred two days earlier by the forces of the Mahdi. The entire episode was seen as a national humiliation and cast a cloud over Gladstone's second ministry.

Gladstone's major domestic problem was Ireland, where economic grievances joined with Irish nationalism to make the island ungovernable. Gladstone's policy was to reconcile Ireland to the Union by redress of economic grievances, but he found that the Irish, led by Charles Stewart

Parnell, wanted both land reform and self-government, or Home Rule. Parnell's methods were to encourage violence in Ireland and to use the Irish members of the House of Commons to disrupt the proceedings of Parliament. Gladstone offered a carrot and a stick. The stick was a Coercion Bill, which gave the authorities sweeping powers to seize and detain persons suspected of violence. The carrot was an Irish Land Act (1881), which gave the Irish peasants the three Fs: fair rent, fixed tenure, free sale. Parnell would settle for nothing less than Home Rule, and violence continued, although the murder of the new British secretary in a Dublin park shocked both the British and Irish into some restraint. The growing power of Parnell, both in Ireland and as leader of the Irish Nationalists in the House of Commons, made some resolution of the Irish problem essential.

Faced with stalemate in his domestic reforms, dissension in his cabinet, and open resistance in Ireland, Gladstone's solution to the problem of governing the British Isles was another installment of democracy. In 1884 and 1885 he pushed through Parliament a two-part electoral reform. The Reform Bill of 1884 removed the last important exception to universal manhood suffrage by enfranchising the agricultural workers. A companion measure in 1885 ended the ancient electoral system based on shires and boroughs and established single-member districts. In doing so Gladstone further alienated some supporters, and his problems were complicated by public dismay aroused by the debacle of Gordon at Khartoum. With his parliamentary support in doubt Gladstone resigned and the Conservatives, now led by Lord Salisbury, formed a caretaker government until an election could be held.

In the election of 1885 Gladstone and the Liberals lost ground but were still the largest party in the House of Commons; the Irish Nationalists, now firmly in the grip of Parnell, held the balance. As Disraeli had done for parliamentary reform in 1867, Gladstone stood quietly by, hoping that Salisbury and the Conservatives would take the plunge for Home Rule. Gladstone's cunning was unmasked when his support for Home Rule was revealed by his son. Parnell then gave his support to Gladstone, and when Salisbury resigned early in 1886 Gladstone organized a ministry committed to Home Rule. Gladstone's Home Rule Bill would have continued the supreme authority of the United Kingdom in matters of foreign policy and defense while establishing in Ireland a separate Irish executive and Parliament to deal with domestic matters. Gladstone's bill shattered the Liberal party, for an influential group of Liberals, led by Joseph Chamberlain, opposed Home Rule. In June 1886 the Home Rule Bill was defeated in the House of Commons. When Gladstone appealed to the nation by calling another election, the Liberal party suffered a stinging rebuff. Gladstone resigned, and Salisbury formed a Conservative government that, with the exception of one Liberal interlude, governed Britain until 1905. Gladstone had gambled and lost, and the Liberal party that he led was no longer the dominant force in British politics.

By 1886 the assurance and stability of the mid-Victorian period were passing. Britain had entered into the age of political democracy, and social democracy was not far behind. Prime ministers and cabinets now held office because they were able, through political parties, to win public support. The diplomatic position of Britain was also changed by the unification of Germany and Italy and the growth of imperial rivalries. The British economy faced unaccustomed competition from new industrial nations, and agriculture was depressed by foodstuffs brought from abroad by railroads and steamships. Finally, the optimism and confidence of the mid-Victorian period was slipping. An emphasis on comfort and pleasure replaced the earnest, hardworking striving of the mid-Victorians; the glories of the Victorian noontide passed into the glow of the late-Victorian afternoon.

Suggestions for Further Reading

Two important interpretive works by George Kitson Clark are *The Making of Victorian England* (1962) and *An Expanding Society: Britain, 1830–1900* (1967). Good studies of the mid-Victorian period are W. L. Burn, *The Age of Equipoise: A Study of the Mid-Victorian Generation* (1964) and Geoffrey Best, *Mid-Victorian Britain, 1851–1875* (1971). See also Asa Briggs, *Victorian People: Some Reassessments of People, Institutions, Ideas, and Events, 1851–1867* (1954) and Richard D. Altick, *Victorian People and Ideas* (1973).

For political history James B. Conacher, ed., provides introductions, documents, and modern views of the reform bills in *The Emergence of British Parliamentary Democracy in the Nineteenth Century: The Passing of the Reform Acts of 1832, 1867, and 1884–5* (1971). Conacher has done two solid studies of mid-Victorian politics, *The Peelites and the Party System, 1846–52* (1972) and *The Aberdeen Coalition, 1852–1855* (1968). These works lead into John Vincent, *The Formation of the British Liberal Party, 1857–1868* (2nd edition, 1976). The leap to democracy is studied by Maurice Cowling in *1867: Disraeli, Gladstone, and Revolution: The Passing of the Second Reform Bill* (1967).

Mid-Victorian rural England is well served by F. M. L. Thompson, *English Landed Society in the 19th Century* (1963) and Gordon Mingay, *Rural Life in Victorian England* (1978).

The development of working-class organization is traced in Henry Pelling, *A History of British Trade Unionism* (3rd edition, 1976). For working-class political movements see Trygve Tholfsen, *Working Class Radicalism in Mid-Victorian England* (1977). A good survey of changes in the lives of women is Jane Lewis, *Women in England, 1870–1950: Sexual Divisions and Social Change* (1985).

Victorian intellectual life is studied by Gertrude Himmelfarb in *Victorian Minds*

(1972). For the influence of Darwinism see William Irvine, *Apes, Angel, and Victorians* (1955) and Michael Ruse, *The Darwinian Revolution* (1979).

A selection of biographies includes Peter Stansky, *Gladstone: A Progress in Politics* (1979), Robert Blake, *Disraeli* (1966), Keith Robbins, *John Bright* (1979), F. S. L. Lyons, *Charles Stewart Parnell* (1977), Maurice Cranston, *John Stuart Mill* (1958), Joseph Hamburger, *Intellectuals in Politics: John Stuart Mill and the Philosophic Radicals* (1965), and Cecil Woodham-Smith, *Florence Nightingale, 1820–1910* (1950).

15

Democracy and Imperialism

1886–1914

*I*n 1886 an observer of the British scene would be most likely to notice the continuities with the past, especially in contrast with the continent, which had been transformed by the establishment of the Third Republic in France, the unification of Germany and Italy, the formation of the Dual Monarchy of Austria-Hungary, and the emancipation of the serfs in Russia. Across the Atlantic the United States had strengthened its central government but only after a bitter civil war. In Britain the institutions and achievements of the previous seventy years seemed undisturbed. The prestige of the monarchy was secure; cabinet government and the two-party system were well established; a democratic electorate was a source of strength to traditional institutions; British industry still led all competitors; Britain was the world center of finance and trade; the pound sterling was the acceptable medium of exchange around the globe; the sun never set on the British Empire; and Britannia ruled the waves. Yet there were many changes in the wind that, from our perspective, can be seen as anticipations of modern Britain.

Political Leaders and Parties

Lord Salisbury and the Conservative Party. If Queen Victoria was the symbolic grandmother of the age, Lord Salisbury was its father figure. Salisbury was a strong and thoughtful aristocrat whose goal was to maintain stability and to resolve the tensions generated by the previous twenty years of political conflict and institutional change. With the exception of a three-year period of Liberal rule (1892–1895), Salisbury served as prime minister from 1886 to 1902. He concentrated his attention on foreign and imperial affairs. On domestic matters he relied heavily on his nephew, Arthur Balfour, a cool, polished intellectual who had abandoned philosophy for a career in politics. Under Salisbury the Conservative party took on a new character, preserving its base in the aristocracy and landed gentry but adding an increasing number of wealthy business and professional men. The Conservative party became the champion of the rights of property holders, whether by commercial, industrial, or landed interests. It claimed to be the patriotic party, which defended British interests in foreign and imperial affairs with unique vigor. It also attracted an important minority of the working-class vote, especially in Lancashire, where English workingmen disliked Liberal industrialists and Irish laborers, and in London, where moralistic Liberal reforms such as restricting the sale of drink irritated the working population. Salisbury also had the support of the Liberal Unionists, who had followed Joseph Chamberlain in the break from Gladstone over Home Rule. While supporting Salisbury's foreign and imperial policies, the Liberal Unionists gave the government a thrust toward social legislation, which was lacking in Salisbury's more conservative followers.

The dominance of the Conservative party under Salisbury was, to some extent, a result of the Liberal split in 1886, but it was also in accord with the mood of the country. Salisbury's concern for foreign affairs and the Empire was shared by much of the public. The Conservatives were widely supported in their determination to preserve the union of Britain and Ireland. Conservative policy toward Ireland was embodied in the Ashbourne Act (1885), which sought to reduce Irish discontent by assisting tenants to purchase their land ("killing Home Rule with kindness"); this policy had some effect. The Salisbury ministry continued Disraeli's policy of concern for social problems in an effort to win working-class support. Legislation passed under Salisbury did not break new ground but included another factory act (1891), the abolition of fees for elementary education (1891), workmen's compensation (1897), and legislation in 1902 that reorganized the school system and provided for the further development of secondary education. Encouraged by Chamberlain's Liberal Unionists, the Salisbury ministry sponsored the Local Government Act of 1888, which established elected councils for county government and a similar form of government for sixty-one urban centers (county boroughs) and the London metropolitan area (the London County Council).

The Liberal Party. In the meantime the Liberal party, split by Gladstone's commitment to Home Rule and consigned to opposition, also began to develop a new character. Normally a major political party in such circumstances would seek new leadership, but such a development was forestalled by the amazing intellectual and physical vitality of Gladstone and by the loss of Chamberlain. The departure of the Liberal Unionists gave an opportunity to Liberals who advocated a new thrust. The established Liberal goals—political democracy, institutional reform, civil liberties—had been largely achieved. The new Liberals were concerned with economic and social problems that could not be regarded as solely matters of individual responsibility. They looked to government to intervene in the life of the nation by providing "the ladder and the net"—opportunity for individual advancement with minimal standards guaranteed for everyone. Liberalism kept its Nonconformist and libertarian flavor and maintained a strong sense of moral crusade against privilege, wasteful public expenditure, and abuse of power.

In 1891 Gladstone accepted the need to appease the Radicals, the Nonconformists, and the Celtic fringe of Wales and Scotland. He adopted as party policy the Newcastle Program, which had originated as resolutions passed by the National Liberal Federation, an organization of constituency activists. The Newcastle Program included the promise of disestablishment of the churches in Wales and Scotland, municipal control over water and other services for London, land reform, free elementary education, and a popular referendum to allow localities to prohibit the sale of alcoholic drink. Irish Home Rule continued to head the Liberal party program.

In 1892 Gladstone and the Liberals, supported by the Irish Nationalists, returned to power. In his last ministry Gladstone attempted to achieve some of the social goals of the Liberal party, but Parliament, and probably the majority of the nation, was unreceptive. Ireland was again Gladstone's major concern, and Ireland again proved to be his downfall. In 1893 Gladstone succeeded in getting a Home Rule Bill through the House of Commons, only to have it defeated in the House of Lords. Shortly thereafter he suffered a severe stroke and resigned, to be succeeded by Lord Rosebery, a genial peer who was spokesman for the moderate wing of the Liberal party. In 1895 Rosebery resigned, and an election returned power to Salisbury and the Conservatives, supported by Chamberlain and the Liberal Unionists. But Gladstone's last ministry had contributed to the new direction taken by the Liberal party. Throughout his long political career Gladstone had given to British politics intellectual power, moral fervor, and a rare ability to recognize and respond to new needs. It was these qualities that helped to mold a new Liberal party, which won a sweeping national mandate in 1906.

The Condition of the People

Agriculture and the Landed Interest. Late Victorian Britain was a wealthy land, enjoying the fruits of Britain's industrial leadership. Yet contempo-

Bluegate Fields by Gustave Doré *(BBC Hulton Picture Library)*.

raries worried about what they called the "Great Depression," which historians normally date as extending from 1873 to 1896. This "Great Depression" was not a dramatic economic collapse, like that which began with the stock market crash of 1929 and extended until World War II. Rather, it was a general decline of prices, profits, investment, and interest rates, with effects that varied from one industry to another. Agriculture was hardest hit, for a dramatic fall in farm prices resulted from opening up new agricultural areas in the American Middle West, the prairie provinces of Canada, the pampas of Argentina, and the interior of Australia. Development of the railroad, steamship, and refrigeration made it possible to bring these products to market in the industrial centers. Britain's free trade ("cheap food") policy meant that British agriculture was totally unprotected. To some extent British agriculture was able to adjust by turning away from wheat and wool and by producing fresh dairy products, meat, fruits, and vegetables for urban markets, but such changes required additional changes in agricultural skills, farm equipment, land use, and landlord-tenant relations.

Despite the decline of agricultural rents, laments for the landed aristocracy and gentry would be premature. By the late Victorian period much of the wealth of the aristocracy had been invested in gilt-edged securities or well-established industries, and with the fall of prices the purchasing power of fixed-income investments was increasing. The growth of population and towns meant that the value of urban properties or land suitable for urban development increased. By the time-honored process of upward social mobility, successful businessmen and professional men, or their heirs, were drawn into the upper class, bringing with them their investments. Lord Randolph Churchill, for example, younger son of the duke of Marlborough, found that marriage to an American heiress could freshen the family coffers. Declining wages and living costs made it possible for the upper class to continue to maintain large numbers of domestic servants. On the periphery of this upper class lived a great many younger sons, maiden aunts, dowered widows, and other dependents with similar social status, although modest incomes. These were the comfortable people, parodied by Oscar Wilde and gleefully dissected by George Bernard Shaw.

Industry. British industry was not affected to the same degree as agriculture, but clearly it was not keeping pace with industrial growth in rising industrial nations such as Germany and the United States. In 1900, for example, both the United States and Germany passed Britain in the production of steel. Other industries where Britain had formerly held unchallenged supremacy, such as textiles, shipbuilding, coal, and engineering, were also meeting stiff competition. British investors, finding profits in domestic industries declining, were attracted to investments overseas, which promised higher returns. Although Britain developed new industries producing consumer goods, the basic industries upon which her industrial leadership had been based were losing ground to newer and more progressive producers elsewhere.

Why this decline in industrial competitiveness? Many reasons can be cited: Britain's factories and machines were old and British industry did not keep pace with technological developments; the growing power of trade unions inhibited change; the export of capital drained Britain of resources needed to remain competitive; Britain's free trade policy injured the economy when her major competitors were protecting their home markets with protective tariffs. In 1896 Ernest E. Williams published a book, *Made in Germany*, that was widely read. Williams argued that the German economy was gaining on the British because the Germans had a domestic market protected by tariffs, because they were aggressive in selling their products abroad, and because they had excellent technical education. In 1902 a similar book by Fred McKenzie, *The American Invaders: Their Plans, Tactics, and Progress* urged British businessmen to develop new products and methods of manufacture and to sell their products aggressively. The message seemed clear: British businessmen were complacent and unprogressive and were already paying for it in lost profits and reduced domestic investment.

The Middle Class. The deflationary trend that was the dominant feature of the "Great Depression" was generally advantageous to the middle class, whose numbers and influence increased notably. The growth of the government bureaucracy, of large-scale business firms, and of retailing, publishing, and service occupations resulted in an increase of salaried persons, while declining prices made it possible to maintain a middle-class life with modest investments. Although the term middle class is difficult to define, Englishmen in the late Victorian period had a reasonably clear idea of what it meant. To some extent the term middle class referred to income: below a certain income it would be difficult to maintain a middle-class lifestyle; above a certain income the life of the gentleman beckoned, with its powerful attraction to the Englishman. The middle class can also be defined in terms of work: the middle class man applied himself to a business or profession and he ordinarily wore a suit and white shirt to his place of employment. But the Victorian middle class was best identified by lifestyle: the husband went regularly to work; the wife stayed home to manage the house; there was some domestic help; the parents gave careful attention to the nurture, education, discipline, and manners of the children; emphasis was given to family activities such as churchgoing, visits to relatives, parlor games, and seaside holidays. Although the middle class advocated economy in government, they were civic-minded and willing to support local improvements, such as town halls, libraries, museums, and hospitals. They were quickly aroused by social issues, such as education, poor relief, and the evils of drink and prostitution.

Questioning of Values. The opulence of the aristocracy and the comfort of the middle class were accompanied by nagging anxieties about matters formerly considered to be certain. Most fundamental of these was the conflict between science and religion. Already weakened by the ideas of Darwin and Huxley, the authority of traditional Christianity was further eroded by Biblical criticism, which undermined faith in the divine inspiration of the Bible. The elegant and poetic *Life of Jesus* by the French theologian Ernst Renan was translated into English in 1888 and became a great success. Renan depicted Jesus, not as the Son of God, but as a man—generous, sensitive, dedicated, at one with nature and all mankind. The naturalistic view of religion was strengthened by James Frazer's *The Golden Bough* (1890ff.), an anthropological study of primitive religion, which showed the extent to which Christianity shared motifs common to early paganism. Perhaps the most telling demonstration of the waning influence of Christianity was the decline of church attendance and the increasing use of Sundays for recreation.

As religion waned it was replaced by a new value system, which looked to society, instead of God, to fulfill the lives of men. In an age of growing secularism the Victorian conscience remained, stung by the disparity between the lives of the comfortable classes and the poverty of a large portion of the population. John Ruskin, an art historian turned social commentator, strenuously denied that most of the population should be condemned to privation in the interests of economic growth. He appealed to the sense of community and fair play so deeply ingrained in the British public. George Gissing, a journalist, gave middle-class readers an insider's view of London life in a series of realistic novels, the best known of which is *Grub Street* (1891). Somewhat later a detailed picture of life in the pottery manufacturing district was presented in the novels of Arnold Bennett. In the theater Oscar Wilde made a name for himself by spoofing conventional Victorian attitudes in *The Importance of Being Earnest*. Another Irishman, George Bernard Shaw, used the stage to criticize Victorian social values in plays such as *Arms and the Man* (the romantic view of war), *Mrs. Warren's Profession* (prostitution and the economic system that encouraged it), and *Major Barbara* (capitalism and war). William Morris—poet, artist, craftsman, radical politician—called his countrymen back to the virtues, skills, and human satisfactions of the preindustrial age. Morris detested the ugliness of machine-manufactured products and gave particular attention to "the lesser arts" such as pottery, weaving, furniture, and

London flowergirl (*BBC Hulton Picture Library*).

wallpaper, which formed taste and gave either beauty or vulgarity to everyday life. In short, the characteristic Victorian beliefs in progress, competitive capitalism, economic growth, and laissez-faire were being challenged by some of the most thoughtful and persuasive writers of the time.

The Status of Women. Another aspect of the questioning of traditional values was the changing status of middle-class women. The Victorians idealized women as creatures of great delicacy and tender feelings who must not be exposed to the rough-and-tumble of everyday life. At the same time women were expected to assume a wide range of responsibilities in the home and bear up under a host of personal and physical privations. The middle-class woman did not work outside the home and was expected to devote herself to the role of wife, mother, and manager of the household. At best, the Victorian middle-class woman was a powerful influence in shaping the values of the nation, and in the age before modern household appliances she performed or directed an enormous amount of useful and necessary work. At worst, these women lived empty, dependent lives as elegant decorations, symbolic of the material success of the head of the household, and filled their time with visits, light reading, shopping, and feeling "under the weather." Women's fashions contributed to limiting the lives of these women, for the clothing was impractical and extravagant and was characterized by numerous petticoats, huge bustles, and trailing skirts. A still more disabling fashion was tightly laced corsets, which reduced many women to suffocation in pursuit of a twenty-inch waist. There was great reticence to discuss frankly the body and its functions, and sexuality was not supposed to cross a woman's mind, although society accepted it as a preoccupation of men. Nevertheless the size of middle-class families declined as knowledge of birth control spread, thus freeing women from the servitude and dangers of frequent pregnancies and childbearing.

Despite traditional notions, increasing numbers of middle-class women found it possible to free themselves from the trammels of conventional views. To attain independence women needed jobs with decent pay in comfortable surroundings, which could not be obtained without education and a change in the attitude of employers. Improvements in secondary education and the establishment of women's colleges opened up new opportunities for women. Teaching and nursing were the most common careers; in 1891 there were more than 53,000 women nurses and over 146,000 women teachers. Well-raised middle-class young women obtained employment in offices as secretaries and "typewriters" (stenographers). The telegraph and telephone provided many jobs for women, since before direct dialing it was necessary to call a central office to be manually connected through a switchboard. By the end of the century 40 percent of those employed in the telegraph and telephone services were women.

Women of the upper and lower classes also began to seek political and legal rights. In this respect, as in so many others, John Stuart Mill was in the vanguard of his time. In *The Subjection of Women* (1869) Mill argued that "the legal subordination of one sex to the other—is wrong in itself, and now one of the chief hindrances to human improvement; and that it ought to be replaced by a principle of perfect equality." He emphasized especially the almost total authority of the husband over his wife, with the potential for abuse that this entailed. Despite ridicule and angry denunciation, progress was made. In 1891, in the Jackson decision, the courts ruled that a husband could not coercively confine his wife to his home. In 1883 Parliament gave wives the right to sell or dispose of their property as they wished, and in 1893 a wife's property or contracts became her own legal responsibility. In 1894 women became eligible to hold office and to vote in local government, and in 1897 a women's suffrage bill for parliamentary elections made some progress. In the same year a number of women's suffrage organizations joined in the National Union of Women's Suffrage Societies. The very conventional woman who reigned over the kingdom, Queen Victoria, vehemently opposed the notion of equal rights for women with no sense of the paradox of her position.

Working-class housing, Newcastle-upon-Tyne *(E. A. Reitan).*

The Working Class. One of the puzzles of the "Great Depression" is its effect on the British working class. In general, it appears that the industrial worker with steady employment was better off: his wages did not fall as much as prices, and thus his purchasing power was increased. Factory acts improved the conditions and safety of industrial employment. The working week was still long, but a half day on Saturday and Sunday off were almost universal. Better housing was available; municipal governments energetically improved civic services such as streets, water, sewers, parks, and libraries; elementary education was provided and in some towns additional technical education for adults was provided. These advances were seen in the extent to which the "respectable" working class adopted middle-class values, for men in the upper levels of the working class, such as shop foremen or skilled machinists, were able to support their wives at home, enjoy a neat house and hot meals, relax with friends and neighbors in the evenings or on Sundays, attend church or chapel, and read a daily newspaper. For such members of the working class the most dreaded hazard of all was the poorhouse, usually as a result of old age, sickness, disability, or unemployment, for they had little to live on except their weekly wage.

For those workers, which included most women then in the labor force, who were unskilled or whose employment was insecure, poverty of the most extreme kind was the normal existence. The sweated workers—those who were paid piece wages—lacked even those modest supports that factory workers had gained from the factory acts or their trade unions. Then there was the great mass of wretched people, especially in large cities, who had no steady means of support and lived a hand-to-mouth existence based primarily upon crime, vice, begging, or casual labor. In 1890 William Booth, founder of the Salvation Army, published a book with wide impact, *In Darkest England and the Way Out*, which told of the lives of these people. The next year Charles Booth (no relation to William Booth) published the first of seventeen volumes entitled *The Life and Labour of the People of London*, supporting with copious detail his conclusion that approximately one-third of the population of London lived in degrading poverty, insecurity, and ugliness. In York, Seebohm Rowntree, member of a wealthy family of chocolate manufacturers, found similar conditions. The Victorian conscience was shocked and was no longer willing to accept the premise of earlier generations that such conditions were an inevitable concomitant of an advanced economy.

Working Class Movements. One important factor in changing the conditions of working-class life was the growth of trade unions. The organization of skilled workers had proceeded steadily in the 1850s and 1860s, and in 1872 trade union membership numbered about 400,000 workers. In the 1880s the focus of unionism turned to the "operatives"—workers with some skill, such as railway workers and miners, but who were not trained through the apprenticeship system, as in the craft unions. By the end of the decade "the new unionism" was organizing unskilled workers, including those with irregular or piecework employment. The plight of unskilled workers was dramatized by a series of spectacular strikes: the women match workers of London (1888), the London gasworkers (1888), and the London dock strike of 1889. Earlier a group of craft unions had formed the Trades Union Congress to bring about cooperation between unions both in political activities and in collective bargaining. By 1900 the trade union movement had grown to almost 2,000,000 members. Women workers remained largely unorganized, as did most pieceworkers. Hostility to trade unions was strong among employers, who attributed some of their competitive problems to union demands and restrictions. The middle class in general disapproved of the conflict that erupted sporadically during organizing efforts and strikes. In 1901 there was widespread satisfaction when the courts, in a celebrated decision, held the unions responsible for damages resulting from a strike at the Taff Vale railway in Wales. Nevertheless, when Queen Victoria died trade unions had become an important part of British life.

The working class was also able to make its influence felt through political action. Political democracy meant that the two major parties had to compete for the working-class vote, and both parties supported the process by which government accepted increasing responsibility for public health, safety, and poor relief. In the 1880s the ideas of Karl Marx began to have some influence in Britain, and in 1884 H. M. Hyndman organized the Social Democratic Federation, a Marxist political party appealing to the workers. The Fabian Society, founded in 1884, was a small body of middle-class intellectuals dedicated to democratic socialism. Leaders of the group were Sidney Webb, Beatrice Potter (later Mrs. Webb), and the playwright, George Bernard Shaw. Their goal was to replace private ownership of major industries with public ownership. They advocated the use of democratic processes to achieve their purpose and relied on books and pamphlets to spread their ideas. Keir Hardie, a Scottish coal miner, was a leader in founding the Independent Labour party, which in the 1890s succeeded in electing a handful of members of Parliament on a vaguely socialistic platform. In 1900 a Labour Representation Committee met to consider forming a political organization for the election of labor candidates to Parliament. This group soon turned to association with the Liberal party as the most practical means of exerting political influence. Through trade unions and political action the British working class began to make its presence felt. But British workers were not revolutionary; they preferred to work through existing institutions.

Foreign Policy and the Empire

The Foreign Policy of Salisbury. While gradual changes were taking place in Victorian society, a disturbing change had taken place in Britain's external relationships. Salisbury was already an experienced diplomat when he became prime minister. During his ministries foreign and imperial affairs remained his major concern. He was uneasy as he observed the rise of international tensions, militarism, and alliances. The unification of Germany in 1871 had created in central Europe a powerful new state with a strong military tradition. The German chancellor, Bismarck, was primarily concerned with consolidating his gains, but in doing so he faced the enmity of France, smarting from her defeat in the Franco-Prussian War of 1870 to 1871. In 1881 Bismarck attempted to stabilize relationships in eastern Europe and to check the intrigues of France by forming an alliance among Germany, Austria, and Russia, but this goal was frustrated by the rivalry between Austria and Russia for influence in the Balkans. Forced to choose between the two, Germany strengthened her ties with Austria. France and Russia responded by making an alliance in 1894 that aroused

German fears of "encirclement." Thus the major powers of Europe were divided into two camps, each heavily armed and each suspicious of the other.

Salisbury wanted to avoid involvement in continental conflicts, but he did not wish to be without friends in such a menacing situation. His major efforts in Europe consisted of a series of overtures to Germany, which he hoped would reduce German anxieties and permit a relaxation of European tensions, but these overtures were unsuccessful. Salisbury worked to eliminate causes of friction with the United States, which was becoming recognized as a potential great power. Steps were also taken to reduce imperial rivalry with France. In 1902 the Salisbury government stunned public opinion by making an alliance with Japan, the rising power in East Asia. Directed against Russia, the Anglo-Japanese alliance was a clear recognition that, in that part of the world, Britain could no longer maintain her interests alone. When Salisbury retired in 1902 the Conservative government, now led by Arthur Balfour, abandoned hope of good relations with Germany, turning instead to France. The result was an entente with France in 1904 that consisted of an agreement to maintain friendly relations and to avoid imperial conflicts. Although the entente was not an alliance and was not specifically directed against Germany or any other power, it led to Anglo-French military conversations dealing with cooperation if war should break out in Europe. The age of "splendid isolation" was drawing to its close.

Imperial Rivalries. Britain also faced new challenges in the imperial world, as the major powers sought to improve their diplomatic leverage, military potential, and economic competitiveness by acquiring colonies overseas. France tried to balance the power of Germany by developing new sources of manpower and wealth in North Africa, West Africa, and Southeast Asia. Germany began building a navy and picking up whatever bits of colonial territory were still available. As a result of the Spanish-American War the United States acquired the Philippines and Puerto Rico. In 1895 Japan entered upon a career of imperialism by defeating the moribund Chinese empire and acquiring Formosa (Taiwan). Suddenly Britain's imperial supremacy, unchallenged since the Congress of Vienna, was seriously threatened. Britain's industrial economy was predicated upon easy access to overseas food, raw materials, and markets. In an age of protective tariffs, each new acquisition by an industrial competitor cut off British access to an existing or potential area for trade. Another major factor in imperial expansion was the search for secure places for long-term investment, since the return on capital at home was declining. Capitalists were unwilling to invest money in long-term projects unless they were assured of political stability and a sympathetic government. The ambitions of politicians, sol-

Africa in the Age of Imperialism

diers, and leaders of the existing empire contributed to the pressures for expansion. Newspaper editors, now appealing to a mass market, needed stories and crises to generate sales, while the books and lectures of travellers and the determination of churches and missionaries to Christianize and civilize the heathen added to imperialist fervor. "God, Gold, and Glory" led the industrial nations of Europe into imperial rivalries with costs that were far out of proportion to the substantial benefits (if any) to be derived from colonies.

In the 1880s imperialism was at its height. After occupying Egypt in 1882 Britain consolidated her control of the Egyptian government and economy. In 1898 Britain occupied the Sudan, which was regarded as vital to the security of Egypt. At the battle of Omdurman a British force defeated the poorly armed forces of the Mahdi with modern rifles and artillery, concluding the battle with a dashing cavalry charge in which young Winston Churchill participated. In East Africa the British navy had a base at the island of Zanzibar that was used for patrolling the Indian Ocean, but Britain had not shown interest in establishing colonies on the mainland. In 1885, however, the Germans claimed the East African territory of Tanganyika (now part of Tanzania). Salisbury reacted by asserting British control of Kenya. In 1888 the British East Africa Company was chartered to begin the development of Kenya, and in 1890 internal disorder in Uganda led the Company to establish its authority there. A year later conflicts with Arab slave traders persuaded the British to occupy Nyasaland (now Malawi). Diplomatically, Salisbury's main concern was to establish good relations with Germany, and in 1890 another Anglo-German agreement further defined their respective territories in East Africa.

In West Africa France was the principal imperial rival. The British had maintained trading stations in West Africa since the later eighteenth century, but the abolition of the slave trade had made these stations of little value and at times proposals were made to abandon them. By the 1880s, however, West African territories had become valuable for palm oil and rubber, and intense economic competition began between the British and French for position in the region. In 1886 the Salisbury ministry gave a charter to the Royal Niger Company to develop trade in the area of the Niger River. The Company extended its influence vigorously until 1900, when the British government took control of Nigeria. By that time the French were seeking British support against Germany in Europe and were eager to settle disputes with Britain concerning West African possessions. A momentary crisis arose in the Sudan at Fashoda, where the British force sent to deal with the Mahdi encountered a small French detachment that had travelled from French West Africa to stake a claim. For a time it appeared that an Anglo-French clash would take place, but the French, much more concerned with Germany than the Sudan, gave way. The Fashoda incident led to resolution of other imperial conflicts between Britain and France and contributed to the improved relations that resulted in the Anglo-French entente of 1904.

Southern Africa. Southern Africa produced the most difficult problems for British imperial policy. In the Cape Colony tensions existed between the two principal white populations, the British and the Boers. The situation was further complicated by a large black population, which provided labor for the farms, mines, and factories. The colony of Natal, to the east of the Cape Colony, was dominated by British planters using African or East Indian laborers. The most pressing problems of the area grew out of the relationships between the two British colonies and the Boer republics (see page 339). The Orange Free State and the Transvaal maintained a frontier existence with loose central authority. Relations had been aggravated by Disraeli's annexation of the Boer republics in 1877 and Gladstone's withdrawal from the Transvaal in 1881.

The man who attempted to resolve this tense situation was Cecil Rhodes, who rose to dominance of the diamond mines in the interior and also rose to political control of the Cape Colony. Rhodes was an imperialist who dreamed of a broad band of British territory linking southern Africa with the British possessions in East Africa, the Sudan, and Egypt. He was also a skilled propagandist, who could play effectively upon imperialist sentiments in Britain. In 1888 he received a concession from Lobengula, king of the Matabele, to settle the territory to the north of the Boer republics, which became Rhodesia. In 1889 the Salisbury government chartered the British South Africa Company to develop the area. In 1893 Lobengula led a revolt of the Matabele which was crushed, and thereafter the settlement of Rhodesia proceeded rapidly.

As a result of Rhodes's expansive policies, the Boer republics were trapped between the Cape Colony and Rhodesia. The Boers were led by the tough president of the Transvaal, Paul Kruger, who saw the Boer way of life jeopardized by the influx of outsiders (Uitlanders) who came into the Transvaal to develop the gold mines. Kruger resisted the claims of the Uitlanders for political rights, and in 1895 the Uitlanders, supported by Rhodes, plotted to overthrow Kruger. The plot was revealed prematurely when Rhodes's agent in Rhodesia, Dr. Jameson, led a party of men into the Transvaal before the Uitlanders were ready to rise. As a result of the Jameson Raid, as it was called, Rhodes was driven from office in the Cape Colony and Kruger began preparing for war, hoping to obtain German aid.

The fall of Rhodes and the prospect of German involvement in the Transvaal changed the views of the Salisbury government. The colonial secretary was Joseph Chamberlain, leader of the Liberal Unionists. Chamberlain was a strong imperialist, but he had mistrusted Rhodes and his highly personal form of imperial expansion. As the grievances of the Uitlanders mounted, the Salisbury government decided that it was necessary to overthrow Kruger to prevent extension of German influence into the region. Kruger in turn decided that the time to drive out the British was now or never. The Boer War began in 1899 and consisted of three phases: Boer invasions of Natal and the Cape Colony, which were repulsed; British invasion of the Orange Free State and the Transvaal, which led to the destruction of the Boer army; and a period of guerrilla warfare as British troops hunted down Boer commandos. By the time the war ended in 1902 Rhodes was dead and Kruger died shortly after.

In Britain the Boer War created a heated political controversy, especially within the Liberal party, as patriots and imperialists supported the war while opponents depicted it as the action of a swaggering bully. The war that had been entered into so lightly produced long lists of dead and wounded, and the efforts of a professional army to put down desperate guerrillas led inevitably to atrocities. As reports reached the newspapers of British concentration camps in which large numbers of women and children had died, public opinion in Britain turned against the war. Although Britain won the war in southern Africa the opponents won the war of words at home. The Boer War discredited the imperialistic policies of the previous twenty years as well as the Conservative government that had been principally responsible. Five years earlier Rudyard Kipling, the British writer who best understood the nature and problems of Britain's far-flung empire, warned in his *Recessional* (1897) of the retribution that came to peoples whose pride was swollen by the transitory experience of dominion over others. "Far-called, our navies melt away," he wrote, thinking of the future. "On dune and headland sinks the fire: Lo, all our pomp of yesterday/Is one with Nineveh and Tyre." He concluded with a prayer:

> Lord God of Hosts, be with us yet,
> Lest we forget—lest we forget!

Chamberlain and Imperial Federation. During his years as colonial secretary Joseph Chamberlain's major concern was to draw the self-governing parts of the empire together in an imperial federation. Threatened by the rise of international tensions and the declining competitiveness of the British economy, Chamberlain tried to redress the balance by taking steps toward greater imperial unity. The Golden Jubilee of Queen Victoria in 1887 and the Diamond Jubilee ten years later were used by Chamberlain to bring the political leaders of the self-governing colonies to London to discuss closer relationships. Chamberlain's proposals fell upon unsympathetic ears. Having gained the right to manage their own affairs, the colonial leaders were unwilling to commit themselves to closer ties. One result of Chamberlain's search for imperial unity was the federation of the Australian colonies into the modern nation of Australia in 1901. Chamberlain also worked to improve the productivity of the dependent colonies in Africa and the British West Indies through encouragement of investment, development of new crops, and the conquest of tropical diseases. In 1903 Chamberlain, still seeking the elusive goal of imperial unity, took a bold step. He defied accepted free trade doctrines and the political attractions of "cheap food" by proposing a protective tariff with preferential rates for the colonies. Having done so, Chamberlain discovered that the colonies were unenthusiastic and that he had unleashed a disastrous political crisis at home.

The Edwardian Age

A New Century Dawns. When Queen Victoria died in 1901 there was a strong sense that one age had passed and another was beginning. The revered queen was succeeded by her handsome and pleasure-loving son who became King Edward VII (1901–1910). Under Edward VII the British monarchy reached the peak of splendor and magnificence, and the king set the tone for an upper-class way of life that turned away from Victorian earnestness to emphasize pleasure and show. The gay social season in London in the winter was varied by long stays at elegant country estates in the summer, trips to continental resorts or the Riviera, sometimes protracted residence in milder climates such as Italy and the south of France, and always the long English weekend, devoted to visits, shooting, picnics, parties, horse races, long walks and talks, reading novels, and other generally pleasant leisure activities. For those fortunate enough to be born, married, or accepted into that social milieu it was a pleasant life indeed, soon to be gravely wounded by World War I.

Edwardian Britain boasted a broad middle class, some of whom had secure incomes and lived in solid comfort while many others, striving to maintain a middle-class standard of living, found life a constant and often unrewarding struggle for respectability. The condition of the working class may have improved marginally, but the aspirations of ordinary working people had risen considerably. They were no longer willing to accept the privations of industrial society. The spread of literacy and the proliferation of inexpensive books and newspapers brought questions of national policy to the attention of a broad public, and the achievement of democracy meant that these questions became a crucial part of the political process.

A new century was heralded by a galaxy of brilliant writers. H. G. Wells, a product of an impoverished background, gained prominence as a writer of science fiction through *The Time Machine* and *The War of the Worlds.* Wells was fascinated by technology, which he saw as the principal means of human improvement. A political and social radical, he advocated socialism, world government, emancipation of women, and free love. His enormously popular *An Outline of History* (1920) presented historical evolution as the story of progress. George Bernard Shaw, who was born and raised in Dublin, early sought a literary career in London. He failed as a novelist, succeeded as a music critic, but found his place as a playwright, using his plays to attack conventional Victorian views. John Galsworthy, educated at Oxford and admitted to the bar, wrote plays dealing with social problems, but he is best known for *The Forsyte Saga,* a series of novels chronicling the lives of an upper middle class family. In philosophy and science new ideas shattered established views, from Albert Einstein's new concept of the nature of matter to the explorations of Sigmund Freud, the Viennese psychiatrist, into the depths of human personality. The automobile, airplane, and radio appeared, introducing the revolution in communications that has been such a notable feature of the twentieth century. It was clear to perceptive observers that the new century would be much different from the old.

The Liberal Revival. A year after the accession of Edward VII Lord Salisbury, the last of the great Victorians, retired due to ill health. Leadership of the Conservative government passed to lesser lights: Salisbury's cool, intellectual nephew, Arthur Balfour, who had acted almost as deputy premier in Salisbury's later years and the willful, impulsive Joseph Chamberlain, leader of the Liberal Unionists. Sir Henry Campbell-Bannerman, whose forthright opposition to the Boer War had appealed to many Liberals, was recognized as the spokesman for those elements in the Liberal party who were committed to progressive ideas. In 1903 the Liberals and the Labour Representation Committee agreed to support each other's candidates against the Conservatives in the next election. A new yeastiness was entering into the body politic.

The Conservatives contributed significantly to their own downfall. In 1902 they passed an Education Act that reorganized the schools by placing them under the control of the counties and county boroughs. The act also gave these authorities responsibility for secondary and technical education. In many respects the act was a rational and forward-looking step, but it offended the local school boards previously responsible for schools and it infuriated Nonconformists by giving financial support to voluntary (private) schools, which were mainly Anglican. Another Conservative measure, the Licensing Act of 1904, further inflamed the Nonconformists. The bill reduced the number of pubs, an outcome with which most Nonconformists heartily agreed, but it did so by protecting the remaining pubs from local licensing authorities and by compensating publicans whose licenses were revoked. This was seen by temperance activists as a compact with Demon Rum. The vital blow to the Conservatives, however, was dealt by Joseph Chamberlain when he announced in 1903 his conversion to a protective tariff with imperial preference. Chamberlain's proposal attacked the twin foundations of Victorian economic policy—free trade and cheap food. Many Conservatives broke with their leaders on the issue, including a promising young member of Parliament, Winston Churchill. In 1905 Balfour resigned. The Liberals took office and prepared to carry their case to the people in an election. The long Conservative dominance had ended.

The Liberal government that took office in 1905 was exceptionally tal-

David Lloyd George and Winston Churchill *(BBC Hulton Picture Library)*.

ented. As prime minister, Campbell-Bannerman displayed unexpected qualities of idealism and practical political sense and was capable of recruiting and leading a cabinet of remarkable individuals. When ill health forced Campbell-Bannerman to retire in 1908 he was succeeded as prime minister by Herbert Asquith, previously chancellor of the exchequer. Asquith brought to the office keen intelligence, a head for figures, and a Nonconformist background diluted by an Oxford education and a wealthy marriage. In some respects the most striking member of the ministry was the fiery young Welshman, David Lloyd George, whose intense personal ambition was fuelled by sympathy for the poor and antagonism toward aristocracy and privilege. Early in 1906 the Liberals called an election, which was one of the most decisive of modern times. In the new Parliament the Liberals held 377 seats, the Conservatives, 157, the Irish Nationalists, 83, and Labour members, 53, some elected as Liberals and others under the auspices of the Labour Representation Committee. Although the issues were confused and the positions of the major parties were far from clear, the election revealed an important shift in the mood of the electorate.

The Liberals and Social Legislation. The Liberals took office determined to come to grips with the main problems of industrial society while maintaining, as much as possible, their historic principles of low public expenditure and reliance on individual responsibility. Trade unions were seen as the best way for industrial workers to promote their own well being. The Trade Disputes Act (1906), passed to overturn the Taff Vale decision, gave trade unions freedom to engage in strikes and other forms of industrial action without fear of suits for damages. The Miners Eight-Hour Day Act was justified as regulation of an abuse that could not be left to collective bargaining. While employed workers could normally be expected to look after themselves, old age and sickness were hazards for which the worker could not be held personally responsible. The Old Age Pension Act (1908) was one of the few pieces of Liberal legislation that drew upon the Treasury, for it provided modest assistance to the elderly in the form of five shillings per week for persons over seventy, a sum not so large as to reduce the inducement to save but large enough to help those who had some personal or family resources to draw upon.

In dealing with loss of income due to sickness, disability, or unemployment, the Liberals faced problems that had been traditionally thought of as matters of personal responsibility. Liberal policy on these matters was much influenced by a young journalist named William Beveridge, who wrote *Unemployment: A Problem of Industry* (1909). Beveridge pointed out that much unemployment was the result of economic forces for which the individual could not be held responsible, including cyclical fluctuations and technological change. Since this kind of unemployment was the result of industrial factors, Beveridge argued that the cost of coping with it should be borne by industry. This principle was adopted in the National Insurance Act (1911), which established a system of insurance to pay benefits to workers who were victims of sickness, disability, or unemployment. Workers and employers contributed to a fund from which benefits would be paid, and thus the cost did not fall on the Treasury. Provision for workers in occupations not covered by the act and for those suffering from long-term unemployment was still the responsibility of the poor relief system.

Liberal doctrines of economic individualism had always recognized the special claims of those who could not be considered free agents, such as women and children. As the Liberal ministers proceeded in their investigations of industrial problems they became aware of two kinds of workers who needed special assistance—casual laborers and workers in "sweatshop" industries, who were paid by the piece. These workers were protected neither by the factory acts nor by trade unions. Their position in a competitive job market was weak, and they could scarcely be expected to bargain for themselves. Winston Churchill, who joined the Cabinet as president of the Board of Trade in 1908, played an important part in dealing with these problems. Advised by Beveridge, Churchill obtained legislation establishing a system of labor exchanges, which served a useful purpose in helping casual workers find employment. Churchill also responded to the needs of "sweated" workers by proposing the Trade Boards Act (1909), which was vigorously supported by the women's labor movement. Under the act boards were established to set minimum wages in piecework industries such as the making of clothing. Another example of the readiness of the Liberal government to give assistance to those who needed it, as long as the government was not expected to pay, was the Provision of Meals Act, which permitted local school authorities to provide one meal a day for school children. Thus the Liberal government preserved the principles of public economy and individual responsibility where possible while responding to those aspects of life in an industrial society where that premise could clearly be seen to be inoperative.

The Liberals and the Lords. As the Liberal government proceeded on its course, a major point of constitutional conflict emerged—the power of the House of Lords, in which the Conservatives were strongly entrenched. The Conservatives, who had a long tradition of concern for social problems, were not strongly opposed to Liberal measures to deal with the pressing evils of industrial society, but the Conservative majority in the House of Lords rejected Liberal measures dealing with voting, schools, licensing of pubs, and other schemes dear to the hearts of certain Liberal constituencies. It was clear that other Liberal goals that were even more controversial, such as Home Rule for Ireland or disestablishment of the Anglican Church in Wales, would encounter a fight to the death in the Lords. But the battle was fought on the question of the budget. In 1909 Lloyd George, who had succeeded Asquith as chancellor of the exchequer, was confronted with the need to raise more revenue, both for naval rearmament and to meet the costs of social legislation. His budget included taxation that fell principally on the wealthy: a progressive income tax, increased death duties (inheritance taxes), and new taxes on land. Stung to fury by Lloyd George's antiaristocratic and "soak the rich" pronouncements, the House of Lords rejected the budget, thus challenging the long-established doctrine that public finance was the exclusive concern of the House of Commons.

The Liberals, with Lloyd George in the vanguard, now had a popular issue with which they hoped to defeat the Conservatives in the election of January 1910. They were disappointed. Lloyd George's attack on the House of Lords may have been of some electoral benefit, but the Liberals lost heavily and became dependent on the support of the Irish Nationalists and forty Labour members. Although the peers agreed to pass the budget, the Liberals decided to seize the nettle and proposed a Parliament Bill that would curtail the powers of the upper house. In the midst of this controversy King Edward VII died and was succeeded by his son, George V. A second election was held, which was indecisive. When the Lords tried to amend the Parliament Bill Asquith came forward with the promise of the new king to create the number of peers needed to pass the bill. In circumstances of high excitement enough Conservative peers abstained or voted for the bill to permit it to pass. The Parliament Act of 1911 provided that the House of Lords could delay a bill for three years, but if passed in three consecutive years by the House of Commons a bill became law without consent of the Lords. Another provision of the act reduced the maximum term for elections from seven to five years, and separate legislation provided salaries for members of Parliament. The inevitable effect of the Parliament Act was to reduce further the political power of birth and privilege and to increase the power of political parties and party leaders. Although the delaying power of the House of Lords was still important, essentially the hereditary aristocracy had followed the monarchy into a role that was more ornamental and advisory than effective.

The Empire. The Liberals brought to the government of other peoples their historic confidence in self-government, replacing the Conservative emphasis on authority and paternalism. Many Liberals, including Campbell-Bannerman, had opposed the Boer War, and their solution to the problem of South Africa was reconciliation of British and Boers, cemented by political unity in a federation. With the death of Kruger the Boers found leaders in Louis Botha and Jan Christian Smuts who were ready to accept these principles as the basis for a political settlement. The result was the Union of South Africa, formed in 1910, which established a federal union of the Cape Colony, Natal, the Orange Free State, and the

Mrs. Pankhurst arrested at Buckingham Palace, 1914 *(BBC Hulton Picture Library)*.

Transvaal, with Botha as its first prime minister. The major objection to the Union in Britain came from persons concerned with the future of the black population, who saw the Union as a coalition of the whites to maintain superiority over the blacks. In South Africa many of the Boers did not share the commitment of Botha and Smuts to participation in the British Empire. Both of these problems returned to haunt the Union of South Africa at a later time.

British control of India created the conditions for its own decline. To govern India the British developed an educational system using the English language, which trained Indians for employment as civil servants. In so doing the British brought to India their ideas of liberalism and nationalism and gave the Indians a common language in which they could communicate these ideas to each other. The predictable result was that an Indian independence movement arose, led primarily by high-caste, educated Hindus who coveted the pomp and power held by the British raj. In 1885 the Indian National Congress was formed to seek self-government within the British Empire using constitutional means. In 1907 a more radical group came to power within the Congress. They demanded swaraj (independence) and were prepared to use all means to obtain it. One problem was India's large Moslem minority, who preferred British rule to an independent government dominated by Hindus. The Moslems had not adopted British education to the extent of the Hindu leaders, but since they were an important element in the Indian army their views had to be taken seriously. In India, as elsewhere, the Liberal government believed that an installment of political responsibility was the best answer to nationalist movements, and the Government of India Act (1909) provided for elected Indian members of the central and provincial legislative councils. Separate representation was included for Hindus and Moslems. As a further expression of good will King George V visited India to receive the title emperor of India, and the capital of India was moved from the seething cauldron of Calcutta to the historic capital of the Mogul Empire, New Delhi. As in South Africa, these measures gave some satisfaction at first but in the long run whetted the appetite of nationalist leaders for more.

Ireland. As always, the nearest and most difficult problem was Ireland. The Act of Union had brought political unity to the British Isles, but the bulk of the Irish Catholic population had developed its own distinct sense of nationality. The Liberals were committed to Home Rule as the answer to Irish national feeling, but here they faced the opposition, not only of the Conservative party but of the Irish Protestants who, like the Moslems in India, did not wish to find themselves a minority in their own country. With the Parliament Act of 1911 the way was now clear for the Liberals and their Irish Nationalist allies to pass a Home Rule Bill. The Conservatives, who could no longer rely on the blocking power of the House of Lords, fought Home Rule by appealing to public opinion. The center of resistance to Home Rule was in Ulster (northern Ireland) and especially in Belfast, the principal city of Ulster. The Ulster Protestants formed a paramilitary body called the Ulster Volunteers and prepared to fight to keep from being engulfed in a self-governing Ireland dominated by Catholics. Using the slogan, "Ulster will fight and Ulster will be right!" the Ulster Protestants were supported by many prominent Conservatives who attended mass meetings in Belfast, London, and elsewhere. The Irish Nationalists also prepared to fight, and attempts by the Liberal government to prevent civil war met with insubordination in the army. The Conservatives decided to make a last-ditch stand in the House of Lords, despite the Parliament Act and the Liberal-Irish Nationalist majority in the House of Commons. The Home Rule Bill was passed by the Commons in 1912 and again in 1913. Each time it was rejected by the Lords, using the delaying powers reserved by the Parliament Act. The bill was passed for the third time in 1914, after which it became law without consent of the Lords, but by then war had broken out in Europe and it was thought prudent to suspend the operation of the act. Thus in Ireland, India, and South Africa Liberal principles achieved an uneasy peace until nationalist feelings were further aroused by World War I.

Domestic Unrest. The partisan conflict unleashed by the controversial Liberal program was matched by other forms of public unrest. A series of strikes by the large unions—such as the miners, railway workers, Lancashire cotton workers, London dockers, and the transport workers—showed that the labor movement was impatient with the slow progress of normal bargaining procedures and was determined to display its strength. The women's suffrage movement also came to a climax. Although most of the suffragists sought to achieve their goals by the normal means of political persuasion, a militant group led by Mrs. Emmeline Pankhurst and her daughters, Sylvia and Christabel, adopted more extreme tactics. They heckled Liberal speakers, broke windows in main shopping streets, put acid in mailboxes, and set fire to empty houses. When imprisoned they went on hunger strikes, and their jailers resorted to forced feeding. Whether dealing with Ulster, strikers, or suffragists, the authorities made themselves look weak and foolish by an ineffectual mixture of conciliation and coercion. It appeared as if the political system was becoming less able to resolve political and social issues by the established methods of persuasion and voting.

The Road to War

Alliances. The greatest failure of leadership was not at home. It was the failure of European diplomacy to resolve the international tensions that eventually led to war. The Salisbury ministry had sought to safeguard Britain through the entente with France, which led to conversations between the two military staffs. The French, who had an alliance with Russia, worked zealously to bring their two friends together. After Russia was defeated in 1904 to 1905 by Britain's ally, Japan, the Russians became more amenable. Russia was more acceptable to Britain as an ally because the Revolution of 1905 had set that great empire in the direction of constitutional government. In 1907 Britain and Russia came to an agreement that resolved their imperial conflicts in Persia (Iran) and Afghanistan, thus forming the Triple Entente of France, Russia, and Britain. The Germans, in turn, clung even more tightly to their alliance with Austria-Hungary, which, since it nominally included Italy, was called the Triple Alliance.

From the British perspective the greatest danger was the naval rivalry with Germany. At the time, sea power was a vital factor in national power, and thus Germany, already the strongest land power in Europe, began building a powerful navy. The British could see only one reason for such a navy—to threaten the British position in the North Sea and the English Channel. The Liberal government responded with an ambitious naval-building program, an undertaking made more necessary by changes in naval technology and design that made many of the British ships obsolete. The question of sea power, which was vital to Britain but of secondary importance to Germany, did more than anything else to poison relations between the two countries and keep Britain firmly in the camp of the Triple Entente.

The Outbreak of War. World War I was preceded by a series of preliminary conflicts. In 1908 Austria-Hungary, supported by Germany, annexed the province of Bosnia, thus provoking violent protests from Serbian nationalists who viewed Bosnia as an important part of the greater Serbia which they sought to achieve. In 1911 Britain and France stood together to protect the French position in Morocco against German threats. In 1912 and again in 1913 wars broke out in the Balkans, and finally another Balkan crisis led to the outbreak of general war.

On June 28, 1914, Archduke Franz Ferdinand, heir to the Austro-Hungarian monarchy, visited Sarajevo, capital of Bosnia, where he was assassinated by Serbian nationalists. The Austrians were determined to make an example of Serbia and issued an ultimatum that was tantamount to a declaration of war. The Serbians turned to their allies, the Russians, who decided that support of Serbia was essential to maintain their influence among their "little Slavic brothers" in the Balkans. The Germans gave full support to Austria-Hungary, which was their only reliable ally. The French felt it essential to support the Russians, thus confronting Germany and Austria with a two-front war. The Austrians declared war on Serbia on July 28, and the Russians began mobilizing their forces. At this point the Germans became anxious, for their plan of battle was to strike hard at France, relying on the slow Russian mobilization to give them time to deal with the French before turning eastward to meet the Russians. Thus, every day given the Russians to mobilize was a day lost on the western front. When the Russians refused to stop their mobilization, the Germans attacked France through Belgium. World War I had begun.

Britain and the Crisis. The Liberal government was deeply divided as it faced the mounting European crisis. The ententes with France and Russia were not alliances, and the conversations between British and French military staffs carried no formal obligations. Britain had one clear commitment—a guarantee of Belgian neutrality made in 1839. However, as the crisis unfolded Britain had a larger concern—the possibility that the European continent might be dominated by one power, as in the days of

Philip II of Spain, Louis XIV of France, or Napoleon, that might use the Channel coast as a springboard for invasion. Beyond these strategic considerations lay the Liberal belief in international law, which appeared to be threatened more by Germany than by any other power. The hazards of war were great: business leaders worried about the effects of war on British banking and trade; increased labor unrest at home and nationalist agitation in Ireland could be expected; the support of the empire for a land war in Europe was doubtful. Some argued that Britain could serve better as a mediator than as a belligerent.

The German attack on Belgium settled the matter, for a German victory and a French defeat would result in a Europe dominated by one military power. Britain declared war. When Sir Edward Grey, foreign secretary, was called upon to explain the policy of his government he used such arguments as national honor, the sanctity of treaties, the balance of power, and international law. Although these noble words undoubtedly concealed a good deal of muddle, there is reason to believe that in his mind, and the minds of his countrymen, these concepts were worth fighting for.

Suggestions for Further Reading

Two of the major figures of the late-Victorian period are covered in Aubrey L. Kennedy, *Salisbury, 1830–1903: Portrait of a Statesman* (1953) and Peter Fraser, *Joseph Chamberlain: Radicalism and Empire, 1868–1914* (1966). The continuing influence of Gladstone may be followed in Peter Stansky, *Gladstone: A Progress in Politics* (1979) and Michael Barker, *Gladstone and Radicalism: The Reconstruction of Liberal Policy, 1885–1894* (1975).

The growth in numbers and importance of the urban working class may be followed in David Kynaston, *King Labour: The British Working Class, 1850–1914* (1976) and Standish Meacham, *A Life Apart: The English Working Class, 1890–1914* (1977). Growing public involvement with working-class problems is the subject of three works by Henry Pelling: *A History of British Trade Unionism* (3rd edition, 1976), *A Short History of the Labour Party* (6th edition, 1978), and *Popular Politics and Society in Late Victorian Britain* (2nd edition, 1979). Reactions against popular democracy are covered in Benjamin E. Lippincott, *Victorian Critics of Democracy* (1938).

The problem of Ireland reached one of its periodic climaxes from 1886 to 1914. In addition to general works such as J. C. Beckett, *The Making of Modern Ireland* (3rd edition, 1966) and Lawrence J. McCaffrey, *The Irish Question, 1800–1922* (1968), see F. S. L. Lyons, *Ireland Since the Famine* (2nd edition, 1973) and Nicholas Mansergh, *The Irish Question, 1840–1921* (3rd edition, 1975).

For a general overview see C. C. Eldridge, *Victorian Imperialism* (1978). C. J. Lowe refutes the idea of a mania for colonies in *The Reluctant Imperialists, 1870–1902* (1968). Differing interpretations of imperialism are reviewed in *British Im-*

perialism: Gold, God, and Glory, ed. Robin Winks (1963). See also J. C. Lockhart and C. M. Woodhouse, *Cecil Rhodes: The Colossus of South Africa* (1963).

The best introduction to the twentieth century is Alfred F. Havighurst, *Britain in Transition: The Twentieth Century* (4th edition, 1985). Another good general book is Trevor Lloyd, *Empire to Welfare State: English History, 1906–1976* (2nd edition, 1979). For the two major political parties see Chris Cook, *A Short History of the Liberal Party, 1900–1976* (1978) and Robert Blake, *The Conservative Party from Pitt to Churchill* (1970). The origins of the Labour party are examined in *The First Labour Party, 1906–1914*, ed. K. D. Brown (1985). Bentley Gilbert, *The Evolution of National Insurance in Great Britain: The Origins of the Welfare State* (1966) studies one of the key features of "the New Liberalism." Reading on this period should include a stimulating but controversial work by George Dangerfield, *The Strange Death of Liberal England* (1935). Another of Dangerfield's lively works worthy of attention is *The Damnable Question: A Study of Anglo-Irish Relations* (1976).

There is a vast literature on the coming of World War I. A readable brief account is Laurence Lafore, *The Long Fuse: An Interpretation of the Origins of World War I* (1965). Two books by Barbara Tuchman tell vividly the tale of the march to disaster: *The Proud Tower: A Portrait of the World before the War, 1890–1914* (1966) and *The Guns of August* (1962).

King Edward VII has evoked good biographies by Philip Magnus, *King Edward the Seventh* (1964) and Keith Middlemas, *The Life and Times of Edward VII* (1972). Other useful biographies are Ruddock F. MacKay, *Balfour: Intellectual Statesman* (1985), Stephen Koss, *Asquith* (1976), Keith Robbins, *Sir Edward Grey* (1971), and Kenneth O. Morgan, *Keir Hardie: Radical and Socialist* (1975). Biographies of Lloyd George and Winston Churchill are given in Chapter 16.

16

An Era of World Wars

1914–1945

*T*he First World War was a cataclysm that rocked Europe. The great empires of the East—Germany, Austria-Hungary, Russia, and the Ottoman Empire—collapsed, setting off radical and nationalist revolutions. France was deeply wounded, and two decades later she had not recovered sufficiently to stand up against a resurgent Germany under Adolf Hitler. Italy, politically and economically weak, floundered during the war and shortly thereafter came under the control of the first of the Fascist dictators, Benito Mussolini. Britain created the largest army in her history and mobilized her industry to produce unprecedented quantities of military supplies. She sacrificed large numbers of ships and seamen to German submarines and extensive overseas investments to the insatiable financial demands of war in an industrial sociey. The war scarred millions of lives and intensified old problems while creating new ones. There was little pride or joy in a victory of exhaustion, and, twenty years later, Britain had to fight again, under much less favorable auspices. The two world wars destroyed the old Britain, changed completely her relations with the outside world and her empire, and led to the Britain we know today.

The War of Attrition

When Germany attacked France through Belgium in August 1914, the nations of Europe expected a short war: either a quick German victory over France and Russia (as the Germans planned) or an Allied check to the German advance, followed by a peace conference. Britain sent a small expeditionary force to France to bolster the French forces and ordered her fleet to bottle up the German fleet, thus keeping the Channel and the sea lanes open. The Germans found they had taken on more than they could handle. British and French forces stopped the German juggernaut at the Marne River in France and at Ypres in Belgium. In the meantime the Russians, utilizing the railroads that had been built in the previous decade, were able to mobilize more quickly than the Germans anticipated. When Russian forces threatened Prussia the Germans were compelled to shift forces to the eastern front, weakening their attack sufficiently to enable the Allied lines to hold. Both sides began digging trenches that eventually stretched from the Channel coast to the Swiss border. While the Germans were annihilating vast Russian forces in a war of movement in the east, stalemate set in on the western front.

By 1915 the leaders of the combatant states had two choices: a compromise peace or vast, desperate efforts for victory. They chose the latter. Britain made preparations for a larger and more protracted war. The Territorial Army, the equivalent of the American National Guard, was sent into the trenches, and Britain began recruiting a large volunteer army. Lacking room for maneuver and without the mobility of World War II, generals on both sides made desperate efforts to break through the trenches, taking frightful losses to no effect. Until the fighting ended in November 1918, fruitless attacks came one after another—deafening artillery barrages were followed by infantry assaults through barbed wire and mine fields. Machine guns chattered their deadly refrain, and the crunch of mortar shells sounded among the troops rushing across no-man's-land. Surviving attackers who leaped with bayonets into the trenches to grapple face-to-face with the enemy rarely accomplished much—at best the other army was pushed back a few miles into a new line of trenches. When Germany finally cracked in 1918 as a result of four years of attrition, the battle lines had changed very little in the West, although eastern Europe and the Middle East had fallen into chaos.

The western front devoured a generation. The British armed forces swallowed up nearly 6,000,000 men, a third of the male population between their teens and midforties. By 1916 volunteers were insufficient, and national conscription was adopted. The war cost the lives of nearly 750,000 British fighting men—more than had been killed in all her previous wars combined. The Empire sacrificed another 200,000 lives. Thousands more were permanently crippled by wounds, poison gas, or mental breakdown.

Politicians and diplomats, unwilling to admit the disaster into which they had led their nations, and generals determined to have victory at all costs, looked vainly for alternatives that would still preserve their reputations. The British public, as in other belligerent nations, was whipped to fury by national pride and tales of enemy atrocities. Few generals on either side gained distinction as strategists, for all believed in the efficacy of the offensive when modern weapons had given the advantage to the defensive.

British and French soldiers in the trenches *(BBC Hulton Picture Library)*.

Sir Douglas Haig, who from 1915 commanded the British Expeditionary Force, was a cavalryman like many British generals. Hoping for a breakthrough and the cavalry charges that never came, Haig kept thousands of horses behind the front, eating vast quantities of hay. Seeking an alternative to head-on offensives that got nowhere, Winston Churchill at the Admiralty organized an attack on the Turks at the Dardanelles, hoping to come to the assistance of the Russians by that route. Despite the sacrifices of thousands of Australian and New Zealand soldiers on the beaches of Gallipoli, this venture also ended in failure. The only major battle between the British and German fleets, near Jutland in 1916, was indecisive. Britain retained control of the seas, and the German surface fleet was no longer a factor in the war. Both sides used sea power for economic war. The British used their characteristic blockade of a European land enemy and the Germans used a new and deadly weapon—the submarine. New weapons changed warfare: the first extensive use of the deadly machine gun; poison gas, which was as dangerous to the user as the intended victim; the tank and the airplane, which became effective only in World War II. Britain and France persuaded Italy to enter the war on the Allied side in 1915, a step that led to savage battles with the Austrians in the north of Italy. The Germans incited the Irish to rebel; the British incited the Arabs to rise against the Ottoman Empire of the Turks. Even as the Russian Empire was collapsing on the eastern front the United States, under President Woodrow Wilson, entered the war in the West, bringing new manpower and economic resources that eventually tipped the balance.

War Socialism. World War I was a conflict of industrial power as much as military power, and the home front had to be organized to manufacture and transport enormous quantities of military supplies. Slowly and reluctantly the government, with the cooperation of businessmen, created a kind of war socialism in which the government controlled industry and trade. Military victory seemed more important than the peacetime principles that had guarded property rights and personal liberties. The government acquired sweeping discretionary powers under the Defence of the Realm Act, personified as the meddlesome Aunt DORA. Industry was called on to supply vast quantities of military equipment such as rifles, gas masks, and munitions. In 1914 the British army had approximately 1,300 machine guns; over the next four years it acquired an additional 240,000. Government arsenals and private contractors could produce only a fraction of the needed armaments. The government set up a special Ministry of Munitions under David Lloyd George that built large new factories employing more than a million workers. War socialism eventually brought victory. Its success helped undermine the cult of laissez-faire and inspired a new faith in centralized planning and government by experts.

Wartime Political Leadership. In 1914 the Liberals and the Conservatives had an equal number of seats in the House of Commons, but with Labour and Irish support the Liberals controlled the government. The political situation strengthened national unity, because the Conservatives strongly supported the war while the Liberals, who were responsible for conducting it, contained in their coalition most of those members of Parliament who were skeptical or opposed. As the war dragged on dissatisfaction with its management compelled the Liberals to bring Conservative and Labour members into the ministry. Herbert Asquith, the Liberal prime minister, a superb peacetime politician, lacked the leadership and vigor needed in war, and his management of the war was increasingly criticized by the press, the public, and even his own colleagues. A replacement was at hand in one of Asquith's colleagues, the aggressive and dynamic Welshman, David Lloyd George. Lloyd George combined an appetite for power with a shrewd and determined capacity for solving problems. Like William Pitt in 1757, Lloyd George knew he was the man to lead Britain to victory, and he did not hesitate to give secondary weight to personal and party loyalty. In 1916 Lloyd George intrigued with the Conservatives and some of his Liberal colleagues to force Asquith to resign. Lloyd George then became prime minister, largely with Conservative support. The majority of the Liberals were bitter at Lloyd George's treatment of Asquith and his apparent lack of principles. Lloyd George was undoubtedly the man to lead Britain to her eventual victory, but in so doing he split the Liberal party and poisoned British politics for a generation.

The new prime minister became one of Britain's greatest war leaders. He was prepared to marshall the full human and material resources of the nation to win the war. The Conservatives who had hated Lloyd George as a radical supported the quick-witted Welshman when he identified himself with a military policy of decisive victory and abandoned his schemes of domestic reform. Lloyd George had the self-confidence to surround himself with talented and independent-minded men and women. He had great personal charm and a genius for arousing enthusiasm. He was also a master of political and personal manipulation. He insisted on action in the stuffy and hidebound administrative departments and created new administrative structures where needed. He was a master of improvisation, a pragmatic solver of crises, and a man of compromises who worried little about consistency. He was also a man with a great zest for life, including an abundant love life, which he managed to keep secret despite his place at the center of public affairs.

Under the traditional system, government policy was shaped by a Cabinet comprised of approximately twenty men, nearly all of them burdened with departmental administration. Lloyd George established a type of democratic dictatorship, headed by himself and supported by a War Cabinet of about five men, most of whom were freed from departmental duties that would distract them from setting general national policy. In 1917 Lloyd George brought Winston Churchill, his former Liberal colleague, back into office, although Churchill had been made the scapegoat for the failure at the Dardanelles two years earlier. He also recognized the importance of Labour party support and gave its leader, Arthur Henderson, a seat in the War Cabinet. Ramsay MacDonald, one of the founders and leading figures in the Labour party, resigned his leadership post in 1914 in opposition to the war but found few supporters within his party.

War and Society

The Labor Shortage. In 1916 the Asquith government ordered conscription of men when volunteers proved too few to satisfy the appetite of the western front. Even earlier the dwindling number of available men in the labor force gave women opportunities to enter jobs previously closed to them. Employers who hired women paid them about half the wages earned by men who did the same work. About 800,000 additional women worked in industry, 250,000 in farming, and 100,000 in transport. Offices and retail shops offered women jobs with greater permanence. About 200,000 women took jobs in government offices, and more than twice this number worked in private offices. Hundreds of thousands of women became retail sales clerks. Domestic service, which had been the most important form of employment open to women, declined greatly as women found better opportunities. The role of women in the war helped change the minds of former opponents of women's suffrage. Wartime life also gave women much more personal freedom, since they had money of their own and freer social contacts at work and elsewhere.

The scarcity of labor compelled the government to court the working class. Labour party leaders were included in the wartime coalition governments, and grievance boards were created on which union leaders served with management. Employers competed for workers, not only with higher wages but by providing amenities such as canteens that served inexpensive hot food. Strikes took place despite these gestures of appeasement. Senior trade union officials usually cooperated with the government, but shop stewards, who combined ordinary employment with local union responsibilities, gave disgruntled workers militant leadership. The discontent of industrial workers was not ideological but grew out of local grievances such as high rents and a sense that the opportunity to advance their interests should not be missed.

The introduction of many new people into the labor force, including women, aroused the concern of established workers, who felt their jobs and work rules were at stake. Trade unions threatened to strike to keep out anyone who had not performed the normal apprenticeship, which would have barred most available men and virtually all women. The government persuaded the trade unions to accept the wartime dilution of skilled workers with the unskilled by promising that the practice would be temporary. In fact, unskilled and semiskilled workers remained numerically dominant, and their wages rose more than the wages of skilled craftsmen.

Social Consequences of the War. During the war some of the old distinctions in the class structure became blurred. Before the war only the upper and middle classes had paid income tax, but during the war the better-off workers paid too. The scarcity of domestic servants forced many middle-class families to do their own cooking and cleaning and made it virtually impossible for the aristocracy to maintain their great stately homes and former comfortable life-style. To encourage productivity and reduce absenteeism the government attacked drunkenness, a favorite issue of the Liberals. Taxes on alcoholic beverages, especially whiskey, were increased, and public houses ("pubs") were required to close in midafternoon on weekdays, a requirement baffling to American visitors. The government also considered prohibition but feared that the people loved their beer more than they hated the Germans. Sinkings of British ships by German submarines led to shortages of food, inflated food prices, and long queues of shoppers. In 1918 there was loosely enforced rationing of meat and other scarce foods. The sacrifices of war, in the trenches and at home, were rewarded by the Representation of the People Act (1918), which removed virtually all restrictions on the vote for adult males and gave the vote to women over thirty, although it was primarily younger women who had served in the factories and on the farms.

To stimulate cooperation with its war policies the government combined propaganda with censorship. As public radio broadcasting did not exist, the mass circulation newspapers exerted the greatest influence, showing their support for democracy by debasing the fund of knowledge and reason upon which democracy depends. The newspapers depicted the Germans as a subhuman race that threatened western civilization—cruel Huns who executed innocent civilians, raped women, and tossed babies on to their bayonets. The royal family, which traced its ancestry to George I, patriotically changed its name to Windsor, an example followed by many others with German names. Those who opposed the war were stigmatized as traitors. As the war dragged on and the casualty lists lengthened, the initial enthusiasm for the war was replaced by a dogged determination.

A minority rejected the official propaganda. Many who supported the war disliked conscription, and sentiment in favor of a compromise peace grew in the Labour party after the revolutions of 1917 in Russia. To justify terrible military losses and the sacrifices of civilians the government promised great rewards after the victory: national security, social justice, an enduring peace, and a better world. When peace came the government lacked the will and perhaps the ability to honor its commitments. The people considered themselves cheated, and there was widespread cynicism about politicians and skepticism about the war. Underlying particular complaints were doubts about the old beliefs in the basic goodness of man and a universe ruled with justice and compassion. The intellectuals were the most openly shaken as they considered the holocaust created by nations that had counted themselves as centers of civilization, but their disillusionment spread in less visible ways into the general public.

The Lloyd George Coalition

Lloyd George and the Peace. As soon as possible after the war ended Lloyd George called an election to capitalize on the glories of victory and to give him a strong political base for his role in the peace settlement. Lloyd George and the Conservative leader, Andrew Bonar Law, agreed to continue their wartime cooperation by not opposing each other's candidates. The Liberals split. Those who followed Asquith did not receive the endorsement ("coupon") given to the candidates of the coalition government. The Labour party left the coalition and for the first time appeared as an independent major party, adopting a socialist platform written by Sidney Webb. Lloyd George pulled out all the stops in using his talents for demagoguery, uttering cries of "Hang the kaiser" and "make Germany pay." The election was a landslide victory for the Lloyd George coalition government, but most of Lloyd George's supporters in the new House of Commons were Conservatives. The Labour party came in second, even though its socialist platform was objectionable to many of its working-class supporters. The Irish Nationalists virtually disappeared, since most of the Irish members of Parliament showed their commitment to an independent Ireland by refusing to take their seats. The Asquith Liberals lost heavily and ceased to be a major political force. The war and Lloyd George had destroyed the great Liberal party, with its commitment to popular democracy, personal freedom, free trade, and a humane but non-socialist approach to social problems.

The Peace Conference met at Versailles, outside Paris, and here Lloyd George's talents as a problem solver and mediator were taxed to the fullest. The American president, Woodrow Wilson, came to Versailles with visions of democracy, national self-determination, and international cooperation, which he naively thought applied to a Europe fallen into chaos and drenched in blood. The French, on the other hand, were primarily concerned to prevent a revival of German military power and were determined to make Germany pay the massive cost of rebuilding. Despite his election rhetoric, Lloyd George attempted to be a mediator between the two points of view. A stable Europe and a prosperous Germany were important to the British economy, but Britain also had to make certain that the sacrifices of war were not in vain.

The Peace of Versailles left Germany intact, although France regained Alsace-Lorraine and German territory was given to Poland to provide an outlet to the sea. At the insistence of France, heavy reparations were imposed on Germany. Germany was disarmed, and the German border with France in the Rhineland could not be fortified. Britain insisted that the German navy be drastically reduced. Germany lost her colonies, including strategic islands in the Pacific, which were given to the victorious powers as mandates of the League of Nations. The collapse of the Russian and Austro-Hungarian Empires led to the establishment of quarrelsome, unstable states in eastern Europe. By this time Russia had come under control of Lenin and the Bolsheviks, who carried out a violent revolution that shocked Europe and seemed to provide a model for proletarian revolutions elsewhere. The fall of the Ottoman Empire set the Arab world ablaze. Britain and France assumed control of Palestine, Iraq, Syria, and Lebanon as mandates, and Britain continued her control of Egypt, thus accepting a role in the Middle East that led to endless trouble. In 1917 Britain, in order to win the support of the Zionist Movement, had issued the Balfour Declaration, which stated British approval of a Jewish national "home" in Palestine as long as the rights of the Arabs were respected. This principle was also incorporated into the peace settlement and became the legal basis for Jewish immigration into Palestine. Woodrow Wilson salvaged something with the establishment of the League of Nations, but the U.S. Senate rejected the Versailles Treaty and refused to join the League. Public approval of the idea of the League was strong in Britain, which for the next twenty years was its strongest supporter.

With Germany humbled, Britain seemed to be more powerful than ever. She had blocked any immediate threat of German supremacy in Europe, destroyed the German fleet, and made herself dominant in the Middle East. In fact, Britain had passed the peak of her power. Britain's wartime allies no longer supplemented her strength: France was in despair, Russia was in revolution, and the United States had turned to isolation. Concerned at Japanese imperialist designs on China, the United States insisted that Britain abandon her alliance with Japan. At the Washington Naval Conference of 1920 to 1921 Britain accepted naval parity with the United States, which left Australia, New Zealand, Britain's East Asian colonies, and the Pacific Ocean to American protection. Britain still had important commercial and imperial interests throughout the world but no longer had the strength to defend them.

The Empire. The state of the British Empire illustrated the contrast between the illusion of power and the reality of long-term decline. The white-dominated self-governing dominions—Canada, Australia, New Zealand, South Africa—had supported the mother country in the war with men, money, and supplies. Some Britons hoped that wartime unity foreshadowed greater political and economic cooperation in the postwar world. Instead, the dominions emerged as fully independent nations joined to Britain by ties of sentiment and self-interest. In 1926 an imperial conference described the United Kingdom and the dominions as "autonomous communities within the British Empire, equal in status, in no way subordinate to one another." In the Statute of Westminster (1931) Parliament renounced its legislative authority over the dominions.

A different situation existed in the parts of the Empire with populations that did not have experience in self-government. Here small, educated elites sought political power for themselves by using the rhetoric of free-

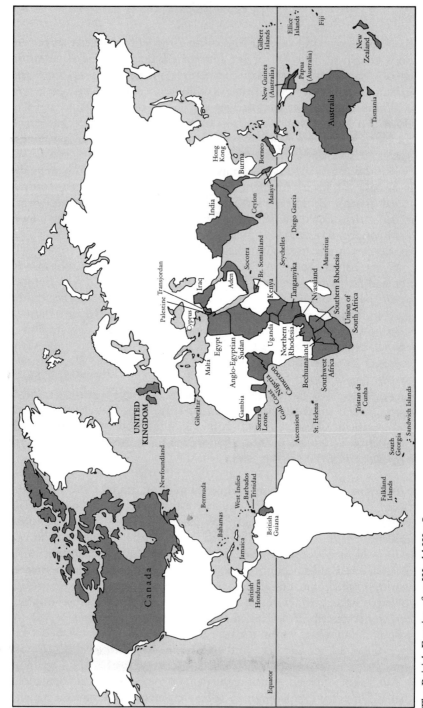

The British Empire after World War I

dom and democracy. In India the Congress party, comprised almost entirely of educated Hindus, came under the leadership of Mohandas K. Gandhi, who won the support of the Hindu peasants by his ascetic lifestyle and appeals to native traditions of self-sufficiency. The goal of the Congress party was independence (swaraj), which Gandhi sought to achieve by nonviolent civil disobedience, such as boycotts of British goods, violations of the salt monopoly, refusal to pay taxes, and hunger strikes. Despite Gandhi's commitment to nonviolence, violence broke out frequently. In 1919 soldiers of the Indian army fired on demonstrators at Amritsar, which provided the Congress leaders with martyrs and a British atrocity that could be used to arouse Indian public opinion. A major problem in India was antagonism between the Hindus and the Moslem minority, for the Moslems preferred British rule to domination by the Hindus in an independent India. The Moslems, who were numerous in the Indian army, formed the Moslem League to protect their interests. The Government of India Act (1919) sought to satisfy Indian leaders by increasing Indian participation in government, but by this time moderation and slow progress were unacceptable to the Congress party. Resistance to British rule continued.

The Irish Crisis. World War I brought to a head the long-simmering problems of Ireland, heightened by the ideals of national self-determination espoused by Woodrow Wilson at the Versailles Conference. The Irish sense of nationalism was strengthened by the movement, Sinn Fein, which fostered interest in the Gaelic language, Irish history and culture, and modern Irish poets and playwrights. As always, Irish nationalism was opposed by Ulster Protestants who, like the Moslems in India, did not favor independence, which would put them in a minority. In 1916 a small group of militant Irish nationalists attempted an uprising that began with the seizure of the General Post Office in Dublin on Easter Monday. The rebellion, known since as the Easter Rising, did not arouse the broad public support its leaders had expected, and it was crushed by government forces. The rebels were booed by bystanders as they marched through the streets to prison, but the execution of their leaders transformed them into heroes and martyrs and radicalized Sinn Fein into a party of violent revolution. To appease American public opinion, the British spared Eamon de Valera, the Brooklyn-born son of a Cuban father and Irish mother, who had been raised in Ireland.

In the elections for Parliament in November 1918 Sinn Fein won almost every seat outside Ulster. The Sinn Feiners refused to sit in the British Parliament and convened in 1919 to declare themselves the legislature of an independent Irish republic. To defend it they created a military force called the Irish Republican Army (I.R.A.). While de Valera was in America raising money for the Irish Republic, the I.R.A. fought a guerilla war using ambush, kidnappings, and assassinations. Informers were viewed as traitors to Ireland and were punished by shooting off their kneecaps. Sympathetic Irish-Americans contributed money to the I.R.A. for the fight against the British. When the British launched an indiscriminate counterterror the Irish public accepted the actions of the I.R.A. as justified. After many of the Royal Irish Constabulary resigned, the British recruited a new police force from among demobilized soldiers. Known as "Black and Tans" because of the color of their uniforms, they lacked the discipline of the army and committed atrocities that rivaled those of the I.R.A. The climax of terror came on Bloody Sunday in November 1920. In the morning, the I.R.A. murdered a number of British officers in their homes while their families watched. In the afternoon the Black and Tans fired at random into a crowd at a football match.

The I.R.A. was no match for the British militarily, but they had a powerful ally in the war weariness of the British people. Lloyd George, as usual, played the role of problem solver. Late in 1921 he arranged negotiations in London with the leaders of the Irish insurgents. He offered to concede virtual independence to Ireland as a free state within the British Empire if the rebels would accept nominal allegiance to the crown and the partition of Ulster from the rest of Ireland. In so doing, Lloyd George alienated many of his Conservative supporters and did not satisfy those committed to a united and independent Ireland.

Most of the Sinn Fein negotiators accepted the terms as the best they could get. When they returned to Ireland with the Treaty they faced strong opposition from de Valera and his supporters. A majority in the Irish legislature endorsed the Treaty, and the voters supported the pro-Treaty party in new elections. The adherents of the Treaty set up the Irish Free State with its capital in Dublin. Then came the ultimate tragedy as Irish patriots fought each other. De Valera and his followers rebelled against the Free State in June 1922, and again Ireland was torn by civil war. By April 1923, the government of the Irish Free State had established its authority, and de Valera was again a prisoner. Remnants of the I.R.A. continued to function as an underground terrorist organization.

The Fall of Lloyd George. Lloyd George thrived in the hectic atmosphere of the years immediately after the war, devoting his political shrewdness and vast energies to peace in Europe, pacification of Ireland and India, and the problems of postwar reconstruction. Property owners, professional men, and the solid middle class relied on him to save them from socialism at home and Bolshevism abroad. The end of the war did not mean the end of crisis; an influenza epidemic killed 150,000 people in Britain, and the threat of mutiny forced the government to scrap its complicated plans to

Eamon de Valera *(The Bettmann Archive)*.

delay demobilization until jobs existed for the soldiers. Halfhearted military intervention against the Bolsheviks in Russia embarrassed Britain abroad, frustrated Lloyd George's Conservative supporters, and upset working-class and radical opinion.

The demand for consumer goods from a world starved by wartime austerities produced for a short time abundant jobs, high wages, and strikes. Skillfully mediating industrial disputes, Lloyd George postponed confrontation with the trade unions until unemployment weakened them. He pacified the coal miners with the appointment of a commission to study the problems of the industry, but, when a majority of the commission recommended one form or another of nationalization, Lloyd George used the disagreement over specifics as an excuse not to act. To fulfill the promise of "homes fit for heroes" the government paid local authorities and private builders generous subsidies to build houses.

Then in 1921 to 1922 the economy collapsed, spoiling Lloyd George's strategy for killing socialism with kindness. The old export industries such as steel, coal, and textiles suffered most. During the war American, Japanese, and other producers had invaded established British markets, and after the war German reparations payments and intergovernmental debts snarled international finance and trade. By mid-1921 there were more than two million people out of work in Britain, and until the beginning of World War II unemployment never fell below a million. At first unemployment compensation assisted the workers, but when those benefits ran out the government provided modest money payments ("the dole"), which enabled them to survive. The government did little to provide new jobs. Economy replaced reform as the official watchword, and expenditures for housing, education, and other programs of social reconstruction were drastically cut.

As problems mounted, rank-and-file Conservatives rebelled against Lloyd George, although their leaders still saw him as the popular figure who could keep them in office. Back-bench Conservatives criticized the cost of subsidies for working-class housing, complained that wartime controls restricting business and industry continued too long, and above all resented the settlement in Ireland. They worried that Conservative leaders might accept a permanent merger of the Coalition parties. They saw Lloyd George as a corruptor of British politics, for he expanded the practice of rewarding generous contributors with titles of nobility and he maintained a substantial political fund collected by Coalition Liberals to use as he liked.

Lloyd George sought to save his position by a diplomatic triumph. He tried to conciliate Germany at the expense of France, but instead the Germans signed an ominous treaty of friendship with Russia. Next he intervened in a war between the Turks and the Greeks. The Turks, under a bold leader named Mustapha Kemal, sought to drive the Greeks out of the territory along the Turkish coast, which was granted to them in the peace settlement. Lloyd George threatened to fight when the Turks marched on their prewar capital, Constantinople, which was still occupied by the Allies. The French would not support Lloyd George against the Turks, who refused to back down in the face of his threats. When the Turks were victorious, Conservative backbenchers decided they had had enough of Lloyd George's frenetic activity.

In 1922, over the opposition of most of the Conservatives in the Cabinet, a caucus of Conservative members of Parliament at the Carlton Club decided that the party should withdraw from the Coalition and return to politics as usual. The Conservative leaders yielded, and Lloyd George was forced to resign. The ailing Bonar Law came out of a brief retirement to lead a purely Conservative government. Repudiated by the Conservatives and mistrusted by most Liberals, Lloyd George, like William Pitt, continued to be the dynamic politician who disrupted where he could not lead. He never held office again.

The Twenties

The Politics of Mediocrity. When Lloyd George resigned in 1922 he was succeeded by the Conservative leader, Sir Andrew Bonar Law, who called an election that resulted in a three-way split between Conservatives, Liberals, and Labour, although the Liberals were further split between followers of Asquith and Lloyd George. A few months after taking office Bonar Law retired and was succeeded by Stanley Baldwin, a shrewd political operator who dominated British politics for the next fourteen years. Prime Minister Baldwin lacked Lloyd George's energy and imagination, but he understood the Conservative party and the ordinary voter. He practiced the politics of conciliation—supporting moderate reforms more than some Conservatives liked—and through the new medium of radio he impressed the public with his straightforwardness and honesty. Almost immediately Baldwin made an important decision when he came out in favor of a protective tariff and called an election on that issue. The Liberals, historically devoted to free trade, were reunited in opposing protectionism. When no party won a majority the Liberals allowed Ramsay MacDonald, leader of the Labour party, to form a government with their support.

MacDonald had been a leader in forming the Labour party prior to World War I and had gained respect for his principled opposition to Britain's involvement in the war. In domestic policy his socialist ideals inspired vague, eloquent speeches, but his dependence on the Liberals made socialist legislation impossible. In foreign affairs he extended diplomatic recognition to Soviet Russia and worked to strengthen cooperation between Britain and France. For all his limitations as a policymaker, MacDonald stood out as the ablest parliamentary tactician in his party. Despite being born the illegitimate son of a penniless maidservant, his good looks, elegant manners, and Scots accent—which bore no working-class taint—enabled him to enter the society of duchesses and millionaires. His career illustrates how the aristocratic embrace could tame humbly born radicals.

In an effort to strengthen his hand politically, MacDonald called an election in 1924. The election centered on the issue of Bolshevism, which was pressed hard by Baldwin and the Conservatives. The government was accused of leniency toward a Communist editor who supposedly had tried to subvert the loyalty of the army. During the election campaign a forged letter showed that a Russian official, Zinoviev, expected armed revolution in Britain. The Conservatives won the election with ease and again the Liberals, whose following was whittled away from the right and the left, were the biggest losers. An imaginative program for economic reform drafted under the leadership of Lloyd George in the middle and late 1920s failed to revive the Liberals as a major party.

Baldwin was able to put together a much stronger government in 1924 to 1929 than in his first ministry. Those Conservatives who had earlier supported Lloyd George now fell in line behind Baldwin, as did ex-Liberal Winston Churchill, whose opposition to Soviet Bolshevism and domestic socialism was intense. As chancellor of the exchequer, Churchill returned the pound to the gold standard, unfortunately at an overvalued rate, which harmed British exports. As foreign secretary, Austen Chamberlain, son of the Liberal Unionist leader, Joseph Chamberlain, led in negotiating the Locarno Treaties (1925), which breathed a spirit of reconciliation by mutual guarantees of borders in western Europe. Germany joined the League of Nations, and Allied occupation forces were withdrawn from the Rhineland. Neville Chamberlain, younger brother of Austen, led in legislation to reform local government finance and to improve pensions for the elderly, widows, and orphans. The Conservatives were also active in building housing for low-income people. The Tory Democracy of Disraeli was still alive in the Conservative party.

The General Strike of 1926 was the most dramatic event of the second Baldwin government. The strike grew out of a dispute in the coal industry: the owners wanted to reduce wages to compete with cheap foreign coal, and the government wanted to end its subsidy that kept wages up. The miners refused to accept any cut in pay, even when a royal commission proposed to couple a reduction with reorganization of the industry. After the coal miners called a strike, the Trades Union Congress decided to support them with a national walk out, a long-discussed move that union

Food convoy, General Strike, 1926 *(BBC Hulton Picture Library)*.

leaders thought would be a decisive blow. The General Strike backfired. Despite rank-and-file solidarity in the unions, the government maintained essential services with the help of middle-class volunteers who drove trucks, soldiers who unloaded ships, and sailors who shoveled coal at power stations. After nine days Baldwin maneuvered the Trades Union Congress into calling off the strike without obtaining anything in return. The coal strike continued until hunger broke it later in the year.

In 1929 an election was due. Baldwin and the Conservatives ran on the slogan "Safety First." Lloyd George made his last major effort with a program for national reform and revival that foreshadowed the American New Deal, but to no avail. The voters turned to Labour, which became the largest single party in the House of Commons, although MacDonald still needed Liberal support to form his second ministry. The MacDonald government soon staggered under the assault of the Great Depression, which began with the 1929 stock market crash in he United States and became a general breakdown of international finance and trade, upon which Britain depended more than any other nation. By the end of 1930 the unemployed in Britain numbered two and one-half million, with no relief in sight.

The MacDonald government had difficulty in paying its bills, and it had to cut spending to obtain loans from bankers fearful of socialism. Philip Snowden, the Labour chancellor of the exchequer, believed that the revival of Britain's export industries required low taxes and expenditures and that the pound based on gold was essential to Britain's trade throughout the world. Despite pressure from his Labour party colleagues, Snowden was unwilling to approve large expenditures for relief of the unemployed. Some of the Labour members of the Cabinet refused to abandon their working-class constituency to the demands of the bankers and economic experts. Unable to agree on a policy, the MacDonald government resigned.

Throughout the 1920s the lack of strong leadership, the absence of well-defined issues, and the existence of three political parties made the idea of coalition attractive. In this crisis another political coalition seemed the way to obtain national unity in the face of economic disaster. King George V asked MacDonald and Baldwin to form a coalition government, perhaps the last time a monarch played an important role in the political process. To the surprise of his Labour party colleagues, MacDonald agreed and was expelled from his party. Although most Liberals and a few Labour members of Parliament supported the National Coalition Government, the Conservatives were dominant.

The National Government was pledged to maintain the gold standard, but as international bankers feverishly converted their sterling balances into gold it became necessary to suspend payments. A peaceful mutiny in the navy—really a strike—persuaded the government to limit the proposed cuts in the pay of the armed forces, the police, and the teachers. The National Government called an election in October 1931 in which it asked the voters for a "doctor's mandate." The result was a sweeping victory over the Labour party, shattered by MacDonald's "betrayal" and the impact of devastating unemployment. The next year Neville Chamberlain succeeded where his father had failed when the National Government abandoned Britain's historic free trade policy and introduced a protective tariff. Britain's most distinguished economist, the Liberal John Maynard Keynes, advocated increased government spending to "prime the pump," policies adopted by Franklin D. Roosevelt in the New Deal but anathema to Britain's Conservatives. Furthermore, British dependence on foreign exchange and trade made this approach less viable than in the United States. Thus Britain floundered while the world sank into economic depression and eventually another world war.

Life in the Twenties. The 1920s bear some resemblance to the Restoration. After a period of high idealism and great sacrifices the trendsetting elements of society placed more emphasis on personal pleasure and sensual gratification. This new attitude was seen in the "flappers," young women who defied conventions about dress and behavior and who, it was sus-

London flappers, 1925 *(BBC Hulton Picture Library)*.

pected, violated the conventional prohibition of premarital sex. The flappers cultivated a boyish appearance, with breasts flattened, slender figures, bobbed hair, skirts just below the knee, flesh-colored silk stockings, high-heeled shoes, bold lipstick, rouge-tinted cheeks, bare arms, and rejection of the whalebone corset that had confined the bodies of proper Victorian women. Slenderness became an enduring feminine ideal, which condemned to diets the full-figured women considered beauties in the Edwardian era.

Despite obtaining the vote, women exercised little political influence after the war. For young, middle-class women social and economic changes mattered more. Though women failed to keep their wartime industrial jobs, many continued to work in offices and retail establishments. Their social freedom grew in relatively superficial things, such as smoking in public, and in more fundamental matters, such as having smaller families. Acceptance of contraception, at least among the comfortable classes, owed much to the efforts of Dr. Marie Stopes, author of *Married Love* (1918) and founder in 1921 of Britain's first birth-control clinic.

American influences were important in the development of a more open and less-inhibited life-style. Jazz bands became fashionable for dancing, and the American practice of smoking cigarettes conquered the country. Hollywood films contributed to American influence in slang, dress, and manners, as attending the cinema became a ritual with all classes of society. Another American practice that took root in Britain was the newspaper gossip column, which tyrannized public figures to titillate the many.

In contrast, radio (the "wireless") created a new, distinctively British institution. Radio became a monopoly controlled by a semiautonomous institution, the British Broadcasting Corporation (BBC), chartered by the government. Though criticized as stuffy, puritanical, and paternalistic, the BBC established high standards in broadcasting, unencumbered by commercials. The BBC acted as a middle-class schoolmaster by letting its audience have what was good for them, introduced by announcers with impeccable upper-class accents.

The working class acquired recreations more to their own taste with the rapid growth of professional sports, especially Association Football (soccer) and boxing. Horse racing, greyhound racing, and football pools fostered the British mania for betting.

The Thirties

The National Government. The National Government organized in 1931 was formed to preserve the gold standard and free trade; within a year it had abandoned both. It was supposed to bring together the ablest individuals from all parties to deal in a nonpartisan way with the financial and economic crisis. In fact it was led by mediocrities: the well-meaning but increasingly fuzzy-minded MacDonald, the steady but uninspiring Baldwin, and the hard-working Neville Chamberlain. The two most dynamic men in public life, David Lloyd George and Winston Churchill, were not asked to join because lesser men feared their energy, persuasiveness, and ambition. Despite its Labour prime minister, the National Government was dominated by Baldwin and the Conservatives, and its adoption of a protective tariff in 1932 caused many of the more independent-minded Liberal and Labour members to withdraw.

The National Government's first priority was financial retrenchment. It balanced the budget in 1931 by cutting social programs, the pay of public employees, and unemployment benefits. The National Government adopted no massive program of public works to create employment, as was done in the United States under Franklin D. Roosevelt. A few innovative economists, such as John Maynard Keynes, and a few politicians proposed that the government organize or plan economic development. In 1934 the government tried to persuade industrialists to locate factories

Hunger marchers, 1936 *(BBC Hulton Picture Library)*.

in especially depressed areas, and it made small grants to subsidize training centers and other services to the unemployed. In addition, private schemes of "rationalization" were encouraged to reduce production in the most afflicted industries by closing old and inefficient plants. The Conservatives served their landed constituency by organizing agricultural marketing boards and showed their interest in the middle class by lower interest rates, which made it easier for house buyers to get mortgages.

The major problem of the National Government was the millions of men and women for whom the depression of the 1930s meant unemployment, poverty, frustration, and crumbling self-respect. Even in good times working-class life was a grinding struggle to get by, often with the help of the neighborhood pawnshop and credit at the local shops. In 1932 nearly three million people were unemployed, and even after the worst was over almost two million people remained unemployed. The north of England, industrial Scotland, and northern Ireland suffered most. These areas depended heavily on declining industries—textiles, shipbuilding, coal—which had been losing ground to foreign competition even before the collapse of the world market. The young moved away or lived on the dole in poverty and idleness. In 1931, as part of its economy drive, the National Government reduced the number of weeks for unemployment insurance benefits, cut the dole and excluded most married women from it, and subjected the dole to the unpopular household means test, which reduced payments when any member of the household received any income.

Despite unemployment, extremist political movements failed to attract mass support. Sir Oswald Mosley, an eccentric aristocrat who was once a Labour minister, organized the British Union of Fascists in 1932 but had few working-class followers. Within a few years the anti-Semitism and brutality of his Blackshirts also repelled middle-class sympathizers. Working-class militants rallied behind the National Unemployed Workers' Movement in which Communists provided much of the leadership. Hunger marches from the distressed areas to London dramatized the plight of the unemployed, but the marchers never reached a revolutionary size. Though bitter about the events of 1931 the Labour party remained committed to democratic, parliamentary institutions. The trade unions disliked radical intellectuals who talked about a socialist dictatorship and a proletarian state. In 1935 a dedicated and mild-mannered moderate, Clement Attlee, was chosen leader of the Labour party.

Revival and Renewal. The thirties were not entirely negative in British economic and social developments. The economic distress inflicted by the depression on certain areas and industries obscured a shift in the British economy away from the export-oriented heavy industries of the north to light manufacturing, retailing, and service industries in metropolitan London and nearby counties. Unemployment in those sectors of the economy that served the domestic market was lower, but most of the jobs paid low wages and trade unions were weak. The middle class grew in numbers, especially those who were salaried employees of central and local government or large business firms.

The cheapness of imported raw materials and food contributed to a modest economic revival in the midthirties. The prices of meat, grain, and cotton fell even more than prices for the manufactured goods that Britain sold abroad. Cheap building materials, low wages for construction workers, and low interest rates for mortgages stimulated housing. After 1932 the National Government stopped nearly all the subsidies that had enabled local councils to build houses for rental to working-class families. The construction industry became dominated by private contractors who built homes for sale to middle-class persons with secure jobs. Before World War I the middle class had usually rented the houses in which they lived; in the 1930s large numbers of them became homeowners.

The middle class and the more fortunate of the working class enjoyed new comforts in the 1930s, which contrasted with the poverty of those who subsisted on the dole. The industries that prospered in the 1930s produced consumer goods such as automobiles, radios, household appliances, and furniture. In 1930 there were about one million automobiles in Britain, and within the decade the figure doubled. Gas and electric cookers (stoves) replaced coal ranges. The electric power industry increased enormously to meet the needs of offices, shops, industries, and homes. Leisure became a profitable business. By the end of the 1930s paid annual vacations became common for working men, which were often taken at seaside resorts such as Brighton, Bournemouth, or Blackpool. The dream world of the cinema provided relaxation and escape. After the development of talking pictures in the late twenties, a quarter of the population went to film shows twice a week.

Appeasement and the Road to War. Ever since World War I British leaders and the public considered another such conflict as inconceivable. Britain looked to conciliatory diplomacy and the League of Nations to resolve international problems before they led to catastrophe. Early in 1933 two leaders came to power who were to have a great influence on Britain: Franklin D. Roosevelt was inaugurated as president of the United States and Adolf Hitler became chancellor of Germany. Hitler quickly established himself as a dictator and began his long-stated plans to rearm Germany, undo the Versailles settlement, and make Germany the dominant power of Europe. Ever since 1919 British leaders had regarded the Versailles Treaty as needlessly harsh toward Germany, but efforts to modify the Treaty had foundered on French determination to keep Germany weak and defenseless. Although the British view might have been helpful in the 1920s, when Germany was governed by a democratic republic, such an approach became suicidal when Germany came under Hitler. Nevertheless, Britain tried to avoid war by redressing German grievances, a policy known as "appeasement." Another reason for seeking good relations with Hitler was fear of the Soviet Union and Communism, sentiments especially strong among Conservatives. The situation was further complicated by Benito Mussolini, the Fascist dictator of Italy, who was at first a rival of Hitler and might become a valuable ally.

Hitler immediately began secretly arming Germany, and in 1935 he threw off the mask when he introduced national conscription. The French were in one of their frequent cabinet crises and did nothing; the British decided that Germany had as much right to an army as her heavily armed neighbors. Britain showed its good will by an Anglo-German naval agreement that permitted the Germans to increase the size of their navy. The British public began to feel uneasy about rising militarism in Europe, but Stanley Baldwin faced an election in 1935 and he ignored the issue so that voters might not be unduly aroused. The Conservatives won the election handily, and Baldwin became prime minister.

In the meantime Mussolini attacked Ethiopia to expand his empire in Africa. Britain's delegate to the League of Nations, Anthony Eden, protested strongly against this violation of international law, but behind the scenes British and French diplomats considered it wiser to yield to Mussolini in order to gain his support against Hitler. Armed with modern weapons the Italians destroyed an Ethiopian army bearing spears and shields. The prestige of the League of Nations and the ideal of collective security had vanished.

In 1936 Hitler threw down the gauntlet when he sent German troops into the Rhineland and began to fortify the German border. If permitted, this action would prevent France from intervening in Germany or aiding her eastern European allies. Both France and Britain were preoccupied—the French were in the process of forming a new government, and Baldwin was confronted with a crisis in the royal family. The esteemed King George V died and the new king, Edward VIII (1936), wished to marry a glamorous American divorcee, Mrs. Wallis Warfield Simpson. Furthermore, the Germans had not invaded anyone; they were simply entering their own backyard. One of the few British political figures to sound the alarm concerning German intentions was Winston Churchill, but he was at this time viewed as a discredited maverick of extreme views, an opinion strengthened by his quixotic support of the king's desire to marry Mrs. Simpson. In any case, Baldwin forced the king to abdicate ("to marry the woman I love"). Edward VIII was succeeded by his brother who became King George VI (1936–1952). Churchill's warnings went unheeded. The next year Stanley Baldwin retired with the plaudits of a grateful nation. He was succeeded as prime minister by his longtime colleague, Neville Chamberlain.

By 1938 Hitler had rearmed and fortified Germany, and he turned to absorbing additional German-speaking areas into his Third Reich. In March 1938 he moved quickly to annex his homeland, Austria. In September he insisted on annexing the German-speaking part of Czechoslovakia, known as the Sudetenland. Chamberlain was determined to avoid war. He thought that one more bold, generous act might convince Hitler that all reasonable German grievances would be redressed. While war hysteria gripped Britain Chamberlain met with Hitler, Mussolini, and the French premier at Munich. Hitler was given the Sudetenland, the Czechs were told to yield, and Chamberlain returned to a cheering crowd, announcing that he brought "peace in our time." A sense of relief swept over the nation, but the feeling remained that a showdown had only been delayed. Chamberlain accelerated the process of British rearmament. When Hitler took over the rest of Czechoslovakia the next spring, Chamberlain made treaties with other threatened states of eastern Europe and announced that further German aggression would mean war.

As the European crisis grew the Labour party had little to offer in the way of constructive criticism. Although they hated Hitler, Mussolini, and the Japanese militarists, the Left was firmly opposed to war and distrusted the Baldwin government. In principle the Labour party favored strong action against an aggressor through the League of Nations or a collective security agreement in which Russia would take part. They opposed rearmament, for they believed that armaments led to war. Some on the political Left were pacifists, holding that war was never justified. The Left was profoundly affected by a civil war that broke out in Spain in 1936. Generalissimo Francisco Franco, the Fascist leader of conservative forces in Spanish life, led an uprising to overthrow the Spanish republic, which was controlled by democratic and socialist groups supported by Communists. Hitler and Mussolini sent aid to Franco, which aroused the British Left to fury and persuaded some that a war against Fascism was justifiable and inevitable.

A major factor in the European scene was the Soviet Union, which was viewed by the British and French governments as a threat as dangerous as Germany. Soviet participation in the crisis over Czechoslovakia was refused. By 1939, however, Britain decided to seek Soviet support in resisting further aggression by Hitler, who made it clear that he was determined to reclaim German territories given to Poland at Versailles. Stalin was doubtful of Britain's determination or ability to fight. While negotiations with Britain proceeded, he secretly agreed with Hitler to partition Poland. In August the German-Soviet Pact was announced, and, on September 1, 1939, Hitler's forces attacked and quickly overran Poland. Britain and France declared war on Germany, although there was little they could do. Two weeks later Stalin invaded Poland to take his share. World War II had begun.

World War II

The Phony War and Norway. When Britain and France declared war they took up defensive positions and watched apprehensively as the German blitzkrieg (lightning war) ran roughshod over the Poles. The French had drawn the conclusion from World War I that modern weaponry gave the advantage to the defensive. They based their military planning on vast fortifications along the Franco-German border called the Maginot Line. The border with Belgium was not fortified because the French planned to enter Belgium when war was declared and to fight the Germans there. The area around Luxembourg known as the Ardennes was rough and wooded; this line was lightly held on the assumption that a modern army could be easily stopped in such rugged country. The British, who were reluctant to fight a land war on the continent at all, accepted the French plan, and when war was declared they sent an expeditionary force to join the French

Evacuation of London children, 1940 *(BBC Hulton Picture Library)*.

along the Belgian border. Since the Belgians did not want to fight at all, the Allies were not permitted to cross the border to take up defensive positions.

In the meantime the British had been preparing for a different kind of war. No nation believed more strongly that air power would be the decisive factor in modern warfare. The Royal Air Force emphasized big bombers, giving secondary attention to fighter planes such as the Spitfire and Hurricane. It was a truism among British military planners that "the bomber will always get through," and for this reason the Chamberlain government gave priority to defense against German air raids. They built bomb shelters and evacuated from London and other large cities more than a million children, mothers of small children, pregnant women, and teachers. When the bombs did not immediately fall most of the evacuees drifted back from the countryside and small towns where they had been sent. Middle-class families who took in working-class children were shocked by lice, skin diseases, flimsy clothing, cheap shoes, and bad language. This experience contributed to the national determination that all children should be better cared for.

The only important military actions taken were the result of the energy of Winston Churchill, who was finally admitted to the Chamberlain government as first lord of the Admiralty. Churchill put the fleet into motion, blockading Germany and seeking means to cut off German imports of Swedish iron ore that was shipped out of the Norwegian port of Narvik and along the Norwegian coast. Hitler forestalled Churchill's plans by a sudden invasion of Norway and Denmark in April 1940. The British landed forces to aid Norwegian resistance, but in vain. Churchill's first venture was a dismal failure that brought back memories of Gallipoli. Blame for the defeat fell on Chamberlain, and when a vote in the House of Commons showed a serious loss of support among members of his own party Chamberlain resigned. Churchill, whose vigor and pugnacity could not be denied, became prime minister in May, just as the Germans fell with full fury upon France and the Low Countries.

A year earlier Churchill had been considered an ageing has-been, his vigorous opposition to appeasement dismissed as a sign of his chronic aggressiveness. Churchill had no doubt that he was the right man to lead Britain. His bulldog-like chin, his cigar, and his fingers raised in a V-for-victory salute made him the wartime image of John Bull. He came to symbolize his country's courage, stubbornness, and zest for life. In the crisis year of 1940 he offered only "blood, sweat, toil, and tears." His carefully prepared speeches, delivered with an aristocratic lisp, brought home to the British people the gravity of the dangers they faced and instilled confidence in eventual victory. The prime minister spent most of his time on military and diplomatic affairs, with the Labour party ministers having a major influence on domestic matters. The leader of the Labour party, Clement Attlee, became deputy prime minister, and Ernest Bevin, leader of the Transport Union, took the lead in organizing the labor force for war as Minister of Labour. Their accomplishments during the war gave them prestige, which stood them in good stead when the war came to an end.

The Fall of France. In May 1940, the Germans attacked with highly mobile forces emphasizing tanks, motorized infantry, and dive bombers. As they rolled into the Low Countries the British and French forces moved into Belgium, as planned. They had walked into a trap. The German panzers (motorized forces) squeezed through the supposedly impassible Ardennes and dashed unobstructed across France, cutting off the Allied force from its base. The French army crumbled, the politicians fled in panic from Paris to the south, and the British decided the best thing to do was retreat to the ports along the Channel. Churchill made desperate efforts to en-

Winston Churchill during the Blitz, 1941 *(BBC Hulton Picture Library)*.

courage the French to renew their resistance in the south of France, for large French forces were still sitting useless in the Maginot Line, but all was in vain. Instead, a motley armada of warships, channel ferries, and small civilian boats evacuated about 225,000 British troops and over 100,000 Frenchmen from the port of Dunkirk. Britain had suffered a staggering defeat. Britain's army had lost most of its equipment, but her men were safely back on their island and their leader was full of fight. It was vitally important to Britain to control the sea, and in this respect the French fleet was important, for it must not fall into German hands. When the French in Algeria would not sail their warships to British ports the British navy entered the harbor of Oran and sank them. Many were killed. It was the ultimate deed in a bitter tragedy.

After Dunkirk Britain's concern was invasion by the triumphant German army. At first Hitler hoped that Britain would also cave in, but he failed to reckon with the defiant spirit of Winston Churchill and an aroused British people. When the British bombed Berlin Hitler ordered an invasion. As the British prepared to defend their island the key factor was air power, for without control of the air Hitler's armada could not sail. In July and August a desperate struggle took place over the Channel ("The Battle of Britain") as the pilots of the Royal Air Force, in their Spitfires and Hurricanes, threw back the German air force. In September Hitler called off invasion plans and began preparations to attack the Soviet Union instead.

The Blitz. With German invasion plans checked, Air Marshall Hermann Göring assured Hitler that the resistance of the stubborn British could be broken by bombing. The German "Blitz," as the British called it, began in September 1940 and continued through May 1941. London was the main target, although other cities were hard hit. When German planes became easier targets during daylight bombing, the Germans turned to bombing at night, their bombers following the silvery Thames to the target, which was lighted by fires set by incendiary bombs.

The Germans made one out of six Londoners homeless, and the government had to organize emergency shelter, clothing, and meals. Bombs tore up gas and electric lines; air raids and false alarms disrupted industrial production. Thousands worked by day in essential war industries and spent their nights as wardens watching from the rooftops and putting out fires. Those who were easily frightened left London, which perhaps explains why morale did not break. Thousands of Londoners huddled night after night in the underground stations, where musicians and entertainers brightened the scene. The East End slums near the docks were hit hard, but no place was safe. King George VI and Queen Elizabeth remained in London throughout the war, sharing the experiences of their subjects when Buckingham Palace was hit. Other industrial towns were bombed, with surprisingly little effect on war production. Production of tanks in Coventry returned to normal within six weeks of a devastating raid. The Germans also bombed places without military importance, such as the cathedral town of Canterbury. The Blitz fostered national unity and determination to resist, for all were in it together.

Britain Fights Back. As soon as Churchill knew that Britain was safe from invasion he looked for a place to fight back, which was provided by Hitler's inept ally, Benito Mussolini. After the defeat of France Mussolini attacked Greece, and his forces in Libya attacked Egypt. Churchill sent all available forces he could spare to Egypt, and the Italians were driven pell-mell back to where they came from. It seemed that Mussolini might lose his entire North African empire. When Mussolini's forces were stopped by the Greeks, Churchill rashly diverted British forces from North Africa to Greece, which brought down upon them Hitler's panzers, who for a second time drove the British into the sea. Hitler sent General Erwin Rommel and his *Afrika Korps* to aid Mussolini in North Africa. In 1941 Rommel drove the weakened British forces back to Egypt in a masterful display of blitzkrieg.

American Aid. In the meantime there were more pressing problems. German submarines were sinking British ships faster than they could be replaced, and Britain faced starvation. In the United States President Franklin D. Roosevelt decided that Britain could not be permitted to fall, but in 1940 he was locked in a presidential campaign and was opposed by powerful isolationist forces. From the time he became prime minister Churchill engaged in a frank correspondence with Roosevelt, making clear Britain's desperate situation. In the summer of 1940, when German invasion loomed, Roosevelt cleared out U.S. arsenals and sent thousands of rifles to Britain. Later in the year he arranged the transfer of fifty overage destroyers to aid the British navy in fighting submarines. Early in 1941, after the election, Roosevelt proposed Lend-Lease, by which the United States would send war supplies to Britain without cost. It was useless to provide Lend-Lease goods that would be sent to the bottom of the ocean by submarines, so the U.S. navy provided convoys for British merchant ships. Thus Britain was able to survive and to hope for a better day.

Britain's prospects changed dramatically in 1941, for Hitler attacked the Soviet Union in June and Japan attacked the United States on December 7. The Japanese onslaught brought heavy blows to Britain in the loss of Hong Kong, Malaya, and the great naval base at Singapore. The security of Australia and India was threatened. Shortly after Pearl Harbor Churchill travelled to Washington, D.C., where the United Nations Alliance was proclaimed. British and American military staffs met and decided to give primary attention to the war in Europe while holding the line against Japan.

The American generals wanted to build up a large force in Britain for a head-on invasion of the continent, but Churchill, fearing a repetition of the stalemate of World War I, urged an attack on Germany and Italy through the Mediterranean. Since the United States was not ready to invade Hitler's empire, Churchill's strategy was adopted and the decision was made for an offensive in North Africa. In November 1942 an Allied army commanded by General Dwight D. Eisenhower landed in French North Africa. A month earlier the British Eighth Army in Egypt, under General Bernard Montgomery, broke through Rommel's lines at El Alamein and drove across the desert to link up with the main Allied force. Hitler sent large reinforcements, and, when his army in North Africa surrendered in May 1943, he suffered a serious defeat with heavy losses.

General Bernard L. Montgomery *(The Bettmann Archive)*.

Allied Conferences. In January 1943 victory was in sight in North Africa, the Russians had trapped a German army at Stalingrad, the submarine menace was coming under control, and the United States had taken the first step on the long road back in the Pacific with a victory at Guadalcanal. Roosevelt and Churchill met at Casablanca to plan their next moves. Roosevelt announced that the goal of the Allies was the "unconditional surrender" of the enemy. Despite American desire for a direct attack on Germany through France, it was decided to continue in the Mediterranean by invading Sicily and then Italy. In November 1943 Roosevelt and Churchill met with Stalin at Tehran. By this time the Red Army had taken the offensive, and Stalin complained that the western Allies had let the Russians do most of the fighting. He was promised that the great invasion of Hitler's Reich would come in the spring of 1944. After the conference General Eisenhower was named supreme allied commander, and preparations for the invasion began in earnest.

Victory. In the first half of 1944 vast Allied forces assembled in Britain for the invasion. It was remarked that all that kept the island from sinking under the weight were the barrage balloons. On June 5 it was announced that Allied forces in Italy had entered Rome. The next day General Eisenhower's forces landed in Normandy, and for six weeks a bitter struggle took place in the hedgerows. The artificial harbors, or "mulberries," developed by British engineers allowed the Allies to unload huge quantities of supplies without the control of a major seaport. At the end of July German resistance broke, and the Allied armies raced across France and into Belgium. In August American and Free French forces from Italy landed in southern France and swept up the Rhone Valley to join with the main Allied armies. The smell of victory was in the air. Then the attack stalled as German resistance stiffened and supply lines lengthened. General Montgomery tried to shorten the war by dropping paratroopers into the Netherlands, but his plan failed. In December Hitler assembled his last resources and counterattacked through the Ardennes, which, despite the lesson of 1940, were lightly defended. "The Battle of the Bulge" was frightening but in actuality provided the Allies with the opportunity to wipe out Hitler's last army. In the meantime the Russians rolled up great gains on the eastern front.

Another part of Allied strategy was a massive bombing attack on Germany. The British bombed by night, attacking population centers. The Americans bombed by day, seeking targets related to the German war effort but in most instances bombing the general population too. After the war a careful study of the results of bombing showed, as in Britain, that its effect on war production was modest. German morale held strong to the bitter end. Late in 1944 and early in 1945 the Germans struck back at

The Normandy landings *(The Bettmann Archive)*.

British civilians with the V-l, a pilotless plane or buzz bomb. This was followed by the V-2, a rocket that could be neither seen nor heard. These "vengeance weapons" had no effect on the outcome of the war, but they killed a considerable number of people and a large number of homes were destroyed before the Allies captured the launching sites. They were forerunners of the awesome missiles of today.

In March 1945, the western Allies invaded Germany in overwhelming force while the Russians drove toward Berlin. German resistance collapsed and, facing capture by the Russians, Hitler committed suicide. A few days later the Germans surrendered unconditionally. The war in the Pacific continued until August when two atom bombs persuaded Japan, which was already beaten, to surrender. Although the atom bombs were built and dropped by the Americans, British scientists played a major role in their development.

Churchill had led Britain through her darkest hours and to her greatest victory. In June 1945 it was time for an election, for the electoral process had been suspended during the war. The British people admired Churchill as a war leader, but they did not see him as the man who could fulfill their aspirations for the postwar world. The Labour party was led by Clement Attlee, whose service in the Cabinet during the war had gained widespread

British Involvement in World War II

respect. Other Labour party leaders had shown leadership and a capacity for government. The Labour party promised a better Britain for all while Churchill campaigned poorly, railing against the dangers of socialism. The result was a landslide victory for Labour. Churchill resigned and was replaced by Clement Attlee and a Labour government. The United States also had a new leader, for President Roosevelt, Churchill's friend and Britain's powerful ally, died in April 1945 and was succeeded by Vice-President Harry Truman. By this time the wartime cooperation of the western Allies and the Soviet Union was dissolving in quarrels and recriminations. The joy of victory was replaced by the bitterness of the Cold War.

Suggestions for Further Reading

The period of the two wars is covered in an outstanding volume in the *Oxford History of England* by A. J. P. Taylor entitled *English History, 1914–1945* (1965). Good surveys are W. N. Medlicott, *Contemporary England, 1914–1964* (1967), Robert Blake, *The Decline of Power, 1915–1964* (1985), Max Beloff, *Wars and Welfare in Britain, 1914–1945* (1984), and Bentley Gilbert, *Britain Since 1918* (2nd edition, 1980).

Britain's role in World War I must be studied in relation to other combatants. Cyril Falls, *The Great War, 1914–1918* (1959) is a good introduction to the conflict. See also Ian F. W. Beckett and Keith Simpson, *A Nation in Arms: A Social Study of the British Army in the First World War* (1985). The social influences of World War I are presented in Arthur Marwick, *The Deluge: British Society and the First World War* (1965) and *Women at War, 1914–1918* (1977) and in J. M. Winter, *The Great War and the British People* (1986).

Britain's foreign policy can be followed in W. N. Medlicott, *British Foreign Policy since Versailles, 1919–1963* (2nd edition, 1968), Bernard Porter, *Britain in Europe and the World, 1850–1982: Illusions of Grandeur* (1983), and F. S. Northedge, *The Troubled Giant: Britain among the Great Powers, 1916–1939* (1967).

Studies that deal with key aspects of British policies prior to World War II are Arnold Wolfers, *Britain and France between Two Wars* (1940) and Martin Gilbert, *Britain and Germany Between the Wars* (1964). On "appeasement" see Martin Gilbert, *The Roots of Appeasement* (1967) and William R. Rock, *British Appeasement in the 1930s* (1977).

The best general history of the interwar period is Charles L. Mowat, *Britain Between the Wars, 1918–1940* (1955). Good surveys of social history are Arthur Marwick, *Britain in the Century of Total War, 1900–1967* (1968) and John Stevenson, *British Society, 1914–1945* (1984). Interesting accounts of life and manners are Robert Graves and Alan Hodges, *The Long Weekend: A Social History of Great Britain, 1918–1939* (1940) and two books by Noreen Branson, *Britain in the Nineteen Twenties* (1975) and (with Margot Heinemann) *Britain in the Nineteen Thirties* (1971). Two important studies of the mass media are Stephen Koss, *The*

Rise and Fall of the Political Press in Britain, Vol. II (1984) and Asa Briggs, *History of Broadcasting in the United Kingdom* (4 vols., 1961–1979).

World War II spawned an enormous body of military history and personal memoirs, the first of which was the splendid work by Winston Churchill entitled *History of the Second World War* (6 vols., 1948–1954). A thoughtful work by one of Britain's best military historians is J. F. C. Fuller, *The Second World War, 1939–1945* (1959). Good general books are Henry Pelling, *Britain and the Second World War* (1970), Angus Calder, *The People's War: Britain, 1939–1945* (1969), and Arthur Marwick, *The Home Front: The British and the Second World War* (1977).

Harold Nicholson, *King George the Fifth, His Life and Reign* (1952), has written a fine biography of King George V (1951) and J. W. Wheeler-Bennett, *King George VI, His Life and Reign* (1958), of King George VI (1958). For the life of Lloyd George see biographies by Thomas Jones, *Lloyd George* (1951), Peter Rowland, *David Lloyd George: A Biography* (1975), and John Grigg, *Lloyd George, the People's Champion, 1902–1911* (1978). The remarkable career of Winston Churchill spans the period. The official biography is by Randolph Churchill, continued by Martin Gilbert. Pelling's *Winston Churchill* (1974) is a useful one-volume overview.

17

Recovery and Crises

1945–1979

Worland War II transformed Britain more completely than any event since the Norman Conquest. Two superpowers, the United States and the Soviet Union, dominated the world. Britain was now a second-rank power, diplomatically and economically. She could no longer hold her empire. Britain's political institutions had again proved their worth, but her people had changed. They were concerned less with Britain's place in the world and more with making a good life for all in their island home. Perhaps the sacrifices of two world wars had taught them an important lesson.

The Labour Government, 1945–1951

Austerity. The Labour government, led by Clement Attlee, came to office with an agenda of reform developed in the 1920s and 1930s, but for most of their six years in office they were confronted with the problem of survival in a world that had changed drastically to Britain's disadvantage. A multitude of financial and economic problems confronted Labour. Britain had diverted most of the country's economy into wartime production, relying on Lend-Lease from the United States to supply food and other essential goods for her population. Most of the country's civilian economy was gone, and what was left was obsolete or bombed to pieces. The task of reconstruction was enormous, especially since American assistance was no longer available. When World War II ended with the defeat of Japan, the Americans suddenly forgot the mutual sacrifices of war, stopped Lend-Lease, and required Britain to pay in dollars for everything they imported from the United States. With difficulty the British negotiated a large American loan only to see the money they had borrowed shrink rapidly

Ernest Bevin and Clement Attlee *(The Bettmann Archive/BBC Hulton).*

because of postwar inflation. When the Cold War convinced the American public that it needed strong European allies, the United States offered substantial aid for reconstruction. In 1947 the American secretary of state, General George Marshall, proposed that aid be given for the reconstruction of Europe, and in 1948 the Marshall Plan began to pump billions of dollars of assistance into Britain and other war-ravaged European countries.

Britain had enormous material needs. German bombs had destroyed or damaged hundreds of thousands of homes and during the war ordinary construction and repair had been suspended. British industry had been distorted by the war: the peacetime aircraft industry, which had produced more than 20,000 planes a year, had excess productive capacity. Britain had lost many of her prewar markets to competitors, and other former customers had no way of paying. Only the United States could supply much of the manufactured goods, raw materials, and food that Britain needed, and these imports required dollars that Britain did not have.

The British people had fought in hope of a better life, not merely for a return to prewar conditions. Perhaps only a party identified with the working class could have obtained acceptance of the sacrifices that the postwar years required. Bread and potatoes were briefly rationed, which had never happened during the war when American Lend-Lease provided many of Britain's needs. Meat was rationed until the mid-1950s. In the late 1940s declining productivity in the mines, a shortage of railroad cars to move the coal, and an exceptionally severe winter combined to create a desperate fuel shortage. Factories had to be closed in 1947 for lack of fuel, idling millions of workers and undercutting the effort to export goods overseas. The use of electricity at home was prohibited between nine and noon and between two and four in the afternoon. In a new kind of black-out street lights were turned off and the BBC suspended its fledgling television service.

In November 1947 Sir Stafford Cripps became chancellor of the exchequer. This intense, austere man preached self-denial with religious fervor. He continued the wartime rationing and, to curtail consumption further, he let prices rise. In 1949 Cripps devalued the pound by about 30 percent, which made exports cheaper and imports more expensive. Lacking dollars to buy from the United States, Cripps had to depend largely on products from the Empire, where the pound sterling was still the medium of exchange. Consequently he downplayed any British role in European economic cooperation that might weaken the sterling bloc.

Nationalization and Welfare. The Labour government came to office pledged to socialism and the welfare state. By socialism they meant public ownership of selected basic industries, and the process of nationalization proceeded systematically. Most British industries were in desperate condition and required massive investment that only the government could provide. The Bank of England, which had long served as a quasi-public institution, was nationalized, giving the government full control of the supply of money and credit. Public ownership of the fragmented and inefficient coal industry raised the hope that its productivity and labor-management relations might improve. Electricity, gas, railroads, scheduled airlines, overseas cables, buses, and most long distance trucking also were brought under national ownership. The old owners were compensated. Some of them, such as the gas companies, had been municipal authorities.

There was little change in the operation of the nationalized firms. Semi-autonomous public boards, largely recruited from the old managers, ran the public industries; workers and consumers had little influence. The work force was not incorporated in the civil service so that strikes to enforce wage demands were legal. Morale did not improve, and the problem of absenteeism continued. One argument for nationalization was to provide funds for modernization, but in the distressed circumstances of the time capital investment had to be delayed to meet the costs of national reconstruction. Furthermore, the workers wanted steady employment doing what they had been doing, not modernization that might reduce jobs and change their cherished and inefficient work rules. In general the Conservatives had little complaint about the industries that the Labour government nationalized. These industries were old and inefficient, with a dubious future. The Labour government found that it had engaged in "lemon socialism," nationalizing problem industries to preserve jobs while the private sector looked for better opportunities elsewhere.

The major controversy over nationalization arose when the Labour government attempted to nationalize the iron and steel industry. Labour wanted at least one industry under public control that had a chance for economic success. Iron and steel was a basic industry, and it needed government help for expansion and modernization. Since it took the Labour government several years to develop a specific plan, it feared that the House of Lords might use its powers to postpone the nationalization bill beyond the next general election. For this reason the government passed legislation reducing the power of the Lords to delay bills passed by the Commons to a single year. The industry was finally nationalized in 1951, but then the Conservatives came to power and repealed the legislation.

The other major objective of the Labour government was to establish the welfare state, by which they meant a combination of compulsory insurance and free services to meet the basic needs of the people "from the cradle to the grave." The social welfare legislation that the Labour party enacted affected the lives of ordinary people more than did the nationalization of a few industries. Since these reforms grew out of a national consensus the Conservative party did not oppose the Labour proposals in principle. Improved insurance schemes offered incomes for the elderly, the unemployed, the sick, and the victims of industrial accidents. For those inadequately provided for by the insurance system there was a catchall program of national assistance. The cost of these welfare services exceeded that of previous social programs far less than was expected. In the 1930s massive unemployment had cost large sums for the dole and other forms of relief. Labour's policy of full employment saved this money, which could be spent on other public services.

The creation of a free National Health Service was the most popular of the new social programs with the ordinary public. It was also the most controversial because of the opposition of the medical profession, and in the long run it was the most difficult to finance. Beginning in 1948 British residents became entitled to free medical, dental, and hospital care as well as free drugs, eyeglasses, and dentures. The minister of health, Aneurin Bevan, the eloquent, hot-tempered leader of the Labour left wing, had difficulty persuading the British Medical Association to cooperate. Though the specific disputes concerned how doctors would be compensated, the physicians disliked any lay control over the practice of medicine. The system adopted was for individuals to sign up with general practitioners for their basic medical care. The general practitioners would refer them to specialists as needed. Doctors were permitted to engage in private practice in addition to the work they did for the National Health Service. In its early years the National Health Service was swamped by a vast backlog of unmet medical needs, and there were great shortages of medical resources. Although individuals abused the system, it provided far better medical care than the British people had received under private medicine. In later years the hospitals provided the greatest problem for the National Health Service. Most were old but expensive to replace, and their staff complained of low pay, long hours, and poor conditions.

Labour's Foreign Policy. With the end of World War II, Britain's foreign policy situation was changed: the United States and the Soviet Union dominated world affairs and Europe was divided and devastated. The Soviet Union established control over eastern Europe and encouraged Communist parties in western Europe to foment revolution and to support the foreign policy of the Kremlin. The British foreign secretary, Ernest Bevin, was a tough-minded union leader who had fought Communists for years in the labor movement. When the Cold War broke out between the United States and the Soviet Union, Bevin led Britain into alliance with the United States. Led by Bevin, Britain joined the United States and France in resisting a Russian blockade of the allied enclave in West Berlin through an airlift of vital supplies. In 1949 Britain became a charter member of the North Atlantic Treaty Organization, the military alliance that opposed the Russians in Europe. As Socialists, many members of the Labour party, for ideological reasons, tended to sympathize with the Soviet Union and to extenuate its brutal dictatorship and denial of personal freedoms. George Orwell's *Animal Farm* (1946) and *Nineteen Eighty-Four* (1948) were written to refute that pro-Soviet point of view.

Palestine was Bevin's bitter failure. He followed Britain's traditional pro-Arab policy despite the Jewish sympathies of the American government and many members of the Labour party. He attempted to restrict postwar Jewish immigration to the British-controlled territory even when that meant herding refugees from Hitler into new concentration camps. Serving as a buffer between the Arabs and the Jews in Palestine cost the British money and lives and confronted Britain with a problem to which there was no peaceful solution. Unable to work out a settlement, Britain withdrew from Palestine in 1948. In the war that followed the new state of Israel established its control over most of Palestine. This embittered the Arabs, who blamed their fate on Britain; Britain gained no credit with the Israelis.

India provided the Labour government with a triumph of principle, although the cost in Indian lives and social disruption was enormous. From early in the century successive British governments had gradually extended participation in government to the Indians. The crucial problem was the lack of unity in India, which was divided into countless castes, regions, nationalities, languages, and religions. Divisions were especially acute between the Moslems and the predominantly Hindu Congress party, which made it difficult for the British to withdraw without condemning the subcontinent to civil war. The leaders of the Congress party, Jawaharlal Nehru and Mohandas K. Gandhi, had refused to cooperate with Britain during World War II. In 1947 Lord Louis Mountbatten, the last viceroy of India, used the threat of unilateral withdrawal to persuade the Congress party and the Muslim League to agree to a partition: the Muslims were to form the new state of Pakistan and Congress was to take control of the non-Moslem parts of India. As a result, full-scale religious warfare was avoided, but hundreds of thousands died in communal riots and millions more fled to the part of the subcontinent assigned to their religion. When the dust settled, India and Pakistan existed as separate states, and native leaders held the political power formerly exercised by the British. But the population had paid a great price for this change of rulers.

The Labour party won another general election victory in 1950. The margin of victory was very narrow and a weary, divided ministry found it difficult to proceed. Cripps died and Ernest Bevin retired. Bitter disputes broke out in the Labour party in 1950 when Britain joined in the Korean War and supported the decision of the North Atlantic Treaty Organization to rearm West Germany as an ally against the Russians. To help finance these moves the Labour government imposed small charges on eyeglasses and dentures. Aneurin Bevan, devoted to his beloved National Health Service, resigned in protest at a government that placed the Cold War ahead of the well-being of its own people, thus depriving the government of one of its most dynamic leaders and the support of the Labour party's left wing. The Labour government forced a new election in 1951 in an effort to get a clear mandate to rule, but instead it lost a close election to the Conservatives, still led by Churchill and blessed with a corps of attractive younger leaders.

The fall of the Labour government in 1951 marked the end of the immediate postwar era. As a symbol of Britain's recovery the government organized a national celebration called the Festival of Britain. Modernistic buildings arose on the site of a bombed-out dock district on the South Thames to house a series of performances and exhibits. Britain was still threadbare, the streets still pockmarked with bomb craters, and the sausages had little meat in them, but the road to prosperity and a better life for all seemed open.

Recovery and Social Change

The Standard of Living. Despite Britain's underlying economic problems, since the 1950s the British people have enjoyed a rising standard of material comforts and a wide range of personal and social freedoms. Britain has shared in the benefits of the greatest period of economic growth the world has ever known. At moments of crisis newspaper headlines screamed about economic disaster, and sometimes government policies intended to strengthen the national economy pinched the average person, but ordinarily the problems of the economy troubled only the experts. Britain moved into an age of affluence for the majority with the comprehensive services and subsidies of the welfare state for everyone. Virtually full employment and improved wages struck hard blows at the prewar culture of poverty. By the middle 1950s a third of all the pawnshops that had flourished a generation earlier had closed for lack of customers.

British businessmen courted the increasingly prosperous mass market with intensive advertising and with installment credit for the purchase of television sets, refrigerators, and washing machines. Multiple-branch retail chains such as the Marks and Spencer clothing stores standardized quality at a high level and kept prices down. Self-service supermarkets replaced the numerous small shops that had made shopping a social occasion but far from efficient economically. New technologies created frozen foods, synthetic fabrics that were easy to wash, cheap plastics, and television.

The new products and the new stores eased the household burdens of women. Prepared foods attractively packaged simplified cooking, not a strong suit in England anyway, and the automatic washer, the laundromat, detergents, and permanent press fabrics greatly reduced the chores of washing and ironing. The rising proportion of women who married, usually at a young age, forced the civil service and the schools to abandon in the early 1950s the old rule that women retired when they married. Popular women's magazines reflected and reinforced the forces for change. In the early 1950s one magazine, *Woman*, added a million sales with a how-to format ranging from cookery to child rearing, cosmetics to sex.

Leisure changed greatly: there was more of it, more money was spent on it, and more of it was enjoyed at home or in cars, which were extensions of home. The television set quickly changed from a luxury to a necessity for all classes of the population. Television viewing took people out of the pubs, as the increase in the sale of bottled beer showed. At first the state-owned British Broadcasting Corporation, financed by license fees, enjoyed a monopoly. Beginning in 1955, the Independent Television Authority offered an advertising-financed alternative. It attracted many working-class and lower middle-class households away from the BBC with a schedule of light entertainment and American adventure and crime programs. Competition from television forced many cinemas to close, and the diversion of advertising revenues reduced the number of newspapers.

A Changing Society. Some people criticized the changes that were transforming British society. They complained that Britain was becoming Americanized and losing its national character. In the late 1950s and the early 1960s church membership declined drastically. The special English vice of gambling grew more conspicuous after 1960 when Parliament legalized gambling casinos and offtrack betting. The young, who had the most time and discretionary income to devote to leisure, developed a subculture in which recorded music played a prominent part. Helped by improved record players and inexpensive discs the record industry sold four times as many records as before the war. A climax of the frenetic years of social and cultural rebellion came in the middle and late 1960s. A young group of musicians and singers, the Beatles, represented the explosion of talent and defiance. Beginning in 1964 their vigorous music and Liverpool accents sold millions of records on both sides of the Atlantic. In 1965 the queen honored them for their contribution to exports by granting them membership in the Order of the British Empire.

Swinging London replaced the staid image of the British as old-fashioned and almost Victorian. Although reality lay somewhere between the old and new images, gaudy boutiques on Carnaby Street and King's Road, unisex clothing, long-haired males, and miniskirted girls provided outward signs of a new cult of revolt and material gratification in which the young acted as trendsetters. Pornographic books, magazines, and films and live sex shows grew commonplace. Though street solicitation was prohibited in 1956, prostitution itself was legal, and many brothels thinly disguised as saunas advertised in the newspapers. By the mid-1960s two out of three children born to mothers under twenty had been conceived out of wedlock. Before the decade ended homosexual acts and abortion

Shopping center in Croydon, Surrey *(E. A. Reitan)*.

The Beatles *(Michael Ochs Archives)*.

were legalized, and capital punishment was abolished. Respect for law and order declined; in 1965 only 79 policemen were victims of assault in Britain, but ten years later the number had grown to 2,835. The old rules often seemed forgotten.

Other social changes that developed more quietly had greater significance than pop singers and short skirts. In 1901 only a quarter of women aged twenty to twenty-four were married; by 1966, a majority were married. In 1911 only 14 percent of women who worked were married; in 1966, 55 percent worked. Between 1911 and 1966 the number of blue-collar workers remained comparatively stable, despite an increase in population, while white-collar workers increased by 176 percent. In 1948 there were fewer than two million private cars; in 1968, there were nearly eleven million. Though the proliferation of the automobile gave a new mobility to drivers it forced a reduction in railroad service and changed the countryside. In 1970 eighteen year olds received the right to vote, and another statute required employers, beginning in 1975, to pay women equal pay for the same work.

Education changed dramatically to meet the needs of a technological age and a decidedly different younger generation. By the standards of virtually every other industrial country it remained highly stratified by social class. Many boys from well-off families attended fee-charging private schools, misleadingly called public schools. Students in the state system were sorted out, on the basis of an examination taken at age eleven, between university-oriented grammar schools and other less prestigious schools. In the 1960s and 1970s comprehensive schools that offered both grammar school and other secondary school curricula were created in some towns. Higher education grew rapidly through the expansion of Oxford, Cambridge, and the Victorian "red brick" universities and by the establishment of new universities with handsome buildings and innovative curricula. An important new factor in higher education was the establishment of polytechnic schools that offered career-oriented programs. Government grants made possible a doubling of the number of full-time students in higher education from 1963 to 1970, but despite financial aid few working-class children continued their studies beyond their mid-teens.

A new problem with ominous implications for the future was the growth in racial tensions. One of the legacies of an empire was the emigration to Britain of hundreds of thousands of black people from the West Indies and Asians from India and Pakistan. In the late 1950s there were racial riots in the Notting Hill section of London. Recognizing the problems created by racial tensions, Parliament in 1963 passed the first of a series of Commonwealth Immigration bills, which made it difficult for immigrants to enter Britain from the nonwhite parts of the Commonwealth but allowed people from the white Commonwealth to immigrate with relative ease. A right wing Tory, Enoch Powell, called for the compulsory repatriation of nonwhites. Despite these problems, the nonwhite immigrants made a valuable contribution to the British economy. They were willing to keep their shops open late, they were indispensable to the operation of London Transport, and they added new foods, music, and customs to British life. Parliament also enacted a Race Relations Act to protect the nonwhites who had already settled in Britain from discrimination. By the middle 1970s one in every thirty-three inhabitants of the United Kingdom was nonwhite.

From the Old Politics to the New

The New Generation of Leaders. In the 1950s the problems spawned by World War II and its aftermath began to disappear, and there was a new

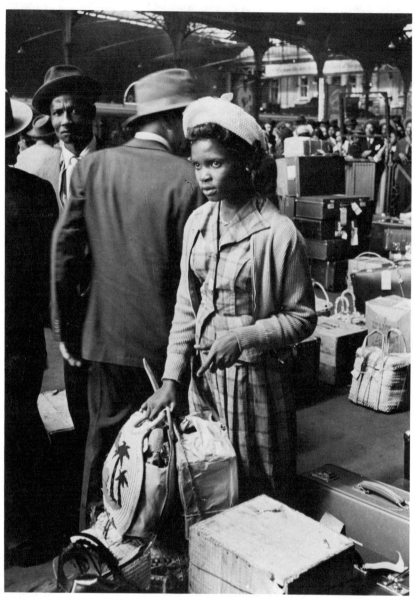

West Indian immigrant at Victoria Station, London *(BBC Hulton Picture Library)*.

sense of optimism in the air. The emergence of new leaders contributed to
the sense of change. In 1952 King George VI died, to be succeeded by
his daughter, Queen Elizabeth II (1952–present). Her impressive coronation in 1953 symbolized the emergence of a new era. In 1955 Winston
Churchill, who had been born in the age of Gladstone and Disraeli, retired
as prime minister. He was succeeded by the handsome, dapper Anthony
Eden, foreign secretary during World War II and in Churchill's second
administration. Clement Attlee, born in Mr. Gladstone's second ministry
and a veteran of Labour politics since the days of King Edward VII, retired to the House of Lords, a body he had long wished to abolish. After
a bitter struggle between moderates and left wingers, the Labour party
leadership went to Hugh Gaitskell, in some respects the embodiment of
the intelligent, forward-looking, pragmatic new generation of politicians
whose ideas were shaped not by the class conflicts of the past but by postwar political ideas and problems. Gaitskell's counterpart in the Conservative party was R. A. ("Rab") Butler. In a nonideological age when almost
everyone accepted Keynesian economics, moderate Labourites and moderate Conservatives supported a mixed economy that combined capitalism
in most industries with an active government role in the economy and
provision of a wide range of social services. This nonpartisan approach to
domestic policy was called "Butskellism." Gaitskell died and Butler was
passed over by his own party; thus neither of them became prime minister.

The Conservative government formed by Churchill in 1951 preserved
most of the achievements of the Attlee government, both in the nationalized industries and the welfare state. Of the nationalized industries only
iron and steel and long-distance trucking were sold back to private enterprise. Though the Conservatives established small fees for dentistry and
prescriptions, they accepted in principle the National Health Service financed by general taxation. They kept many wartime restrictions (meat
rationing continued until 1954) and retained rent control of most
working-class housing. They differed from Labour by enlarging the proportion of homes built for owner-occupiers. Thus continuity was maintained while the Conservatives reaped the benefit of an improving
economy.

Suez and the Illusion of World Power. While the Labour party emphasized
domestic policy, the Conservatives, who traditionally presented themselves
as the "patriotic" party, were in tune with most public opinion when they
sought to maintain Britain's place as a great power. Seeking to retain an
independent role in world affairs, the Churchill government rejected
membership in a proposed European Defense Community, an idea scut-
tled by the French two years later. Another symbol of great power status
was the first British atomic bomb, detonated in 1952. Conservative deter-

Coronation of Queen Elizabeth II, 1953 *(BBC Hulton Picture Library)*.

mination to retain an imperial role was shown when British soldiers crushed the Mau Mau terrorists in the East African colony of Kenya and Communist guerillas in Malaya. Britain's influence in the Middle East was damaged in 1952 when King Farouk of Egypt, in most matters a British puppet, was overthrown by Colonel Gamal Abdel Nasser, a charismatic prototype of many Third World leaders to follow. Under pressure from Nasser, the British left Egypt in 1954 in return for Nasser's guarantee of free navigation of the Suez Canal.

The Suez Crisis of 1956 shattered the myth of British power. When Nasser failed to get an American loan for a dam to exploit the waters of the Nile, he asked the Soviet Union for help and nationalized the canal. Then war broke out between Egypt and Israel. After the Israelis had routed the Egyptian army, the British and French sent troops into the former Canal Zone on the pretext that the war endangered the operation of the waterway. Anthony Eden, who had recently succeeded Churchill as prime minister, saw Nasser as a kind of Hitler, someone to be crushed before he became too dangerous. The United Nations and the Eisenhower administration denounced the Suez intervention as an act of aggression. Britain and France lost their nerve and dared not defy the United States and world opinion. They withdrew in humiliation, Nasser having already blocked the canal with sunken ships. Anthony Eden had a nervous breakdown and resigned as prime minister in 1957. His Conservative followers were aghast at the humiliation he had brought upon Britain and the Conservative government.

Harold Macmillan and the Restoration of Confidence. Eden's successor, Harold Macmillan, restored Conservative morale and public confidence. Born into a distinguished family of publishers, socially and educationally Macmillan came out of Britain's top drawer. He had distinguished himself in the 1930s as one of a progressive group of young Conservatives and an opponent of appeasement; he had served with distinction in a diplomatic role in World War II; and in the 1950s he emerged as a poised, shrewd, tough-minded political leader who always seemed in control of the situation. In the struggle for power in 1957 he shouldered aside his rival, R. A. Butler, who lacked Macmillan's ambition and determination. A newspaper cartoonist pictured Macmillan as "Supermac," a kind of Superman with moustache and drooping eyelids.

Under Macmillan's leadership the Conservative party again presented itself as the natural ruling party, led by practical men unbothered by the ideological disputes that characterized Labour. In the general election of 1959 Macmillan skillfully used television and national prosperity in his campaign, reminding the voters that they "never had it so good." The divided Labour party was badly beaten, and for the third successive election the Conservatives had increased their majority. The future of the Labour party appeared bleak.

Although the Conservative party was historically the advocate of imperialism, Macmillan presided urbanely over the dissolution of most of what remained of the British Empire. In 1960 he warned white South Africans that "The wind of change is blowing through this continent, and, whether we like it or not, this growth of national consciousness is a political fact." After Ghana became independent in 1957 Britain took steps to grant independence to Nigeria (1960) and other African colonies, Jamaica and other Caribbean possessions, Singapore, and Malaysia. The Central African Federation broke into its constituent parts, Rhodesia (now Zimbabwe), Zambia, and Malawi. The white regime in the Union of South Africa found the new Commonwealth uncongenial and left it.

Britain took pride in her role as leader of a multiracial family of nations, a bridge between the rich and the poor. The existence of the Common-

Harold Macmillan *(The Bettmann Archive/BBC Hulton)*.

wealth disguised the disintegration of the Empire and made it easier for the British to accept the new reality or ignore it. In practice the Commonwealth became little more than periodic conferences of prime ministers. The British hoped that they had firmly planted their own political institutions: government responsible to the people, a representative legislature, a nonpolitical civil service and judiciary, military institutions subject to civilian control, and freedom of the press—in short, constitutional government. The results of independence were often quite different: one-party states, charismatic dictatorships, military coups, and communal violence among religious, language, ethnic, and tribal groups. The English language and the British school system survived as factors unifying small ruling elites. Perhaps white-ruled Rhodesia provided the most telling example of Britain's inability to shape the futures of her former colonies. In 1965 the white settlers in the small southern African colony declared their independence to prevent Britain from imposing a government that gave control to the black majority. Despite many bitter words and an economic boycott, the white Rhodesians led by Ian Smith and supported by the Union of South Africa maintained their power until 1980, when a constitutional conference finally established the black-dominated state of Zimbabwe with special privileges for the white settlers.

In military affairs old views were swept away by recognition of new realities. Britain drastically reduced the number of men in uniform, ended conscription, and closed overseas bases. There were painful rows when historic regiments were amalgamated. The most divisive issue was Britain's development of nuclear weapons, an issue intensified in 1957 when Britain exploded a hydrogen bomb. An articulate and influential segment of British public opinion rejected nuclear weapons as immoral and demanded that Britain set an example by renouncing them. Thousands of men and women from all walks of life and representing a wide range of political opinions joined in the protest marches of the Campaign for Nuclear Disarmament. The debate was in one sense irrelevant, for Britain had nuclear warheads but she did not have an adequate missile to deliver them. In 1962, when the United States cancelled the development of a missile that Britain had decided to use for her nuclear warheads, the fact of dependence could not be avoided.

The European Economic Community. Despite the relative prosperity of the Macmillan years, the British economy failed to grow as rapidly as that of its neighbors. Property speculators and retail-chain entrepreneurs sometimes accumulated large fortunes. The lower middle class and working class bought second-hand cars and travelled on package tours to Spanish seaside resorts. But the standard of living in other countries grew faster. The European Economic Community (known as the Common Market) successfully combined the West European nations into a single economic system without barriers to trade among members. Britain refused to join the Common Market when it was formed in 1957, citing her "special relationships" with the United States and her Commonwealth. By 1960, however, those relationships were wearing thin, and the Macmillan government applied for membership.

Britain wanted to join the European Economic Community for political as well as economic reasons. Many anticipated that European economic unity would lead eventually to political unification. In an age of superpowers Britain could hope to count for something as part of a united Europe, but not alone. When the United States pulled the rug out at the time of the Suez Crisis, it was evident that Britain's ally of World War II was no longer reliable. Macmillan hoped that Britain would find a new sense of national power and purpose within the Common Market, but her application was vetoed in 1962 by President Charles DeGaulle of France, who was convinced that the British could never be good Europeans.

The Fall of the Tories. For Macmillan 1963 was the year of reckoning. His political magic was losing its potency, and in the preceding year he earned the nickname "Mac the Knife" by purging one third of his colleagues from the Cabinet. In 1963 a scandal broke growing out of an affair between John Profumo, the debonair secretary of state for war, and Christine Keeler, a young model who was also involved with a Russian naval officer. Profumo at first told the House of Commons that the charges were false, then admitted them and resigned. Investigations revealed that Profumo was part of an unsavory world of call girls, drugs, and violence. Although Macmillan was not personally involved, the episode communicated the image of decadence and incompetence in high places.

Later in the year a serious medical operation convinced Macmillan that he must resign as prime minister and leader of the Conservative party. Macmillan announced his retirement when the annual party conference was meeting, which added to the drama of the struggle for the succession. The Conservatives had no procedure for electing a leader, who traditionally had emerged out of a consensus of prominent party members. Most of the Cabinet probably favored R. A. Butler, but to general surprise Macmillan and other party leaders preferred the foreign secretary, the Earl of Home (pronounced Hume), even though he was a member of the House of Lords. A recent change in the law enabled Lord Home to renounce his title, becoming Sir Alec Douglas-Home, and thus he was eligible for election to the House of Commons. Macmillan's triumph in imposing Sir Alec as his successor was short-lived. The new prime minister was a competent, likeable man, but he was old-fashioned and out-of-touch. In the election called the next year (1964) Labour appeared to be the party with new leaders and new ideas. Hugh Gaitskell and his bitter rival, Aneurin Bevan, were both dead, and Harold Wilson had seized the reins. Wilson won a close contest, and the long Conservative dominance of British politics had ended.

Harold Wilson. Wilson attended grammar school, and he was educated in a state secondary school rather than in a prestigious public (i.e, private) school. Unlike Attlee and Gaitskell and nearly all the Conservative leaders who were part of the old elite of public school boys, Wilson represented the new meritocracy of men and women who climbed the scholarship route from grammar school to university. The son of a Yorkshire pharmacist, Wilson studied at Oxford, taught economics there, spent the war as a civil servant, and was elected to Parliament in the Labour landslide of 1945. A few years later he became the youngest member of Attlee's Cabinet, and in 1950 he was one of the left-wing ministers who followed Aneurin Bevan out of office. When Gaitskell's death made the leadership of the Labour party available, Wilson was the candidate of the left. Nevertheless, Wilson was a pragmatist who cared little about theoretical arguments. Supremely confident, he dominated his Cabinet, few of whom had any previous experience in office.

In the election of 1964 Labour barely defeated the Conservatives, but Wilson led as if his tiny majority had been ten times as large. He won the loyalty of Labour's socialists by boldly renationalizing the iron and steel industry. Otherwise, Wilson was the advocate of a new approach to managing the economy, using control of money, credit, and interest rates instead of Labour's traditional emphasis on public ownership. In 1966 Wilson called an election to strengthen his support in Parliament and was rewarded with a comfortable majority. The public saw Labour as the party of younger leaders with fresh ideas.

Harold Wilson was a political juggler who had to deal with a variety of contradictions as Britain moved into a different kind of world. He had to manage a national economy, the paramount goal of the Labour party, when Britain was increasingly dependent on the world economy. He had to win the support of the growing salaried class of white-collar workers while holding his political base in the wage-earning workers of the declining manufacturing industries. The welfare state was an established fact and one of Labour's most cherished achievements, but the nation was increasingly unable to pay for it. Britain had become a consumption-oriented society while productivity and competitiveness declined. In attempting to resolve these problems Wilson got a reputation for slipperiness, which was only partially deserved. Any other political leader would have to face the same problems, although some might have been more frank about them.

Although the unflappable Wilson seemed to know what he was doing,

Harold Wilson *(The Bettmann Archive)*.

his policies were undercut by the problems of the British economy. In 1967 he was forced to devalue the pound, an admission that the British economy was still weak in comparison with other industrial nations. To fight inflation the Wilson government used its control of the nationalized industries to cut back capital investment, hold down prices, and resist wage demands. The government supported drastic reductions of train service, despite the complaints of the unions and the public. Wilson proposed legislation to decrease the number of strikes by encouraging mediation and restricting wildcat strikes. Predictably, the trade unions, which were still the backbone of the Labour party, were opposed to Wilson's policy on strikes and forced the government to abandon this idea. A nation grown self-indulgent in the buoyant years of the early 1960s needed economic growth to sustain its standard of living, while Wilson's policies, despite his fair words, were a prescription for national discipline and cutbacks.

In 1970 Wilson called another election, which he expected to win. The new Conservative leader, Edward Heath, resembled Wilson in that he too was a grammar-school boy who attended Oxford on a scholarship, supplementing his income by playing the organ. During the war Heath strengthened his middle-class status by attaining the rank of colonel. He was handsome and earnest, and his sincerity at times made him dull. His campaign managers made effective use of television; Wilson was content to run on his reputation and to look thoughtful while puffing his pipe. In an election that "Americanized" political campaigning, Heath won an upset victory. Although Harold Wilson later returned to office, British politics would never be the same.

The Difficult Seventies

Edward Heath and the Politics of Growth. Heath took office committed to the view that Britain would have to abandon the nationalist policies which had characterized both parties, and come to grips with the need to compete in the world economy that had developed since World War II. Heath's goals were to preserve the standard of living gained since the war and to present the Conservative party as the guardian of the social programs that encouraged the wide sharing of prosperity. His prescription was economic growth, which would develop new industries and jobs while making it possible to maintain high levels of consumption and the security offered by the welfare state.

Heath's government recorded one great accomplishment: the successful negotiation of Britain's entry into the European Economic Community, effective on New Year's Day, 1973. It was a controversial decision. Some Conservatives disliked the sacrifice of national sovereignty. Within the Labour party socialists objected to joining a capitalistic economic entity, while trade unionists feared that their established powers and work rules would be eroded by partnership with nations that were less sympathetic to unions. Food prices rose as Britain accepted the protective agricultural policies of the Common Market, although British farmers, among the most efficient in Europe, benefited from policies aimed at supporting the small farms of France and West Germany. There were other changes that caused grumbling: the coinage was changed to a decimal system, metric weights and measures were greatly extended, and the Celsius (centigrade) temperature scale replaced Fahrenheit. Underlying the sense of unease created by Heath's policy was recognition that Britain was no longer master of her own destiny. The island people who had held out against Philip II, Louis XIV, Napoleon, and Hitler now found it necessary to capitulate to friendly but highly competitive rivals.

Heath found that his commitment to economic growth created great disruptions in the national life. The government allowed the money supply to increase rapidly to encourage investment; the result was profiteering and inflation, which Heath attempted to check by imposing wage and price controls. In 1972 the Organization of Petroleum Exporting Countries, a new factor in the world economy, achieved a dramatic increase in oil prices, which hit hard at the economies of industrial states and developing nations. The drastic increase in the price of petroleum forced the Heath government to let the pound float down to its international value, thus increasing the cost of imports. Heath's commitment to competition meant that some industries would be allowed to fail, but when the prestigious Rolls Royce Corporation faced bankruptcy Heath let it be sold to keep its identity; similarly, he supplied funds for the shipbuilding industry of Scotland. Competitiveness as an abstract concept was one thing; the national and human consequences were something else.

It was generally agreed that economic growth was choked by the restrictions imposed by organized labor and especially by strikes. Heath tried to resolve these problems by an Industrial Relations Act; organized labor resisted this Act with crippling strikes on the railroads, at the electric power stations, and in the coal mines. A worldwide energy crisis was precipitated by the Organization of Petroleum Exporting Countries' oil embargo of 1973. When the coal miners refused to work overtime Heath ordered business and industry to go on a three-day week to save energy. Street lights were turned off and television broadcasting was reduced. When the miners called a strike Heath, driven to desperation, called for an election to determine "who governs Britain." The public, tired of confrontation and crisis, turned back to the imperturbable Harold Wilson, who won a slim majority in the election of 1974. The Conservative party was outraged by Heath's rashness in provoking a showdown with the miners in the middle of an energy crisis and his decision to appeal to the electorate for support. They began looking for a new leader.

Northern Ireland. One of the most serious problems to face Britain during the difficult seventies was the wave of terrorism and violence that wracked

Northern Ireland. When Ireland became a separate state after World War I, the six northern counties (Ulster) remained united to Great Britain. The Protestant majority of Ulster looked to the union as a guarantee that they would not become subject to an Ireland dominated by Catholics and powerfully influenced by the Roman Catholic Church. Northern Ireland had its own ministry, civil service, police, and Parliament, and also elected members to the Parliament in Westminster. Its people participated fully in the benefits of the British welfare state. Irish nationalists, however, insisted that they would never be satisfied until all of the island was united under the government in Dublin.

Influenced by struggles for civil rights in the United States, in the late 1960s a civil rights movement sprang up among the Catholics of Northern Ireland, who experienced discrimination in jobs, housing, and political power. An attractive young woman, Bernadette Devlin, became a prominent leader of Catholic students in marches and demonstrations that provoked violent clashes with the police. The civil rights movement was concerned with changes in Ulster, but its efforts were complicated by the activities of a revived Irish Republican Army (I.R.A.). The I.R.A. advocated political unity of the entire island, using its familiar weapons, the bomb and the revolver. The shootings and bombings of the I.R.A. and the unpopularity of the Ulster police led the British government to send troops into Ulster to preserve order until a political resolution of the conflict could be achieved. The Ulster Protestants viewed the army as sent to support the status quo, while the Catholics resented this new assertion of British power. Neither side was much interested in reconciliation or compromise.

As was likely in such a volatile situation, violence increased, capped by a new Bloody Sunday in 1972 when British paratroopers, trying to preserve order, killed thirteen Catholics in a riot at Londonderry. When Britain attempted to guarantee the civil rights of the Catholics, Ulster Protestants complained that those who were loyal to the union were not being supported. In 1972 Heath, who did not shrink from confrontations, suspended the Protestant-controlled government of Ulster and announced direct rule from London, a policy that outraged both Protestants and Catholics. Angry at the failure of the authorities to suppress the I.R.A., Protestant paramilitary organizations began a counterterror.

Wearily the British government searched for a way in which the peoples of Ulster could live together. In 1974 Britain introduced a new provincial government in which the two religious communities would share power. Leaders of the Protestant majority did not wish to share power, and working-class Protestants organized a widespread strike that forced the collapse of this experiment. An attempt in 1975 to draw up a new constitution failed.

Meanwhile sectarian murders struck down hundreds on crowded Belfast streets and lonely rural roads, in homes darkened for sleep and in noisy bars. The I.R.A. extended the terror into Britain. Seven died and 120 were injured when two Birmingham pubs were bombed in 1974. Late that year the I.R.A. called a holiday truce, which was extended in return for the gradual release of interned suspects. The truce slowed but did not stop terrorism. In 1975 London was struck by a series of bombings at the Tower of London, Harrod's department store, the Hilton Hotel, and several underground stations. There were dozens of frightening hoaxes as well. The British government, press, and people roundly criticized Americans, primarily of Irish extraction, who sent weapons and financial aid to the I.R.A. Britain found that a policy of direct rule and martial law did not accomplish its purpose and only brought the problems of Ulster closer to home.

Devolution. Even in Britain, disunifying tendencies threatened to unravel the proud Union Jack. In the middle 1970s nationalist movements arose in Scotland and Wales, which were seeking "devolution," meaning delegation of some powers of the central government to parliaments established for those regions. Devolution was weak in Wales, for Welsh nationalism centered on a language that few spoke and the poverty of Wales made the notion of a separate political structure impractical. Scottish nationalism was strengthened by a long national history, separate administrative, legal, and religious institutions, and a national culture that included such distinctive elements as kilts and bagpipes. Furthermore, Scotland's financial prospects looked good with the development of offshore oil and natural gas, most of which was landed on the Scottish coast. The movement for devolution was specially threatening to the Labour party, which had much of its strength in Scotland and Wales. Unwilling to alienate potential supporters, both parties reluctantly agreed to submit the issue to the decision of the areas concerned. When referenda were held in Scotland and Wales it was found that most of the population was uninterested, and the devolution movements waned.

Wilson Again. When Heath called an election in 1974 to determine who ruled Britain, he discovered the answer was the resourceful Harold Wilson, whose slim majority had to be eked out by the support of minor parties. Wilson ended the coal strike with a settlement favorable to the miners, whose complaints were found by most of the British public to be justifiable. Later in the year Wilson called another election, which gave him a paper-thin majority. To check the continuing decline of British manufacturing industry, the Labour party left wing, led by Anthony Wedgwood Benn, Minister of Industry, advocated further nationalization. Continuing Labour's propensity for "lemon socialism"—nationalizing failing industries that would drain the Treasury—the bankrupt automaker, British Leyland, was nationalized and proposals were made to nationalize shipbuilding and the aircraft industry. By this time nationalization had lost its appeal to the public as well as to many Labour party leaders, but, politically, Wilson had no choice but to go along with the left wing of his party.

Wilson's opportunism was again demonstrated on the issue of British membership in the European Economic Community. British membership was opposed in the Labour party by left wingers, who were primarily concerned to establish socialism at home, and in the Conservative party by nationalists who objected to the loss of British sovereignty. Moderates in both parties supported membership. Nimbly, Wilson avoided taking a stand by proposing a referendum on the issue. The voters gave overwhelming approval to continuance in the Common Market, and that question was finally settled.

By 1976 the master political juggler had had enough. Harold Wilson announced his decision to resign on the ground that he should give others in his party a chance to lead the country and to promote their political futures. Wilson had brought about the revival of the Labour party, but at the same time his political legerdemain had concealed the fact that its prescriptions for the country had either been discredited (nationalization) or accomplished (the welfare state). The new ideas in the Labour party came from the radical left and were too extreme to have credibility with the voters. Wilson's successor as prime minister was James Callaghan, a party wheelhorse, whose genial disposition was devoted to the difficult task of reconciling the differences within his own party.

Callaghan, as prime minister, continued Wilson's economic policies, trying to make Britain's resources stretch to cover the commitments the country had made to the North Atlantic Treaty Organization, the European Economic Community, the developing nations, and her own people. To keep the system going, Callaghan had to convince business to turn from speculation to investment, to persuade the trade unions to moderate their wage demands, to restrict spending for popular programs, and to justify a high rate of unemployment as the price of the fight against inflation. Even nature failed to cooperate: in the summer of 1976 Britain suffered the worst drought in history. Inflation remained higher than in most industrial countries. Unemployment exceeded the worst figures since World War II. The pound fell to a record low on foreign exchanges, which increased the cost of what Britain bought without improving sales of her export goods. The International Monetary Fund provided a credit of almost four billion dollars in exchange for humiliating controls on public spending and unpopular restraints on consumption. When Callaghan called an election in 1979, Britain seemed to have reached the end of the line.

By that time the Conservatives had a new leader, Mrs. Margaret Thatcher, the first woman to head a major party in a large industrial country. Mrs. Thatcher's father was a small-town grocer active in local politics. She was educated at the local grammar school and earned a degree at Oxford, with the support of scholarships. Her husband, a wealthy businessman, provided her with the financial means to pursue a political career. Under Heath she had held the second-rank office of Minister of Education, where her attempt to reduce the cost of school lunches gained her the sobriquet, "Thatcher, the milk snatcher." She was a strong advocate of free enterprise, self-help, and sturdy British patriotism, which contrasted sharply with the Tory democracy and internationalism of Heath, still her principal rival within the Conservative party. Her victory in the election of 1979 inaugurated a new era in British politics.

As Mrs. Thatcher prepared to introduce her version of Conservatism, observers contemplated the cause and nature of "the British disease." While pundits saw decline from former greatness, visitors saw that Britain looked better than ever. The people bustled about their business; the children were bright eyed and lively; the ill, handicapped, and aged were looked after; schools, roads, libraries, and other public facilities were improved and modernized; new universities and polytechnic schools added to the opportunities for higher education; Britain excelled in theater, films, and television; British rock groups created a massive new industry. The usual answer to the dilemma was that Britain was living on borrowed time and money, a reaction which overlooked the intelligence and resourcefulness of the country's people. Mrs. Thatcher promised a new broom, and as Britain moved into the 1980s she looked the part of the strong-willed political housekeeper that Britain needed.

See combined Suggestions for Further Reading for chapters 17 and 18, which follow chapter 18, on pages 453–455.

18

Britain under
Margaret Thatcher

from 1979

The Thatcher Ministry

Margaret Thatcher. When Mrs. Thatcher took office in April 1979 Britain was a troubled nation. The decline of the country's industries, high inflation and unemployment, the bad-tempered and disruptive disputes of employers and workers, the alienation of youth, the interminable violence in Northern Ireland, and the rise of racial conflict had created problems that the ministries of Heath, Wilson, and Callaghan seemed to aggravate. Britain had joined the European Economic Community but almost as a suppliant and on terms that many thought were unfair. Devolution seemed to be eroding the foundations of the United Kingdom itself.

Mrs. Thatcher brought to the office of prime minister a trained intelligence, a quickness in debate, a firm adherence to well-articulated principles, and a sturdy courage that earned the respect of her Cabinet, the support of her party, and the confidence of the nation. She communicated a strong sense of British character and national pride, and it was these qualities that enabled the British people to accept and to adjust to a position in Europe and the world that changed forever the World War II concept of Britain as the island nation that stood alone.

Economic Policy. Mrs. Thatcher took office convinced that the British economy had become lazy and inefficient and needed the bracing effects of competition. Britain's economic problems were compounded by the world recession of the 1970s, but Thatcher, undaunted, took steps to return Britain to a free-market economy. Britain's high rate of income tax was reduced to encourage private investment, and taxes were raised on

Margaret Thatcher *(The Bettmann Archive/BBC Hulton)*.

purchases to discourage consumption. The money supply was tightly controlled to bring down inflation. These policies required severe cuts in public spending, which fell heaviest on public employment and the social services such as health, education, and public housing. Mrs. Thatcher was committed to reversing Labour's socialist policies, and she took steps to sell off nationalized industries such as British Airways and British Petroleum. Other nationalized industries were expected to become profitable, even at the cost of eliminating many jobs at a time of high unemployment. In October 1986 Britain's financial institutions were deregulated, creating a wide open market for securities from all over the world. In December British Gas was sold to private investors in a mammoth sale of stock, sparked by special inducements for small investors to promote Mrs. Thatcher's idea of a "people's capitalism." Despite threats from the Labour party to renationalize the corporation at the first opportunity, the sale was a great success.

Mrs. Thatcher's policies were introduced at a time of a severe world recession as unemployment rose to a postwar high of 13 percent. Under these economic pressures British manufacturing industry (nationalized and private) declined, and the British economy became increasingly dominated by service industries. Fortunately for Britain, the financial cushion provided by North Sea oil enabled the government to maintain unemployment benefits and to ease some of the strains of the recession. Agriculture, always a favorite constituency of the Conservatives, prospered with the aid of the high price supports of the European Economic Community.

The Welfare State. There were fears that Mrs. Thatcher might seek to dismantle the broad range of social services known collectively as "the welfare state," but this did not happen. Old age pensions were maintained as before, and reduction of unemployment benefits was impossible with joblessness at a high level. The decreasing number of school children made possible modest decreases in school expenditures, and government support for higher education was cut severely, including increased tuition costs for foreign students. One of Mrs. Thatcher's major objectives was to reduce the involvement of government in housing. Housing subsidies were cut, and tenants in public housing were encouraged to purchase their houses at low prices, a popular policy that converted large numbers of working-class voters to homeowners and Conservative voters.

The National Health Service continues to be supported but reforms have been introduced that are intended to make it more economical and efficient. There are long delays in providing medical treatment for ailments that can be deferred, such as tonsillectomies, but the National Health Service is quick to respond to emergencies. Private medicine continues in Britain, and increasingly those who can afford it go to private doctors for prompt treatment of everyday medical needs, turning to the National Health Service only for high-cost surgery or treatment of catastrophic illness.

Northern Ireland. Britain's most intractable problem continues to be Northern Ireland, where the Protestant majority is determined to hold power and continue as part of the United Kingdom and the Catholic minority seeks equal rights or, in some instances, union with the Republic of Ireland. This long-standing dispute has led to numerous local conflicts and riots and unending terrorism by elements of the Irish Republican Army (I.R.A.). Mrs. Thatcher found it necessary to continue direct rule of Northern Ireland from London, supported by the British army, but disorders and assassinations continued. In 1981 Lord Mountbatten, an uncle of Prince Philip and a hero of World War II, was assassinated by the I.R.A. In 1981 imprisoned members of the I.R.A. went on hunger strikes, claiming that they should be treated as political prisoners, not criminals. In 1985 the I.R.A. set off a bomb in the Brighton Hotel where Mrs. Thatcher planned to stay while attending the annual conference of the Conservative party.

Mrs. Thatcher has attempted to outflank the I.R.A. by diplomacy. The British are convinced that substantial financial support for the I.R.A. comes from Irish-Americans, especially in New England, and have urged the United States to impose stricter controls. Mrs. Thatcher also sought closer relations with the Republic of Ireland to deprive the I.R.A. of a source of support and a place to hide. In November 1985 Mrs. Thatcher signed an agreement with the prime minister of Ireland to establish procedures by which British and Irish leaders would meet to discuss the problems of Northern Ireland, especially in regard to the security and rights of Catholics there. The agreement was strongly opposed by the Protestants, and the violence continued. Since much of the world takes a highly selective approach to terrorism, condemning some terrorists and supporting others, it is questionable how successful these efforts will be. It appears that the Irish problem will continue.

The Falklands War. The Falklands War dramatically improved Mrs. Thatcher's political standing and gave a boost to British morale, which had been shaken by Britain's poor performance in the world economy and dependence on other countries. In April 1982 Argentine troops invaded the Falkland Islands. The claims of Britain and Argentina to the islands were lost in obscurity and the islands have little value, but there could be no question that the people were British and had no desire to be ruled by

Casualty of the Falklands War. The destroyer *HMS Sheffield* was hit by an Argentine missile and later sank with the loss of twenty lives *(UPI/Bettmann Archive)*.

a military dictatorship noted for the "disappearances" of thousands of its own people. Mrs. Thatcher responded like a lioness aroused by danger to her cubs. After a full debate in Parliament Britain declared war, and a hastily improvised armada of ships, planes, and soldiers was sent to the rescue. The Labour party deplored the resort to force and Conservatives criticized the government for failing to foresee the Argentine invasion, but Mrs. Thatcher held to her course with Churchillian determination.

With important logistical support from the United States, the British fleet sailed more than 7,000 miles, engaged Argentine naval and air forces, landed troops in the Falklands, and forced the surrender of Argentine troops. The Argentine dictators fell from power, and Mrs. Thatcher had won a classic military victory. She had also asserted British national power in a manner that pleased the British people but did not change Britain's dependence on others in most aspects of her external relationships.

Thatcher and Europe. Mrs. Thatcher came to power with the long-established Conservative view of foreign policy: commitment to the North Atlantic Treaty Organization, continuing good relations with the Commonwealth, opposition to Soviet expansion and troublemaking, and coolness toward Britain's membership in the European Economic Community. In her view, Sir Edward Heath had been too idealistic and enthusiastic about joining with Western Europe; Harold Wilson had been weak and vacillating. She was determined to maintain Britain's membership of the European Economic Community but to play a strong role in shaping it more to Britain's liking.

"The Iron Lady," as some European leaders called her, aroused a furor by the aggressive manner in which she insisted that Britain could not afford to pay the contribution required by the terms of her membership. She also aroused concern by her strong anti-Soviet views, since Western Europe had learned to live in proximity to the Russian Bear without undue alarm. The other members countered by raising questions about the sharing of North Sea oil, fisheries, and other objects of contention. Nevertheless, they stood by Britain in the Falklands War, the British contribution to the Community was reduced, and Britain's relations with Europe were strengthened. The most dramatic example of the growth of trust is the recent commitment to build a tunnel under the Channel from Britain to France, a project that some feared would make Britain vulnerable to invasion and others disliked because it tied Britain even more closely to the continent.

British Government

One of the great achievements of the British people through the centuries has been a system of government that has preserved existing institutions while adapting them to new needs and expectations. By the 1970s British government was not working well. The attempt to maintain a large, costly government with heavy commitments in foreign policy, defense, industrial development, and social services was hampered by a declining economy and domestic unrest. Joining the European Economic Community was one response to a sense of dissatisfaction, but complaints and ideas were being generated that supported Mrs. Thatcher's determination to initiate another period of governmental reform.

Institutions. One institution that is gaining strength is the monarchy. Queen Elizabeth and her consort, Prince Philip, carry out the role of the monarchy with dignity and warmth. The royal family gained popular appeal with the marriage of Charles, prince of Wales, to Lady Diana Spencer in "the wedding of the century." After sowing a wild oat or two and serv-

Prince Charles & Princess Diana *(The Bettmann Archive)*.

ing in the Falklands War, Prince Andrew married Lady Sarah Ferguson (they became the duke and duchess of York), adding youth and attractiveness to a royal family that—prior to the royal marriages—some had considered too stodgy for the late twentieth century. In the age of television, the magic of monarchy is more widely diffused than ever before, in Britain as well as abroad.

The general principles of British government as they have developed over the centuries are unquestioned: parliamentary sovereignty, Cabinet government, democratic elections, and the rule of law. Britain does not have one document that is referred to as its "constitution," but it has a constitution nonetheless. The British constitution is found partially in such memorable documents as Magna Carta (1215) and partially in legislation: the Parliament Acts (1911, 1949), the Representation of the People Acts (1918, 1928, 1948), the Riot Act (1715), the Act of Union (1707), the Official Secrets Act (1911), and the Race Relations Acts (1965, 1969). The rule of law is preserved by the courts, which interpret and enforce the law against violation by the authorities, although (unlike the United States) the courts cannot override or declare unconstitutional any act of Parliament. Given the far-flung powers of government departments and local authorities, the role of the courts is important in restricting the actions of government to the letter of the law and in protecting individuals against abuses of power.

The conventions of government are another important part of the British constitution. Although they are unenforceable at law, the conventions rest upon the consensus of the politicians and the people. The most important of these conventions is the rule that the queen must accept the advice of her ministers, which is the principal device by which the monarchy has been preserved in the age of democracy while the executive power has been transferred to the prime minister and Cabinet. For example, the queen has the power to appoint the prime minister, but the conventions of British government require that the person appointed have the support of a majority of the House of Commons, which usually means the leader of the majority party. The prime minister has full discretion in appointing the members of the Cabinet and holders of other political offices, although these appointments are made in the name of the queen. Another convention is that members of the Cabinet must support the decisions of the government or resign, a requirement that greatly strengthens the hand of the prime minister in dealing with the Cabinet, the party, and the media. The prime minister also has the dominant voice in deciding when to dissolve Parliament and when to hold an election. An election can be called at any time, although no Parliament can continue longer than five years. In the age of mass politics the office of prime minister has come increasingly to resemble the American presidency.

The demands placed on government in the twentieth century have brought about a great increase in its size and cost. The prime minister continues to hold the title first lord of the Treasury, and the chancellor of the exchequer serves as the principal spokesman for the government in public finance and economic policy. The foreign secretary is responsible for foreign policy, and with the decay of the Commonwealth the Foreign Office absorbed responsibility for that aspect of Britain's external relations. The home secretary is responsible for law and order and a wide range of domestic services. A Ministry of Defence was established in 1964, which consolidated the War Office (army), Admiralty (navy), and Royal Air Force. The departments of Health and Social Security have been merged (1968), and new departments of the Environment (1970) and Trade and Industry (1983) were established to meet new needs. Important governmental powers are exercised by separate agencies under governmental supervision, such as the Arts Council (funding of artistic projects), the Commission for Racial Equality, and the Gaming Board, which controls legalized gambling. A well-educated, professional civil service is the glue that holds this vast structure of public authority together.

Problems. Some critics of British government are concerned by the unlimited power of the House of Commons, especially since the Commons is so rigidly controlled by party leaders. Proposals have been made for a Bill of Rights, enforceable in the courts, that would limit the extent to which Parliament could interfere with the rights of individuals. In Victorian times the exercise of parliamentary sovereignty was limited by common values that confined government to comparatively limited functions and restrained the power of government over individuals. In the late twentieth century the role of the state has become so widely extended many feel that the freedom of the individual is jeopardized. A Bill of Rights limiting the powers of Parliament is a step toward American principles which would alter in a fundamental way one of the key premises of British government—the sovereignty of Parliament.

Serious questions have been raised concerning the ability of Parliament to represent the nation in view of the great influence given to government and political parties by the economic interests at stake in the political process and the enormous influence politicians can exercise over public opinion, especially in the age of television. The House of Lords continues to serve a useful purpose as a deliberative body that can review legislation free from political pressures. Periodically, efforts are launched to abolish the House of Lords, but without success. The House of Commons is the center of British government, for there the executive (the Cabinet) and the legislative powers are combined. The prime minister and Cabinet explain and defend their policies and answer questions at "Question Time," the initial hour daily of the parliamentary sessions. The opposition leaders, organized in the "Shadow Cabinet," offer criticisms and alternatives. The debates are often sharp and witty and sometimes raucous.

One criticism of the House of Commons is that single-member districts do not represent adequately the variety of views held by substantial elements of the electorate. Single-member districts strengthen the two-party system, for third-party candidates can rarely muster a majority of votes in any district against the entrenched power of one of the two major parties. The result is that a third party may gain 20 percent of the popular vote in the nation but win only a few seats in the House of Commons. This situation has led to proposals for proportional representation, which would give each party seats in the House of Commons in proportion to its share of the popular vote. For obvious reasons, neither of the two major parties favors the proposal. An electoral bombshell would be needed for a third party to gain enough seats to influence parliamentary politics, but, where the two major parties are almost equally divided, even a modest share of seats could give important influence to any third party.

The United Kingdom. One cannot understand the complexity of British government without grasping that the official name of the country is "The United Kingdom of Great Britain and Northern Ireland," which includes four distinct parts: England, Scotland, Wales, and Northern Ireland. The word "British" is usually applied to government and citizenship, while the terms English, Welsh, Scottish, and Irish refer to cultural differences, which include not only the spoken accents of the people but differences in dress, manner, celebration of holidays, foods, religious traditions, and personal mannerisms. England includes 80 percent of the population and is the wealthiest part; concern is often expressed at the steady migration of population to the south of England and the decline of other parts of the United Kingdom. Scotland has its separate Church of Scotland and legal system, and there is a secretary of state for Scotland who is a member of the Cabinet. The Scottish Nationalist Party, which flourished in the 1970s, has declined to insignificance. Wales was absorbed into England by Henry VIII, but many aspects of Welsh nationality are preserved and there is a secretary of state for Wales. The Welsh Nationalist Party is also in decline.

Northern Ireland is the problem child of the United Kingdom. The Government of Ireland Act (1920) gave Home Rule to Northern Ireland, and the present Republic of Ireland became independent two years later. Under Home Rule Northern Ireland had its own prime minister, Parliament, and administration for local affairs, while remaining part of the United Kingdom. The province is torn by conflict between the dominant Protestant majority (approximately 60 percent of the population) and the Catholic minority, who have been excluded from political power and in many respects treated as second-class citizens. In 1972 the Heath government suspended Home Rule and established direct rule from London under the secretary of state for Northern Ireland. The British army was stationed in Northern Ireland to preserve order and secure the rights of the Catholics. Since neither Protestant nor Catholic liked British rule, this approach has not resolved the problem.

Political Parties. Characteristic of British democracy since Gladstone and Disraeli has been a strong party system. The election of 1979 and the victory in the Falklands War brought a Conservative resurgence, culminating in a decisive triumph for Mrs. Thatcher in the election of 1983. Mrs. Thatcher brought to Conservatism a strong ideological commitment to less government, a free-market economy, denationalization of socialized industries, cuts in the social services, and greater reliance on a competitive economy and personal responsibility. Her hectoring tone gave her the nickname "Attila the Hen" and contrasted with the traditional image of the Conservatives as the party of moderation, realism, and pragmatism. Some Conservatives continue unreconciled to her leadership, especially in foreign policy, where they criticize her pro-Reagan and anti-Soviet pronouncements and her confrontational approach to the European Economic Community. With a concern for social welfare going back to Disraeli, many Conservatives are concerned about the substantial cuts she has made in the welfare services, including education.

In the meantime the Labour party has been torn by bitter infighting between moderates and extremists, and the militance of some Labourites has diminished the appeal of that party to the general public. One scene of conflict is the annual Labour party conference, where the Labour members of Parliament, who are usually more moderate, confront local leaders with highly emotional special axes to grind. In an effort to improve its public image, the Labour party leadership has attempted to purge some of the militants from positions of power in the local constituencies, but the controversies that have resulted simply made Labour appear less ready to govern. In the 1970s the Liberal party experienced a minirevival as a progressive, non-Socialist alternative to the Labour party. In 1981 four moderate Labour party leaders, distressed by the direction their party had taken, seceded to form the Social Democratic party. They joined with the Liberals to form the Social Democratic-Liberal Alliance, which began drawing support from moderates in both parties. There is reason to believe that a major realignment of political parties may be in the making, with the Alliance replacing Labour as the second major party.

The European Community. A major new factor in British government is the relationship of the United Kingdom to Europe. When Britain joined the European Community, treaties were signed that committed Britain to a

The European Economic Community and the Warsaw Pact

wide range of rules, which significantly limited her freedom to act for herself as a sovereign state. Britain became part of a union that granted its members free movement of people, money, services, and goods throughout the Community, but in turn the members were subject to the authority of the European Commission on a wide range of matters, primarily economic. The European Economic Community also includes a European council, composed of the political leaders of the member states, a European court of justice to settle disputes concerning the Community, and an elected European Parliament, which is at present a talk shop with advisory powers only. Attempts to move the European Economic Community to greater political unity have failed. The members of the Community are part of the North Atlantic Treaty Organization, and thus they still depend on the United States and other nonmembers of the Community for their defense. The movement for European unity has achieved important success, and Britain's membership in the Community signalled her change from a nation with global interests to a component of an association whose concerns are primarily regional.

The Election of 1987. By June 1987 the British economy was humming, inflation was under control, exports were increasing, denationalization of industries had greatly extended the number of holders of common stocks, and the sale of council houses at rock-bottom prices had created thousands of homeowners of modest means. Unemployment was high, but it was confined mainly to the north of England, while the southeast was thriving with new white-collar, high-technology industries. Mrs. Thatcher called an election for June 1987, which resulted in another Conservative victory. Mrs. Thatcher had rejected the paternalism of the Conservative party and the socialism of Labour, and the electorate confirmed her policies emphatically.

Although the election of 1987 gave Mrs. Thatcher a solid majority of seats in the House of Commons, the Conservatives were a minority of the electorate, polling 43 percent of the popular vote. Despite the moderation of Neil Kinnock, leader of the Labour party, the extreme views expressed by some of his followers undermined confidence in his leadership. The Social Democratic-Liberal Alliance, which had hoped to draw from moderates in both parties, found that Mrs. Thatcher had stolen most of its appeal by a combination of personal toughness and national prosperity. The most ominous result of the election was the political gap between the prosperous south of England and the rest of the United Kingdom, for most of the support of Labour and the Alliance came from Scotland and the north of England where unemployment was high and hopes for the future were dim.

British Society

The Standard of Living. Since World War II the British people have made remarkable gains in their incomes, opportunities, health, and material well-being. By the 1970s, however, problems and discontent were mounting, and it was evident that Britain was not keeping pace with its prosperous neighbors in Western Europe. The question was frequently raised: what went wrong? Obviously many things about Britain today are good, but serious economic and social weaknesses are becoming apparent.

One problem is regional disparities. The population is stable at about 56 million, but there is a steady drain from the depressed North to the more affluent South, especially to the area within 100 miles of London. Scotland has the stimulus of North Sea oil, but the oil industry itself does not create many jobs and falling production and prices may soon reduce the value of this bonanza. The older manufacturing industries of Scotland, such as steel, coal, shipbuilding, and engineering, have declined, but there still is a market for specialties such as tweed cloth and Scotch whisky. The north of England shows a similar picture of industrial decline, in some places rivalling the hard times of the 1930s. The automation of coal mines and the closing of uneconomical pits brought a bitter coal strike in 1984 to 1985, leading to a disastrous defeat for the miners' union. Britain's future lies in the new technological industries, and these are located primarily in the South and East.

The British standard of living improved remarkably in the 1960s, but in the 1970s it stagnated. Undoubtedly the majority of the population enjoys considerable affluence or at least modest comfort, a situation which compounds the misfortune of those who have been left behind. The wide range of British social services guarantees a decent provision for everyone, but inflation has eroded the value of savings and pensions. The rapid increase in house prices and interest rates has excluded many from home ownership, and a declining stock of rental housing (partially due to rent control) means that alternative housing is hard to find. High-rise public housing built in the 1950s and 1960s has become rundown and unattractive. Britain is still a prosperous and comfortable country, with many valuable public services at low cost, but the signs of decay are beginning to appear.

Social Class. It is often remarked that the persistence of class consciousness is a factor that weakens British life. Probably 5 percent of the population comprise the upper class, which still includes some elements from the old aristocracy and gentry but is today comprised primarily of persons born to wealth and social position, whose superior education and culture provide opportunities for power, influence, and prestigious, well-paid employment. The middle class (perhaps 25 percent) have secure employment and social status and incomes that permit a comfortable life, including home ownership and good educational opportunities for their children. The more successful members of the middle class may rise into the upper class, but most middle-class persons do not expect that they or their children will enter into the elite world of the "top people." Sir Edward Heath and Mrs. Thatcher are examples of persons from the middle-class who rose to the top, but their Cabinets and most of the leaders in the civil service, the military forces, and the upper reaches of big business and the media have upper-class origins.

This social anatomy of Britain leaves approximately 65 percent of the population in the working classes. They are employed in manual labor jobs (which are declining), white-collar jobs in offices, or white-coat jobs in the new high-tech industries. Most members of the working class do not expect to rise in the social scale; they assume that they will continue to be employed in jobs that lead nowhere. They hope they will not become unemployed. They expect to earn enough to live decently and enjoy their amusements or hobbies. Their children will probably have the same future. The working class does not earn enough to save very much; the inducement to save is slight, since the welfare state provides for sickness, unemployment, old age, and the nurture and education of their children. Observers of a radical persuasion argue that working class acceptance of the undemanding life that society offers them keeps Britain from the changes needed to thrive in a competitive world. Modern rock music, which is primarily an expression of working-class youth, expresses a different kind of radicalism—alienation from society and the quest for personal fulfillment through love, drugs, music, or other forms of individual experience.

The Family. Britain, like other parts of the industrialized world, has seen rapid changes in the roles of men and women and in the institution in which the sexes are most intimately joined: the family. Marriages continue at about the same rate as before, although divorce has increased—perhaps indicative that people expect more from marriage. Except in affluent families it is usual for both husband and wife to be employed. The number of children per family is normally one or two. The British nanny is hard to find, but child-care centers (many operated by the local authorities) have become common. Watching television is the most common recreation of families, although reading, walking, attending sporting events, and visiting friends and relatives are also important.

Germaine Greer's book *The Female Eunuch* appeared in 1971 and had an enormous influence on the changing role and self-concept of women in Britain and elsewhere. Earlier feminists were interested primarily in obtaining equal opportunities for women in politics, business, and social relationships. Greer's purpose was to change the way women thought about themselves, especially women's dependence on men (primarily husbands) for their sense of self-worth. Her argument was that women are shaped by cultural forces to adopt stereotyped roles and expectations that limit their potential for fulfillment as human beings. She was, in short, a modern Mary Wollstonecraft, calling for a revolution. Whether her book led or followed changes in the lives of women, it became a landmark work.

Race. In the 1960s the British people looked with some condescension on the racial problems of the United States, only to find a decade later that they had problems which were similar. A large black population (mainly from the British West Indies) immigrated to Britain in the 1960s, finding employment in industry and especially in transport. They were joined by

Londoners *(Reuters/Bettmann Newsphotos)*.

immigrants from India and Pakistan, some of them well-educated professional people but most of them working in industries requiring dexterity
and patience or as proprietors of small shops and restaurants. The immigrants found housing in rundown neighborhoods, which brought them
into competition with working-class people, many of whom were not inclined to be tolerant of racial or cultural differences. Today approximately
40 percent of Britain's dark-skinned population have been born in Britain,
but they often find themselves treated as outsiders.

Racial tensions have led to riots, which caused grave alarm. An organization appeared called the National Front, using bullyboy tactics reminis-
cent of the Nazis, and at times gangs of youths roamed the streets engag-
ing in "Paki-bashing." The immigrants fought back, resulting in ugly riots
that seem to have been aggravated by police tactics. A report by Lord
Scarman in 1981 recommended improvements in the recruitment and
training of police, more nonwhite police officers, limits on the use of force
by police, greater responsibility of the police to local authorities, and a

vigorous attack on the social problems that spawn racism and crime. A series of acts restricted immigration from the nonwhite parts of the empire, but acceptance of persons who are racially and culturally distinct proceeds slowly.

Britain Today

The best way to learn about modern Britain is to go there. Britain is an ideal place to begin overseas travel: it is clearly a foreign country but not so foreign as to be intimidating. Apart from an occasional encounter with a cockney cabdriver, there is no significant language barrier. Americans can read signs and timetables, ask directions, order in a restaurant, read the papers, and talk to the people. The British people are generally courteous and helpful to visitors, and the pubs make everyone welcome.

A trip to Britain should begin with London. For centuries London has been the center of British life, and the history of England can still be seen in London and its environs: the Norman Tower of London, the Gothic splendor of Westminster Abbey (with its monuments to political and intellectual leaders of the past), the Tudor glories of Hampton Court palace (unfortunately damaged by fire), the Stuart elegance of Charles I's Banqueting Hall, the simplicity of William III's Kensington Palace, the legacy of Christopher Wren at St. Paul's cathedral and his many splendid churches. The Hanoverians left their mark at Windsor Castle, that most regal of royal palaces. Monuments to Queen Victoria and Prince Albert are everywhere, but especially at the Albert Memorial, the Royal Albert Hall, and the Victoria and Albert Museum. The Victorian Houses of Parliament, splendidly sited along the Thames, remind the visitor of Britain's contribution to democracy and parliamentary government. The statue of Winston Churchill at Parliament Square and his World War II underground headquarters nearby bring back memories of the courage and toughness with which the British people stood alone against the vile empire of Adolf Hitler. The superb Museum of London at the Barbican brings it all together.

Persons whose image of Britain is based on the study of her history or the advertisements of travel agencies will be surprised to discover the "modernity" of Britain. Those who go to Britain looking for castles, cathedrals, stately homes, or thatched cottages will find them, in many cases attractively displayed. But the characteristic features of our modern world are also there. London is a great world city, thronged with people of all races and nationalities seeking profit, knowledge, or entertainment. The tall office blocks of London are the introduction to a world of superhighways, shopping centers, heavy traffic, franchise restaurants (including

MacDonald's), stylish clothing, rock music, and the "punk culture" of young men with eccentric haircuts and black leather jackets and girls with bright green or dark purple makeup. In many respects Britain is a pace-setter for our modern world.

Those who think of the British as prim, proper, and stuffy have a delightful surprise in store for them. The British have become a lively, voluble people. British cookery does not match that of the continent, but good food representative of many nations and cultures is available. British clothing is first class in style and quality. The London theater is unsurpassed, and tickets can still be obtained at reasonable prices. It is possible to travel by rail to most places of interest, and the London Underground provides a fast, convenient means to visit any part of that fascinating city.

The attentive visitor will learn that Britain has some of the best and worst newspapers in the world and will find in the newspapers (good and bad alike) a window to the life of the British people today. The British Broadcasting Corporation is world famous for the accuracy and fairness of its news. It presents a wide range of outstanding programs for radio and television, and its overseas services broadcast in many languages throughout the world. Independent television provides an enjoyable alternative, including many popular American programs.

The student traveller will be interested in visiting British campuses and meeting British students—an articulate and argumentative lot. Oxford and Cambridge have the most prestige, and their magnificent buildings, some going back to the Middle Ages, are among the great sights of Britain. The Victorian "redbrick" universities, located principally in the industrial towns, were expanded after World War II. The postwar period also saw the establishment of "new" universities with modern buildings and new curricula to provide for a large expansion of university enrollments. A distinctive feature of British higher education is the polytechnic schools, which offer programs that prepare students for a wide variety of careers. The visitor from overseas will find that education is a major industry that attracts students from all over the world.

The British countryside is still beautiful, and a modern road network makes it possible for coach (bus) passengers or the visitor with a car to enjoy its delights, including village inns and pubs. The traveller should remember that the land is also a place of work and that British agriculture, supported by the Common Agricultural Policy of the European Economic Community, is flourishing. Many of the villages and cottages of the past retain their quaint appearance, but their interiors have been modernized to provide chic country residences for the well-to-do. Britain is dotted with medieval parish churches; the decline of the rural population has raised the painful question of how many of them can be preserved. The cathedrals of England still retain their medieval splendor, although their soft stone is crumbling due to industrial and automotive pollution. There is special beauty in the grace and dignity of Edinburgh, Wordsworth's lovely Lake Country, and the rugged mountains of Wales with their imposing castles. In short, the past and present are both visible in Britain today, and the student of British history and civilization is urged to go see them.

The End of British History?

There'll Always be an England was a popular song during World War II, and it is likely that the United Kingdom will continue indefinitely to provide for its people a way of life that is free, secure, progressive, and humane. Things will continue to happen in the British Isles that will interest future historians. But British history will no longer be the independent, self-sustaining process, intelligible in itself, which has been recounted in this book. Since Roman and Anglo-Saxon times, British history has been shaped both by indigenous developments and Britain's relationships with the continent and the wider world overseas. In the twentieth century the latter factors began to predominate, and in the 1980s the supremacy of the broader context is probably complete.

In the present world of superpowers and a global economy the nations of Europe—including Great Britain—are too small to stand alone. During World War II Britain depended on the United States, and the notion of a "special relationship" continued long after the interests of the two nations had diverged. Those who looked to the Commonwealth for support found that, like the Cheshire cat, all that was left was the smile. Thus Britain turned to the European Economic Community. The achievement of Mrs. Thatcher was to maintain national character and pride while accepting the loss of Britain's position as a nation with an independent role as a major world power.

Britain maintains her distinctive geographical location, political and social institutions, and national character, but these no longer shape her destiny. As the separate history of Britain draws to a close the creativity of the British people continues to be seen in scholarship, science, technology, medicine, literature, music, popular entertainment, and many other aspects of our rapidly developing world culture. And the influence of Britain's long and remarkable history continues to radiate throughout the world.

Suggestions for Further Reading

Many of the books cited for Chapter 16 continue to be useful for the postwar period. C. J. Bartlett, *A History of Postwar Britain, 1945–74* (1977) is a reliable guide. Alan Sked and Chris Cook, *Post-War Britain: A Political History* (rev. ed., 1984) takes the story through the Falklands War. Arthur Marwick, *British Society since 1945* (1982) is an interesting social history. The annual volumes of *Britain: An Official Handbook* (Central Office of Information, London) contain a wealth of information about the current year.

Good introductions to the Labour government of 1945 to 1951 are offered by Kenneth O. Morgan, *Labour in Power, 1945–1951* (1985) and Roger Eatwell, *The 1945–51 Labour Governments* (1980). Politics in the sixties are covered by Robert R. James in *Ambitions and Realities: British Politics, 1964–70* (1972).

James E. Cronin, *Industrial Conflict in Modern Britain* (1979) deals with one of Britain's most persistent and damaging problems. Almont Lindsey, *Socialized Medicine in England and Wales* (1962) examines one of the landmarks left by the Labour governments. The problems of the welfare state are analyzed in William Breckinridge and Stephen Clark, *Economics and Politics: Poverty and Social Security in Britain since 1961* (1982). A role of the state easily overlooked is traced in George A. N. Lowndes, *The Silent Social Revolution: An Account of the Expansion of Public Education in Britain, 1895–1965* (1969). Catherine Jones, *Immigration and Social Policy in Britain* (1977) deals with a recent problem.

The changing roles of women in postwar Britain are covered by Jane Lewis in *Women in England, 1870–1950: Sexual Divisions and Social Change* (1985). John Colville, *The New Elizabethans, 1959–1977* (1977) reviews broad changes in British life, and Anthony Sampson, *The Changing Anatomy of England* (1981) gives much attention to the movers and shakers. Philip Norman, *Shout! The Beatles in Their Generation* (1977) deals with a phenomenon that has extended Britain's influence in an unexpected way. A good survey of society in the 1980s is Judith Ryder and Harold Silver, *Modern English Society* (3rd edition, 1985). See also two books by A. H. Halsey, *Change in British Society* (2nd edition, 1981) and *Origins and Destinations: Family, Class, and Education in Modern Britain* (1980).

The change in Britain's world role since World War II is discussed in Joseph Frankel, *British Foreign Policy, 1945–1973* (1975), F. S. Northedge, *Descent from Power: British Foreign Policy, 1945–1973* (1974), and two provocative books by Corelli Barnett, *The Collapse of British Power* (1973) and *The Audit of War: The Illusion and Reality of Britain as a Great Power* (1986). One of the great accomplishments of postwar Britain was the peaceful dissolution of her empire, which can be followed in Colin Cross, *The Fall of the British Empire, 1918–1968* (1968).

Memoirs and biographies are especially important for recent history, where many of the essential sources are not available. The continuing popularity of the monarchy is better understood after reading Robert Lacey, *Majesty: Queen Elizabeth II and the House of Windsor* (1977). Good biographies are Kenneth Harris, *Attlee* (1982), Alan Bullock, *Ernest Bevin* (3 vols., 1960–1983), David Charlton, *Anthony Eden: A Biography* (1982), and Nigel Fisher, *Harold Macmillan: A Biography* (1982). The *Memoirs* of Harold Macmillan (6 vols., 1966–1973) are of exceptional interest. For Mrs. Thatcher, see Russell Lewis, *Margaret Thatcher: A*

Personal and Political Biography (rev. ed., 1984). For the Falklands War see Max Hastings and Simon Jenkins, *The Battle for the Falklands* (1983).

There are a number of bibliographies that list scores of books and articles, usually arranged by subject headings such as Political History, Cultural and Intellectual History, and Religion. The most comprehensive bibliographies are those jointly produced by the American Historical Association and the Royal Historical Society: Edgar B. Graves, *A Bibliography of English History to 1485* (1975), Conyers Read, *Bibliography of British History. Tudor Period* (2nd edition, 1959), Mary Frear Keeler, *Bibliography of British History. Stuart Period* (2nd edition, 1970), Stanley Pargellis and D. J. Medley, *Bibliography of British History. The Eighteenth Century, 1714–1789* (1951), L. M. Brown and I. R. Christie, *Bibliography of British History 1789–1851* (1977), H. J. Hanham, *Bibliography of British History, 1851–1914* (1976). A series of bibliographic handbooks prepared under the auspices of the Conference on British Studies is shorter but particularly valuable for citations to articles in scholarly periodicals. These are: Michael Altschul, *Anglo-Norman England, 1066–1154* (1969), DeLloyd J. Guth, *Late-Medieval England, 1377–1485* (1974), Mortimer Levine, *Tudor England, 1485–1603* (1968), William L. Sachse, *Restoration England, 1660–1689* (1971), Josef L. Altholz, *Victorian England, 1837–1901* (1970), and Alfred Havighurst, *Modern England, 1901–1970* (1976).

A good series of historical maps is in Martin Gilbert, *British History Atlas* (1969) and in Chris Cook and John Stevensen, *Longman Atlas of Modern British History* (1977). Useful guides to the types of records that exist, and the limitations on understanding the past that result, are to be found in the series "The Sources of History: Studies in the Uses of Historical Evidence." These, which deal with England in whole or part, are: G. R. Elton, *England, 1200–1640* (1969), T. H. Hollingsworth, *Historical Demography* (1969), and C. L. Mowat, *Great Britain Since 1914* (2nd edition, 1977). A bibliography of articles recently published in historical journals appears three times a year, including a section on "British Commonwealth and Ireland," edited by Frederic A. Youngs, Jr. and Michael E. Moody, in *Recently Published Articles* (published by the American Historical Association). A critique of historical writings since World War II is in G. R. Elton's *Modern Historians on British History, 1485–1945. A Critical Bibliography, 1945–1969* (1970). W. B. Stephens' *Sources for English Local History* (1973) can help develop a fuller understanding of English communities. The principal historical journals that deal particularly in English history are *English Historical Review, Historical Journal* (formerly *Cambridge Historical Journal*), *Bulletin of the Institute of Historical Research, Past & Present, Economic History Review, History, Journal of British Studies,* and *Albion,* the last two published in the United States.

APPENDIX

Kings and Queens of England

Bretwaldas

ca. 560–591	Caelwin, king of the West Saxons
560–616	Ethelbert, king of Kent
ca. 600–616	Raedwald, king of East Anglia
616–632	Edwin, king of Northumbria
633–641	Oswald, king of Northumbria
654–670	Oswiu, king of Northumbria

King of Mercia

757–796	Offa

Kings of the West Saxons

802–839	Egbert
866–871	Ethelred
871–899	Alfred *—Anglo Saxson Chronicle*
899–924	Edward the Elder

Rulers of England

959–975	Edgar the Peaceful
978–1016	Ethelred the Unready *—horrible*
1016–1035	Canute *— Viking invader*
1042–1066	Edward the Confessor *— religious devotion - prob. w/ Godwin*
1066	Harold Godwinson *— 6 mons - Battle of Stamford Bridge*

Normans

1066–1087	William I *Doomsday Book, feudal system*
1087–1100	William II *struggle w/ Aselm of Canterbury*

457

son of Wm I — 1100–1135 Henry I — lion of justice, charter of liberties

nephew — 1135–1154 Stephen — problems with Matilda and Geoffrey

Angevins-Plantagenets
grandson Wm I — 1154–1189 Henry II — red energy, Anjou empire, Constitutions of Clarendon — law w/ juries, circuits — à Becket

son — 1189–1199 Richard I — "the Lion Hearted," military strength

son — 1199–1216 John — Magna Carta June 15, 1215, pope Innocent II

son — 1216–1272 Henry III — De Montford + Parliament, Provisions of Oxford

son — 1272–1307 Edward I — model parliament, codified law, Confirmation of ch.

son — 1307–1327 Edward II — absolutely horrible, forced to abdicate

son — 1327–1377 Edward III — House of Commons + Lords – 100 yrs. War

son — 1377–1399 Richard II — Merciless Parliament, abdicated

Lancastrians
cousin — 1399–1413 Henry IV — put down Clarence rebellions

son — 1413–1422 Henry V — victory at Agincourt 1415

son — 1422–1461 Henry VI — lowest pt. in foreign + domestic affairs — puppet and totally inept, mad

Yorkists
son — 1461–1483 Edward IV — restored monarchy, increased yield from crops,

1483 Edward V — minor, killed w/ brother in tower of London

brother — 1483–1485 Richard III — tried to impose control over local officials — Killed in the Battle of Bosworth Field

Tudors
1485–1509 Henry VII — secured Tudor regain, debt of nobles. Court of Star Chamber

son — 1509–1547 Henry VIII — six wives, Act of Supremacy of 1534, dissolution of mona.

son by Jane Sey. — 1547–1553 Edward VI — minor, Book of Common Prayer, d. of Northumb.

daughter by Cath A. — 1553–1558 Mary I — m. Philip of Spain, persecuted Prot. – 300 burnings at

daughter by Anne Boleyn — 1558–1603 Elizabeth I — defeat of Spanish Armada, Anglicanism despite Puritan + Presy. pressure, Renaissance – Jonson, Shakespeare, Pacification of Ireland by mountjoy, growth of London

Stuarts
son of Mary q. of Scots — 1603–1625 James I — King James Bible, prob. w/ Parliament, Frederick's

son — 1625–1649 Charles I — ruled w/o Parl. 11 years, French style court, Long Parlia.

son — 1649–1660 Commonwealth and Protectorate — led by Oliver Cromwell, Rump

son — 1660–1685 Charles II — Catholic, Treaty of Dover, Exclusion Parliaments, 'Barebones' Parliament

brother — 1685–1688 James II — Restoration, Cavalier Parl., Declar. 2nd Indulgence decla.

nephew — 1689–1702 William III and Mary II — daughter, Bank of Eng. Wars of Spain, Cabinet

daughter — 1702–1714 Anne — triumph of Godolphin, Marlborough, Harley — wars of Spanish succession, mercantilism, immigration, Union w/ Scottish Parliament

Hanoverians
1714–1727 George I — Whig dominence, Jacobite Uprisings, Stanhope, Walpole

son — 1727–1760 George II — Treaty w/ Spain, Aix-la-chapelle, Age of Reason and

grandson — 1760–1820 George III — Lord North's ministry, revolution in America, French Rev.

1820–1830 George IV — William Pitt, Tory liberalism, political discontent, Peterloo

1830–1837 William IV — Reform Bill Crisis, Corn Law

1837–1901 Victoria — m. Prince Albert of Saxe-Coburg, ministry of Peel, Potato famine in Ireland, Reform Bill of 18', made empress of India, went into a long mourning, becoming more and more of a figure head

1901–1910 Edward VII *splendor and magnificence, posh lifestyle*
1910–1936 George V (House of Windsor) *Parl. Bill for H.of L., WW I, died 9*
1936 Edward VIII *wanted to marry his American divorcé, stepped down*
1936–1952 George VI *WW II*
1952– Elizabeth II — *little left to monarchy, impressive coronation*

son, son, son, brother, daughter
symbol of a new era

Prime Ministers of England

375 – 1297 - Hammer of the Scots

1721–1742	Sir Robert Walpole	
1742–1744	John Carteret	
1744–1754	Henry Pelham	
1754–1756	Duke of Newcastle	
1756–1757	William Pitt, the Elder	
1757–1761	Pitt the Elder and the Duke of Newcastle	
1761–1762	Duke of Newcastle and Lord Bute	
1762–1763	Lord Bute	
1763–1765	George Grenville	
1765–1766	Lord Rockingham	
1766–1768	William Pitt, Lord Chatham	
1768–1770	Duke of Grafton	
1770–1782	Lord North	
1782	Lord Rockingham	
1782–1783	Lord Shelburne	
1783	Charles James Fox and Lord North	
1783–1801	William Pitt, the Younger	
1801–1804	Henry Addington	
1804–1806	William Pitt, the Younger	
1806–1807	Lord Grenville	
1807–1809	Duke of Portland	
1809–1812	Spencer Perceval	
1812–1827	Lord Liverpool	Tory
1827	George Canning	Tory
1827	Lord Goderich	Tory
1828–1830	Duke of Wellington	Tory
1830–1834	Earl Grey	Whig
1834	Lord Melbourne	Whig
1834–1835	Sir Robert Peel	Tory
1835–1841	Lord Melbourne	Whig
1841–1846	Sir Robert Peel	Tory
1846–1852	Lord John Russell	Whig
1852	Lord Derby and Benjamin Disraeli	Tory
1852–1855	Lord Aberdeen	Coalition
1855–1858	Lord Palmerston	Liberal
1858–1859	Lord Derby and Benjamin Disraeli	Conservative
1859–1865	Lord Palmerston	Liberal

(handwritten marginalia: Crecy-Poitiers; huge amount of land; er; James, Cromwell; More, Cranmer; stake; dominant; civil wars; after legislation of 1642; abdicate; professions, press; Townsend; 7 yrs. war; Enlightenment; Napoleonic war; Tory - integrity. Railway Act 1844, comb; Crimean war; peace, stability, contain Russia; Italian war; sym. 4 Italy, Am. civil war; 1st w/ South, then slavery and the North)

1865–1866	Lord John Russell	Liberal
1866–1868	Lord Derby and Benjamin Disraeli	Conservative
1868–1874	William E. Gladstone	Liberal
1874–1880	Benjamin Disraeli	Conservative
1880–1885	William Gladstone	Liberal
1885–1886	Lord Salisbury	Conservative
1886	William Gladstone	Liberal
1886–1892	Lord Salisbury	Conservative
1892–1894	William Gladstone	Liberal
1894–1895	Lord Rosebery	Liberal
1895–1902	Lord Salisbury	Conservative
1902–1905	Arthur Balfour	Conservative
1905–1908	Sir Henry Campbell-Bannerman	Liberal
1908–1916	Herbert H. Asquith	Liberal
1916–1922	David Lloyd George	Coalition
1922–1923	Andrew Bonar Law	Conservative
1923–1924	Stanley Baldwin	Conservative
1924	J. Ramsay MacDonald	Labour
1924–1929	Stanley Baldwin	Conservative
1929–1931	Ramsay MacDonald	Labour
1931–1935	Ramsay MacDonald	National Government
1935–1937	Stanley Baldwin	Conservative
1937–1940	Neville Chamberlain	Conservative
1940–1945	Winston Churchill	Conservative
1945–1951	Clement Attlee	Labour
1951–1955	Winston Churchill	Conservative
1955–1957	Sir Anthony Eden	Conservative
1957–1963	Sir Harold Macmillan	Conservative
1963–1964	Sir Alec Douglas-Home	Conservative
1964–1970	Harold Wilson	Labour
1970–1974	Edward Heath	Conservative
1974–1976	Harold Wilson	Labour
1976–1979	James Callaghan	Labour
1979–	Margaret Thatcher	Conservative

[Handwritten marginal annotations appear throughout the right margin, e.g. "Proposed Reform Bill of, twilight", "1867", "secret ballot, education", "measures of soc...", "Mahdi massacre, Ref...", "caretaker gov't.", "defeat of Home...", "father figure, A...", "national unrest...", "genial moderate", "imperialism i...", "Education Act", "idealism, great...", "intelligence, Noncon...", "Split liberal party", "3 way split...", "moderation, co...", "socialist, opposed to...", "General Strike of...", "assault of Great Depres...", "called by cri...", "appeasement", "Munich meeting", "WWII, great military...", "welfare state, nationalization", "Festival of Britain", "Suez crisis, ret...", "confidence, dissol...", "old fashioned, at...", "new approach to econ...", "E. Econ. Comm.", "nationalization, ma...", "finances in disarr..." Left margin: "Industrial Relations Act" beside 1974–1976.]

[handwritten annotations at top of page:] disest. of church in Ireland free trade reform, preserve auth. in Ireland, 'sue [?] Land Congress of Berlin. Africa Bill of 1884, Irish Land Act, defeat of Home Rule

Index

[handwritten annotations:] bourne act, Local Gov't Act 1888; Home Rule defeated, stroke, mold a new Liberal party, Africa and Boer War, rise of industrial middle class, change invales Licensing Act, cool intellectual cabinet, practical political sense, decisive 1906, election head for figures – Liberal legislation, great politician dynamic, democratic dictatorship w/ War Cabinet, Coalition gov't, Irish free India conservatives, liberals, Labor

461

The English Heritage, Second Edition, was copyedited and
proofread by Martha Kreger. Brad Barrett was production
manager and photo editor. The index was compiled by
Schroeder Editorial Services. Maps were rendered and revised by
James A. Bier. Graphic Composition, Inc., typeset the text,
and the book was printed and bound by Edwards Brothers, Inc.

Text and cover design by Roger Eggers.